The Big Book
of Holiday Plays

The Big Book

of

Holiday Plays

31 *one-act plays, curtain raisers, and adaptations for the celebration of holidays and special occasions round the year*

Edited by

Sylvia E. Kamerman

Publishers   PLAYS, INC.   *Boston*

CAUTION

NOTICE FOR AMATEUR PRODUCTION

NOTICE FOR PROFESSIONAL PRODUCTION

Library of Congress Cataloging-in-Publication Data

The Big book of holiday plays / edited by Sylvia E. Kamerman.
    p.   cm.
Summary: Thirty-one plays for the celebration of fourteen holidays, including, in addition to the commonly-known ones, Book Week, Black History Month, Mother's Day, and St. Patrick's Day.
  ISBN 0-8238-0291-4 : $16.95
    1. Holidays—Juvenile drama. 2. Children's plays, American.
[1. Holidays—Drama. 2. Plays.] I. Kamerman , Sylvia E.
PS627.H65B564 1990
812.008'033—dc20   90-7615
                                             CIP
                                             AC

Manufactured in the United States of America

Contents

Christmas

Black History Month

Lincoln's Birthday

Valentine's Day

Washington's Birthday

St. Patrick's Day

Easter

Arbor Day

Mother's Day

The Big Book
of Holiday Plays

Prologue to Adventure

by Graham DuBois

Columbus risks royal displeasure to realize his dream. . . .

Characters

CHRISTOPHER COLUMBUS
BARTHOLOMEW, *Christopher's brother*
DIEGO, *Christopher's son*
PEDRO, *a Spanish sailor*
SUZANNA, *a maid*
GARCIA FERNANDEZ, *a Spanish physician*
JUAN PEREZ, *his friend, a member of the Spanish clergy*
LANDLADY
MESSENGER

TIME: *January, 1492.*
SETTING: *A room in a small inn outside Granada, Spain.*
AT RISE: PEDRO *is seated on bench,* DIEGO *on stool at* PEDRO'*s feet.*
DIEGO (*Enthralled*): And you say the island was rising from the water? It really came up from beneath the waves?
PEDRO: Of course it did. We sailors could see it as plainly as I see you now. Our ship rocked so much in the heavy swell made by the island that we could hardly stand.
DIEGO: Did you turn back?

3

PEDRO: Turn back? I'll say we didn't, my lad! We landed.

DIEGO: Landed? On that island? Weren't you afraid?

PEDRO: Not at all. Though we had a little trouble with the sea-beasts before we could land. Ugly monsters they were, huge, with spouts between their eyes that shot up great streams of water.

DIEGO: Did they follow you ashore?

PEDRO: No, we frightened them off.

DIEGO: They must have been strange creatures!

PEDRO: They were—but not half as strange as the tiny people we met on that island.

DIEGO: You saw people there?

PEDRO: Thousands of them! I stepped on half a dozen of them as I landed.

DIEGO: That was cruel!

PEDRO: I didn't mean to. But they were so small, I couldn't see them at first in the tall grass. (*Pauses*) And they had only one eye!

DIEGO: Only one eye?

PEDRO: Yes, right in the middle of their foreheads. And they were so tiny, I could hold three of them on the palm of my hand, and at least six on each shoulder when they showed us where the food trees grew. (SUZANNA *enters and shakes her head in disbelief at* PEDRO.)

DIEGO (*Amazed*): The *food* trees?

PEDRO: Everything on that island grew on trees. The people never had to cook. When they were hungry, they just picked what they wanted. I'll never forget those delicious cakes. I ate so many that—

SUZANNA: Enough, Pedro! (*To* DIEGO) Come child, go out and play in the sun.

DIEGO (*Rising*): All right. (*To* PEDRO) But you mustn't go, Pedro. I want to hear more of your adventures later.

PEDRO: You shall, my lad! I'll tell you about the people who always walk on their heads, and—

SUZANNA: No more, Pedro! (*To* DIEGO) Go now, Diego. Your father will be angry if he finds you still indoors when he returns. (DIEGO *exits*.)

PEDRO: How he loves my yarns!

SUZANNA: Yarns? Monstrous lies, you mean. (*Crosses to window and looks out*)

PEDRO: Well, I'm glad he's taken a fancy to me. That may help me win favor with his father.

SUZANNA (*Suspiciously*): What do you mean?

PEDRO: I want to sail with him.

SUZANNA (*Incredulously*): Do you mean to tell me that you believe in the wild ideas of Christopher Columbus? Do you think there's really land somewhere out there in the sea?

PEDRO: I certainly do. And if we sail westward, we'll find it.

SUZANNA: If you sail westward! I'll show you what will happen if you sail westward. (*Takes apple from bowl and rolls it along the table so that it drops to the floor.*) That's what's in store for you. You'll fall off the earth.

PEDRO: You don't understand. (*Takes apple from bowl*) You are supposing that the earth is flat. But this is what will happen. If we sail westward, we can come right back to the point from which we started. (*Traces his finger from stem, around apple, and back to stem.*)

SUZANNA (*Stunned*): You believe that the earth is round?

PEDRO (*Nodding*): Better men than I believe it. (SUZANNA *shakes her head, goes to window and looks out.*)

SUZANNA: Such as Christopher Columbus? Humph! Come here to the window. (*Points*) Look, there he is now, pacing the ground like a caged animal. (PEDRO *moves to window and looks out.*)

PEDRO: He's stopped now. He's making marks in the dirt with his cane.

SUZANNA (*Tapping her forehead suggestively*): Crazy, he is. Do you want that to happen to you, Pedro?

PEDRO: I see what he's doing! He's drawing maps.

SUZANNA: Mad! The poor gentleman is quite mad, I tell you. (PEREZ *enters, holding a letter.*)

PEREZ: I must speak to Senor Columbus at once. It is a matter of the utmost importance.

SUZANNA: Yes, senor. I'll call him. (*Exits.* PEDRO *rises and walks toward door.*)

PEREZ: One minute, Pedro. There is no reason you should not hear what I am about to say to Senor Columbus. You may be of some assistance to us.

PEDRO (*Taking his seat again*): I am at your service, senor. If it's my voyages you'd like to hear about, I've much to tell. I have been to far places and seen strange things.

PEREZ (*Dryly*): So I understand. (COLUMBUS *enters.*) Ah, here you are, Senor Columbus. I have glorious news for you. I have just received word from Queen Isabella. (*Holds out letter*) She is willing to grant you an audience.

COLUMBUS (*Obviously disappointed*): I have had several audiences with her already—with what results you know.

PEREZ: But I feel that this time it will be different. She has had time to weigh her decision, now that she and the king are no longer occupied with a war.

COLUMBUS: I am grateful to you—truly grateful, but sometimes I feel that I cannot bear another disappointment at the court of Spain.

PEREZ: You talk nonsense, man. You must act without delay. I have been working night and day for this opportunity. There is no time to lose. Take my horse.

COLUMBUS: Out of appreciation for all you have done for me, I'll pay one more visit to their majesties, but this is the last! I am expecting word from my brother, Bartholomew, in France. I believe the French will look with favor on my plans.

PEREZ: Make haste. Don't keep the queen waiting, my friend. (COLUMBUS *exits.*) And now, Pedro, you and I can have a chat while we're waiting for Senor Columbus to return. (*Stops himself*) But wait—I must call Senor Fernandez. (*Goes to door and calls*) Fernandez! Fernandez! I'd like to see you a moment. (*Returns to seat*) How many years have you followed the sea, Pedro?

PEDRO: Thirty years or more. Ever since I was a small child.

PEREZ: You must have learned much about the world in that time. You can probably tell us a great deal about tides and rivers and islands.

PEDRO: I think I can, senor. (FERNANDEZ *enters.*)

PEREZ (*To* FERNANDEZ): Please, sit down. (*Indicates chair*) I want to discuss Columbus's ideas with you. You'll be happy to know that even now he is on his way to see the queen.

FERNANDEZ (*Sighing*): I can only hope he will meet with success this time.

PEREZ: I am convinced he will. I think I know the queen's mind. Despite the war, she would have raised money for the voyage if it had not been for the king.

FERNANDEZ: He has always been too easily influenced by Talavera. He presided over the committee that reported Columbus's ideas were foolish and hopeless. How unfortunate that Duke Celi was not in a position to help Columbus carry out his great plan.

PEREZ: The duke?

FERNANDEZ: Of course! He was enthusiastic. He even considered providing three or four ships, but he finally decided that the scheme was too costly and too ambitious for a subject and should be undertaken by the court of Spain. It was he who brought Columbus to the attention of the queen.

PEREZ: For years Columbus has tried to convince someone to supply him with sailors and ships. What persistence the man has! But he is almost without hope. So many years of discouragement and failure would be enough to break anybody's heart.

FERNANDEZ (*Sighing*): And don't forget his experience at the Court of Portugal. How he was fêted and encouraged—and tricked. King John listened to his plans, and then secretly, without Columbus's knowledge, sent a ship out. But the sailors lost heart and insisted on turning back. I'm afraid that something like that may happen now.

PEREZ: What do you mean?

FERNANDEZ: I don't trust that man Talavera. Columbus is much too naïve. He lets almost anybody see his maps and plans. Talavera has had ample opportunity to examine the papers; he could even copy them if he wished.

PEREZ (*Incredulously*): Are you suggesting that—

FERNANDEZ: Yes, I am suggesting that Talavera is not above using the plans and maps for his own venture, just as King John did.

PEREZ: I think you're wrong. Talavera is too cautious a man to risk so much on any enterprise that may fail. I believe he is convinced that what Columbus proposes will never succeed.

FERNANDEZ: Then he must be more stupid than I had thought.

PEREZ: You have always believed in Columbus, haven't you?

FERNANDEZ: I have, and do completely.

PEREZ: And you really do believe the earth is round, and that there is land to be discovered?

FERNANDEZ: A great deal of land. And, given a chance, Columbus will discover it.

PEREZ: You are a physician, senor, and a keen student of geography. I have, as you know, accepted your views. But we read the books of scholars. What of the many who never consult books or speak to learned men? Who will convince them?

FERNANDEZ: I have met hundreds of seamen who believe in Columbus's ideas.

PEREZ (*Pointing to* PEDRO): Here's an honest sailor we can put to the test. Pedro, what is the shape of the earth.

PEDRO: It is round, senor.

PEREZ: There are many who say otherwise.

PEDRO: I am not an educated man, senor, but I know what I know.

FERNANDEZ: And what do you know?

PEDRO (*Gesturing*): I have watched ships far at sea. It is the hull that disappears first, and then the sails.

PEREZ: But is there land to be discovered? Have you any evidence that it exists?

PEDRO: I have indeed, senor. Once, when I was sailing with Martin Vicente, the Portuguese, we saw—

PEREZ (*Laughing*): Now, let us have none of those wild tales you tell little Diego.

PEDRO (*Placing his hand on his heart*): This is the truth, senor. Four hundred leagues to the west of Cape St. Vincent we found a piece of strange wood in the sea. A westerly gale had been blowing for days. The wood was cut from a kind of tree that does not grow in any known part of the world, and it was carved in a fashion that none of us had ever seen before.

FERNANDEZ (*Nodding*): I have heard of similar cases. (LANDLADY, *excited, enters.*)

LANDLADY (*Breathlessly*): Excuse me for interrupting you, gentlemen, but I am terrified.

PEREZ: Calm yourself, my good woman, and tell us what has frightened you.

LANDLADY: A man—a brooding, dark man has been walking around outside, looking up at the windows.

FERNANDEZ: Come, come, now. This is an inn—all kinds of people come here.

LANDLADY: But this man didn't come to the door like other people.

PEREZ: A beggar, no doubt. Offer him some food or a few coins, and he'll soon be on his way.

FERNANDEZ: It's probably one of our discharged soldiers.

LANDLADY: But this isn't one of our men, I'm sure. I'm afraid he may be an escaped prisoner. Look! (*Points to window*) There he is now. (*A face is pressed against the window.*)

PEREZ: Pedro, go ask that fellow what he wants.

PEDRO: Yes, senor. (*Rises and exits*)

PEREZ (*To* LANDLADY): I will talk to this man. I think he will not annoy you further.

LANDLADY: Thank you, senor. (*Bows and exits.*)

FERNANDEZ: There is nothing to be alarmed about. The land is overrun with poor vagrants these days. (PEDRO *enters, leading* BARTHOLOMEW *by the arm.*)

PEDRO: Here he is, senor; but he's not a beggar, and he's not a discharged soldier.

PEREZ: What, then?

PEDRO: He is Senor Columbus's brother, Bartholomew.

FERNANDEZ: What!

PEREZ (*To* BARTHOLOMEW): Pray, be seated, senor. (BARTHOLOMEW *sits on bench beside* PEDRO.)

FERNANDEZ: May I ask why you were skulking around the inn and peering through the windows?

BARTHOLOMEW: I beg your pardon, gentlemen. Perhaps I am overcautious. But I have just come from France on a confidential mission for my brother, Christopher. I must see him as soon as possible, and in the utmost secrecy.

PEREZ: Your brother is not here at present; he is having an

audience with Queen Isabella. I am Juan Perez, and this is Dr. Garcia Fernandez. Perhaps you have heard your brother speak of us.

BARTHOLOMEW: Many times. I am happy to meet you.

PEREZ: You need not hesitate to speak openly before us. Your brother has frequently discussed his plans with Dr. Fernandez and me. We are eager to know how the French court looks upon your brother's proposals.

BARTHOLOMEW: You will pardon me, gentlemen, but I can discuss my brother's affairs only in his presence. As you know, Christopher has never learned to guard his tongue. I go to the other extreme. After all, you have no proof that I am Bartholomew Columbus, and I have no proof that you are Senor Perez and Dr. Fernandez.

FERNANDEZ (*Laughing*): Excellent! I only wish that your brother had adopted some of your caution years ago. . . . Now, Pedro, will you show Senor Bartholomew to a comfortable room? He will want to rest after his long journey. (PEDRO *rises.*)

BARTHOLOMEW (*Rising and following* PEDRO *to door*): Thank you, doctor. Please let me know when my brother returns.

FERNANDEZ: Of course. (PEDRO *goes out with* BARTHOLOMEW.)

PEREZ: Do you suppose the French have outwitted us?

FERNANDEZ (*Nodding*): It is quite likely that they will appreciate the wonderful opportunity that Columbus has to offer.

PEREZ: But we must not let such a prize drop into the lap of France. Isn't it possible to win over Talavera to our side?

FERNANDEZ: I'm afraid not. He is an obstinate creature.

PEREZ (*Going to window and looking out anxiously*): Perhaps their majesties will not be swayed by Talavera's objections this time.

FERNANDEZ: Even if they are not, I am not too hopeful. It takes immense sums to provide men and ships for such an expedition. Our treasury is depleted from years of war.

PEREZ (*Firmly*): But it is our patriotic duty to see that the funds are raised, even if we have to ask for private contributions from the rich. (*Sounds of galloping horse*)

FERNANDEZ: That may be Columbus now.

PEREZ: It's much too soon for him to be back.

FERNANDEZ: Not if he didn't succeed. (COLUMBUS *enters, dejected.*)

PEREZ: How do matters stand, my friend?

COLUMBUS (*Sighing deeply*): I have failed.

FERNANDEZ: I am sorry, very sorry.

PEREZ: This is a keen disappointment to me. But I won't give up hope. I am quite sure that I can arrange another audience.

COLUMBUS: Spare yourself the trouble, senor. (*Proudly*) If their majesties want to see me, they can send a representative here. I have pleaded for the last time.

FERNANDEZ: Don't censure them too severely. The expedition takes vast amounts of money and—

COLUMBUS: It was not a question of money. The queen even offered to sell her jewels.

FERNANDEZ (*Excitedly*): To sell her jewels? She was convinced, then?

COLUMBUS: She was enthusiastic.

PEREZ: What about the king?

COLUMBUS: He finally consented—reluctantly.

FERNANDEZ: And Talavera? Did you succeed in persuading him?

COLUMBUS: No, he argued heatedly against me, but they overruled him.

PEREZ (*Puzzled*): I don't understand. If the king and queen gave their consent, how could you have failed?

COLUMBUS (*Firmly*): They would not agree to my terms.

PEREZ: Your terms? (*Incredulous*) You insisted on terms? What did you ask?

COLUMBUS: I asked for the rank of admiral. I insisted on the title of Admiral of the Ocean in every island, sea, and continent that I may discover; the viceroy of such discoveries; and one tenth of all precious metals found within those realms.

PEREZ (*Angrily*): Why, that's preposterous! You must compromise.

COLUMBUS (*Heatedly*): Never! For twelve years I have labored and suffered—and waited. I left my old father in Genoa to toil at his looms without my aid. I have seen my wife sicken and die. I have dragged my little son from one port to another until he hardly knows the meaning of home. And what have I received for my pains? I have been called imposter and mad man. I have had mockery and sneers and insults. If I am to have recognition now, if will be on my own terms. (BAR-THOLOMEW *enters.*)

BARTHOLOMEW: I thought I heard my brother's voice. (COLUMBUS *turns toward him.*) Ah, Christopher, at last. (*They embrace.*)

COLUMBUS (*Excitedly*): Bartholomew! What news? (BAR-THOLOMEW *sits*) We have much to say to each other. (*Sits*) I never understood just why you decided to leave England. (*Pauses*) You can speak frankly. (*Gestures*) All these gentle-men are my friends. Wouldn't King Henry listen to you?

BARTHOLOMEW: Yes. I had many audiences with him and his advisors. They always received me kindly and entertained me royally, but month after month they questioned and pondered and debated until I despaired of ever receiving assistance from them.

COLUMBUS: Another failure! That word is engraved on my heart.

BARTHOLOMEW: So I decided to take ship for France. I found men at court there whom I could trust. When I laid my plans before them, they were most sympathetic. They promised to consider them.

COLUMBUS: Promised! Portugal, Spain, England, France—every-where it is the same. Promises can't sail the seas. I need money and men and ships.

BARTHOLOMEW: You jump to conclusions too fast, Christopher. I have reason to believe that the decision of France will be favorable.

COLUMBUS: You mean they will provide funds for the expedition?

BARTHOLOMEW: I think they will—under one condition.

COLUMBUS (*Suspiciously*): And what is that?

BARTHOLOMEW: You must be at the French court to carry on negotiations yourself.

COLUMBUS (*Rising*): Agreed! Where is Diego? I shall sail for France at the first opportunity. (PEDRO *enters.*)

PEDRO: Senor Columbus, there is a gentleman to see you.

COLUMBUS: Show him in. . . . And, Pedro, please find Diego and ask Suzanna to pack our things at once.

PEDRO: Yes, senor. (*Exits*)

COLUMBUS: Well, gentlemen, I am sorry that I couldn't sail for the court of Spain. You have been so kind to me that I wish the expedition were for your nation.

PEREZ: Please don't be hasty. I'm sure you can come to a satisfactory agreement with the queen—(MESSENGER *enters.*)

MESSENGER (*To* COLUMBUS): I represent her majesty, Queen Isabella. She bids me invite you to return to court. She asks me to say that she is willing to meet your terms. Papers will be ready for your signature. There are horses at the door. I shall await you there. (*Bows and exits*)

COLUMBUS (*Sinking into chair*): At last! Half my life I have been waiting for this.

BARTHOLOMEW: Well, then, I suppose you have no further need of me.

COLUMBUS: I have, indeed! I am going to entrust to you the task of raising crews. Pedro is sailing with us. He will help you.

PEREZ (*Rising*): I salute you, Admiral of the Ocean!

FERNANDEZ (*Rising*): And Viceroy of Undiscovered Kingdoms. (*Excitedly paces about*) What a day for Spain is this!

COLUMBUS: Not only for Spain, but for the entire world. We shall sail into waters where no ship has ventured before. (*Quick curtain*)

THE END

A Compass for Christopher

by Deborah Newman

Gift to Columbus points the way to his future. . . .

Characters

CHRISTOPHER COLUMBUS, *9*
BARTHOLOMEW, *his brother, 7*
LUIS
ANTONIO
ISABEL
BEATRIZ
DON PEDRO
MARIA ⎤
SUSANNA ⎦ *his young daughters*
CAPTAIN TORRES

TIME: *1455.*
SETTING: *A part of the harbor at Genoa, Italy.*
AT RISE: ISABEL, BEATRIZ *and* ANTONIO *sit on kegs, holding a large net. While* ANTONIO *examines it for holes, the girls pretend to twist and tie the fibers together.*
LUIS: (*Calling from offstage*): Christopher! Christopher Columbus! (*He enters, breathless, and looks around.*) Antonio! Where is Christopher?

ANTONIO (*Shrugging*): Where is Christopher Columbus? Where should Christopher be?

ISABEL (*Sharply*): He *should* be home combing the wool his father will weave into cloth.

BEATRIZ: Luis, have you asked Christopher's mother?

LUIS: Of course. She thinks Christopher and Bartholomew are down here at the harbor.

ANTONIO: That is the answer I would have given you, too. When Christopher Columbus is nowhere to be found, he's down at the harbor, of course! Poking that red head into barrels and boxes, talking to sailors, begging for a visit on board ship, looking at maps . . .

LUIS (*Interrupting*): But Antonio, that's just it. Francisco's father will let us come on board his ship—all of us, so I *must* find Christopher!

BEATRIZ: Christopher would never forgive us if he missed this chance.

ANTONIO (*Excited*): Didn't Francisco's father just return from Africa?

LUIS: Yes—with a whole cargo of wonderful things in the hold— even (*Dramatically*) gold dust!

ISABEL (*Rising*): Oh, let's go.

LUIS: We must find Christopher first. (*Calls*) Christopher! (*Looks offstage*) I don't see him. (ANTONIO *rises*.)

ANTONIO (*Pointing offstage*): Look—isn't that his red head, down there by that caravel? Yes, that's Christopher, and Bartholomew is beside him. (*Calling*) Christopher! Christopher! Come here!

ISABEL (*Sighing*): Poor Christopher. He wants to be a sailor more than anything else in the world, and he is to be apprenticed to a weaver.

BEATRIZ: I'm not sure Christopher will ever be a weaver. (CHRISTOPHER *and* BARTHOLOMEW *enter.* CHRISTOPHER *carries a bolt of blue cloth.*)

CHRISTOPHER: What is all the shouting about, Antonio?

LUIS: Listen, Christopher. Francisco's father has said all of us can come on board his caravel.

BARTHOLOMEW (*Excited*): Oh, Christopher! That's wonderful.

CHRISTOPHER (*Enthusiastically*): That's worth shouting about, Antonio. Francisco's father's ship is big, with many sails. (*Pauses; then sighing*) But I cannot go. (*He holds up bolt of blue cloth.*) I must try again to sell my cloth.

ISABEL: Why not let your father take care of it?

BARTHOLOMEW: This is special cloth. Christopher wove it himself.

CHRISTOPHER: Yes, and I must sell it. I want money to buy little Johnny a toy. He has a fever, and Mother says it is because I took him down to the harbor and he got a chill. So I want to give him something.

BEATRIZ: Surely you can sell it to one of the wool merchants— Don Nino or Don Mendoza.

CHRISTOPHER (*Shaking his head*): No, I asked all of them. No one is interested. (*Firmly*) But I must sell it somehow.

BARTHOLOMEW (*Pleading*): Christopher, couldn't we go to the ship and try to sell the cloth later?

ISABEL (*Teasing*): Francisco's father might be able to answer your questions about the sea, Christopher—you know, about the sea monsters and the shipworms that eat up the bottoms of ships.

LUIS: Francisco's father does not believe those stories. I know, because I asked him myself.

CHRISTOPHER (*Eagerly*): You have talked to him, Luis? And does he think the earth is flat—does he think that on the other side of the earth there are lands where men go about with their feet above their heads?

LUIS: Come and ask him yourself, Christopher. Let's go down to his ship now.

CHRISTOPHER (*Hesitating*): I would like to go—(*Firmly*) but no. I must try to sell my cloth.

BARTHOLOMEW: Oh, Christopher!

CHRISTOPHER: You go with them, Bartholomew. You can tell me all about it later.

ISABEL: Yes, if Christopher won't come, I'll take you, Bartholomew.

BEATRIZ: Christopher, sometimes I cannot understand you. (*Shrugs*) Well, if you have made up your mind about selling that cloth, then I know you will not change it. (*Children exit.* CHRISTOPHER *stares after them, waves his hand, and then sits down on a keg.*)

CHRISTOPHER (*Fingering the cloth*): Poor little piece of cloth. Is Christopher Columbus such a bad weaver that no one will buy you? I made you blue, the color of the sky and the water on a sunny day. And here are bits of white—like the clouds and the foam on the waves as they break in Genoa's harbor. (*Shakes his head sadly, as* DON PEDRO, MARIA, SUSANNA *and* CAPTAIN TORRES *enter. They do not see* CHRISTOPHER *at first.*)

CAPTAIN TORRES: I tell you, Don Pedro, Genoa is growing each day. She shall again be known as a great harbor. Look at our map makers, our ship builders—(*He notices* CHRISTOPHER.) Why, hello—it's Christopher Columbus, son of Domenico, the master weaver. But why do you look so sad, Christopher?

CHRISTOPHER (*Rising*): My friends have gone on board a caravel, Captain Torres.

MARIA: Then why didn't you go with them?

CHRISTOPHER (*Embarrassed*): I—I could not go.

CAPTAIN TORRES: I have never yet heard you refuse to go on board a ship. (*Turns to* DON PEDRO) Christopher, this is Don Pedro, owner of the good ship *Castilla*. And these are his daughters—(*Introducing them*) Maria and Susanna.

GIRLS (*Curtsying*): Hello, Christopher.

DON PEDRO: Good day, young man.

CHRISTOPHER: Good day.

CAPTAIN TORRES: Don Pedro, this lad would make you a fine sailor when he grows up.

SUSANNA: I would like to be a sailor when *I* grow up.

MARIA: Susanna! Girls do not become sailors.

DON PEDRO: So you would like to become a sailor, Christopher?

CHRISTOPHER (*Politely*): I am afraid that sons of weavers, like girls, do not become sailors, Don Pedro.

SUSANNA: Do you know how to weave? I would like to know how.

CAPTAIN TORRES: I think my young friend prefers the roar of the sea to the rattle of the loom.

DON PEDRO: As do I. There is not much choice between the smell of wool and the smell of the sea.

SUSANNA (*Pointing to cloth* CHRISTOPHER *holds*): Did you weave this cloth?

CHRISTOPHER (*Eagerly*): Yes, I did. Do you like it?

SUSANNA: Oh, yes, I think it is fine cloth.

MARIA: But not as fine as the cloth Father gives us.

CHRISTOPHER (*Disappointed*): No, I suppose not. I thought perhaps—(*He shrugs.*)

DON PEDRO: What did you think, Christopher?

CHRISTOPHER (*Bursting out*): I thought perhaps you might like to buy it. I want to sell it to get the money for a toy for my little brother, Johnny. He is ill, and I think it is my fault.

MARIA: But we do not need your cloth. Why, we have dresses made of silk from India.

DON PEDRO: It is not nice to boast, Maria. But my daughter is right, lad. I am sorry, but they have all the cloth they need.

CHRISTOPHER (*Nodding*): I understand. Well, I must be off. I shall try to sell my cloth to one of the sailors. (*He starts to exit.* SUSANNA *hesitates, then runs after him.*)

SUSANNA: Wait! (CHRISTOPHER *turns.*) I would like to have your cloth, after all.

CHRISTOPHER: But your father said you do not need it.

SUSANNA (*Looking at her father*): Father, could I buy his cloth?

MARIA: You have no money, Susanna.

SUSANNA (*Thoughtfully*): No, I have no money. But wait! (*To* CHRISTOPHER) Could we trade? (*She fumbles in her pocket, draws out a small compass.*) See, I have a compass. It would make a fine present for your little brother. I will give it to you if you give me your cloth.

CHRISTOPHER (*Coming forward, looking at compass*): A compass! I have always wanted to have one of these. (*Draws away*) But it is worth far more than my poor cloth.

DON PEDRO: If Susanna wishes to give it to you in exchange for the cloth, it is all right.

CHRISTOPHER (*Smiling broadly*): I would like that. (*Holds out cloth, which* SUSANNA *takes. She gives him the compass.*) This will be Johnny's—but I think he will let me use it sometimes.

SUSANNA: Yes, and you are a *real* sailor if you have a compass.

CHRISTOPHER (*Hopefully*): I might become a real sailor some day.

I *must* become a sailor! (*He looks at compass happily.*) Now I will go and join my friends. Thank you very much. (*He exits.*)

DON PEDRO (*Shaking his head and smiling*): He is like all the boys of Genoa—crazy for the sea and the life of a sailor.

CAPTAIN TORRES: No, Don Pedro. Young Christopher is not like the others. He is a boy with a strong will and a passion for the sea.

SUSANNA: Do you think he *will* become a sailor someday, Captain Torres?

CAPTAIN TORRES: I would not be surprised.

MARIA (*Haughtily*): Is it so wonderful to be a sailor?

SUSANNA: He could be more than a sailor. Why, he could even be an admiral! He could sail away and—and find new lands at the edge of the world!

DON PEDRO: Admiral Christopher Columbus? New lands? (*Laughs and pats* SUSANNA'*s head*) A fine future you have imagined for this young redhead, Susanna.

MARIA: Father, we must be getting home. Come on Susanna. (*They exit, but* SUSANNA *lingers and looks out over harbor. She drapes cloth around her.*)

SUSANNA (*Dreamily*): Admiral Christopher Columbus. And I gave him his first compass.

MARIA (*From offstage*): Susanna, are you coming? (SUSANNA *smiles, hugs the cloth to her, and then exits. Curtain.*)

THE END

The New Broom

by Mildred Hark and Noel McQueen

Witches make a clean sweep of an old house. . . .

Characters

MR. JONES, *a real estate agent*
MRS. ELEANOR COOPER
MR. FRED COOPER
NORA, *13* ⎫
BOB, *10* ⎬ *their children*
JANIE, *8* ⎭
1ST WITCH
2ND WITCH
3RD WITCH
4TH WITCH

TIME: *The present. Halloween.*
SETTING: *The living room of a very dirty old house. A few old chairs and tables are scattered around.*
AT RISE: *Door center rear opens, and* MR. JONES *enters, followed by* MR. *and* MRS. COOPER *and their three children.*
MR. JONES (*As they enter*): I'm sorry, Mr. and Mrs. Cooper, but

20

this is the only house I have to show you near your children's school.

MR. COOPER: A friend told us you knew every piece of property around.

MR. JONES (*Shaking his head*): This is the only vacant house in the neighborhood.

MRS. COOPER: It doesn't look as though anyone has lived here for years.

BOB: They must have left in a hurry. They didn't even take their furniture!

MR. JONES (*Laughing*): Well, I might as well be truthful. Some folks say this house is haunted.

NORA: Haunted?

MR. JONES: Oh, don't worry, Nora. There's no such thing. It's just old and needs a lot of fixing up.

MRS. COOPER (*Looking around; sighing*): I really don't see how we could live here, do you, Fred? We'd practically have to rebuild.

MR. COOPER: It does seem pretty bad . . .

MRS. COOPER: But we just *have* to find something—

NORA: Oh, Mother, I'm so tired.

BOB: My legs feel like rubber. (*He flops down in chair, then gets up again, coughing and brushing off pants.*) This dust is awful!

NORA: It's just a horrible place!

JANIE (*Suddenly*): I don't think so. I like it!

MRS. COOPER (*Surprised*): You like this house?

NORA (*With a shudder*): It's about the spookiest place I've ever seen.

JANIE: I'll bet it wouldn't be if we moved in. We'd fix everything up, and after we'd lived here and laughed and had fun—you'd see—it would be a nice house.

MR. JONES (*To* JANIE): I could use you as a salesman!

MRS. COOPER: Janie sees some good in everything.

MR. JONES (*Looking around doubtfully*): I suppose this place might not be so bad once it was all cleaned up. My crew was suppose to come over and do just that—(*He points to a broom leaning against table.*) You see, I even bought a new broom.

MR. COOPER (*Shaking head*): I really don't think there's much use, do you, Eleanor?

MRS. COOPER: No, dear. . . . We might as well go back to the hotel.

NORA (*Sighing*): And hope that something turns up soon!

MR. COOPER: Maybe there'll be something advertised in the evening paper. (JANIE *wanders around room, touching various items.*)

MR. JONES: Well, I'm certainly sorry I couldn't be more help.

BOB: We've just got to find something!

MRS. COOPER: Yes, we have to move out of the hotel tomorrow. That fair nearby has brought hundreds of tourists.

JANIE: Mother, please, why can't we stay right here? You know tonight is Halloween. It's the perfect house for Halloween.

MRS. COOPER: I'm sorry, Janie, but we just can't stay here.

MR. COOPER: Eleanor, who don't you and the girls go back to the hotel, and Bob and I will keep on looking. Maybe we'll see a "For Rent" sign somewhere.

MRS. COOPER (*Sighing*): If you think so. Nora, Janie, come along with me. (*They all exit. After a moment* JANIE *re-enters smiling.*)

JANIE (*To herself*): I really like this place. I feel right at home. If I can just get it straightened up by the time my parents come back looking for me—oh, but I'm so sleepy. (*Lies down on sofa behind table, where she can't be seen well*) I hope I can keep my eyes open. (*Yawns. After a moment,* 1ST WITCH *enters right.* 2ND WITCH *enters left. They wear black robes, masks, and pointed hats and carry brooms.*)

1ST WITCH: Good timing, sister.

2ND WITCH: Where are the others?

1ST WITCH: They should be here any minute. We agreed to meet here at the haunted house on Halloween. (3RD WITCH *enters left, also with broom.*)

3RD WITCH: Happy birthday, weird sisters.

2ND WITCH: By the toad's great toe, this *is* our birthday isn't it?

3RD WITCH (*Annoyed*): Of course. Halloween is always the witches' birthday. How could you forget that?

2ND WITCH: Ever since I passed the two hundred mark, I don't like to think of birthdays. After all, I'm a woman, too, even if I am a witch.

1ST WITCH: Nonsense! The older we get, the more skillful our tricks and spells.

2ND WITCH: Absolutely. This is going to be the best birthday party we've ever had. I've been thinking up new charms and spells all the year.

3RD WITCH: Where can our other sister be?

1ST WITCH: Perhaps she's mending her broomstick. I had a lot of repairs to make on mine. I practically wore it out last Halloween with all our tricks.

3RD WITCH: How shall we begin? Should we turn all the fresh milk sour? Or change all the children's pets into garter snakes? (4TH WITCH *enters right without a broom.*)

4TH WITCH: Hail, weird sisters!

2ND WITCH: Where have you been? The owl hooted a long time ago.

4TH WITCH: I'm sorry I'm late, but I've been trying to buy a new broom.

3RD WITCH: A new broom?

4TH WITCH: Yes, and I couldn't find one anywhere. My old one broke.

2ND WITCH: Why didn't you mend it?

1ST WITCH: This is a fine kettle of frogs. What will you do without a broom?

4TH WITCH (*Spying broom leaning against table, and taking hold of handle*): Look—here's one—a fine new broom!

3RD WITCH: But will a new broom work as well as an old one?

1ST WITCH: Of course it won't. You can't cast evil spells with a new broom.

4TH WITCH (*Happily*): But a new broom sweeps clean, and why do we have to cast evil spells anyway? Why can't we change all that?

2ND WITCH (*Horrified*): Are you suggesting we reform?

3RD WITCH (*Firmly*): Witches never reform. They go on doing tricks and casting spells forever and especially on Halloween. (*Briskly*) Now we'd better get busy and make our plans.

1st Witch (*Cackling*): There's no place like a haunted house for planning mischief.

4th Witch: But why do we have to make mischief?

1st Witch: We wouldn't be witches if we didn't. People expect it of us.

4th Witch: But couldn't we do something good for a change?

2nd Witch (*Stunned*): Something good? That new broom has affected her mind.

3rd Witch: She's got bats in her belfry!

4th Witch: And you all have cobwebs in your brains—and I wish I could sweep them away with my new broom. (*She waves it.*)

1st Witch: Stop—stop—this is Halloween. Time for mischief-making!

4th Witch: But Halloween is such a nice holiday. Why don't we do good deeds instead of evil ones?

1st Witch: Because that's the witch tradition! The first witch that ever lived had an evil spell cast over her, and that has been handed down—from generation to generation—

3rd Witch (*Impatiently*): Everyone knows that witches are bad.

4th Witch: Well, maybe if someone would say something good about us, that would break the spell. (Janie sits up and speaks half-dreamily.)

Janie: Who is there? (Witches *jump in surprise.*)

1st Witch: Black bats and cats, I hear a voice.

2nd Witch: Who would come here—to the haunted house?

3rd Witch: We'll have to disappear, scat, vanish—

1st Witch: Away on our broomsticks. (Janie *gets up and comes forward.*)

Janie: Wait, please, don't go. Who are you?

1st Witch: You mean you don't recognize us?

Janie: Oh, I will in a minute. I'm awfully glad you came.

2nd Witch: But—what are *you* doing here?

Janie: Well, I sort of ran away. My mother thinks I went with my father, and my father thinks I'm with my mother. I suppose it wasn't right, but I had to come back. I like this house.

3rd Witch: But this house is haunted.

4th Witch: I don't think so. I feel something different about this house—it's changed somehow.

JANIE: Oh, I wish I could make my parents see that it's a nice house. It's the people that live in a house that make it a home, and I've got the nicest family.

4TH WITCH: You want to live in this house?

JANIE: Oh, yes. I know it needs cleaning up, but I thought maybe I could do that.

4TH WITCH: Well, that settles it. Do you know what I'm going to do this Halloween? I'm going to use my new broom to clean up this house so people can live in it. I'm going to sweep cobwebs away. (*She begins sweeping.* WITCHES *crowd around, trying to stop her.*)

3RD WITCH: No, you can't do that—

2ND WITCH: That would be a good deed.

JANIE (*Suddenly*): Now, I know who you are! You're the good fairies who live in this house, aren't you? You're good fairies in disguise!

1ST WITCH (*Puzzled*): What?

2ND WITCH (*Slowly*): What did you say?

3RD WITCH: Did you say what I thought you said?

JANIE: Every nice house has good fairies. I knew all along—you *are* good fairies, aren't you?

1ST WITCH: Did you hear that? She said something good about us. (*Removes her mask*)

2ND WITCH: So she did. (*Removes her mask*)

3RD WITCH: I feel so different. (*Removes her mask*)

4TH WITCH (*Removing mask*): She broke the spell!

1ST WITCH: Quickly—let's change this house with charms and chants!

2ND WITCH: Let's brighten every corner.

3RD WITCH: Yes, let's get rid of that haunted feeling.

4TH WITCH: We'll chase away the cobwebs with our magic brooms! (WITCHES *rush about using brooms to clean wall, etc.*)

WITCHES:
Folderol and Fiddle-dee-dee,
We have no time to waste.
To rid this house of so much trash,
we witches must make haste. (*They sweep rubbish offstage,*

rushing back and forth. JANIE *stands clapping her hands and smiling.*)

JANIE: You're wonderful! You're wonderful! (WITCHES *continue their furious cleaning; they sweep cobwebs off ceiling, take gray covers off furniture and push them offstage with their brooms, as they chant.*)

WITCHES:
Hocus pocus, mumbo jumbo,
Cobwebs all take heed.
Our magic spell will banish you
With hurly-burly speed!

JANIE: Oh, how different everything begins to look. It's magic! (WITCHES *rest their chins on the handles of their brooms.*)

1ST WITCH (*Shaking her head*): The room still needs something.

2ND WITCH: It looks a bit dreary.

3RD WITCH: It needs some more magic.

4TH WITCH: (*Waving her broom with a flourish; as she chants, lights brighten*):
Magic broom, magic broom.
Chase away the grime and gloom.
Make the house all bright and cheery.
Leave no trace that might be eerie.
(WITCHES *nod approvingly.*)

1ST WITCH: It certainly looks clean and bright.

4TH WITCH: A new broom sweeps clean!

JANIE (*Happily walking around room*): Oh, it's beautiful. I knew this was a nice house!

1ST WITCH: It's because of you, little friend.

2ND WITCH: You made it into a nice house.

3RD WITCH: It was you who chased the gloom away.

4TH WITCH: You made us realize that good tricks are more fun than mischief.

JANIE: But I didn't do anything. *You're* the good fairies.

1ST WITCH (*Surprised*): You don't know who we really are, do you?

2ND WITCH: Shall we tell her?

3RD WITCH: I think we'd better.

4TH WITCH (*To* JANIE): We're not good fairies at all. We're witches!

JANIE: But of course you are—Halloween witches! And Halloween witches are just good fairies in disguise. (*Voices are heard off.*)

1ST WITCH: Listen—voices! We'll have to scat, disappear, vanish—

JANIE: Oh, but please don't go! It's probably my family, and I'd like you to meet them!

2ND WITCH: No, we'd only frighten grown ups. (WITCHES *mount their broomsticks, ready to leave.*)

JANIE: Will you come back sometime—please?

4TH WITCH: Next Halloween! (WITCHES *rush off left and right just as door at rear opens, and* MR. *and* MRS. COOPER *hurry in, followed by* MR. JONES, NORA, *and* BOB.)

MR. COOPER (*Rushing over to* JANIE): Janie, you're here!

MRS. COOPER: Oh, Janie, we've been so worried—

JANIE: I'm sorry, but I just had to come back here.

BOB: Come back to this old dump? (*Stops and looks around*) Hey, what's happened to it?

NORA (*Amazed*): It looks so different, all cleaned up and sparkling.

MR. COOPER: Why, so it does. I'd never know it was the same house.

MR. JONES (*Looking around*): My crew must have gotten over here and cleaned up the place while we were gone, but, frankly, I'd never have thought it would look like this!

JANIE: It wasn't your crew, Mr. Jones. It was the witches who cleaned it up.

MR. COOPER: Witches? Janie—

JANIE (*Earnestly*): Yes. The Halloween witches. They cleaned it up with their magic brooms.

MRS. COOPER: Janie, you must have been dreaming. Did you fall asleep while you were here?

JANIE: Yes, but it was after I woke up that the witches came.

MR. JONES: Say, you folks wouldn't want to reconsider renting this place. . . .

MR. COOPER: Would we? I think it's as good as done. (*To* MRS. COOPER) What do you say, Eleanor?

MRS. COOPER: Why, Fred, I don't see how we could do better. (*Happily*) It's really a homey old place.

NORA (*Delighted*): A house at last!

BOB: A home of our own again!

JANIE (*Excitedly*): You mean we can really stay and live in this house?

MRS. COOPER: Yes, Janie.

JANIE: Then maybe the witches will come and see me again.

BOB: Now, wait a minute, Janie. We don't want witches.

JANIE: Oh, but these are good witches, and they only come on Halloween. (*Curtain*)

THE END

The Hound of the Maskervilles

by Helen Louise Miller

Ghouls foil plans to bulldoze Hag Hollow. . . .

Characters

SABILLA ⎫
AURILLA ⎬ *witches of Hag Hollow*
VANILLA ⎭
LADY MASKERVILLE
BRIDGET ⎫
FIDGET ⎭ *her maids*
QUIVER ⎫
QUAKE ⎭ *her footmen*
GHOULFINGER, *Master of the Haunt*
HEADA CHOPPER
BINGO ⎫
BONGO ⎭ *gangsters*
MAYOR
FANG, *the Hound of the Maskervilles*
MASQUERADERS

SETTING: *A clearing in front of witches' cave in Hag Hollow. Entrance to cave at right has a big "Welcome" sign over it, festooned with orange and black streamers. Nearby are several tree stumps.*

AT RISE: AURILLA *is stirring large black pot, right, as* SABILLA *sets long table, left, with plates of sandwiches, crackers, cups. Halloween decorations adorn table.*

SABILLA: Do hurry up with that Baboon Punch, Aurilla. Lady Maskerville will be arriving any minute.

AURILLA: Don't get yourself so stirred up, Sabilla. The Broomstick Special is never on time. Besides, Vanilla will be there to meet her.

SABILLA: It's all so exciting for us to be entertaining one of Britain's most famous ghosts, right in our own cave! We'll give Lady Maskerville a reception Hag Hollow will never forget. (*Nibbling at cracker*) Um-m! These Crocodile Crackers are good! And the ladybug sandwiches are delicious! Have you tried them?

AURILLA: *I've* been much too busy. What about your guest list? Is it complete?

SABILLA: Not quite. We need two more men, but where we'll get them on such short notice, I have no idea. Have you any suggestions?

AURILLA (*Tartly*): That, my dear sister, is *your* problem! After all, it was *your* idea to invite Lady Maskerville to spend the winter with us.

SABILLA: But think what it will mean to our Vanilla! If we entertain Lady Maskerville as our Foreign Exchange Ghost, World-Wide Haunts will send Vanilla to one of the great haunted houses of Britain. Think of the prestige!

AURILLA: I'm not so sure I like the idea of having Vanilla living in one of those musty old dungeons! And besides, what about *our* prestige, if we're put out of our cave this winter?

SABILLA: I'd just like to see anybody try it!

AURILLA: You know the Mayor is threatening to run a new road through Hag Hollow, and if he does—wham! Our cave will be blasted to bits with the first stick of dynamite!

SABILLA: He wouldn't dare!

AURILLA: Maybe not, but—(*Loud whirring noise is heard from off left.*) Listen! I think I hear the Broomstick Special!

SABILLA: They're coming! They're coming! (*Nervously*) I'm so excited! How do I look?

AURILLA (*Flatly*): Same as usual.

SABILLA: Now, remember to make a proper curtsy!

AURILLA: I'll do no such thing! Think of my rheumatism! (*Whirring sound stops.*)

SABILLA (*Looking off left*): They've landed! There's Vanilla (*Waving*), and that must be Lady Maskerville! Here they come! (VANILLA *enters left with* LADY MASKERVILLE, *who wears flowing, white robes. They are followed by* QUIVER *and* QUAKE, *who are dressed as skeletons and carry a black coffin.* BRIDGET *and* FIDGET *enter, carrying a chest.*)

VANILLA (*Leading* LADY MASKERVILLE *center*): Come this way, Lady Maskerville. My sisters are so eager to meet you. (*Introducing her*) Lady Maskerville, may I present my sister, Sabilla (SABILLA *makes a wobbly curtsy*), and my sister, Aurilla. (AURILLA *nods stiffly.* SABILLA *pokes her, and she manages to curtsy.*)

SABILLA *and* AURILLA: Welcome to Hag Hollow, your ladyship.

LADY MASKERVILLE (*Speaking with English accent*): Thank you, my dears. So good of you to receive me. (*Looking about*) Ah, what a charming spot! Quite like our summer place at Hangman's Hill in Surrey, is it not, Bridget?

BRIDGET: Quite, your ladyship.

VANILLA: I'm sure my sisters have arranged everything for your comfort, Lady Maskerville, and for the comfort of your staff.

AURILLA (*Amazed*): Staff! You mean all these people (*Indicates footmen and maids*) are your staff?

LADY MASKERVILLE: I'm sorry I could not bring more of my household, Lady Aurilla, but I will try to be as little trouble as possible. If you will tell Quiver and Quake where to put my coffin, I will send Bridget and Fidget to unpack.

SABILLA (*Looking at coffin doubtfully*): Dear me! I'm afraid that coffin may be a bit large for our cave!

LADY MASKERVILLE: Never mind, my dear. There's nothing I like better than to sleep out of doors under a full moon. Just put it down there, boys. (*Indicates a spot up center*) Then you may go have a look around the village. (*Shaking her finger at them*) But mind you, none of your tricks! (*They place coffin up center, then exit left.*) Now, if you will show Bridget and Fidget where to hang up my shrouds and put away my jewels—

AURILLA (*Leading way to cave*): Right in here, please. (*She exits with* BRIDGET *and* FIDGET. *Blast of hunting horn is heard off left.*)

VANILLA *and* SABILLA (*Startled*): What's that? (*They huddle together, frightened.*)

LADY MASKERVILLE: It's only Ghoulfinger, my faithful Master of the Haunt. He loves blowing that horn of his. (GHOULFINGER, *in hunting costume and carrying hunting horn, enters left, leading* FANG. *They stand silently beside* LADY MASKERVILLE.)

SABILLA: A dog! (*Reproachfully, aside to* VANILLA) You didn't tell me she brought a dog, too!

AURILLA (*Entering, from right*): I showed the maids where to— (*Sees* FANG *and screams*) A dog! Help! Help! (*Runs about wildly, then jumps up on a tree stump*)

VANILLA: Do be quiet, Aurilla! The dog belongs to Lady Maskerville, and she won't let him hurt you.

AURILLA: But what about Screech?

SABILLA: That cat can take care of himself, Aurilla. (*To* LADY MASKERVILLE) Aurilla is devoted to Screech.

LADY MASKERVILLE: I promise you Fang will not hurt your precious cat. Fang is the Hound of the Maskervilles, you know. A purebred haunting-hound. I never go anywhere without him (*Pats dog's head*), and Fang never goes anywhere without Ghoulfinger, so we three are always together. Ah, forgive me for not introducing you. This is Ghoulfinger, Master of the Haunt, ladies. Ghoulfinger, our American hostesses, Lady Aurilla, Lady Sabilla, and Lady Vanilla.

GHOULFINGER (*Bowing very stiffly*): Charmed, I'm sure.

LADY MASKERVILLE: You had best take` Fang for a walk, Ghoulfinger, but see that he doesn't trouble the villagers. He hasn't had his dinner yet.

GHOULFINGER: Very good, your ladyship.

LADY MASKERVILLE: And leave your haunting-horn with me, so I can call you if I need you.

GHOULFINGER: Certainly, your ladyship. (*He hands horn to her and exits left with* FANG.)

SABILLA (*Sharply*): They've gone, Aurilla. You can come down off that stump now. (*To* LADY MASKERVILLE) You must excuse my sister. She's terrified of dogs.

AURILLA (*Stepping down from stump*): Lady Maskerville, please forgive me.

LADY MASKERVILLE: It was nothing, Lady Aurilla. I am sure you and Fang will be great friends when you get to know each other. And now, I believe I would like to go inside for a bit.

AURILLA: Of course. And do let me make you a nice cup of hemlock tea with a spot of viper juice.

LADY MASKERVILLE: An excellent idea. It's just what I need. (*They go right, into cave.*)

VANILLA: Oh, Sabilla, isn't she wonderful?

SABILLA: Very nice, my dear, but that awful dog and all those people!

VANILLA: We'll manage. How is the reception coming along?

SABILLA: I still need two more men. Will you fly over and try to get Mortimer Monster and Captain Cutlass?

VANILLA: I'll try, but I doubt if they'll come at this late date.

HEADA CHOPPER (*Calling from off left*): Yoo-hoo! Anybody home?

SABILLA: Oh, dear! It's Heada Chopper. What a nuisance! I promised her she could interview Lady Maskerville.

VANILLA: I'll ask Lady Maskerville to come out, then I'll slip out the back way and try to find Mortimer and Captain Cutlass. (*She exits right, as* HEADA CHOPPER *enters left.*)

HEADA: There you are, Sabilla, my dear! I have a million questions for your Ghost of Honor.

SABILLA: Try to make it short, Heada. The reception will be starting soon. (LADY MASKERVILLE *enters right, carrying a teacup.*) Ah, Lady Maskerville, I want you to meet Miss Heada Chopper, who writes the Guillotine Society Column for the *Goblin Gazette*. She wants to interview you.

HEADA: How do you do, Lady Maskerville?

LADY MASKERVILLE: Delighted to meet you, Miss Chopper. Won't you sit down? (*She and* HEADA *sit on tree stumps.*) Lady Sabilla, could we trouble you for a cup of tea for Miss Chopper?

SABILLA: Of course. I'll have Aurilla bring some right away. (*She exits right.*)

HEADA: Naturally, Hag Hollow is simply agog with excitement over your visit, Lady Maskerville. There are so many things we all want to know about you. Tell me, how do you like our American haunts?

LADY MASKERVILLE (*Sipping her tea*): I really can't say yet. I've only just arrived.

HEADA: Of course. My readers are all dying to know what your specialty is. Do you glow in the dark, clank chains—or what?

LADY MASKERVILLE (*Loftily*): I really do very little haunting myself. You see, my man Ghoulfinger is Master of the Haunt. He makes all the arrangements. And then there's Fang.

HEADA: Fang? Who is Fang?

LADY MASKERVILLE: Fang is the Hound of the Maskervilles. Surely you have heard of him.

HEADA: Oh . . . oh, yes, yes, indeed. (*Looking around nervously*) Is he here now?

LADY MASKERVILLE: No, not at the moment. (AURILLA, *followed by* SABILLA, *enters carrying teacup.*)

AURILLA: Hello, Heada. (*Hands her cup*) What have you been poking your nose into these days?

HEADA: Nothing much, Aurilla, except the bank holdup, of course—

LADY MASKERVILLE: Bank holdup? How exciting!

HEADA: The two who did it got away, and when I was at City Hall this morning, I heard that the Town Council is offering a large reward for their capture.

AURILLA: You were at City Hall this morning?

HEADA: Yes. It's a bit out of my line, but I did so want to hear about the new road.

AURILLA: The new road? I hope they're not going through with it.

HEADA: I'm afraid they are, my dear. I heard the mayor say the dynamite crew will start next week.

AURILLA *and* SABILLA (*Crying and sobbing ad lib*): Oh, no! It can't be! Our cave! (*Etc.*)

LADY MASKERVILLE: What is the matter? Tell me. Perhaps I can help.

AURILLA: There's nothing you can do!

HEADA (*To* LADY MASKERVILLE): The town is going to build a new road that will go right through Hag Hollow. The witches' ancestral cave will be blown to smithereens.

SABILLA: We'll be homeless!

LADY MASKERVILLE: Don't cry, my dears! Surely something can be done. Perhaps if I were to talk to the Mayor . . .

HEADA: The Mayor is a very stubborn fellow.

SABILLA: Nothing can stop him now!

AURILLA: I feel faint! I must lie down.

SABILLA (*Putting her arm around her*): Come, sister, I'll help you to bed. (AURILLA *and* SABILLA *exit.*)

HEADA: This is a dreadful shock, poor things! I think I'd better go. We can continue our chat later at the reception. (*She stands, as* VANILLA *enters left.*)

VANILLA: Hello, Heada.

HEADA: Vanilla, my dear, I was just leaving. I'll see you later. Goodbye, Lady Maskerville. (*Exits left*)

LADY MASKERVILLE: Vanilla, your sisters are in the cave, and I think you had better go to them. They've had a bit of bad news.

VANILLA: My own news isn't too good. Neither Captain Cutlass nor Mortimer Monster can come to the reception, so we're still short two gentlemen guests.

LADY MASKERVILLE: How awkward! But don't bother to tell your sisters. They are so upset now about the new road.

VANILLA: Don't tell me the Mayor has finally decided to run that new road through Hag Hollow!

LADY MASKERVILLE: I'm afraid so, my dear.

VANILLA (*Sighing*): I never thought we'd come to this. I'll go to my sisters at once.

LADY MASKERVILLE (*As* VANILLA *exits*): Please send Bridget and Fidget to me. (*To herself*) I really must find a way to help. Surely there is some way to persuade the mayor to drop this ridiculous project. (BRIDGET *and* FIDGET *enter right.*)

BRIDGET: You sent for us, your ladyship?

LADY MASKERVILLE: Something rather distressing has come up, a nasty problem to be solved.

FIDGET: Then we will help you to your couch, madam. You always think more clearly when you are lying down.

LADY MASKERVILLE: Thank you, Fidget. (FIDGET *opens the coffin lid*) It will feel good to stretch out for a while. (*Climbing in*) But, wait! I have just thought of something, Fidget. Please bring me my notepaper. (FIDGET *exits.*) You may prop those pillows behind my back, Bridget. (*She does so*) There! That is quite comfortable. (FIDGET *enters with paper and pen.*)

FIDGET: Here you are, milady.

LADY MASKERVILLE: Thank you, Fidget. (*She begins to write.*) To the Right Honorable Lord Mayor . . .

BRIDGET: Begging your pardon, milady, but I believe the Americans address their mayor as Mister rather than Honorable Lord.

LADY MASKERVILLE: Thank you, Bridget. I must brush up on these American forms of address. (*Writing busily and signing it with a flourish*) There! That should do the trick. (*Folding letter and handing it to* BRIDGET) Now, you two hurry down to the village and deliver it to the mayor. Then look around for Quiver and Quake. Tell them I want the mayor here immediately. If he won't come under his own power, they'll know what to do.

FIDGET: Very good, madam.

LADY MASKERVILLE: Now I would like to take a short nap. (BRIDGET *and* FIDGET *adjust pillows.*)

BRIDGET: Are you quite comfy?

LADY MASKERVILLE: Fine. Cover me with my sheet and then get on with your errand. (*She lies down out of sight and maids cover her with sheet, then exit left. After a moment,* BINGO *and* BONGO *enter, wearing ordinary clothes and half-masks.* BINGO *carries a briefcase, and* BONGO *has a violin case. They look around furtively as they enter.*)

BINGO: Is this the place?

BONGO: Looks like it. Yup—there's the cave.

BINGO: I wonder who put up the Welcome sign?

BONGO: Some of the boys must have a sense of humor.

BINGO (*Spotting food on table*): And look! Refreshments! (*Takes plate of sandwiches and sits on ground beside coffin*)

BONGO: Wait a minute! Wait till we stow the cash in the cave before you start eating.

BINGO: Who cares about that now? We made a perfect getaway. Robbing a bank on an empty stomach is hard work. (*Leans against coffin and begins to eat*) Um-m! These are good.

BONGO (*Looking around nervously*): Just the same, we should hide the loot. Hey, what's that you're leaning against! It looks like a coffin!

BINGO (*Eating calmly*): You're crazy. It's just a storage box— probably full of old junk.

BONGO (*Going to coffin and kicking it*): Pretty sturdy. We might even hide the bank loot in it. Sure does look like a coffin, though. (LADY MASKERVILLE, *her head covered with sheet, slowly raises herself to a sitting position.*) Bingo, it *is* a coffin— and there's something in it! (BINGO *scrambles to his feet, and they clutch each other in terror.*)

BINGO *and* BONGO (*Together*): It's alive!

LADY MASKERVILLE (*Removing sheet*): For goodness' sake, keep quiet! You'll wake the dead!

BONGO: Let's get out of here! (*They start to exit.*)

LADY MASKERVILLE: Just one moment, gentlemen. (*They stop.*) If one of you will give me a hand, and help me out of here, perhaps we can get better acquainted.

BONGO: You help her, Bingo.

BINGO: No thanks.

LADY MASKERVILLE: I *command* you, both of you, help me out. (*As they gingerly take her hands, she steps out.*) Thank you, gentlemen. I am Lady Maskerville, and I suppose you are the two gangsters who just robbed the town bank. I have always wanted to meet some American gangsters.

BINGO: She's on to us, Bongo! Let her have it!

LADY MASKERVILLE (*As* BONGO *stoops to open violin case*): Now, there's not a bit of use opening that thing. I know very well there's a sawed-off shotgun inside, and you might as well know I am completely bullet-proof. (*To* BINGO) Young man, I'll thank you for a plate of those sandwiches. (*As he fills a plate from table*) Not too many, because we must leave plenty for the other ghosts.

BINGO *and* BONGO: Ghosts!

LADY MASKERVILLE: I meant to say *guests*. There's to be a reception, you know.

BINGO: A reception! For us? (*He hands her plate.*)

LADY MASKERVILLE: Certainly not. It's for me. (*Eating sandwich*) Aren't these ladybug sandwiches delicious?

BINGO (*Weakly*): Ladybug sandwiches?

LADY MASKERVILLE: How tiresome the way you repeat everything I say! These are ladybug sandwiches with a wee bit of grasshopper dressing!

BINGO (*In great distress*): And I ate some of them! Bongo, I think I'm going to be sick!

BONGO: Pull yourself together, Bingo.

LADY MASKERVILLE: Please, gentlemen. We must have a little talk. I am sure we have much in common. Some of my family have had considerable dealings with highwaymen, pirates, and outlaws in general. The name of Maskerville is well known on Tower Hill, Execution Dock, and Tyburn Tree. In fact, our present country place, Hangman's Hill, is named for one of my more illustrious ancestors.

BINGO: Don't listen to her, Bongo. She's some sort of witch!

LADY MASKERVILLE: Oh, come now, do I look like a witch?

BONGO: Well, no, but what do you want with us?

LADY MASKERVILLE: I merely want you to do me a small favor.

BINGO: Like what?

LADY MASKERVILLE: I want you to stay for my reception. My hostesses needed two extra warlocks—but gangsters will make a delightful substitute!

BONGO: We don't have time for receptions, lady.

LADY MASKERVILLE (*Sternly*): I am not accustomed to refusals.

BINGO: Look, lady, I don't know who you are or what you are, but we're not staying to find out. Come on, Bongo. (*As they start to exit,* GHOULFINGER *enters, blocking their way.*)

GHOULFINGER: Your ladyship, something terrible has happened.

LADY MASKERVILLE: Later, Ghoulfinger, later. Just collar these two men and make sure they don't get away. (BINGO *and* BONGO *try to dive under* GHOULFINGER'S *arms, but he grabs each one by the collar.*) These louts have had the discourtesy to refuse my invitation to the reception, Ghoulfinger, so I suggest you have Fang take care of them. They will be a change from his Grave-burgers, and they seem to have plenty of meat on their bones.

GHOULFINGER: But, your ladyship—

LADY MASKERVILLE: Do as I bid you, Ghoulfinger, but take them outside. Fang has such atrocious eating habits!

BONGO: Who's Fang?

LADY MASKERVILLE: You'll find out soon enough.

BINGO *and* BONGO (*Struggling to escape, ad lib*): Help! Let go! (*Etc.* QUIVER *and* QUAKE *enter with* BRIDGET *and* FIDGET.)

GHOULFINGER (*To* QUIVER *and* QUAKE): Give me a hand with these fellows. They're tough customers. (*As* QUIVER *and* QUAKE *hold prisoners,* BRIDGET *and* FIDGET *approach* LADY MASKERVILLE *nervously.*)

FIDGET: Your ladyship, we could not deliver your invitation. The mayor is nowhere to be found.

BRIDGET: He has disappeared! Vanished!

LADY MASKERVILLE: How extremely awkward! But first things first. Ghoulfinger, you three may take the prisoners to Fang now.

GHOULFINGER: But, your ladyship, I was about to report when I came in that Fang has run away.

LADY MASKERVILLE (*Upset*): Run away! How could you let such a thing happen?

GHOULFINGER: Just as I was about to give him his Grave-burgers, a big black cat came out of the bushes and he immediately gave chase!

LADY MASKERVILLE: Horrors! That must have been Lady Aurilla's cat, Screech. Why didn't you call him back?

GHOULFINGER: The horn, milady—I left it with you.

LADY MASKERVILLE: So you did. (*Handing horn to him*) Sound it at once. We must get Fang back before he devours any of the villagers, to say nothing of Screech! Blow, Ghoulfinger, blow! (*He blows several loud blasts.*) If that doesn't fetch him, nothing will. (*Points to* BINGO *and* BONGO) Meanwhile, we must find another way to dispose of these wretches. (*She walks about, thinking.*)

BINGO: Just a minute, folks. Why can't we talk this whole business over in a nice, friendly way?

BONGO: My pal means we've decided we would be delighted to attend your reception.

BINGO: In fact, we're dying to come.

LADY MASKERVILLE: Well, methinks they have changed their tune! Now, listen to me, you two. Put that violin case and briefcase into my coffin. Quiver and Quake will stand guard. (QUIVER *and* QUAKE *march* BINGO *and* BONGO *over to coffin; they put violin case and briefcase inside.*)

QUIVER (*As he closes lid*): Now, sit down and keep quiet. (BINGO *and* BONGO *sit on lid.*)

QUAKE: One false move and it will be your last! Understand?

BINGO: We get the message.

GHOULFINGER: I'm worried about Fang, milady. He's always come at the sound of the horn.

LADY MASKERVILLE: Try another blast, Ghoulfinger. (*As* GHOULFINGER *blows horn,* VANILLA, SABILLA *and* AURILLA *enter from cave.*)

VANILLA: What is that dreadful noise? What's happening?

LADY MASKERVILLE: Nothing to worry about, my dears. It's only Ghoulfinger, calling Fang. He's wandered off, and we don't want any trouble.

SABILLA (*Pointing to* BINGO *and* BONGO): Who are those two?

LADY MASKERVILLE: Vanilla told me you needed two more gentlemen to fill up your guest list, so here they are. Bingo, Bongo, you may greet your hostesses, the ladies Aurilla, Sabilla, and Vanilla.

BINGO *and* BONGO (*Standing, bowing stiffly*): Nice to meet you!

AURILLA (*Suspiciously*): You must be new around here.

SABILLA: I thought we knew everyone in Hag Hollow.

BINGO: We were just passing through, ma'am.

VANILLA: How nice. Do have a glass of Baboon Punch and a Crocodile Cracker.

BINGO (*Hastily*): No, thank you, ma'am. My buddy and I are on a diet! (*Sound of barking and snarling and cries of help are heard off left.*)

GHOULFINGER: It sounds like Fang! (*He dashes off left, as* MAYOR *stumbles in, clutching a blanket around his waist. On his head is a stuffed black cat.* AURILLA *rushes up to* MAYOR *and removes cat, cradling it in her arms.*)

AURILLA: Screech! My darling Screech, where have you been? (*She strokes cat.*) There, there. What has the nasty old man been doing to you?

MAYOR (*Indignantly*): What have *I* been doing to *him*? He practically scratched my eyes out!

AURILLA: Never mind him, Screech. You need some nice warm milk. (AURILLA *exits with cat.*)

MAYOR (*As barking continues*): Somebody call off that horrible hound! He's after me, too!

LADY MASKERVILLE: You may rest easy, sir. My man will soon have him under control. (*Barks cease.*) There.

MAYOR: Does that terrible beast belong to you, ma'am?

LADY MASKERVILLE: I am proud to say that I am his owner.

MAYOR: Then you are under arrest!

ALL (*Ad lib*): Under arrest! Not Lady Maskerville! (*Etc.*)

MAYOR: On three charges: Number one: Permitting a mad dog to run loose.

LADY MASKERVILLE: Fang is not a mad dog!

MAYOR: Number two: Not having a proper license for that vicious brute!

VANILLA: But she's only just arrived in the United States!

MAYOR: Number three: Endangering the safety of our citizens and destroying property.

SABILLA: And just what property has been destroyed?

MAYOR: Look at me, ma'am. Do you think I am in the habit of going about wrapped in a blanket? That beast of hers has torn the seat out of my second-best trousers! (*All laugh.*) You'll find it no laughing matter when she is locked in the county jail!

LADY MASKERVILLE: And just who are you to make such dire threats against a subject of the Queen?

MAYOR: I am the mayor, that's who I am!

BINGO *and* BONGO: The mayor! (*They leap up, avoiding* QUIVER *and* QUAKE, *and rush off left.*)

MAYOR (*Shouting*): Hey, I recognize those two! They're the bank robbers! Don't let them get away!

LADY MASKERVILLE: Don't worry. They won't get far. Fang is right outside. (*Offstage barking is heard, followed by loud cries, and* BINGO *and* BONGO *run in again, into the arms of* QUIVER *and* QUAKE.)

BINGO: We surrender!

BONGO: Another minute and that brute would have torn us apart! (AURILLA *enters right.*)

AURILLA: What is the meaning of this? These men are our guests.

MAYOR: In that case, you're *all* under arrest—for harboring criminals and obstructing justice! These gangsters held up the town bank this morning. I received a tip they were heading in this direction. I was on their trail when that beast out there and that cat of yours attacked me.

LADY MASKERVILLE: I understand there is a reward for their capture.

MAYOR: Five thousand dollars. And I mean to claim it, since I captured them single-handedly.

LADY MASKERVILLE: May I remind you that the bank robbers were already in my custody when you arrived on the scene. *My* men were standing guard, and *my* faithful hound just now prevented their escape.

MAYOR: And I suppose you think that entitles you to the reward!

LADY MASKERVILLE: Precisely!

MAYOR (*Angrily*): Now, listen to me—

LADY MASKERVILLE: Besides, you don't know where the loot is.

MAYOR: The money! Where is it? (*To* BINGO *and* BONGO) What have you scoundrels done with the bank notes?

BINGO: We're not talking till we get a lawyer.

BONGO: We know our rights!

MAYOR (*Lunging at them awkwardly, still holding blanket*): Why, you . . .

LADY MASKERVILLE: There's no need for violence, sir. The money is quite safe.

MAYOR: Then hand it over immediately.

LADY MASKERVILLE: Rest assured I will return the money and relinquish any and all claims to the reward in exchange for a simple favor.

MAYOR: What sort of favor?

LADY MASKERVILLE: I merely want you to sign a statement that you will immediately and permanently abandon all plans for running a road through Hag Hollow.

VANILLA, SABILLA and AURILLA: Hooray! Hooray!

MAYOR: This is blackmail!

LADY MASKERVILLE: Nonsense! It's merely a friendly negotiation. Bridget, my writing paper. Fidget, my pen, if you please. (*They exit right.*)

MAYOR: And what makes you so sure I'll sign any such agreement? The law is on my side.

LADY MASKERVILLE: But Fang is on *our* side. I hate to think what would happen to you and your so-called prisoners, if you were to take one step in his direction.

MAYOR: I'll have the police destroy the beast.

LADY MASKERVILLE (*Shaking her head sadly*): You're a stubborn man, Mr. Mayor. (*Calling off left*) Ghoulfinger . . . Ghoulfinger!

GHOULFINGER (*From off left*): Yes, milady?

LADY MASKERVILLE: When I count three, please unleash Fang and send him in here. (BRIDGET *and* FIDGET *return with paper and pen.*)

BINGO *and* BONGO (*Clutching each other; ad lib*): No! Help! Anything but that! (*Etc.*)

MAYOR (*Looking fearfully off left*): Bring the paper. I'll sign.

LADY MASKERVILLE: A very sensible decision. Now, sit down over there (*Indicating coffin*), and write as I dictate. (FIDGET *and* BRIDGET *supply him with writing equipment.*) "I faithfully promise (*Pauses as* MAYOR *writes*) to abandon all present and future plans (*Pause*) for running a road through Hag Hollow (*Pause*) or to engage in any other construction (*Pause*) that would endanger the peace and quiet of this spot." Now sign it.

MAYOR (*Signing*): This is ridiculous! (BRIDGET *takes paper from him and hands it to* LADY MASKERVILLE.)

LADY MASKERVILLE: If you fail to keep this agreement, you will be haunted by the Hound of the Maskervilles for the rest of your life. (*Whispers to* BRIDGET, *who exits right*) Lady Sabilla, this paper will ensure the safety of your property. (*Hands it to* SABILLA)

SABILLA: Oh, thank you, thank you, Lady Maskerville!

AURILLA: You have saved our home!

VANILLA: We shall be eternally grateful.

MAYOR: Now, where's the money?

LADY MASKERVILLE: You are sitting on it, sir.

MAYOR (*Leaping up*): What?

LADY MASKERVILLE (*Pointing to coffin*): If you will just lift the lid—(MAYOR, *clutching his blanket with one hand, opens lid and withdraws briefcase.*)

MAYOR: Confound this blanket! I need both hands to count the money. (BRIDGET *enters with long, red velvet robe.*)

LADY MASKERVILLE: There is no need for that, your honor. But I must confess I hate to see a man of your dignity in such an awkward position. If it pleases you, you may attire yourself in the state robe of my great-grandfather, who was twice Lord Mayor of London. My maids will assist you. (BRIDGET *and* FIDGET *place robe over his shoulders, permitting him to dispose of blanket.*)

AURILLA: What a handsome figure!

SABILLA: Would you do us the honor of staying for our reception, Mayor?

VANILLA: Oh, please do! It will be one way of showing our gratitude.

MAYOR: But my prisoners—

LADY MASKERVILLE: Quiver and Quake will turn them over to the proper authorities. And in view of your generosity to my friends, I will be proud to stand beside you in the receiving line.

MAYOR: In that case, ladies, I shall be delighted to join you.

VANILLA: Listen! (*The sound of music is heard off left.*) Our guests are on their way.

LADY MASKERVILLE (*To* QUIVER *and* QUAKE): Take those creatures (*Points to* BINGO *and* BONGO) away before the company arrives. (QUIVER *and* QUAKE *drag* BINGO *and* BONGO *off.*) And now, my Lord Mayor, if you will give me your arm, we will prepare to receive the populace. (MASQUERADERS, *led by* HEADA CHOPPER, *troop in left, talking excitedly among themselves. If desired, some of them may be playing musical instruments as they enter.* MASQUERADERS *shake hands with* MAYOR *and* LADY MASKERVILLE, *then go to table, where* AURILLA, SABILLA *and* VANILLA *serve them cups of punch, and* BRIDGET *and* FIDGET *serve sandwiches, etc.* When everyone has a cup, AURILLA *steps forward and raises her hand for silence.*)

AURILLA: Ladies and gentlemen, this is a great day for all of us at Hag Hollow.

SABILLA: You may have heard rumors of a new road that was to have destroyed our happy haunting grounds.

VANILLA: But we have good news for you. The mayor himself will make the announcement.

MAYOR (*Stepping forward and addressing the group*): It has recently been brought to my attention that you good people of Hag Hollow would have been seriously inconvenienced by the proposed new road. We have, therefore, decided to abandon all such projects, not only for the time being, but for all time to come.

ALL (*Ad lib*): Hurray! Three cheers for the mayor! (*Etc.*)

VANILLA: And we owe our good fortune not only to our friend, the mayor, but also to our Ghost of Honor, the distinguished banshee from Britain, Lady Maskerville. (*All cheer.*)

SABILLA: But most of all, we are indebted to the greatest haunting-hound of all time. Without him, none of this would be possible. (GHOULFINGER *enters, leading* FANG *on leash.*)

AURILLA: Ladies and gentlemen, I propose a toast—to the immortal fame of our four-footed friend, Fang, the Hound of the Maskervilles!

ALL (*Raising their cups*): To the Hound of the Maskervilles! (*Curtain*)

THE END

Happy Haunting!

by Lewy Olfson

Finding the "right" school for ghouls . . .

Characters

MISS MAGICIA, *Headmistress*
MISS GOBLINETTE, *her secretary*
MRS. SPECTRE
WILMA WITCH
FANNY PHANTOM
POLLY POLTERGEIST

SETTING: *Office of Miss Magicia, in Seminary for Young Ghouls. Large desk, with chair behind it and one beside it is left center. At right, there are four straight chairs arranged in a semicircle. There is a telephone on desk. Back wall is covered with pictures and hanging bookcase filled with books. There is a door at right.*

AT RISE: MISS MAGICIA *is seated at her desk. Phone rings, and she answers it.*

MISS MAGICIA (*Into phone*): Miss Magicia's Seminary for Young Ghouls. . . . Yes, this is Patricia Magicia speaking. . . . No, I'm sorry, but I absolutely cannot give interviews . . . (*Indignantly*) No, I do *not* care to comment on the rumor that my

46

school is going to merge with the Massachusetts Institute of Demonology. (*Sharply*) Young man, I don't care if every ghost academy in the country goes coeducational. Miss Magicia's Seminary for Young Ghouls has always been an all-female institution, and it will remain an all-female institution . . . (*Slams down receiver.* MISS GOBLINETTE, *her secretary, enters, carrying typed letters.*) Honestly, Miss Goblinette, these newspapers seem to think that the headmistress of a school has nothing better to do but answer a lot of foolish questions. And today of all days, with the alumnae arriving for homecoming.

MISS GOBLINETTE: Terrible, isn't it? Here are the letters you dictated earlier, Miss Magicia. (*Puts letters on desk*)

MISS MAGICIA: My goodness, but you've typed these quickly.

MISS GOBLINETTE: It's the new electric Ouija Board I'm using.

MISS MAGICIA: Oh, is it working out, then?

MISS GOBLINETTE: I should say so! Why, it's the greatest piece of office equipment since the spirit duplicator! Now, if you'll just sign these, I can hand them to the eleven o'clock apparition. That way they'll go air-mail.

MISS MAGICIA: Good! (*Signs letters*) Has Mrs. Spectre arrived yet?

MISS GOBLINETTE: Yes, she's waiting to see you now. (*Takes letters*)

MISS MAGICIA (*Excitedly*): Do you know she's one of the most exclusive ghosts in the country! She haunts only the best houses. And she's thinking of enrolling her two daughters in my school. What a blot on the school's escutcheon *that* would be!

MISS GOBLINETTE: I'll show her in.

MISS MAGICIA: Do, please, do! (MISS GOBLINETTE *goes to door and opens it.*)

MISS GOBLINETTE (*Speaking at door*): Miss Magicia will see you now. (*Ushers in* MRS. SPECTRE, *a "grande dame" with a lorgnette.*) Miss Magician, Mrs. Spectre. (MISS GOBLINETTE *exits.* MISS MAGICIA *stands.*)

MISS MAGICIA (*Gushing*): Do be seated, Mrs. Spectre, and make yourself uncomfortable. Can I get you some refreshment? A cup of hemlock, perhaps?

MRS. SPECTRE (*Imperiously*): I am not here to socialize, Miss
Magicia. (*Sits in chair beside desk*) Let us get down to business
at once. As you know, I am thinking of enrolling my daughters
in your school, but before I reach my decision, I have some
questions to ask. (MISS MAGICIA *sits*.)

MISS MAGICIA: I am sure your daughters could not get a better
education than at Miss Magicia's Seminary for Young Ghouls.

MRS. SPECTRE: Hm-m, I'm not so sure. I've heard very good
things about the Academy of Hades for Unearthly Young
Ladies.

MISS MAGICIA (*Disparagingly*): Oh, they have *some* sort of repu-
tation, I grant you . . . but your daughters would find the
living accommodations there most uncomfortable. Here at
Miss Magicia's, we have the finest dormitories available.
Every room always has a fresh supply of cobwebs, and, of
course, a skeleton in every closet.

MRS. SPECTRE: Well, that does sound nice. But what I'm really
interested in is your curriculum. I insist on the highest aca-
demic standards for my daughters. After all, I myself was Phi
Beta Cadaver.

MISS MAGICIA (*Ingratiatingly*): And I'm sure you graduated
magna cum laudanum, too. I assure you, Mrs. Spectre, we
offer only the most advanced studies. In the freshman and
sophomore years, all the students take the same program:
Introduction to Haunting, Basic Invisibility, Problems of Demonology—you know, a general survey of the Inhumanities.
But in their junior year, they get to choose a major: Home
Wreckonomics, Ancient Mystery, that sort of thing. Inciden-
tally, if your daughters are athletic, we have an excellent
program in broom riding.

MRS. SPECTRE (*Indignantly*): Broom riding! You don't think that
I, who have haunted some of the finest houses in the country—
I, who am a direct descendant of the Headless Horseman of
Sleepy Hollow, and can trace my lineage all the way back to
the Witch of Endor—would allow my daughters to do anything
so common as riding brooms!

MISS MAGICIA (*Meekly*): They could ride side-saddle.

MRS. SPECTRE (*Rising*): No, Miss Magicia, I'm afraid that you have a very mistaken idea of what would be acceptable to me for their education.

MISS MAGICIA (*Pleading*): Oh, wait, Mrs. Spectre. I'm sure if you met some of our star pupils you'd be convinced that the Seminary is just right for them. (*Picks up phone, presses buzzer, and speaks into receiver.*) Miss Goblinette, ask a few of our honor students to come to my office to meet Mrs. Spectre. (*Hangs up*)

MRS. SPECTRE (*Sitting down again*): Well, they'll have to be spectacular if they're going to impress me.

MISS MAGICIA (*Confidently*): My dear Mrs. Spectre, our pupils have made the National Halloween All-Stars for the past nine years! (*Door opens*) Ah, here they come now. (WILMA WITCH, POLLY POLTERGEIST, *and* FANNY PHANTOM *enter and sit in the first, second, and fourth chairs at right.*) Thank you for coming, girls. I would like you all to meet Mrs. Horrible Nasty Spectre.

MRS. SPECTRE (*Quickly*): The third.

MISS MAGICIA: Mrs. Spectre, may I present Wilma Witch . . . (WILMA *rises, curtsies, and sits.*) Polly Poltergeist . . . (POLLY *rises, curtsies, and sits.*) Gertrude Ghostess . . . (*Points to empty chair*) and (*Quickly*) Fanny Phantom. (FANNY *rises, curtsies, sits.*)

MRS. SPECTRE (*Puzzled*): Excuse me, Miss Magicia—but you mentioned four girls. I see only three.

MISS MAGICIA: Oh, I'm sorry. I should have remembered that Gertrude Ghostess has been doing her term paper on invisibility—and she's completely wrapped up in her work.

MRS. SPECTRE (*Skeptically*): I admit, Miss Magicia, that I would be very much impressed with your school if I thought you could really teach the art of invisibility. But I'm afraid I'm not easily fooled. (*Points to empty chair*) There's nobody sitting in that chair.

MISS MAGICIA: You're right! There's no *body* sitting in that chair. (MRS. SPECTRE *glares at her.*) Ha, ha! Just my little joke. (*Calling*) Gertrude! Demonstrate to Mrs. Spectre that you are really in the room. (MRS. SPECTRE *begins shrieking and jerk-*

ing her head, as though her hair were being pulled.) There! You see? We don't call Gertrude the school spirit for nothing!

MRS. SPECTRE (*As if trying to move out of reach*): Stop it! Stop at once! (*Recovering*) My! (*In admiration*) She certainly is the ghostess with the mostest! Though she could have demonstrated her skills less violently.

MISS MAGICIA: (*Soothingly*): Well, ghouls will be ghouls, you know. Now, who wishes to be next to show Mrs. Spectre what she has learned here at the seminary?

WILMA (*Waving her hand*): I will, Miss Magicia.

MISS MAGICIA: Very well, Wilma. (*To* MRS. SPECTRE) Wilma is majoring in languages. As a matter of fact, she won the National Witch Open Spelling Bee. Wilma, show Mrs. Spectre how well you can spell.

WILMA (*Rising*): Yes, Miss Magicia. (*Waves her hands as she speaks*)
Tail of monkey, funeral knell,
None escape this witch's spell.
Wing of bat and eye of newt,
Let this lady now be mute.
(*She sits down primly.*)

MISS MAGICIA (*Enthusiastically*): Wasn't that a wonderful spell, Mrs. Spectre? My, it takes me right back to the dear, dead days of the Middle Ages!

MRS. SPECTRE (*Unable to speak*): Mm-f! Mm-f!

MISS MAGICIA: What was that, Mrs. Spectre?

MRS. SPECTRE (*Trying desperately to speak*): Mm-m-mf-f-f! Mm-m-f-f!

MISS MAGICIA: Oh, of course! You can't speak because of Wilma's spell! She left *me* quite speechless, too! (MRS. SPECTRE *glares at her.*) Just a little joke. Wilma, dear, undo your spell, so Mrs. Spectre can talk again.

WILMA: I don't feel like it.

MISS MAGICIA (*Overly sweet*): Wilma, dear, do as I ask—or I'll have to put you on short rations. You know what that means, dear. No bones for a month—and no cream in your coffin, either.

WILMA (*Petulantly*): Oh, all right. (*Chants*)
Griffin's liver, lion's lung,
Let Mrs. Spectre use her tongue.

MISS MAGICIA: That's better.

MRS. SPECTRE (*Enthusiastically*): Oh, that was wonderful! Wonderful! I really must remember that—how did it go? "Tail of monkey, funeral knell . . ."

MISS MAGICIA (*Interrupting*): Now, Fanny Phantom, show Mrs. Spectre what you've learned in Shriekology. (FANNY *gives a cackling laugh and a blood-curdling scream.*)

MRS. SPECTRE (*Shivering*): Marvelous! Marvelous! Why, she positively made my blood run warm!

MISS MAGICIA: Yes, she's very talented. Although I must admit I can't take all the credit for Fanny's skills. She took part in our Junior Year Abroad program—spent last semester studying at some of England's most notable haunted castles.

FANNY (*Proudly*): I even took a graduate seminar at the Tower of London.

MISS MAGICIA: And now it's Polly Poltergeist's turn. Polly, show us what you can do.

POLLY (*Timidly*): I—I'm not sure I can, Miss Magicia. I've been sick.

MISS MAGICIA: Oh, I'm sorry to hear it.

POLLY: I went on a field trip—and I'm afraid I caught a warm.

MISS MAGICIA: Well, try, dear. I'm sure Mrs. Spectre will understand.

POLLY: Very well. (*In a timid voice*) Sha-zam.

MRS. SPECTRE (*Loftily*): And what, may I ask, was that supposed to be?

POLLY: It—it didn't work.

MISS MAGICIA: Try again, dear. And really put some umph into it.

POLLY: Sha-zam. Sha-zam, sha-zam, sha-zam! (MISS MAGICIA's *desk lifts slightly off the floor.* MISS MAGICIA *does this with her foot.*)

MISS MAGICIA (*Enthusiastically*): Did you see that, Mrs. Spectre? My desk jumped.

MRS. SPECTRE: Humph! I am *not* impressed.

MISS MAGICIA (*Hastily*): Polly, dear, as you're not feeling well, maybe you ought to try something a little less strenuous than table-lifting. How about a nice little remote knocking?

POLLY (*Tentatively*): I'll try. (*Recites*) Abra, cadabra, knock, knock, knock. (*There is a loud knocking on door right.*)

MISS MAGICIA (*Happily*): Good, Polly! (*Loud knocking is repeated.*)

MRS. SPECTRE: Well, I must admit that was a good deal better. (MISS GOBLINETTE *enters right.*)

MISS GOBLINETTE: Excuse me for just walking in, Miss Magicia—but I knocked twice, and nobody answered.

MRS. SPECTRE (*Rising indignantly*): Well! So it wasn't Polly's doing after all. (*Icily*) Miss Magicia, if this is the level of skill your seminary practices, I'm afraid there isn't a ghost of a chance of enrolling my daughters here.

MISS MAGICIA (*Upset*): Oh, Mrs. Spectre, I'm sure we can settle this to your complete satisfaction. Let me just see what my secretary wants . . .

MISS GOBLINETTE: It's the alumnae, Miss Magicia. (*To* MRS. SPECTRE) They've begun to arrive for our annual Halloween Homecoming. (*To* MISS MAGICIA) Apparently there's been some mixup over the housing arrangements.

MISS MAGICIA: Oh, dear! What seems to be the trouble?

MISS GOBLINETTE: Well, Queen Elizabeth the First and Bloody Mary both insist on staying in the Dormitory of the Seven Gables—but I can't get the girls from Salem to give up their rooms.

MRS. SPECTRE (*Impressed*): Did you say Queen Elizabeth and Bloody Mary?

MISS GOBLINETTE (*Continuing*): Then there are the graduates who belong to the Demons of the Ancient Regions . . .

MRS. SPECTRE (*Impressed*): The D.A.R.!

MISS GOBLINETTE: And as for the three weird sisters—

MRS. SPECTRE (*Interrupting*): Oh, Miss Magicia, I've changed my mind! My daughters must enroll here. Why, I had no idea that you have educated so many of the most fashionable spirits of all time!

MISS MAGICIA (*Surprised*): Why, Mrs. Spectre, I thought you knew. After all, you know our school motto. Girls?

WILMA, FANNY *and* POLLY (*In unison, hands over hearts*): High Goals—High Society—High Spirits!

MRS. SPECTRE (*Radiantly*): Just think! Why, if my girls come here—they might even end up in "Who's Who in Haunting!" (*Blackout*)

THE END

Voting Against the Odds

by Aileen Fisher

A heated campaign for class president challenges students to make the *right* choice. . . .

Characters

DOUG
RALPH
COLEMAN
PEGGY
NORMA
CELIA

TIME: *After school.*
SETTING: *A living room.*
AT RISE: RALPH *is sitting on sofa, thumbing through comic books.* DOUG *enters, carrying two huge sandwiches, hands one to* RALPH.
DOUG: Here. Peanut butter and honey.
RALPH: Thanks!
DOUG (*Looking at comic books*): Well, what do you think of my comics, Ralph? I'll trade you mine for yours.

RALPH: Maybe. (*He eats as he continues to look at books, and pulls one out*) Say, what kind of comic book is this?

DOUG: Oh, that. (*Laughs*) My mother bought it at a rummage sale, but when she read it, she was furious. The funny thing is, it made me mad, too.

RALPH (*Reading title*): "What's the Matter with the U.S.A.?" (*Looks up*) What made you mad?

DOUG: Turn the page.

RALPH (*Turning page, skimming it*): It's about voting. That's an odd subject for a comic book. (*Reads aloud*) "In an average election not even half of our qualified voters take the trouble to vote." Is that what upset your mother?

DOUG: Partly. The worst is yet to come. Go on!

RALPH (*Reading on*): "America is supposed to be the champion of democracy. Yet every one of the following countries has a better voting record than ours: Sweden, Norway, Italy, Holland, Great Britain, France, Finland, Denmark and Canada." (*Looking at* DOUG) Well, what do you know!

DOUG: The P.T.A. is going to run a "Get Out and Vote" campaign.

RALPH: You'd think that the United States would have the best voting record of all. Well, anyway, our homeroom didn't have any trouble electing a member to the Student Council. Not the way some classes have.

DOUG: My sister told me about that. Her class is having a run-off to cut its list of candidates down to two. The final vote is tomorrow.

RALPH: Peggy's one of the six on the list, isn't she?

DOUG: Uh-huh.

RALPH: Peggy's popular. She should do fine. Who's running against her?

DOUG: Coleman Winter and a couple of others.

RALPH: Wow! That's tough competition. With Coleman's athletic record she'll have to do some campaigning!

DOUG: The funny thing is, Peggy likes Coleman. (*Laughs*) She'd probably vote for him instead of for herself. I think she's crazy. He doesn't care about anything but sports.

RALPH: There's nothing wrong with sports.

DOUG: No, but Peggy has a lot of other ideas. Good ones that would improve things at the school—not just for athletes, but for everyone. She'd be good on the Student Council . . . even if she *is* my sister. (*Pauses*) How about another sandwich?

RALPH: Sure.

DOUG: O.K. I'll get it while you make up your mind about the comic books. (*Exits.* RALPH *looks through more comics. There is a tap on door.* COLEMAN *enters.*)

COLEMAN (*Walking center*): Hi, Ralph. Is Peggy home?

RALPH: Hi, Coleman. No, she's not here.

COLEMAN: Do you have any idea when she'll be back?

RALPH: I don't, but Doug may know. (*Calls off*) Hey, Doug! When's your sister coming home? (DOUG *enters*).

DOUG: Oh, hi, Coleman. Sorry, I don't have any idea. Want to leave a message?

COLEMAN: Well, yes. (*Hesitating*) Will you just tell her I'd appreciate her help in the election? As long as she won't be running against me in the finals.

DOUG (*Surprised*): You mean Peggy lost?

COLEMAN: Celia Upton squeezed her out by one vote. So I'll be running against Celia in the finals tomorrow.

DOUG: Who's Celia Upton?

COLEMAN (*Nonchalantly*): Oh, she's been around. She doesn't make much noise, but she's a real brain. What she doesn't have is Peggy's class. (*Boastfully*) The election ought to be a cinch.

RALPH (*Mischievously*): For Celia?

COLEMAN (*Snickering*): What do *you* think? (*To* DOUG) Tell Peggy I'd appreciate her support. The more votes, the merrier. If she could make a pennant or something . . . with my name on it . . . well, you know, whatever she can think of.

DOUG: Coleman, how do you think the money in the Student Council treasury should be used?

COLEMAN (*Shrugging*): Oh, I'll worry about that *after* the election.

DOUG: But it's the toughest decision the Student Council has to face.

COLEMAN (*Laughing*): It's never hard to spend money, Doug. (*Moves toward exit*) You'll tell Peggy about the pennant, huh? If the kids know she's for me, I'm as good as in. See you later! (*Exits*)

DOUG (*Shaking his head*): He may be a good football player, but. . . . Just a minute, I'll get those sandwiches. (*Exits; RALPH looks at comic books. In a moment, there is another knock on door. It opens, and NORMA enters, carrying books.*)

NORMA (*Calling*): Peggy!

RALPH: She's not home yet.

NORMA: (*Crossing to table*): O.K. I'll wait. (*To RALPH*) Aren't you Shirley Harper's brother? (*Puts books down. RALPH nods.*)

RALPH: Yes, I'm Ralph.

NORMA: Where's Doug?

DOUG (*Entering with sandwiches*): Hi, Norma. Want a snack?

NORMA: No, thanks. When do you think Peggy will be home?

DOUG: Search me. Everybody's looking for her.

NORMA: Everybody?

DOUG (*Sarcastically*): Even Coleman the Great was here.

NORMA: What did he want?

DOUG: He wants Peggy to support him in the election tomorrow.

NORMA: As if he couldn't win against Celia Upton without lifting a finger!

RALPH: Maybe he wants to make it unanimous.

DOUG: What I want to know is how Celia got more votes than Peggy.

NORMA: Only *one* more. And you know how modest Peggy is. She didn't push herself forward at all . . . even though she's done a lot of thinking about what the Student Council should do. I don't know Celia very well, but she's smart—and lots of kids look up to her.

RALPH: Who's getting your vote, Norma? (*PEGGY enters, stands at door unobserved.*)

NORMA: Nobody! I'm not going to vote.

PEGGY (*Entering*): Norma, you have to! Everybody should vote in an election.

OTHERS (*Ad lib*): Peggy! Hi! When did you get here? (*Etc.*)

DOUG: Peggy, I'm really sorry you didn't make the finals.

RALPH: Yes, that's really too bad.

PEGGY: Well, it's a democratic process, and I lost, that's all. I guess I didn't try hard enough to get votes. . . . But Norma, you absolutely have to vote!

NORMA: No, I don't. You were my candidate, Peggy, and if I can't vote for you, I won't vote.

PEGGY: What's the matter with Coleman? He's the most popular boy in school.

NORMA: The most popular *athlete*, Peggy. But he's just a yes-man, haven't you noticed? Not that it makes much difference in football . . . but I wouldn't want him deciding the agenda for the Student Council—not after all the work we put into raising that money!

PEGGY: I don't know why you think he's a yes-man. He's always been awfully nice . . .

NORMA: Being nice has nothing to do with it, Peggy. A candidate has to *stand* for something. What did Coleman say in his speech this morning? It boiled down to absolutely nothing.

PEGGY: What about Celia? What did she say? I was so nervous thinking about my own speech, I didn't really listen.

NORMA: Celia had some pretty good ideas, but she talked so softly I could hardly hear. Anyway, Peggy, if I can't vote for you, I'm not going to vote. I should have done some campaigning for you, but I was sure you were going to win.

PEGGY: Oh, well . . .

DOUG: Coleman was here a little while ago, Peggy. He wants your support. He said something about your making a pennant with his name on it.

NORMA (*Annoyed*): He would! I don't know why I didn't think of putting your name on a pennant, Peggy.

PEGGY: A pennant. Of course I'll do it . . . for Coleman. We've got some scraps of felt here somewhere. I'll be right back. (PEGGY *exits.*)

RALPH (*To* NORMA): You *are* going to vote, aren't you, Norma?

NORMA (*Dejectedly*): I suppose so.

DOUG (*Turning to* RALPH): What about the comic books, Ralph?

RALPH: Sure, I'll trade you.

DOUG: Great! I'll help you carry them over to your house. (*They pick up books.* RALPH *hands* NORMA *voting booklet, as they start to exit.*) Here's one you ought to read cover to cover. (*They exit. In a moment,* PEGGY *reenters, carrying pieces of felt, scissors, etc.*)

PEGGY: I had a hard time finding the right stuff for a pennant. (*Puts things down*) Let's see. (*Counts on fingers*) C-o-l-e-m-a-n. Seven letters. I have just enough scraps here. Want to help?

NORMA: No thanks, I'll watch. I just can't support him, Peggy.

PEGGY: Oh, I think you're being unfair, Norma. (*Begins to cut letters*) Anyone who can play football like that must have a sense of purpose. . . . (*Dreamily*) And anyone who looks like that . . .

NORMA: You know what? I'll bet if I called Coleman up and asked him if he thought it would be a good idea to buy footballs with Student Council money, he'd say yes.

PEGGY (*Laughing*): Not when the library needs books so badly. That's ridiculous. (*Goes on cutting*) But go ahead, call him. See what he says. (NORMA *goes to phone, dials, waits.*)

NORMA (*Into phone*): Hi, Coleman? . . . This is Norma. . . . Look, Coleman, when you get elected to the Student Council, don't you think it would be a good idea to invest all the money in the treasury—you know, the money we raised all year—in footballs and basketballs and sports equipment? . . . I *knew* you'd say that. See you tomorrow. (*She hangs up, turns.*) He agreed with everything I said. Now you call him, Peggy. Ask him about library books.

PEGGY (*Going to phone, dialing; into phone*): Coleman? Peggy. Doug says you stopped by to see me. Sorry I missed you. . . . Well, of course, it's hard when you lose by one vote, but I probably couldn't have won against *you,* anyway. Look, Coleman, one thing I had in my platform was more books for the library. And that international relief program to send books and science equipment to schools abroad. You agree, don't you? . . . Will you? . . . Can I count on it? . . . What a question! Of course I'll support you! . . . O.K., Coleman. Be seeing you. (*Hangs up phone*)

NORMA: He agreed with everything you said, didn't he?

PEGGY: Yes, he did. (*Half-heartedly she goes back to work on pennant.*)

NORMA: And it doesn't take a mastermind to figure out that you can't spend money for *all* those things he agrees to.

PEGGY (*Putting down scissors*): What are we going to do? . . .

NORMA: We don't have to vote. Nobody's going to *make* us.

PEGGY: But that never solves anything. (*Doorbell rings.* PEGGY *goes to door, opens it.*) Why, Celia! (*Hesitates*) Won't . . . won't you come in? Norma is here. (CELIA *enters.*)

CELIA: Hi, Norma.

NORMA (*Trying to be pleasant*): Hello, Celia.

CELIA: I suppose you think I've come to ask you to vote for me tomorrow, but I haven't. I've come to say I'd vote for you, Peggy.

PEGGY (*Amazed*): But I lost. I'm out of the running. Completely.

CELIA: If I withdrew you wouldn't be!

NORMA (*Suspiciously*): But why would you want to withdraw, Celia? You wanted to win, didn't you?

CELIA: Yes, I suppose everyone does. But I realize now that I can't beat Coleman. Not without the support of you and your friends, and I don't have that. We don't even know each other very well.

NORMA: You're scared you'll lose to Coleman, so you'd rather not be in the finals. Is that it?

CELIA (*Embarrassed*): No. It sounds crazy, maybe. But I'm more scared of Coleman's winning than I am of my losing. I mean, it's important for someone to beat him.

PEGGY (*Puzzled*): Why do you say that?

CELIA: Because he's not the kind of person we need on the Student Council. Oh, he's a great athlete, and everybody likes him, but he's always making promises and not keeping them. And whenever he does a good turn, he wants to get something out of it for himself.

NORMA (*Excitedly*): See, Peggy, it's not only that he's a yes-man.

CELIA (*With growing confidence*): We need someone on the Council with ideas about how to help the whole school, and even schools in other countries. You had good ideas in your talk,

Peggy. That library book program, for instance—it's important for everyone in the school.

PEGGY: I didn't even know you thought about it.

NORMA: Too bad you spoke so softly, Celia.

CELIA: I was nervous, too. You see, being here only a year and a half, I still feel like an outsider.

NORMA: You got more votes than Peggy.

CELIA: Only one. And I worked for it. And with the vote split six ways, that's not so surprising. But there's no way I can win against Coleman. Peggy, you're the only one who can.

NORMA (*To* PEGGY; *enthusiastically*): Why don't you do it, Peggy? I think Celia has a good idea. With her friends and ours behind you, you can beat the mighty Coleman.

CELIA (*To* PEGGY): I feel the way you do about the library, and sending science equipment to poor schools abroad. But Coleman isn't a bit interested in things like that. There is a place where he belongs—but it's not on the Student Council.

PEGGY (*Slowly, nodding*): You're right, Celia.

CELIA (*Eagerly*): Then you'll run if I withdraw

NORMA (*Excitedly*): Of course you will, won't you, Peggy? You *have* to!

PEGGY: Celia, you won fair and square, against much greater odds than I had. You deserve to keep your place, and I won't take it. But I will support you. Norma and I will tell our friends how we feel, won't we, Norma?

NORMA (*Enthusiastically*): You bet we will! Celia, I wasn't going to vote because Peggy lost. But I've changed my mind—and I'm *not* voting for Coleman.

CELIA (*Uncertainly*): Well, I don't know what to say. I would have been glad to withdraw. All I can say is that I'll do my best, if I win.

PEGGY: *When* you win. No if's about it! (NORMA, *at the table, is placing letters on pennant.*)

NORMA: What do you know!

PEGGY: What, Norma? (PEGGY *and* CELIA *move to table.*)

NORMA (*Picking up letters*): We can use the letters you cut out for our candidate. C . . . E . . . L . . . A. All we need is an I.

PEGGY (*Picking up scissors and letter M*): Here, I have it. (*As she works*) All we need to do is cut the straight piece from the M. Voilà—an I. (*Arranges letters on pennant*) There. Look, Celia! C-E-L-I-A. That's the pennant we'll be waving tomorrow for the winning side. (*Quick curtain*)

THE END

Hubbub on the Bookshelf

by *Alice Woster*

Bookworms are forced to change their diet—with astonishing results. . . .

Characters

1ST BOOKWORM, *Gangster*
2ND BOOKWORM, *Etiquette*
3RD BOOKWORM, *Red Riding Hood*
4TH BOOKWORM, *Ms. Wise*
5TH BOOKWORM, *Count Dracula*
6TH BOOKWORM, *Rock Superstar*
7TH BOOKWORM, *Knight of the Round Table*
8TH BOOKWORM, *Cowboy*
OLD BOOKWORM

SETTING: *An old bookshelf in an attic. Eight very large "books" (which may be represented by three- to four-foot cut-outs)— "Etiquette," "Grimms' Fairy Tales," "Encyclopedia," "Dracula," "Life of a Rock Superstar," "King Arthur and His Knights," "Tales of the Wild West," and "Arithmetic"—form the background. Each book has a flap at side for exits and entrances.*

AT RISE: 1ST BOOKWORM *enters right, followed by seven other* BOOKWORMS, *identical in appearance.*

1ST BOOKWORM (*Delighted*): It's true!

2ND BOOKWORM: Books and books and books!

3RD BOOKWORM: A paradise for bookworms!

5TH BOOKWORM: That spider told us the truth!

6TH BOOKWORM: No sign of inhabitants!

7TH BOOKWORM: Our long journey has not been in vain!

ALL: Let's eat! (*They start for the books.* OLD BOOKWORM *enters from "Encyclopedia" and stares at them in amazement.*)

OLD BOOKWORM: As I live and wiggle, these are creatures of my own kind! (*Stretches out arms*) Welcome, friends, welcome! (*They are silent.*) What is the matter? I am a Bookworm, too, just like you. Aren't you glad to see me?

8TH BOOKWORM (*Looking at others, disappointed*): We can't stay here. This bookshelf is already occupied!

2ND BOOKWORM (*To* OLD BOOKWORM): We are looking for a new place to settle, because we have been driven from our home downstairs. An old spider told us about this shelf of books in the attic, and we hoped to move in and send for our families. (*Sighs*) Now we have nowhere to go!

3RD BOOKWORM: And we are so hungry!

OTHERS: We are very hungry!

OLD BOOKWORM: But, I am the only one who lives here. There is plenty of room for you.

ALL: Hooray!

4TH BOOKWORM (*To* OLD BOOKWORM): Why do you live here all alone?

OLD BOOKWORM: (*Shrugging*): I grew up here and never knew any other life. There is a rumor that I was kidnapped in infancy by a gypsy moth.

5TH BOOKWORM: How sad!

OLD BOOKWORM: I *have* been lonely. The crickets and centipedes have been kind to me, but all my life I have wished for the companionship of my own people. That's why I am so happy to welcome you. There is nothing I would rather see than a thriving community of bookworms on this old bookshelf.

OTHER BOOKWORMS (*Ad lib*): Thank you! We're happy too! We've found a new home! (*Etc. They walk by the* OLD BOOKWORM *and, one by one, shake his hand. Then they form a group on opposite side of stage.*)

OLD BOOKWORM: Now tell me why you were driven from your homes.

6TH BOOKWORM: There was a dreadful disaster! Perhaps you don't know this, but the household downstairs is a dangerous place for insects. There is constant peril from vacuum cleaners, sprays, and exterminators.

OLD BOOKWORM: How horrible!

7TH BOOKWORM (*Tearfully*): Yes, many of our people have been wiped out by such weapons. But we thought we were safe. We lived in a box of stationery. . . . that belonged to the cook.

8TH BOOKWORM: It was just an old box of stationery—but it was home sweet home to us.

1ST BOOKWORM: We never bothered anyone.

OLD BOOKWORM: Then what great disaster befell you?

2ND BOOKWORM: The cook decided to write a letter.

3RD BOOKWORM: And she screamed so loud at the sight of us that we had to flee. It would have been too dangerous to stay there.

OLD BOOKWORM: You'll be safe here. These books have been long forgotten by the children who used to read them, and you can live here peacefully.

BOOKWORMS (*Ad lib*): Wonderful! Great! Hooray! (*Etc.*)

OLD BOOKWORM: Let's have a meeting so that we can organize our new community, and you can send for your families.

1ST BOOKWORM: But first we have to eat.

4TH BOOKWORM: Yes, we're starving! (*They start for books.*)

OLD BOOKWORM: Wait! (*They stop.*) I'll be happy to make lunch for you.

2ND BOOKWORM: Oh, that's not necessary. There are lots of big books here. We'll just help ourselves.

OLD BOOKWORM: Oh, no! You mustn't do that!

3RD BOOKWORM: Why not?

OLD BOOKWORM: If you have always lived in a box of plain stationery, you're accustomed only to very simple, plain meals.

Some of these books may be too rich for you. They may be hard to digest . . .

4TH BOOKWORM: That's silly!

BOOKWORMS: Ridiculous!

OLD BOOKWORM: I have lived here all my life, and I know.

5TH BOOKWORM (*Firmly*): We're perfectly able to choose for ourselves.

OLD BOOKWORM (*Worried*): If you won't let me help you choose your food, at least let's have the meeting before you eat.

6TH BOOKWORM: We are too hungry.

7TH BOOKWORM: It'll take us only a few minutes to eat. We can have the meeting afterward.

8TH BOOKWORM: The meeting won't take very long. We all agree on our future. We always agree on everything.

1ST BOOKWORM: And after we eat we'll be able to think more clearly.

OLD BOOKWORM (*Solemnly*): I seriously doubt it. I warn you, you are acting against my best advice.

2ND BOOKWORM: We'll be with you in a minute. (*To other* BOOKWORMS) Let's eat.

BOOKWORMS: Yes, let's eat! (*All except* 1ST BOOKWORM *and* OLD BOOKWORM *go into first seven books, leaving only "Arithmetic" empty.* 1ST BOOKWORM *lingers behind.*)

1ST BOOKWORM (*Pulling scrap of blank paper from his pocket*): I still have a piece of stationery left, I brought to eat on the way. I'll finish it first and then try one of the books. (*He sits and munches on paper.*)

OLD BOOKWORM (*Absently*): Suit yourself. (*He paces back and forth, shaking head anxiously.*) I'm afraid there's going to be trouble.

1ST BOOKWORM: Don't you think you're making too much of this? We can digest your big books!

OLD BOOKWORM: I'm sure you can digest them all right. Too well, probably. But you should have let me choose a balanced diet for you. Too much of one thing is bad—

1ST BOOKWORM: All right, then tell me which of those books is the best one, and I will sample it.

OLD BOOKWORM: I cannot say that any one of them is *best*. They are all very good. There is the "Encyclopedia"—I am very fond of that. Especially at dinner time. It is a little heavy for breakfast. I like something lighter at breakfast, this book of "Fairy Tales," for instance. For a heartier repast, here's "Dracula"—that's blood-curdling! "Etiquette"—"King Arthur and His Knights"—"Life of a Rock Superstar"—"Tales of the Wild West"—"Arithmetic"—each one is delectable in its own way. If you take my advice, you'll try a little of each, because you will enjoy them all. There's nothing like a varied diet. And besides, that way you'll all stay out of trouble.

1st Bookworm: You have your mind set on trouble, haven't you? Wait till my friends come out of the books, they'll be fine, just the way they were before.

Old Bookworm: That, my young friend, is unlikely.

1st Bookworm (*Pointing to "Etiquette" book*): Here comes one now.

Old Bookworm: Yes. Out of the book of etiquette. (*Shakes head*) That's a delicate diet. (Amy Etiquette, *formerly* 2nd Bookworm, *comes out of Etiquette book. She wears large, flowered hat, white gloves, and lorgnette, which she peers through in affected manner. She looks at others haughtily through lorgnette.*)

Amy Etiquette: How do you do? (*Gushing*) I'm so *very* happy to see you again! (*She extends her hand to* Old Bookworm, *who shakes it.*)

1st Bookworm: For goodness' sake!

Old Bookworm: I knew this would happen.

Amy Etiquette (*Walking toward* 1st Bookworm, *peering at him through lorgnette*): Why don't you rise when a lady enters the room? It is bad manners to remain seated.

1st Bookworm (*Standing; puzzled*): I don't know what's going on. She never talked this way before. (*Glancing at books*) Look! Someone else is coming out!

Old Bookworm: Yes, from the book of Fairy Tales. (*Book of "Fairy Tales" opens, and out comes* Red Riding Hood, *formerly* 3rd Bookworm, *now dressed in red cape with hood and carrying basket.*)

1st Bookworm: Why is she wearing that red coat?

OLD BOOKWORM: It's really a red hood. "Little Red Riding Hood" is one of the fairy tales in that book.

RED RIDING HOOD: Just see the nice cake I am taking to Grandmother! (*Lifts napkin in basket*) Which is the way to Grandmother's house? This way? (*Skips gaily across stage to left, singing loudly "Over the River," or any song.*) Or this way? (*Skips right, and looks offstage*)

AMY ETIQUETTE: Please stop that silly skipping! Don't you know children should be seen and not heard? Come here and curtsy to me.

RED RIDING HOOD: Why should I?

AMY ETIQUETTE: Little girls should always curtsy to ladies. And I am a lady-bug. (*"Encyclopedia" opens and out comes* 4TH BOOKWORM, *now* Ms. WISE, *wearing black mortar-board and large spectacles.*)

Ms. WISE (*Impressively*): A laser beam can cut through a solid steel girder in fifty-five seconds.

RED RIDING HOOD (*Sarcastically*): What for?

AMY ETIQUETTE: My dear child, that remark was very rude.

RED RIDING HOOD (*Skipping to* Ms. WISE): See my nice cake for Grandmother?

Ms. WISE (*Looking at cake*): It is manifestly a culinary achievement.

RED RIDING HOOD: No, it's not. It's a cake. (OLD BOOKWORM *is shaking his head in dismay. "Dracula" book opens, and* COUNT DRACULA, *formerly* 5TH BOOKWORM, *comes out, dressed in black, with flowing black cape. He stalks around stage, menacingly, swirling his cape.*)

DRACULA (*Heavily accented speech*): Good evening. I am Count Dracula of Transylvania.

1ST BOOKWORM (*In despair*): I'm afraid that his book was not in the best of taste.

COUNT DRACULA (*Menacingly*): Right now I am thirsty . . . very, very thirsty. I must have my crimson brew before morning.

AMY ETIQUETTE: A glass of milk before retiring is all that any proper person should require.

DRACULA: I never drink milk . . . (*Making a face*) Ugh! It is so pale, so white!

RED RIDING HOOD (*Skipping up to* DRACULA): See the nice cake that I am taking to my grandmother.

DRACULA (*Rubbing his hands together*): Did you say that your grandmother was here? Hmmn. . . . I would like to sink my teeth into her neck!

RED RIDING HOOD (*Pointing to "Rock Superstar" book*): Look! Here comes somebody else! (6TH BOOKWORM, *now* ROCK SUPERSTAR, *comes out of book, moving rhythmically, and snapping his fingers. He wears shiny outfit, dark glasses, and carries guitar.*)

ROCK SUPERSTAR (*Striking a pose*): Hold the applause until I finish my act. (*Sings or pantomimes to a record, strumming guitar and gyrating in time to music. Any popular rock record may be used.*)

AMY ETIQUETTE (*At conclusion of song*): That was highly immodest and improper!

RED RIDING HOOD (*In ecstasy*): Oo-o-oh! He's divine!

1ST BOOKWORM (*To* OLD BOOKWORM): What happened to him?

OLD BOOKWORM (*With a sigh*): He has overindulged. (*Book of "King Arthur and His Knights" opens, and* 7TH BOOKWORM, *now dressed as* KNIGHT, *with helmet and sword, comes out.*)

KNIGHT (*Seeing* RED RIDING HOOD, *who squeals*): Ah, a damsel in distress! (*Draws sword; bows to her.*) Fair damsel, tell me who hath made thee weep and wail in sorrow, and by my faith, I will avenge thee!

RED RIDING HOOD (*Pointing to* ROCK SUPERSTAR): It's him!

MS. WISE (*Shaking head*): That pronoun usage is incorrect. You should have said, "It is he."

KNIGHT (*Striding to* ROCK SUPERSTAR): If thou hast in truth distressed this damsel, make ready to defend thyself!

ROCK SUPERSTAR: Cool it, man. I don't know what came over her. I was just singing my song and strumming my guitar.

DRACULA: We have nothing like him in Transylvania. Only the beautiful music of howling wolves . . . (*Book of "Wild West Tales" opens, and out comes* 8TH BOOKWORM, *now* COWBOY, *wearing ten-gallon hat, chaps, vest, boots, spurs, etc.*)

COWBOY: It's mighty lonesome on the range! I'm hankering for a bite of chow.

1ST BOOKWORM: Where did he learn to talk like that?

OLD BOOKWORM: I'm afraid that it was something he ate.

RED RIDING HOOD: I'm taking goodies to my grandmother. She lives in a cottage in the forest.

DRACULA (*Hopefully*): Maybe there are bats in the forest. I like bats!

MS. WISE: Bats are one of the numerous flying mammals, being nocturnal in habit.

RED RIDING HOOD (*Giggling*): How fascinating!

AMY ETIQUETTE: Little girls should not be rude!

OLD BOOKWORM (*Banging on table*): The meeting will come to order. Quiet, please! It troubles me greatly to see how much you have been changed. I feared as much if you ate such a rich diet.

1ST BOOKWORM: That reminds me. I haven't eaten yet myself. I think I'll have a snack.

RED RIDING HOOD: Do try some Fairy Tales. You'll love them.

AMY ETIQUETTE: If you will allow me to suggest, try a bit of "Etiquette."

COWBOY: Pardner, why not saddle up and ride into the Wild West over yonder?

ROCK SUPERSTAR: Read about my life. I drive a gold-plated limousine, and I have thirty-one guitars, one for each day of the month.

KNIGHT: If thou wilt take thy repast at the Round Table of King Arthur, I'm sure thou wilt find it to thy liking.

MS. WISE: I feel confident that you will appreciate the wisdom of the "Encyclopedia."

DRACULA: My book of Dracula is thrilling . . . and chilling!

1ST BOOKWORM (*Waving them away*): I don't want to be like any of you. (*Points*) There's a book at the end that none of you tried—I think I'll sample that. (*Looks closely at "Arithmetic" book*) What's the name of it?

OLD BOOKWORM: That's "Arithmetic," my boy. It's a good book—pretty solid, of course, but very worthwhile. But hurry back, because we must begin our meeting.

1ST BOOKWORM: You start it, and I'll be right back shortly. (*Goes into "Arithmetic" book*)

OLD BOOKWORM (*Gesturing toward left*): Please sit over there. (*All sit in group*) My friends, I am taking it upon myself to begin this meeting because I have recently devoured several books about government and politics. Very dry, they were, but not without some spice. I have learned that it is best to establish some form of government for our new community. Then you can send for your families and build your new homes.

DRACULA: Hear, hear! A dank and gloomy castle makes a wonderful home. And there should be lots of bats in it.

COWBOY: I like to sleep under the stars with my faithful horse.

AMY ETIQUETTE: Every home should have seven monogrammed, linen tablecloths at the very least.

ROCK SUPERSTAR: Southern hospitality is what I like. And my favorite music piped into every room.

RED RIDING HOOD: We must hurry, because I want to bring this food to my dear grandma.

OLD BOOKWORM: I am glad you all agree. Now to proceed. . . .

MS. WISE: A government is an established system of administration of public affairs.

OLD BOOKWORM: Yes, yes, of course. What kind of government do you think we should have?

RED RIDING HOOD: I think it would be nice to have a fairy queen.

KNIGHT: Or perchance a noble king, like good King Arthur.

MS. WISE: A manifestly unwise decision, entailing absolute rule by a monarch.

DRACULA: Why should there be any government? Why can't we all do just as we please, and be as free as bats! When we are thirsty, we can drink . . . (*Howls*)

ROCK SUPERSTAR: Anyone who can play the guitar can be the mayor!

OLD BOOKWORM (*Anxiously*): Perhaps we should first decide what we wish it to do for us.

AMY ETIQUETTE: I think the chief purpose of our community should be to teach everyone good manners.

KNIGHT: I fain would have a goodly company of brave knights, to protect ladies and young damsels, and to slay all dragons, serpents, and giants in the countryside.

COWBOY: We'll have to saddle up and ride the north forty, looking for strays, and keeping the rustlers off our land. Then, at night, we can visit the saloon for some sarsaparilla.

Ms. WISE: My opinion is that we should devote ourselves to the acquisition of knowledge.

RED RIDING HOOD: I think every one of us should have a goose that lays golden eggs and a fairy godmother.

DRACULA: By day we should sleep in our coffins. Then by night we can soar through the skies in search of sleeping victims. (*Howls eerily.*)

ROCK SUPERSTAR: Let's sing rock all night!

Ms. WISE: That idea is ludicrous.

ROCK SUPERSTAR (*Angrily*): What do you know about it?

AMY ETIQUETTE (*To* ROCK SUPERSTAR): Please! Where are your manners? No insulting remarks are permissible.

Ms. WISE: My dear lady, individuals who have really good manners don't talk about them incessantly.

AMY ETIQUETTE: Why the very idea! I've never been so insulted in my life!

KNIGHT (*Drawing sword and going toward* Ms. WISE): Fie on thee! Why dost thou assault this lady!

Ms. WISE: Now, now, Mr. Knight! Your sword is not needed.

KNIGHT: (*Pompously*): Do not insult this lady, or I will smite off thy head. (*Makes menacing gesture with sword.*)

AMY ETIQUETTE: That would not be polite.

RED RIDING HOOD: No, it wouldn't be polite at all. I don't think we ought to have a company of knights in our town. They would be worse than a wolf.

DRACULA: Ah, the howling of a wolf! What a wonderful, spine-tingling sound!

COWBOY: Out on the prairie it's a lonesome sound. I don't hanker to hear any wolf howling, no, siree! Coyotes are bad enough.

DRACULA: How dare you!

COWBOY: You're the orneriest varmint this side of the Rockies.

OLD BOOKWORM: Please, please! This is no time for idle bickering if we are to live together peacefully.

AMY ETIQUETTE: Really, I don't see how you can expect me to get along with persons who are so uncouth!

Ms. Wise: And so ignorant!

Cowboy: Real dudes.

Dracula: So bloodless!

Rock Superstar: So unmusical!

Knight: So lacking in gallantry!

Old Bookworm (*In despair*): We must cooperate.

Amy Etiquette (*Haughtily*): I don't seem to feel very cooperative.

Ms. Wise: Neither do I.

Cowboy: Neither do I.

Dracula: Nor I.

Rock Superstar: Count me out!

Knight: Nay.

Red Riding Hood: I want to go home!

Old Bookworm (*Upset*): This is terrible! Everything is ruined.

Red Riding Hood (*Pointing to "Arithmetic" book*): Look! He's coming out!

Old Bookworm: Maybe he can help us. Arithmetic is solid, substantial! (1st Bookworm *steps out of "Arithmetic" book, now dressed like a gangster. He carries a giant-sized spray can, with a large label reading* INSECT REPELLANT.)

Gangster: Reach, all of you! I've got you covered! (*Everyone slowly raises arms.*) Make it snappy! (*As they comply*) That's better. (*Sternly*) Now, what's going on here? (*To* Old Bookworm) Pops, you should be able to give me the lowdown.

Old Bookworm (*Dismayed*): This is our meeting! Have your forgotten? We're trying to form a new government.

Gangster (*Laughing harshly*): Oh, yes, the meeting. But don't bother about forming a government—*I'm* your government here from now on. All you have to do is just what I tell you. And I'm going to make you an offer you can't refuse.

Dracula (*Aside*): I don't like this! I think I'll sink my fangs into him.

Old Bookworm: Where did he get these ideas? I always had the highest regard for Arithmetic. I can't see how it could have affected him this way.

Red Riding Hood: Maybe he's under the spell of a wicked witch!

KNIGHT: There must be a fearful dragon within that book!

AMY ETIQUETTE: It sounds to me like rudeness, greed, and plain selfishness!

Ms. WISE: It is undoubtedly caused by lack of learning.

GANGSTER (*Waving can*): All of you! Silence!

OLD BOOKWORM: Why do you talk this way?

GANGSTER: Silence, I said! Anyone who refuses to do what I say will soon be wearing a concrete overcoat.

Ms. WISE: This is incomprehensible!

KNIGHT: I, for one, will never pay thee tribute!

AMY ETIQUETTE: If you want me to do anything you'll have to say "please"!

RED RIDING HOOD (*Tearfully*): I want to see my grandmother!

DRACULA: Remember, I have sharp fangs!

ROCK SUPERSTAR (*Singing and strumming guitar*): Never, never, never!

KNIGHT (*Brandishing sword*): Let me deal with him.

GANGSTER (*Sneering*): You wouldn't dare! One blast from this (*Waving spray can*), and you'll be goners!

KNIGHT: Thou boasteth greatly, and speaketh wild words, but I fear thee not! (*Advances on* GANGSTER)

Ms. WISE: No, stop! Your courage is inspiring Sir Knight, but a sword hasn't a chance against this menace.

RED RIDING HOOD: Please, Sir Knight, you might get hurt.

Ms. WISE: Let us—excuse my slang—put our heads together and come up with a plan. (*All seven huddle and whisper, while* OLD BOOKWORM *and* GANGSTER *watch.*)

GANGSTER: Forget it. You don't have a chance against me.

OLD BOOKWORM (*Sadly*): I cannot understand what has caused this terrible change in you. Surely a few bites of Arithmetic couldn't have done it. It is a dreadful mystery.

GANGSTER: No more talk! Pops! (*The huddle breaks up.*)

COWBOY (*To* GANGSTER *in discouraged tone*): Well, you win. We're helpless.

GANGSTER: Now you're talking.

Ms. WISE: Defeat is humiliating, but what can we do? (*Shrugs*)

GANGSTER: Nothing—you can do what I tell you!

DRACULA: I will not bite you now.

GANGSTER: It'll be too bad for you if you do! Good thing you all had enough sense to give up. (*All nod, sadly.*)

RED RIDING HOOD: Yoo-hoo! Grandma! Come right in! (*She waves as if someone were standing behind* GANGSTER. *He whirls around and others quickly pounce on him, knocking the spray can from his hand.*)

DRACULA (*Picking up spray can and pointing it at* GANGSTER): Now you are in our power!

ROCK SUPERSTAR: We've got him!

MS. WISE: Yes, we've got him, all right. But what are we going to do with him?

AMY ETIQUETTE: He should be made to apologize to each of us!

RED RIDING HOOD: I think he ought to be turned into a donkey and be forced to pull a heavy load for a year and a day.

COWBOY: Let's tie him to a cactus and leave him for the buzzards!

ROCK SUPERSTAR: Let him listen to me sing. That will be a real lesson for him.

KNIGHT: I would gladly smite him. (*Waves sword*)

OLD BOOKWORM: Wait—please wait a few moments before you choose a punishment for him. I cannot understand how this could have happened. Let me go into the "Arithmetic" book and see if I can find any clue to this mystery.

MS. WISE: All right, we'll wait a little while, but eventually this hoodlum is going to get what's coming to him. (OLD BOOKWORM *goes into "Arithmetic" book.*)

RED RIDING HOOD: And he used to be a real nice fellow.

KNIGHT: He was of noble and gentle nature.

AMY ETIQUETTE: I cannot imagine what caused him to change.

OLD BOOKWORM: (*Coming out of back*): It is astounding!

COWBOY: What's astounding?

OLD BOOKWORM: It is unbelievable! Do you know, some mischievous youngster who once owned that "Arithmetic" book hid a comic book (*Holds up large comic book*) in the middle of it!

OTHERS (*Ad lib*): Oh! Not really! How could that be? (*Etc.*)

OLD BOOKWORM (*To* GANGSTER): That was what you ate, wasn't it?

GANGSTER (*Sullenly*): What if it was? What's it to you?

OLD BOOKWORM (*To others*): He happened to nibble at the very worst part, and he swallowed every word of it!

OTHERS (*Ad lib*): Oh! How dreadful! No! (*Etc.*)

OLD BOOKWORM (*To* GANGSTER, *waving comic book*): I can't believe you really gorged yourself on this!

GANGSTER: It's none of your business!

OLD BOOKWORM: Poor fellow! You probably have a bad case of indigestion. (*In kindly voice*) Tell me, does your stomach hurt?

GANGSTER (*Suddenly moaning and holding hands on stomach*): Yes, it does! It's killing me! (*Moans*) Oh-h-h!

AMY ETIQUETTE: No wonder, after filling up on all that trash!

GANGSTER (*Moaning*): Oh! My stomach! Help me, someone!

RED RIDING HOOD: The poor fellow! What can we do for him?

MS. WISE: He needs an antidote.

COWBOY (*With a friendly smile at* DRACULA): Maybe he needs a change, and some good books! He should read "Dracula."

KNIGHT: Yes, he should read "Dracula."

RED RIDING HOOD: Some fresh air will be good for him. He should read "Tales of the Wild West."

ROCK SUPERSTAR: How about a bit of "King Arthur's Knights?"

MS. WISE: Some "Etiquette" is always beneficial! (OLD BOOKWORM *is smiling and nodding approvingly.*)

DRACULA: He will benefit from a taste of every book on the shelf.

COWBOY: Yes! Every book on the shelf! That's just what he needs.

OLD BOOKWORM: I believe you have found the right solution.

AMY ETIQUETTE (*To* GANGSTER): Come on, you would-be gangster. We'll cure your indigestion, with a powerful medicine that acts ten times faster than any leading wonder drug. You're going to have a dose of the "Encyclopedia." (GANGSTER *still holding stomach, goes into "Encyclopedia."*) It would do all of us good to vary our diet.

OLD BOOKWORM: Bravo! A sound mind in a healthy body! Now I know that you are off to a good start. Our new town will flourish.

MS. WISE: You're right. A balanced diet of books will make you lively and happy. (*All nod.*)

KNIGHT: It improves the digestion, too.
ALL (*Together*):
Tasty pages are what we need—
We'll dine with pleasure on books to read! (*Curtain*)
THE END

The Case of the Bewitched Books

by Claire Boiko

When fairy tale villains turn the tables on heroines . . .

Characters

WITCH, *from "Sleeping Beauty"*
TWO STEPSISTERS, *from "Cinderella"*
WICKED QUEEN, *from "Snow White"*
THREE READERS
SLEEPING BEAUTY
PRINCE FLORIAN
HERALD
PRINCE CHARMING
CINDERELLA
CHUBBY
SLUMPY
SLOPPY
GROUCHY   *seven dwarfs*
WOOZY
SNIFFLY
MOPEY

SNOW WHITE
PRINCE ROLAND
LIBRARIAN

BEFORE RISE: *Sign reading,* FAIRY TALE FESTIVAL, CHILDREN'S
ROOM OF THE PUBLIC LIBRARY, *stands on easel down right.*
WITCH, TWO STEPSISTERS, *and* WICKED QUEEN *are marching
back and forth on the apron of the stage, carrying picket signs.*
WITCH *carries sign proclaiming,* FAIRY TALES UNFAIR TO
WITCHES. WICKED QUEEN'S *sign says,* MIRROR, MIRROR ON THE
WALL, WE WANT JUSTICE FOR VILLAINS ALL! TWO STEPSISTERS
wear sandwich signs, one reading, SUPPORT YOUR LOCAL STEP-
SISTERS, *and the other,* STEPSISTERS ARE HUMAN, TOO.

ALL (*Chanting*): Boycott the library! Books are unfair to villains!
(1ST READER *and* 2ND READER, *carrying books, enter right,
cross stage, and start to exit through curtain, center, paying no
attention to picketers.*)

WITCH (*To* 1ST READER): Stop! You don't want to go to that silly
old Fairy Tale Festival, do you? (*As* 1ST READER *ignores her and
exits,* WITCH *walks in front of* 2ND READER, *pleading.*) Don't go
in dearie. There's not a word of truth about witches in those
books. (2ND READER *exits without speaking.*)

WICKED QUEEN: They didn't pay the slightest attention to you.
(3RD READER *enters left, with books.*)

1ST STEPSISTER (*To* 3RD READER): Stay away! Every word you read
about stepsisters is a lie! (*As* 3RD READER *exits*) Humph! He
didn't even see me.

2ND STEPSISTER: Of course he didn't see you. You're imaginary.

1ST STEPSISTER: Is that so? Well, if I'm imaginary, you're imaginary, too.

WITCH: We're all imaginary. Nobody can see us or hear us. That's
too bad, because I wore my favorite perfume—Eye of Newt
Number Five—especially to impress the children.

WICKED QUEEN (*To others*): I told you that picketing the library
was a ridiculous idea.

1ST STEPSISTER: Do you have a better plan?

2ND STEPSISTER: How can we make people like us?

WICKED QUEEN: I don't know. I can't understand why people shudder so when they read about us. We're full of personality.

1ST STEPSISTER: Not to mention charm.

2ND STEPSISTER: And beauty.

WITCH (*Thoughtfully*): I think I know what it is.

ALL (*Ad lib*): What? Tell us! (*Etc.*)

WITCH: We're not the *heroines*. We never get the prince.

1ST STEPSISTER: That's right. We get invitations to the ball, but somebody else gets the prince.

WICKED QUEEN: And there's always some silly snip who thinks *she's* the fairest of us all.

WITCH: Exactly. Oh, if only I could be a heroine! Children would adore me.

WICKED QUEEN: Listen, friends. Instead of this useless picketing, let's do the thing we do the best.

WITCH: Aha! You mean—cast a spell?

WICKED QUEEN: Precisely. Cast a spell over all the books of fairy tales. Turn them topsy-turvy. *We* will become the heroines.

ALL (*Ad lib*): Sounds good, Queen. Not a bad idea. (*Etc.*)

WITCH: We'll be popular at last. Come. Put down your signs and form a magic circle. (*All cross left, put signs down, return to center and form a circle, holding hands. As they chant, they circle counter-clockwise.*)

ALL (*Together*):
Fairy tales and legends dim,
Andersen and Brothers Grimm,
You must transform and mutate
Wicked witches full of hate,
Queens of evil, bringing woes,
And sisters silly, now transpose.
Alter, vary, modulate! (*They go faster.*)
Shift and turn and deviate!
Crown for wand, and wand for crown,
Down-side up and upside down,
Backside-to and widdershins,
Turn us into *heroines*.
(*They run offstage left.*)

* * * * *

TIME: *Immediately following.*

SETTING: *The library. Up center is a bookcase labeled* FAIRY TALES. *Librarian's desk and chair stand left. Down right is table with three chairs.*

AT RISE: 1ST, 2ND, *and* 3RD READERS *are seated at table, reading intently. Ominous chords are heard.*

1ST READER (*Holding up book entitled* SLEEPING BEAUTY; *dismayed*): What's happening? The words in this book are changing before my eyes! (*Musical chord is heard.*)

2ND READER (*Holding up book* CINDERELLA): It's all blurry. (*Rubs eyes; chord is heard*)

3RD READER (*Holding up* SNOW WHITE): Something's the matter with "Snow White." The story is all wrong.

1ST READER: Remember the ending of "Sleeping Beauty"? Well, listen to this. (*Reads*) "And then, the noble Prince Florian parted the fence of brambles and came to the castle where everyone had been asleep for a hundred years. . . . (*Lullaby music is played softly in background, as* STAGEHAND *pushes* SLEEPING BEAUTY, *asleep, in wheelchair; another* STAGEHAND *pushes* WITCH *in on chaise. She is covered with a sheet.* PRINCE FLORIAN *enters.*) The prince climbed into a dark tower, where a lovely heroine lay fast asleep. Oh, yes. There was a Princess of no great account in the room, too. . . ."

PRINCE FLORIAN: How strange! The castle seems to be under a spell of some kind. Who could have cast such a cruel enchantment? (*Crossing to* SLEEPING BEAUTY, *he regards her with disfavor.*) Ugh! A beautiful Princess? What a sight! That disgusting curly hair and those gruesome rosy cheeks. I'll bet *she* cast the spell. She looks evil enough to do something like that. (*Crossing to chaise, and pulling off the sheet, then gasping in admiration.*) Oh, what a marvel! That delicate beaky nose! How I long to snag my fingers in her musty, matted hair. And all those lovely little green warts! (*Inhaling*) Ah-h, Eye of Newt Number Five. My favorite perfume. (*Leaning over*) Awake. Awake you heavenly hag.

WITCH (*Opening eyes*): At last, my prince has come. I have you all to myself now. (*She cackles.*)

FLORIAN (*Aside*): Listen to that melodious laughter. Like little silver bells.

SLEEPING BEAUTY (*Waking, reaching out to* FLORIAN): Oh, Prince Florian. (*He turns to her.*) I have waited a hundred long years for you.

FLORIAN (*Grimacing, then as he takes sheet and throws it over* SLEEPING BEAUTY): Why don't you go back to sleep for another hundred years? (*To* WITCH) Come, let the wedding bells ring. (*He exits, leading* WITCH, *cackling happily.* STAGEHANDS *push* SLEEPING BEAUTY, *covered with sheet, offstage.*)

2ND READER (*To other* READERS): I don't understand it. Everything's all mixed up in my book, too. Listen to the ballroom scene in "Cinderella." The Prince is awaiting the arrival of the guests, and the Herald is about to blow a fanfare, opening the ball. . . . (*Rippling chords are heard.* HERALD *enters, stands down right, carrying trumpet.* PRINCE CHARMING *enters, stands up center, arms folded.*)

HERALD (*Blowing fanfare, then speaking*): Let the royal ball of the kingdom of Prince Charming begin. (*Waltz is heard softly in background.*) Announcing the arrival of the mystery princess—Cinderella. (*Fanfare.* CINDERELLA *glides across stage to* CHARMING *and curtsies.* CHARMING *bows, then yawns.*)

CHARMING: What was that name again?

CINDERELLA: Cinderella, Your Highness.

CHARMING (*Yawning again*): Ho-hum. So you're the mystery princess, eh? Mysteries bore me. (CINDERELLA *curtsies again.*) Why the curtsy? You want to dance, is that it?

CINDERELLA: That would be *thrilling*, Your Highness.

CHARMING: Only for you. (*He holds her at arm's length, and they dance a measure or two.* HERALD *blows fanfare.*)

HERALD: Announcing the arrival of two stepsisters. (*Music stops.* CHARMING *gazes, thunderstruck, as* TWO STEPSISTERS *enter. He leaves* CINDERELLA *abruptly and goes to greet* STEPSISTERS.)

CHARMING (*To* 1ST STEPSISTER): Magnificent!

1ST STEPSISTER: Oh! I never, ever thought you'd say that word to *me*, Your Highness.

CHARMING (*To* 2ND STEPSISTER): Beautiful!

2ND STEPSISTER (*With hand to chest*): Be still, my heart. After all these years, he called me "beautiful."

CHARMING (*Aside*): One is more ravishing than the other. With whom shall I dance first? (*Pointing to* STEPSISTERS) You first. No, you. It's no use. I can't choose. I shall dance with you both. (*They join hands and dance, as music plays. Sound of chimes striking twelve is heard.*)

HERALD: Announcing the arrival of midnight.

CINDERELLA: I must go, Your Highness.

CHARMING (*Still dancing with* STEPSISTERS): Don't let me keep you.

CINDERELLA: My coach will turn into a pumpkin.

CHARMING: Trot along, Cinder-whatever-your-name-is. Don't keep your pumpkin waiting.

CINDERELLA: Aren't you going to follow me? Don't you want my glass slipper?

CHARMING: Whatever for? I have a whole drawer full of girls' slippers. They keep falling off at these balls. Hand it to the Herald on your way out. (*To* STEPSISTERS) Now, my beauties, let us go in to the royal banquet. (*Takes arm of each* STEPSISTER, *as they exit left.* CINDERELLA, *holding out slipper, lets out a long wail.* HERALD *takes slipper, puts it in pocket and exits, followed by* CINDERELLA, *still crying.*)

3RD READER (*To other* READERS): You think *your* books are mixed up! I can't believe what I just read about Snow White. Remember when she escapes from the Wicked Queen and goes to live with seven dwarfs? Well, listen to this. (*Lively march music is heard, as* SNOW WHITE, *barking like a drill sergeant, leads* CHUBBY, SLUMPY, SLOPPY, GROUCHY, WOOZY, SNIFFLY *and* MOPEY, *puffing wearily, onstage.*)

SNOW WHITE: Hup, two, three, four. Hup, two, three, four. Pick up your feet, boys. (PRINCE ROLAND *enters left, and quietly watches action, unnoticed. He shakes his head in disbelief.*)

CHUBBY (*Panting*): Please, Snow White. Can't we rest?

DWARFS (*Together*): We're exhausted!

SNOW WHITE: Company, halt! (DWARFS *line up across stage.* SNOW WHITE *reviews them, shaking her head.*) Stand up

straight, Slumpy. (SLUMPY *sighs and stands straight.*) Button
your buttons, Sloppy. (SLOPPY *buttons his tunic.* WOOZY *yawns.*)
Aha, I caught you yawning, Woozy. Bedtime at six o'clock for
you tonight.

WOOZY: But, Snow White, I'm tired because we've been marching
all day.

SNOW WHITE: No buts, Woozy. Listen, everyone, someday my
prince will come, and I want you all to be in tip-top shape.

GROUCHY: We were so happy before you came along, Snow White.
We used to sing and dance. Now all we do is march.

SNOW WHITE: No complaints, Grouchy. Remember—a healthy
dwarf is a happy dwarf. (SNIFFLY *sniffs loudly.*) Don't you have
a handkerchief, Sniffly? (*To all*) Now, stand at attention, while
I go to the top of Lookout Hill to see if my prince is coming.
(*Shading her eyes with one hand, she runs off.*)

ROLAND (*Aside*): Whew! So that's the famous Snow White I've
been searching for. Br-r-r. I may as well marry a drill sergeant!
(WICKED QUEEN, *carrying basket of apples, enters.*)

WICKED QUEEN (*Sweetly*): Apples for sale. Nice, fresh apples for
sale. (*To dwarfs*) Why, you poor dear creatures, all lined up
like statues. Relax. (*Dwarfs sigh and relax.*)

MOPEY: *Relax.* That's the first kind word we've heard all day.

WICKED QUEEN: If you were my little dwarfs, I wouldn't treat you
like this. (*To* CHUBBY) Here. Have an apple, dear.

CHUBBY (*Grabbing the apple*): Oh, thank you. You're much nicer
than Snow White. (*Sinks teeth into apple*)

ROLAND (*Crossing to* QUEEN): Indeed you are. (*Bowing*) I've seen
some fair maidens in my day, but you are the fairest of them
all. (*Extends arm*) Would you care for a stroll?

QUEEN (*Taking arm*): I thought you'd *never* ask. (*They start off
left.*)

GROUCHY: Please, don't leave us here at the mercy of Snow
White.

DWARFS (*Begging; together*): Please take us with you.

ROLAND: Very well. Come along, then. You shall be ushers at our
wedding. (*Reprise of march music is played, as all except* READ-
ERS *exit.* SNOW WHITE *returns, looking left and right.*)

SNOW WHITE (*Puzzled*): Where is everybody? (*Calls*) Dwarfs! If you don't come out this instant, you'll eat bread and water for a week! (*She exits left, as* WITCH, STEPSISTERS, *and* WICKED QUEEN *enter right, gathering around* READERS.)

WITCH: Come on, girls. I can't wait to hear how the readers loved us.

1ST STEPSISTER: You have to admit, our version of "Cinderella" was certainly an improvement.

WICKED QUEEN (*Preening*): Surely they'll agree I was the fairest of all.

WITCH (*Motioning for silence*): Sh-h-h! They're about to say something.

1ST READER (*Pushing book away*): I hate it. "Sleeping Beauty" used to be my favorite fairy tale. I'll never read it again.

2ND READER (*Putting book on top of other*): What a disaster! I used to *dislike* the silly stepsisters—now I absolutely *loathe* them. (WITCH, STEPSISTERS *and* WICKED QUEEN *pantomime dismay.*)

3RD READER (*Putting book on top of pile*): Take this one away, too! Everyone knows the witch and the stepsisters and the wicked queen were great villains.

1ST READER: Right.

2ND READER: But they make terrible *heroines.*

1ST *and* 3RD READERS (*Together*): Absolutely awful heroines. (WITCH, STEPSISTERS *and* WICKED QUEEN *go center and huddle.*)

WITCH: Did you hear that? Our spell was a failure.

STEPSISTERS (*Together*): They hate us.

WICKED QUEEN: But didn't you hear what they said? We are great villains. Now that's what I call a real compliment. Come, let us reverse the spell and return to our former selves. (*They circle around the table.*)

WITCH, STEPSISTERS, QUEEN (*Chanting*):
Fairy tales and legends dim,
Andersen and Brothers Grimm,
Circle, cycle, swivel, spin,
Bring back every heroine.
(*They run off right as* LIBRARIAN *enters, left.* READERS, *waving their books, run to* LIBRARIAN.)

READERS (*Ad lib*): Look at this book. This is terrible. (*Etc.*)

LIBRARIAN (*Holding up hand*): What's the matter?

1ST READER: Our books are all mixed up. (LIBRARIAN *takes books and examines them.*)

2ND READER: It's as if somebody cast a *spell.*

3RD READER: Yes, the stories are all different.

LIBRARIAN: I don't see anything wrong with these books. (*Showing books to each* READER *in turn*)

1ST READER: What happened? The stories are back to the way they should be. Sleeping Beauty is a heroine.

2ND READER: So is Cinderella.

3RD READER: And Snow White is her old sweet self again. What a relief! (*All three rub their eyes.*)

LIBRARIAN (*Laughing*): Perhaps you dozed a little as you were reading, and you had a dream.

READERS (*Ad lib; not quite convinced*): Well, maybe. I guess it could have happened that way. (*Etc.*)

LIBRARIAN (*Crossing center slowly*): After all, *nobody* believes in magic anymore. (*To audience*) Right? (WITCH, STEPSISTERS, *and* WICKED QUEEN *re-enter and cackle loudly as curtains close.*)

THE END

Horn of Plenty

by Helen Louise Miller

Discovering an antique treasure gives everyone something to be thankful for. . . .

Characters

TONY HILL
MRS. KATHY HILL, *his mother*
SALLY, *his sister*
SAM MARINO, *his friend*
AUNT ABIGAIL
OFFICER RILEY
OFFICER DIAZ
MR. RAMSAY
MR. FRANK

SETTING: *The Hill living room.*
AT RISE: TONY HILL *and* SAM MARINO *are piling various items into cartons.*
SAM (*Holding up worn baseball glove*): You'll never get a nickel for this glove, Tony. It has a hole in it.
TONY: Toss it into that box of junk along with the water wings and fire engine. (*Holds up racket*) Don't let Mr. Ramsay give you a cent less than ten bucks for this racket.

87

SAM: Are you kidding? He'll spot the broken string right away.

TONY: Where's your sales technique, Sam? It's all in your approach. You've got to soften him up right at the beginning.

SAM: How do I do that?

TONY: Wish him a happy Thanksgiving, appeal to his generous nature—then shove the racket in with some of the good stuff and hope it gets by.

SAM (*Sarcastically*): Old man Ramsay never heard of Thanksgiving.

TONY (*Ignoring him and holding up small radio*): Try to get ten bucks for this radio, but I'll take five.

SAM: But it doesn't work.

TONY: It will if you give it a good whack right before you turn it on. And be sure not to move the dial. I have it set for the one station it gets.

SAM: Tony, Ramsay's a smart guy. He knows his merchandise.

TONY (*Holding up old typewriter*): Then he'll know a good typewriter when he sees one. Hold out for fifty bucks on this baby.

SAM: You can't sell your typewriter!

TONY: Why not? I bought it.

SAM: But what will your parents say? And how can you type your papers if you sell it?

TONY: Listen, my parents hardly ever go up to my room. They'll never notice it's gone. As for the typing, I can always do it in school.

SAM (*Shaking head*): The more I think about this, the less I like it.

TONY: What do you mean?

SAM: The way he looked at me yesterday, when I took your camera down there—sort of fishy-eyed. It made me feel guilty somehow.

TONY: Guilty? Why? I have a right to sell this stuff.

SAM: Then take it down yourself.

TONY: Sam, I've told you a hundred times why I can't. He knows Mom, and he knows me. I don't want anybody to find out about this.

SAM: How come I always get the dirty end of the deal?

TONY: Look who's talking! It was all your fault the horn was stolen in the first place. You're the one who forgot to lock the car.

SAM: Well, if you hadn't hung around talking to Kim for half an hour . . .

TONY: And if you'd stayed in the car, instead of going for an ice cream.

SAM: If, if, if!

TONY: Look, Sam, do you want to help me, or don't you? Can't you see I'm desperate? I've got to put a hundred fifty bucks on that sousaphone by noon, or it's all over.

SAM: I said from the beginning you should have reported it to the police.

TONY (*Sarcastically*): Oh, sure! And have everybody in town find out I lost a school instrument through sheer carelessness.

SAM: But the school carries insurance. They could collect!

TONY: And in the meantime, Mr. Carl would throw me out of the band so fast I'd bounce.

SAM: You'll have to tell him sooner or later.

TONY: Well, naturally I'm going to tell him much later—*after* the Thanksgiving Day parade. I'm not going to miss that band trip to New York for anything.

SAM: He wouldn't throw you out before the parade. What's a marching band without a tuba player?

TONY: He has Buzzy Jenkins.

SAM: Buzzy Jenkins! He can't even play the school song. I can just see him trying to play the National Anthem!

TONY: Well, I won't be playing it either unless I can replace that horn. Explanations can come later.

SAM: You couldn't have stalled this long if I hadn't dreamed up that story about having the valves fixed.

TONY: Good thing I had Big Bertha on hand for practice. (*Indicates old-style tuba on table left*)

SAM (*Suddenly*): Hey, why don't you use Big Bertha in the parade?

TONY: Are you out of your mind? The Brewster Pilgrims would be the laughing stock of the whole parade!

SAM: Yeah, I guess you're right. I can hardly see Big Bertha on national TV. (*Points to toy bank*) Where did you get that bank?

TONY: Had it ever since I was a kid. It has a combination, but it hasn't worked for years. (*Bangs it open*) That does it! (*Takes out a few bills, coins*) Hm-m. Only $5.60—but every little bit helps.

SAM: Mr. Ramsay has a lot of metal banks in his shop.

TONY: He does? Then take this one along. Maybe he'll buy it. (*Doorbell rings*) Oh, no! Hurry! Get this stuff out of here. Go the back way! (SAM *tries to pick up everything at once. The bank falls to floor, unnoticed.*)

SAM: Give me a break! I'm hurrying as fast as I can. (*As he drops something else*) What do you think I am—an octopus?

TONY (*Picking up box*): Here, I'll give you a hand. Now, hurry and get back here as soon as you can. (*They exit left.* TONY *re-enters; doorbell rings again.*) I'm coming! I'm coming! (*Exits right; re-enters a moment later with* SALLY *and* KIM)

SALLY: Where were you? You took long enough to answer the door.

TONY (*Annoyed*): I was busy, O.K.? You should have remembered your key.

KIM: Why are all the doors locked, anyway?

TONY: Oh, Mom wants us to keep everything locked while Aunt Abby's here for Thanksgiving.

SALLY: Aunt Abby's scared of her own shadow. Tony, do you have any money? Mom sent me to the store with a shopping list a mile long, but she didn't give me enough cash.

TONY: You're asking *me* for money? You know my wallet's in a perpetual state of emptiness. (SALLY *opens desk drawer, removes small change purse.*)

SALLY (*Opening purse*): There's not much in here. I'll check the kitchen. Kim, tell Tony about your dress. (*Exits*)

KIM (*Excitedly*): Oh, Tony, you'll love it! It's blue, so if you make my corsage those tiny French irises . . .

TONY (*Blankly*): Corsage? French irises? What are you talking about?

KIM: Oh, well, if you've already ordered something else, it's all right. Any flowers look pretty with blue.

TONY (*Clapping hand to forehead*): Oh, no!

KIM: What's the matter?

TONY: The dance! You're talking about the dance!

KIM (*Puzzled*): Well, of course I am.

TONY: Listen, Kim, I've got something to tell you. (*Takes her hand, leads her to couch*) Maybe you'd better sit down. Um-m. This will be a shock, but please try to understand.

KIM (*Impatiently*): What are you talking about? Understand about what?

TONY: Well, it's just that . . . well, we can't go to the dance.

KIM (*Shocked*): Can't go! What do you mean? Why not?

TONY: Because I'm broke. Absolutely and totally flat broke!

KIM (*Upset*): But we had a date! You asked me weeks ago!

TONY: I know I did, but . . .

KIM (*Upset*): If I had time to save up for a dress, you could have saved for the ticket!

TONY: If you'd just listen . . .

KIM (*Angrily*): There's nothing you can say to me that I want to hear—not now or ever! (*Runs off right*)

TONY (*Shouting*): Kim! Kim, please come back! I have to talk to you!

SALLY (*Entering with purse*): Thank goodness Mom left thirty dollars in the kitchen drawer. (*Looks around*) Where's Kim?

TONY: Gone! And I've got to catch her. (*Races off right*)

SALLY (*Shrugging*): Crazy people! Well, I guess I'll have to do my shopping alone. (*Tosses empty purse on table left, puts money into her purse*) I'd better take my keys, in case I get home before Mom. (*Takes key from drawer in phone table; phone rings.* SALLY *answers it.*) Hello. . . . No, sorry, Tony isn't here. . . . (*Puzzled*) He's to pick up Susie? I'm sorry. You must have the wrong number. . . . Yes, he lives here, but . . . No, I can't tell you exactly when he'll be back. . . . All right. 'Bye. (*As she hangs up*) So that's it! He's got another girl! Just wait till Kim hears about this. (*Disgusted*) Men! They're all alike. Even my own brother! (*Exits right. After a brief pause,* AUNT ABIGAIL *enters left. She calls offstage.*)

ABIGAIL: I'm sure the kitchen door was locked when we left, Kathy. I checked it myself.

MRS. HILL (*Entering*): You must have been mistaken, Abby. You have to slam it extra hard.

ABIGAIL: But I did slam it, and I tried the lock. (*Ominously*) Kathy, someone's been in this house.

MRS. HILL (*Annoyed*): Honestly, Abby, you're getting downright ridiculous on the subject of locks and doors.

ABIGAIL: Ridiculous or not, someone's been in this house. I can tell.

MRS. HILL: All right. How can you tell?

ABIGAIL (*Looking around*): I don't know exactly, but I have a sixth sense about things like this. There's something in this room that isn't the way we left it.

MRS. HILL: You're just overtired. Go upstairs and lie down. I have a million things to do. If I don't get dinner started, we'll never eat by five o'clock, and the kids won't be ready for the dance on time. (*Starts to exit left*)

ABIGAIL (*Grabbing* MRS. HILL'*s arm*): Don't go upstairs, Kathy!

MRS. HILL: Abby, you're trembling. If you keep on like this, I'm going to have to call the doctor.

ABIGAIL (*Nervously*): Don't you understand? Whoever came in the house might still be up there.

MRS. HILL (*Firmly*): Now, look, Abby, enough is enough!

ABIGAIL: Well, look! (*Points to purse on table*) Isn't that the purse you keep in the kitchen?

MRS. HILL (*Picking it up*): How in the world did that get in here?

ABIGAIL: *Now* do you believe me?

MRS. HILL (*Examining purse*): It's empty! I had thirty dollars in here!

ABIGAIL: Oh, my goodness! You've been robbed! Heaven only knows what else has been taken. Call the police, Kathy!

MRS. HILL: Abby, calm down. We don't want to sound a false alarm. (*Looks around*) Nothing else seems to be disturbed, but maybe we'd better take a look around. You take the dining room.

ABIGAIL: The silver! I'll bet there's not a piece left! (*Exits left*)

MRS. HILL: I don't care what she says. I'm going upstairs. (*Stumbles on toy bank*) What in the world? (*Picks up bank; in amazement*) Why, it's Tony's bank! And it's been forced open!

ABIGAIL (*Re-entering; excitedly*): Kathy! I've found out how they got in! There's a ladder propped up against the dining room windows. Someone must have climbed in through a bedroom window!

MRS. HILL (*Alarmed*): I can't believe this is happening. (*Goes to phone*) I'd better call the police. (*Suddenly phone rings; MRS. HILL answers it.*) Hello. . . . Yes. . . . Oh, Mr. Ramsay, of course I remember you. . . . Why, yes, my son does have a typewriter. It's an old portable, but I'm sure it's in his room. . . . A camera? What kind? . . . Well, yes, he has one like that, but. . . . Look, Mr. Ramsay, I just got home, and there are signs of breaking and entering here, but I haven't checked yet to see what's been taken. If you have a suspicious character there, hang onto him, and I'll call you back. . . . Yes, and thanks so much for calling. (*Hangs up*) Well, Abby, you don't need to worry about our thief hiding upstairs. That was Neal Ramsay from the Swap Shop. He thinks some young thug is trying to unload stolen goods, and he saw Tony's name on the back of a typewriter case. I'm going to take a look upstairs. (*Exits*)

ABIGAIL: Well, I think it's time to call the police. (*Picks up phone, dials; after a moment*) Hello. This is Abigail Simms, 70 Prospect Street. I wish to report a robbery. . . . Yes, my sister— Kathy Hill—and I came home a few minutes ago and discovered someone had broken into the house through a second-story window. . . . Well, I can't tell you exactly what's been taken, but there is very definitely some money missing. . . . Thank you. (*Hangs up*)

MRS. HILL (*Entering*): Abby! Someone's stripped Tony's room practically bare. Everything's cleared out—his camera, typewriter, radio. His baseball stuff and tennis racket are gone from his closet. The toy chest has been rifled, and even his alarm clock is gone!

ABIGAIL (*Upset*): Oh, no! Well, don't worry. I've already called the police. They're sending a patrol car.

MRS. HILL: Good! I'll call Mr. Ramsay. (*Dials*) Hello, Mr. Ramsay? Kathy Hill. Well, you were right. Every one of those items you described belongs to my son. . . . (*In disbelief*) He says he's a friend of Tony's? Ha! That's a likely story! . . . Well, please hold him. My sister just called the police, and I'll send them to your place when they're finished here. . . . Oh, you'll bring him here? . . . Well, if it's not too much trouble. . . . Thanks, Mr. Ramsay. Goodbye. (*Hangs up*)

ABIGAIL (*Dramatically*): It's a miracle we weren't all murdered in our beds!

MRS. HILL: Don't make things worse than they are, Abby. After all, it's broad daylight, and nothing's been touched except the money and Tony's things.

ABIGAIL (*Pointing to tuba*): Let's be grateful they didn't take Uncle Josh's old tuba.

MRS. HILL: Oh, nobody would want that old thing, Abby.

ABIGAIL: Is that so? I'll have you know that's a very valuable instrument—a real antique! I'm surprised you don't make Tony take better care of it.

MRS. HILL: He hardly ever uses it any more except when the school tuba is out for repairs. Poor Tony! I wish we could afford to get him a sousaphone of his own. He should have one next year when he goes to college.

ABIGAIL: Sousaphone! Humph! This old tuba is worth more than a new sousaphone.

MRS. HILL: That may be, but this thing belongs in a museum instead of a modern band. (*Sound of siren is heard.*)

ABIGAIL: The police! I'll let them in. (*Exits right and returns with* OFFICER RILEY) Officer Riley, this is my sister, Kathy Hill.

MRS. HILL (*Shaking* OFFICER'*s hand*): Thanks for coming so promptly, Officer Riley.

RILEY: My partner's checking the ladder at the side of the house. Have you listed the missing articles?

MRS. HILL: Only the money is missing. Everything else was taken from my son's room, and it's all turned up at Ramsay's Swap Shop. Mr. Ramsay's holding the boy who brought them in.

ABIGAIL: And bringing him here for identification.

RILEY: Good. He's probably one of our regulars! (*As* OFFICER DIAZ *enters*) Well, Diaz, what did you find?

DIAZ: The ladder leads straight to an unlocked window. (SALLY *and* TONY *enter.*)

TONY (*Breathlessly*): Mom! What's going on? Why are the police here?

SALLY (*Upset*): Are you all right? What happened?

MRS. HILL: Now, don't panic. No one's hurt. We've just had a robbery.

TONY *and* SALLY (*Together*): A robbery!

ABIGAIL: Maybe after this you won't think it's so unusual to keep the doors and windows locked.

MRS. HILL: Someone broke in through your bedroom window, Sally, and stole practically everything of value out of Tony's room.

TONY (*Collapsing into chair*): Oh, my gosh!

MRS. HILL: It's nothing to be upset about, Tony. Everything but the money has been recovered.

SALLY: The money!

MRS. HILL: Yes. (*Picks up kitchen change purse*) Thirty dollars is missing from the kitchen change purse. (*Points to bank*) Even Tony's toy bank was broken open.

SALLY: But, Mom . . .

ABIGAIL (*To* RILEY): Aren't you going to take fingerprints, Officer?

MRS. HILL: Why should they? The thief has already been caught with the goods.

TONY (*Leaping to his feet*): Caught with the goods! But they can't do this! (MR. RAMSAY *enters, pushing* SAM *ahead of him.*)

MR. RAMSAY: Here he is, Mrs. Hill. The minute I set eyes on him I knew he was up to no good!

ALL (*Except* OFFICERS): Sam!

SAM: You'd better get me out of this, Tony.

RILEY: You know this boy?

TONY: Know him? He's my best friend.

MRS. HILL: Sam, how could you do such a thing? What will your parents say?

DIAZ (*To* SAM): What's your name, young man?

SAM: I'm not answering any questions. It's up to Tony to do the talking. Go ahead, Tony, tell them what happened.

TONY: Listen, Mom, there's been a terrible mistake. Sam didn't steal anything. I sent him down to the Swap Shop to sell that stuff. He was only doing me a favor.

MRS. HILL (*Shocked*): What?

ABIGAIL: But what about the ladder? The window?

TONY: Thanks to your locking and bolting every door in sight, that was the only way I could get into the house. I forgot my key.

SALLY: And as for the money, Mom, I took it! I didn't have enough money for the Thanksgiving groceries, so I came back to the house and took all the money I could find.

SAM (*Shaking his head*): Gee, Mrs. Hill, you should have known I wouldn't steal anything.

MRS. HILL: Of course you wouldn't, Sam. I'm sorry. In fact, I apologize all around. (*To* OFFICERS) You must think my sister and I have overactive imaginations.

RILEY: There's no need to apologize. It's our job to investigate unusual happenings.

ABIGAIL: Then there was no crime after all!

DIAZ: Don't sound so disappointed, ma'am. That's the best news a police officer could hear. But I'm afraid this young man (*Indicates* TONY) has some explaining to do to his mother.

MRS. HILL: What made you do such a thing, Tony? Why would you want to sell your typewriter, your camera, your radio . . .

MR. RAMSAY (*Sternly*): And why didn't you bring them in yourself instead of throwing suspicion on your friend here?

TONY: It's all mixed up, but I had to have money fast.

MRS. HILL: But why? Are you in some kind of trouble?

TONY (*Uncomfortably*): Am I ever! (MRS. HILL *looks alarmed.*) Don't worry, Mom. I guess it's not *that* serious. I had to have the money for a new horn.

MRS. HILL (*Unhappily*): But I promised we'd try to get you one for next year.

TONY: I had to have it now—today! (MR. FRANK *enters with sousaphone.*)

MR. FRANK: Excuse me. I rang, but I guess nobody heard.

TONY (*Surprised*): Mr. Frank!

MR. FRANK: I called a while ago to tell you to pick up the

sousaphone, but the young lady who answered the phone didn't seem to understand.

SALLY (*Suddenly*): Susie . . . sousaphone! (*Shakes head*) I don't believe it. I thought you were talking about a girl. Susie something or other. Oh, Tony, then there's no Susie after all! Kim will be so happy!

RILEY (*To* TONY): Who is this gentleman?

TONY: This is Mr. Frank. He runs the music store in Stratham. I bought the sousaphone from him, or rather, I was going to buy it as soon as I could get the down payment together.

MR. FRANK: But that's what I came to tell you. After reading about the high school band going to New York for the Thanksgiving Day parade, I decided I should do something to help. So you may have the horn without the usual $150 deposit. (*As he places sousaphone on table left, he notices old tuba.*) Where did you get this tuba? It's beautiful!

TONY: Oh, that! It's Big Bertha.

ABIGAIL (*Proudly*): It belonged to Tony's great-uncle Joshua. It's a very fine instrument.

MR. FRANK: I should say it is, and a very rare one. (*Adjusts glasses*) My goodness! I believe this is a genuine Helicon, one of the earliest, in fact, dating back to 1880. (*To* TONY) Tony, why didn't you tell me you had this rare instrument?

TONY: I never thought it was rare or important, Mr. Frank. I just thought it was old.

MR. FRANK: This is the type of tuba used in John Philip Sousa's concert and marching bands.

ABIGAIL: For your information, Mr. Frank, this is not just the *type* that was used in Sousa's bands. It's the real thing. Uncle Joshua inherited it from his father, who traveled through Germany and England with Sousa.

MR. FRANK (*Excitedly*): I can't believe it! Wait till the National Sousa Foundation hears about this! The publicity committee is planning a television documentary on Sousa, and we've scoured the country for a horn like this. Would you consider letting me rent it to use in the show, for, say, two hundred dollars?

TONY: Two hundred dollars! Gosh! What do you think, Mom?

MRS. HILL: It's up to you, Tony. Big Bertha belongs to you.

TONY: Well, you know, if it's so rare, maybe it belongs in a museum, so more people could appreciate it.

MR. FRANK: If you really want to do that, I'm sure I could arrange it.

TONY (*After a pause*): That's what I'd like to do, Mr. Frank—after the TV program, of course.

ABIGAIL (*Happily*): That's just what your Uncle Joshua would have liked.

MRS. HILL: I'm so proud of you, Tony!

RILEY (*Examining sousaphone*): So this is a sousaphone?

MR. FRANK: That's right. Designed according to instructions from Sousa himself.

RILEY (*Impressed*): No kidding! (*To* DIAZ) Isn't this the same kind of horn that guy from upstate brought into headquarters yesterday?

DIAZ: You know, you're right. It looks exactly the same to me.

TONY (*Excitedly*): You mean you have a horn like this at the police station?

RILEY: It was there this morning, unless the owner's claimed it by now.

SAM: How did it get there?

RILEY: Last Wednesday night this salesman from Erie parked his car in front of the civic center, and when he got home, he found a tuba—I mean, sousaphone—in his back seat.

SAM: So that's what happened!

TONY: I can't believe it! Sam, you turkey, you put the horn in the wrong car! I don't believe it!

DIAZ: Do you know who owns the horn, Tony?

TONY: I sure do. It belongs to Brewster High. We played in a concert last Wednesday night, and Sam carried the horn down to my mom's station wagon . . . only he must have put it in the wrong one.

DIAZ: Why didn't you report it to the police?

TONY: I was afraid the band director would throw me out of the band and I'd miss the trip to New York. He's a real demon when it comes to school instruments. Of course, I planned to tell him about it on Monday—*after* the Thanksgiving Day parade.

MRS. HILL: So *that's* why you had to have a new horn in such a hurry.

MR. FRANK: Well, now that the school horn's been found, you won't be needing the sousaphone.

MRS. HILL: Oh, but he will, Mr. Frank. We're hoping he'll be in the band next year at college, and he'll want his own instrument.

TONY: Wow! Thanks, Mom!

MR. FRANK (*Picking up sousaphone and handing it to* TONY): Fine, here you are, Tony.

MRS. HILL: Would you like me to give you a check now?

MR. FRANK: No, that's O.K. I'll be in touch later. Well, I have another call to make, so if you can bring the Helicon down to the store this afternoon, I'll give you a receipt for it. You'll be hearing from the publicity committee in a few days. This will be great news for them and for the museum as well. (*Looks all around*) Good day, all. (*Shakes* TONY's *hand*) And thank you, Tony. (*All ad lib goodbyes.* MR. FRANK *exits.*)

TONY: Oh, wow! Two hundred dollars! Sam, I'm treating you to the dance tonight. You're a real friend.

SAM: Thanks, Tony, but the next time you get into a mess like this, just count me out.

MR. RAMSAY (*To* SAM): I guess I should apologize to you again, young fellow. No hard feelings, I hope.

SAM: That's O.K., Mr. Ramsay.

RILEY: Thanks for being so alert, Mr. Ramsay.

MR. RAMSAY: Thanks. (*Walks right with* OFFICERS)

DIAZ: Goodbye, everyone. Glad we got everything squared away.

RILEY: We'll be watching for you on TV, Tony, so be sure you don't play any wrong notes. (*All ad lib goodbyes.* OFFICERS *and* MR. RAMSAY *exit.*)

MRS. HILL: Well, Abby, if your nerves are settled, I could use some help in the kitchen.

ABIGAIL (*Rolling up sleeves*): I'm ready, Kathy.

SALLY: Who would have thought Big Bertha was valuable?

ABIGAIL: It's turned out to be a real horn of plenty, if you ask me.

MRS. HILL: Sam, will you stay for dinner? It's the least we can do after all you've been through.

SAM: Thanks, Mrs. Hill. That would be great. (KIM *suddenly enters, carrying foil-covered pie.* TONY *rushes over to her.*) Kim! I'm so glad you came back.

KIM (*Brushing past him*): I'm not here to see you. (*To* MRS. HILL) Mrs. Hill, Mom baked a pie for your Thanksgiving dinner. I hope you enjoy it. (*Hands pie to* MRS. HILL)

MRS. HILL: How thoughtful of her! Thanks, Kim. You're a dear to bring it over. (MRS. HILL, SALLY, *and* ABIGAIL *exit.*)

TONY (*Putting hand on* KIM's *arm*): Kim, listen to me. You're wearing orchids to the Thanksgiving Dance.

KIM (*Astonished*): Orchids!

TONY: That's right! No measly French irises for my girl tonight!

KIM: Who says I'm your girl? Besides, I thought you were broke.

TONY (*Pulling her toward tuba on table left*): That was before Big Bertha came to the rescue.

KIM: All I see is a rusty old horn.

TONY: Rusty old horn, is it? You may not realize it, Kim, but *that* is the original horn of plenty! Just right for Thanksgiving!

KIM (*Starting to laugh*): Tony, you are so weird. I don't have any idea what you're talking about.

TONY: Don't worry. I'll explain it all later. Right now, get out your dancing shoes. You and I are going to be the hottest couple at the Thanksgiving dance! (*Swings* KIM *in impromptu dance, as curtain falls*)

THE END

New-Fangled Thanksgiving

by *Mildred Hark and Noel McQueen*

An improvised holiday dinner recalls the pioneer spirit. . . .

Characters

ALEX BROOKS
JANE BROOKS
VICKY ⎫
KEVIN ⎬ *their children*
BILLY ⎭
GRANDPA
GRANDMA

SETTING: *Living room of the Brooks home, Thanksgiving Day.*

AT RISE: ALEX BROOKS, *wearing suit, paces, looks at watch.*
VICKY, *in dress, and* KEVIN *and* BILLY, *in slacks and jackets, sit on sofa.*

MR. BROOKS: If your mother doesn't hurry, we'll be late for our two o'clock reservation.

VICKY (*Excitedly*): Thanksgiving dinner at the Plaza! I can't believe it.

MR. BROOKS: Mom's the one who's really going to enjoy this, after all these years of wearing herself out preparing a big Thanksgiving dinner.

KEVIN: Right. All we do is stuff ourselves and feel miserable afterwards.

VICKY: Don't forget all those dirty dishes!

MR. BROOKS: And all those leftovers. Turkey croquettes, turkey salad, turkey pie, turkey soup.

VICKY: Just think—if Grandpa hadn't hurt his back, he and Grandma would be here right now, and Mom would have insisted on making a big dinner, as usual.

BILLY: Well, I don't want to go to any old hotel, even if Grandma and Grandpa aren't coming.

MR. BROOKS: But Billy, the other day you said you wanted to go.

BILLY: I did, but the other kids are having dinner at home—and that's what I want!

VICKY: Billy, we'll have the same kind of dinner we always have—turkey, stuffing, squash, pies. It'll be just the same as at home.

BILLY: No, it won't. We'll just go to the hotel and then come home. It won't be fun the way it is when we eat here, with lots of people, lots of laughing and fooling around. And besides, I made turkey place cards at school yesterday, and we can't even use them.

MR. BROOKS: Sure we can! We'll take the place cards with us. That will really make it seem like home.

MRS. BROOKS (*Off*): Alex! Is everyone ready?

MR. BROOKS (*Calling*): We're in the living room. (*Quickly, to* BILLY) Now, Billy, you don't want your mom to see you in a bad mood. She's looking forward to going out. (MRS. BROOKS *enters, wearing apron with large turkey on the front*) Ah, there you are, Jane! Are you about ready? We have to leave soon or the hotel won't hold our reservation.

MRS. BROOKS: I just have to put on some lipstick, and I'll be all set.

VICKY: You'd better take your apron off, too, Mom. Why are you wearing it, anyway, when you don't have to cook dinner?

MRS. BROOKS (*Looking down at apron*): Well, I don't know. It's just that I've worn this old apron every Thanksgiving for years. I guess I put it on this morning out of habit. (*She takes apron off.*) You know, it's funny not to smell a turkey roasting in the oven.

MR. BROOKS: You sound as if you wish you were out in the kitchen, cooking dinner as usual.

MRS. BROOKS: Oh, of course not, Alex. I think your plan to eat at the Plaza is fine.

BILLY (*Doubtfully*): You mean you *want* to eat dinner out, Mom?

MRS. BROOKS (*With exaggerated enthusiasm*): Why, of course I do. It's going to be wonderful for a change, not to be stuffing the turkey, making the pies, cooking all the vegetables, and thinking how to use the leftovers, and . . . (*Suddenly*) Well, I'd better hurry and get ready, or we'll be late. (*Exits left*)

MR. BROOKS: Well, I'll go brush the snow off the car. Be back in a minute. (*Exits*)

KEVIN: You know what? I think Mom would rather be staying home today.

VICKY: But why, when she usually has to work so hard? And today we'll have a wonderful dinner in a beautiful restaurant.

KEVIN: I know, but . . . well, to tell you the truth, I'd rather stay home myself.

VICKY (*Angrily*): Kevin, how can you say that? You've been excited about this dinner all week!

KEVIN (*Uncomfortably*): I know, but I've been thinking. We won't be able to watch the football game—it'll be almost over by the time we get back—and what's so great about eating in a hotel restaurant, anyway?

BILLY: Maybe we can convince Mom and Dad that we don't want to go.

VICKY: Now listen, you two, no matter how we feel—

KEVIN (*Quickly*): We? Do you mean you don't want to go, either?

VICKY (*Sighing*): Well, I did at first, but—I don't know. It just seems Thanksgiving ought to be a home day, with all these great smells coming from the kitchen and people running in and out. And there won't be any leftovers. (*Firmly*) But no matter how we feel, we have to pretend that we're having fun. Dad's all excited about going out, and maybe Mom is, too.

KEVIN (*Decisively*): O.K. I'll try to be the life of the party. (*Laughs half-heartedly*) Ha, ha.

VICKY: How about you, Billy? No more talk about wanting to stay home, O.K.?

KEVIN: We couldn't eat home if we wanted to. There's no dinner.

BILLY (*Dejectedly*): O.K. (*Sits.* MR. BROOKS *re-enters right.*)

MR. BROOKS: Isn't your mother ready yet? I wish she'd hurry. (*Phone rings. He answers.*) Hello. . . . (*Smiling broadly*) Ed Neely! What a surprise! Are you in town? . . . (*Disappointed*) Oh, I'm sorry, Ed, but we're going out for dinner. Can you stop by later? . . . Of course. I understand. . . . Listen, if you can manage it, I'd love to have you come over and meet my family. . . . Happy Thanksgiving to you. (*Hangs up*) Well, well. Good old Ed Neely.

KEVIN: Who's that, Dad?

MR. BROOKS: An old buddy of mine from high school. He moved away before you were born. He's visiting his mother and wanted to stop by in half an hour or so, but of course, we won't be here. (*Wistfully*) I did want him to meet all of you and see the house. . . . Well, maybe later. (*With exaggerated cheerfulness*) It sure is a beautiful day! Cold, crisp air. Just right for Thanksgiving. It makes you feel thankful just to be alive!

KEVIN: Dad, that sounds just like your Thanksgiving speech. Are you going to make it at the hotel this year?

MR. BROOKS: Oh, I don't think the other guests would appreciate it.

KEVIN: Sure they would, Dad.

MR. BROOKS (*Sighing*): No, I'm afraid those speeches of mine are strictly for home.

BILLY (*Sadly*): After Dad's speech, we always play the Thanksgiving game.

VICKY (*With enthusiasm*): Yes! One of us goes out of the room and the rest of us have to think of something to be thankful for.

BILLY: Last year I went out first—

KEVIN (*Laughing*): And then you came back and said, "Is it animal, vegetable, or mineral?"

BILLY: I didn't have to ask many questions, though. It was easy to guess—it started with H.

VICKY: I remember. It was "home."

MR. BROOKS (*Pacing nervously*): Where *is* your mother? She knew we wanted to get started on time. (MRS. BROOKS *enters left.*)

MRS. BROOKS (*Walking center*): Here I am, Alex, all ready.

MR. BROOKS (*Sharply*): And it's about time, too. Let's get started.

MRS. BROOKS: Oh—my gloves. I have to run upstairs again.

MR. BROOKS: Forget it. You don't need them.

MRS. BROOKS: Of course I do. It's cold outside.

MR. BROOKS (*Angrily*): Jane, you've had all morning to get ready.

MRS. BROOKS (*Angrily*): And whose fault is that? All this foolishness about going to a hotel . . .

MR. BROOKS (*Astonished*): What do you mean by that? You know I did it to please you. (KEVIN, VICKY, *and* BILLY *exchange nervous glances.*)

MRS. BROOKS (*Incredulously*): To please *me?* You're the one who was pleased. The last thing I wanted to do was have Thanksgiving dinner in a hotel.

MR. BROOKS (*Bewildered*): But you always talk about what a lot of work it is to get ready for Thanksgiving!

MRS. BROOKS (*More calmly*): I know, but I really love every minute of it. I find cooking—well—creative. Why do you think I took that course last spring in nouvelle cuisine? I *like* to cook.

VICKY (*Going over to hug her mother*): Oh, Mom. You're the best.

MR. BROOKS (*Shaking his head*): Well, don't blame the whole thing on me. If you think *I* like being away on Thanksgiving . . .

KEVIN (*Surprised*): But, Dad, you—

MR. BROOKS: I know, I know. I said it so much I almost believed I wanted to go to the hotel. (*To* MRS. BROOKS) I really thought it would please you, Jane.

MRS. BROOKS (*Going over to* MR. BROOKS): Alex, why are we quarreling when we really agree?

MR. BROOKS: I *am* sorry, Jane.

MRS. BROOKS: So am I. (*Sighing*) It's really nobody's fault that we're going out to dinner. We all thought we were doing it to please each other.

VICKY: To tell you the truth, we didn't really want to go, either.

BILLY: And I still don't! I want to eat at home.

MRS. BROOKS (*Putting her hand on* BILLY's *shoulder*): We all do, Billy, but we can't. I didn't buy a thing for dinner.

MR. BROOKS: Let's just go to the hotel and make the best of it. We'll have a good time if we try.

MRS. BROOKS: I'm afraid that's all we can do. (*Voices are heard off.*)

GRANDMA (*Off*): Now, Charles, don't be foolish. I'm sure they're all busy getting dinner ready.

GRANDPA (*Off*): You're probably right.

VICKY: That's Grandma!

KEVIN: And Grandpa! (GRANDMA *and* GRANDPA *enter right.*) What are they doing here?

GRANDPA (*Cheerfully, walking center*): Well, here we are, folks. Not too late for dinner, I hope. (*Sniffing air*) I don't smell the turkey yet. (*All ad lib greetings, embrace, etc.*)

GRANDMA: Grandpa thought one of you might be at the airport to meet us, but I told him you'd have better sense. The place is mobbed with Thanksgiving travelers trying to get their relatives, and besides—(*Laughing*) you know how much Grandpa and I enjoy a taxi ride. Don't have much of a chance to take them in Woodsville Center.

MRS. BROOKS (*Affectionately*): We're really happy to see you. It wouldn't be Thanksgiving without you. (*Concerned*) But, Dad, what about your back?

GRANDPA: Janie, I'm feeling chipper as a chipmunk, now that everything's snapped back into place. The trouble seemed to go away just like that. (*Snaps fingers*) That chiropractor I went to was a miracle worker.

MR. BROOKS (*Surprised*): Well, that's great. We certainly didn't expect to see you this year at all.

GRANDMA (*Perplexed*): Didn't you get our message? (*Suspiciously*) Charles, you *did* call, didn't you?

GRANDPA: Well, of course I did, Madeline. I left a message on that infernal answering machine of theirs—even though I hate the thing.

MRS. BROOKS: Oh, no! That must have been the day the machine wasn't working right, and we didn't get any of our messages.

GRANDMA (*Exasperated*): Well, no wonder you all looked so surprised when we walked in. Sometimes this modern technology is useless!

VICKY (*Going over to hug her*): Never mind, Grandma. We're just glad you're here.

KEVIN: You can watch the game with us, Grandpa, the way we always do.

BILLY (*Taking* GRANDPA's *hand*): And I can show you my new computer game!

GRANDMA: I guess it doesn't matter that we surprised you. I know there's always more than enough Thanksgiving dinner for extra guests.

MR. BROOKS (*Uneasily*): Well, Grandma, I'm afraid there isn't any Thanksgiving dinner at all this year.

GRANDMA (*Incredulous*): Why not?

MR. BROOKS (*Uncomfortably*): Well, you see—we decided to go out to eat this year—at a hotel.

GRANDMA (*Amazed*): Out? On Thanksgiving?

MRS. BROOKS (*Calmly*): Yes, Mother, we're going to eat at the Plaza Hotel. It's very posh. You and Dad will just love it. There'll be music and lots of people around at other tables . . .

GRANDPA: Thanksgiving dinner at a hotel, eh? (*Shaking his head*) This must be some new-fangled notion that hasn't caught up with us yet in Woodsville Center.

GRANDMA (*Puzzled*): You mean you really want to eat Thanksgiving dinner at a hotel?

BILLY: I don't!

VICKY: We wanted to spare Mom all the work of cooking dinner.

KEVIN (*Quickly*): To tell you the truth, no one wants to go now.

GRANDMA (*Decisively*): Then we won't go.

MRS. BROOKS: But it's too late now. There's nothing in the house to eat. I knew we were going out, so I didn't buy a thing.

GRANDMA: When I was a girl, we had to make do with what we had. Things are too easy for us now—we're used to too many frills. (*To* MRS. BROOKS) You say there's *nothing* in the house?

MRS. BROOKS: Well, of course there *is* some food in the freezer, but we couldn't get it ready in time.

GRANDMA: There's no law that says you have to eat Thanksgiving dinner at two o'clock. If we all pitch in we can eat by five or so. What do you have in the freezer?

MRS. BROOKS (*Thinking, then excitedly*): Hey, I just remembered. I froze two chickens I bought on sale last week!

GRANDMA: Fine. Chicken's close enough to turkey.

MR. BROOKS: We'll defrost them in the microwave! It's about time I learned how to use that machine.

BILLY: Can we have stuffing, too?

GRANDMA: I can whip up a batch of my special stuffing in no time.

MRS. BROOKS: Let's see. There's a bag of potatoes in the bin, and some peas and squash in the freezer.

VICKY: Great! That gives us chicken, stuffing, potatoes, peas, squash—

GRANDPA: How about cranberry sauce? Thanksgiving dinner isn't complete without it.

MRS. BROOKS: Don't worry, Dad. I have several cans in the pantry.

KEVIN: Now all we need is dessert.

GRANDMA: Well, you must have some apples in the house.

MR. BROOKS: You bet, Grandma! I always get a bushel at this time of year.

GRANDMA (*Rolling up sleeves*): Then we'll make apple pies as usual!

GRANDPA: And I'll have two pieces as usual.

VICKY (*Happily*): We'll have a wonderful dinner after all—and at home!

GRANDMA: Of course we will. We'll have to use our wits a bit, but then, so did the Pilgrims.

KEVIN: This is fun. Improvising makes me feel like a pioneer!

VICKY: I can decorate the table.

BILLY: I'll use my place cards. And we can play the Thanksgiving game! (*Happily*) I know I can guess everything today—home, family, and Thanksgiving dinner.

GRANDMA: We'd better get started, or we'll never eat!

MRS. BROOKS (*Happily*): I'm so glad we're having Thanksgiving as usual; nothing newfangled. There's a lot to be thankful for.

(She smiles, puts on apron, starts singing "We Gather Together." All start off in various directions, humming and singing. Curtain)

THE END

The Pilgrim Painting

by James Rawls

Appearance of mysterious visitors turns gloom to happiness on Thanksgiving Day. . . .

Characters

MEG LANDIS
DAVID, *her brother*
MRS. LANDIS
MR. LANDIS
MR. MARKS, *school board chairman*
PILGRIM GIRL
PILGRIM BOY
PILGRIM MOTHER
PILGRIM FATHER

TIME: *Thanksgiving Day.*
SETTING: *The living room of the Landis home. Two folding screens hide back center wall. Armchair and end table are right; table set for dinner is left.*
AT RISE: *MEG LANDIS, wearing bright print dress, is seated in armchair, holding old doll. DAVID, wearing red sweater, stands near, bouncing small rubber ball. MRS. LANDIS enters with bowl of fruit, which she places on table.*

MEG: I wish I could buy a new doll. This one is a total disaster.

DAVID: Well, *I* could really use a new bat, ball, and mitt.

MRS. LANDIS (*Arranging table*): Now, you two, that's no way to talk on Thanksgiving. You have a great deal to be thankful for. You're young and healthy, you have a roof over your heads (MEG *and* DAVID *groan*), and you're going to have a good Thanksgiving dinner soon.

DAVID: Yeah—a scrawny old chicken. What's so special about that?

MEG: Most people have turkey. That's what Thanksgiving is for!

MRS. LANDIS (*Firmly*): Well, sometimes you just have to make do with what we have. Be thankful we have this chicken and some of the fixings to go with it.

MEG: Emily Stone's family is having their Thanksgiving dinner catered.

MRS. LANDIS: That's nice, but you know it's more than we can afford, Meg.

DAVID: We can't ever afford anything. Look at this old sweater I'm wearing. I'm so sick of it.

MEG: Well, this dress is worse. It's the newest one I have, and it's already over a year old. (*In trembling voice*) Oh, Mom, why do we have to be so poor? (*She starts to cry.*)

MRS. LANDIS (*Crossing to* MEG, *putting her arm around her shoulder*): Now, don't cry. (*Puts other arm around* DAVID) I know how you feel. You both need new clothes and toys, but we're all making sacrifices until Dad can sell one of his paintings.

DAVID: What about the one he did for the school board?

MRS. LANDIS: I'm afraid they turned that painting down.

DAVID: Oh, no! He paints, paints, paints, but no one ever buys a picture from him. Why doesn't he stop painting pictures and paint houses or something? People pay for that kind of painting.

MRS. LANDIS (*Sharply*): You stop that talk this instant, David. I will not have you children criticizing your father. He gave up a lot to be an artist, and he works hard. Someday he'll make it, but we all have to stand by him until he does. Now, stop this grumbling and be thankful for what we do have. (*She exits.* MR. LANDIS *enters left.*)

MR. LANDIS: Have you two seen my new painting yet? I finished it this morning.

MEG (*Listlessly*): Did you, Daddy?

DAVID (*Dully*): That's nice, Dad.

MR. LANDIS (*Enthusiastically*): It's the best work I've ever done, even if the school board decided they didn't want it. It's right over there behind the screens. (*Points to screens*) Have a look.

MEG: We will, Dad—later. It's too bad the school board doesn't want to buy it.

DAVID: It looks big enough to cover one whole wall in our cafeteria.

MR. LANDIS: Yes, it's life-size, all right—and life-like, too, I hope. I really pushed myself to finish it by Thanksgiving. But, I guess it wasn't worth all the hard work. (*He shakes his head, exits left.*)

MEG: All that work for nothing.

DAVID: Let's take a look at it.

MEG (*Half-heartedly*): Oh, all right, but I don't know why we should bother. It's not going to bring us a Thanksgiving turkey. (*They fold back screens and reveal a framed live tableau of a Pilgrim family sitting at table.* PILGRIM FATHER *and* MOTHER *are at right and left ends of table and* PILGRIM GIRL *and* BOY *sit side by side behind table facing front. On table is a cooked turkey.*) David, those Pilgrims look almost real!

DAVID: Something else looks real, too. That turkey!

MEG: Mm-m-m. I wish it were. If only we could have one like that.

DAVID: You know, the longer you look at those Pilgrims, the more real they seem. I wouldn't be a bit surprised if they raised their heads and said hello. (PILGRIMS *slowly raise heads, then* PILGRIM BOY *and* GIRL *smile at* MEG *and* DAVID.)

MEG (*Stunned*): David, look!

PILGRIM GIRL: Would you share our meal?

PILGRIM BOY: Pray join us. (MEG *and* DAVID *gasp.*)

MEG: Did you hear that?

DAVID: I did, but I don't believe it! (*They start to back away.*)

BOY (*Rising*): I pray you, do not run from us. We are as real as you.

GIRL (*Rising*): Aye, in faith, as surely as this is Thanksgiving Day, 1628.

MEG: But it isn't! I mean, it's Thanksgiving Day, but it's 199–. (PILGRIM BOY *and* GIRL *look at each other, startled.*)

DAVID (*Uneasily*): You're a painting. You're not real. My father painted you.

GIRL (*Coming around table into room, as* PILGRIM MOTHER *rises and exits.*) He painted us well, too. Do but feel the texture of my cape.

BOY (*Coming into room, as* PILGRIM FATHER *exits, taking turkey with him*): And my jacket. Prithee, feel the warmth of it. (*Puts out his arm, as* DAVID *and* MEG *back away.*)

GIRL: Do not be afraid. (MEG *and* DAVID *touch her cape.*)

MEG: It feels rather rough and coarse. It's nice, but isn't it rather plain?

GIRL: It is the only one I have. May I touch your garment?

MEG: Oh, this old dress. I hate it.

GIRL (*Touching fabric*): Why, it feels like a feather on my finger. It has the colors of the rainbow. Truly, it is the most beautiful dress I have ever seen.

BOY (*Fingering* DAVID'S *sweater*): Sister, look upon this overshirt. It is heavy wool and the color of fire.

GIRL: Aye, brother, it is a wondrous thing! See there! (*She points to armchair.*) That object! (*She runs to it.*) Let me guess. It is for sleeping!

MEG (*Laughing*): No, it's a chair—for sitting! (BOY *sits in armchair.*)

GIRL: All our chairs are of wood, hewn with an axe.

BOY (*Bouncing in chair*): It *must* be for sleeping, for it is soft like a bed.

DAVID: No. Our beds are in the bedroom.

GIRL: A separate room for beds?

DAVID: Sure. Next to the bedroom is the bathroom. (*Pointing left*) The kitchen is over there.

GIRL (*Gazing around*): So many rooms! It is like a palace!

MEG: How many rooms do you have?

GIRL: Only one. All families have but one, except the Squire, who is rich, and has three.

BOY: But our cabin is warm, for I sealed the cracks between the logs with grass and clay.

GIRL (*Proudly*): My brother did a fine job. No grown man could have done the task better.

BOY (*Picking up doll*): Look upon this rare little creature. Is it alive?

MEG: Alive? Of course not. That's my old doll. She's ugly.

GIRL (*Taking doll*): No! Why, she is like a real, true child. Real arms, real legs, and real hair, golden as the ripened wheat. She is truly an angel.

DAVID: Do you have a doll, Pilgrim girl?

GIRL: Aye, my doll is a length of wood with a corn husk for a dress, but I love her, for she is mine. (*She gives doll to* MEG.)

DAVID (*Pulling ball from his pocket*): Have you seen one of these? (*He bounces it, as* BOY *and* GIRL *laugh and clap their hands.*)

GIRL: It jumps like magic! Oh, let me make it jump.

BOY: Prithee, friend, take all I possess (*Taking pebbles from pocket*)—these smooth pebbles—but let me hold the ball.

DAVID (*Exchanging ball for stones*): Sure. Here.

BOY (*Bouncing ball*): See, sister, see! I am making it jump!

GIRL: It is magic! (*She walks to table. Others follows.*) Brother, look upon this table. It is prepared for a feast.

BOY: It is prepared for a king.

DAVID: Here, have a banana. (*Hands her banana*)

BOY *and* GIRL (*Examining it*): Bah-nah-nah?

GIRL: It is an odd name.

BOY: A bah-nah-nah. (MEG *and* DAVID *laugh.*) Is that not right?

DAVID: That's pretty close. Taste it. You'll like it.

BOY (*Trying to bite it*): Its hide is thick! (*Bites again*)

DAVID: Wait! You have to peel it first! (*He does so.*) Now taste it.

BOY (*Eating*): Its meat is soft and strangely sweet.

MEG: It's a fruit.

GIRL: Apples and pears and peaches I have seen, but never this.

MEG: What about oranges? Do you have these? (*Hands an orange to* GIRL)

GIRL: It is the magic ball again! Now it will jump for me! (*She tries to bounce it.*) Oh! I have broken it.

MEG (*Picking up orange*): No, an orange won't bounce like a rubber ball. Here, squeeze the juice into your mouth.

GIRL (*As she does so*): Ahh, it is good. Sharp, but sweet.

BOY: You must be very rich to own such treasures: your shirt of fire, the magic ball, the sleeping chair—

GIRL: The angel doll, the rainbow dress, and this strange fruit.

DAVID: No, we're not rich at all. We're poor. (*Doorbell rings. PILGRIM BOY and GIRL are startled. They run to painting.*)

BOY: Heaven protect us!

GIRL: We must go home!

MEG and DAVID (*Ad lib*): No, don't go! Stay here for a while longer! (*Etc. PILGRIM FATHER and MOTHER re-enter rear. All four PILGRIMS sit, resuming their former positions, with heads bowed. Doorbell rings again. MR. LANDIS enters, crosses stage to open door.*)

MR. LANDIS (*To MEG and DAVID, who are standing, stunned*): What's the matter with you two? (*He opens door to MR. MARKS, who carries large package.*) Why, Mr. Marks! What a surprise!

MR. MARKS (*Entering; jovially*): Happy Thanksgiving!

MR. LANDIS: Happy Thanksgiving to you.

MRS. LANDIS (*Entering*): Why, Mr. Marks! Happy Thanksgiving. Let me take your coat.

MR. MARKS (*Putting down package*): No, no. I can't stay. Just stopped by for a moment. Hello, David. What a pretty dress, Meg.

MRS. LANDIS: I'm afraid she doesn't think so.

MEG: Oh, but I do, Mom. It's my favorite dress. See, it has all the colors of the rainbow. (*She twirls around.*)

MR. MARKS: Careful, there. You'll make that doll dizzy spinning her around like that.

MEG: I wouldn't do that. I take good care of my doll. I'm going to make her a new dress and wash her face and comb her hair.

DAVID: I'll fix her leg if you want, Meg.

MRS. LANDIS (*Puzzled*): What's come over you all of a sudden? You just told me earlier you hated that doll.

MEG: No, I love her. She's like an angel to me.

MRS. LANDIS: Next thing we know, David will be telling us he likes his old red sweater.

DAVID: I do like it, Mom. It's still warm, and it hasn't faded a bit. See? It's the color of fire.

MR. MARKS: Well, I would say Mom and Dad are very luck to have children who appreciate their clothing and take care of their toys.

MR. LANDIS: Yes, this time I believe they really mean it.

MR. MARKS: Mr. Landis, to get down to my reason for coming here: I've come in person, because I bring good news. I'm happy to tell you that the school board has re-examined their budget and voted to buy your Pilgrim painting after all.

MR. LANDIS: That's great!

MRS. LANDIS: How wonderful!

MEG *and* DAVID (*Ad lib*): Dad, that's terrific! Congratulations. (*Etc.*)

MR. MARKS: Yes, I convinced the board that along with science and football and video equipment, schools need art. We'll hang your painting in the cafeteria, as planned.

MR. LANDIS (*Shaking* MR. MARKS' *hand*): Mr. Marks, I'm delighted. Thanks so much for your support.

MR. MARKS: Now, here's the check to pay for the Pilgrim painting. (*Hands check to* MR. LANDIS) I know a little unexpected cash comes in handy at the holidays. I'll have someone come by tomorrow and pick up the painting.

DAVID: Oh, no!

MEG: You can't sell it after all, Dad!

MR. LANDIS: What's all this about?

DAVID: We want to keep the painting.

MRS. LANDIS: I don't understand.

MEG: We like the Pilgrim boy and girl. They taught us a lot.

MR. MARKS: Of course, it's true that the Pilgrims gave us our heritage and freedom when they came to this country seeking freedom of worship. But if the painting has taught you all this, don't you think other students at school would want to see it?

MEG: Hm-m. Yes, I guess so.

DAVID: We'd still be able to see the painting every day if it's hanging in the cafeteria.

MEG: I know, David, but what will happen to—you know who?

MRS. LANDIS: Meg, what are you talking about?

DAVID (*Trying to protect* MEG; *quickly*): She doesn't know what she means, Mom. She's just talking.

MRS. LANDIS: Excuse us, Mr. Marks. Sometimes kids do imagine things.

MR. MARKS (*Smiling*): The privilege of youth. Well, I must be going.

MR. LANDIS: Mr. Marks, I don't know how to thank you and the board for accepting my painting. It makes today the happiest Thanksgiving we've ever had.

MR. MARKS: My pleasure. Oh, I almost forgot. A man and woman stopped me in front of your house and asked me to deliver that package to you. They were all dressed up like Pilgrims. On their way to a costume party, I guess. (MEG *and* DAVID *exchange looks.*)

MRS. LANDIS: Thanks for bringing it, Mr. Marks. And Happy Thanksgiving. (*All exchange goodbyes.* MR. MARKS *exits.*)

MR. LANDIS (*Grabbing* MRS. LANDIS *and dancing her around*): We've sold it, Abby, we've sold it! Look at this check!

MRS. LANDIS: Oh, Peter, it's wonderful! Really wonderful!

MEG (*Eagerly*): Mom, Dad—may we open the package now?

MRS. LANDIS: Sure, honey. Go ahead. (MEG *and* DAVID *open package, pull out large cooked turkey.*)

DAVID: A turkey!

MEG: A real Thanksgiving turkey!

MRS. LANDIS: Who would have sent us a turkey?

MEG: Mr. Marks said a man and woman in Pilgrim clothes gave it to him.

MR. LANDIS: Yes, but who would that have been? Do you two know anything about this?

MEG: Well, we . . . we—

MRS. LANDIS: Come on, Meg, out with it.

MEG: You see . . . oh, David, help me!

MR. LANDIS: What is it, David?

DAVID: Dad, we might be able to make a guess, but even if we told you, you wouldn't believe it.

MEG: We don't even know whether to believe it ourselves!

DAVID: So can't we just say that it's a secret? A secret handed down by the Pilgrims?

MR. LANDIS (*Laughing*): O.K. You keep the secret, and I'll keep the turkey. (*Starts toward table*) Bring it to the table, kids, and let's sit down to eat. (MEG *and* DAVID *follow their parents. As they pass painting they hold turkey high.* PILGRIMS *wave and smile.* LANDIS *family sits.*) We have more to be thankful for this Thanksgiving Day than we could ever have imagined. (*He begins to carve turkey, and all ad lib excited conversation, as curtain falls.*)

THE END

The Reform of Benjamin Scrimp

by *Claire Boiko*

A Christmas melodrama inspired by Dickens' "A Christmas Carol" . . .

Characters

CAROLERS, *6 male and female*
PAPER BOY
BENJAMIN SCRIMP, *class treasurer*
PENNY
LORA
KIM
MIKE
RALPH
TINY TOM
PETER
GHOST OF CHRISTMAS PRESENT
GHOST OF CHRISTMAS PAST
GHOST OF CHRISTMAS FUTURE
DOCTOR
BAND LEADER
DEBBIE ANN JEAN MARIE SMITH
FRANKIE BING SCRIMP

JITTERBUG DANCERS, *12 male and female*
BAND

BEFORE RISE: *Sign on easel in front of curtain reads,* AUDITORIUM, CHARLES DICKENS JUNIOR HIGH SCHOOL. *Music to "Christmas Is Coming" begins, and* CAROLERS, *dressed in red and green robes, enter and sing "Christmas Is Coming" as a round.*

1ST CAROLER *(To audience)*: Merry Christmas! Welcome to Charles Dickens Junior High School. I'm sure you remember Charles Dickens.

CAROLERS *(Together)*: "It was the best of times, it was the worst of times . . ."

2ND CAROLER: Naturally, with such a distinguished author as Charles Dickens for our school symbol, we have a tale to tell.

CAROLERS *(Together)*: A Christmas story.

3RD CAROLER: We begin, as all of Mr. Dickens' best stories begin, with a character.

CAROLERS *(Groaning)*: What a character! (BENJAMIN SCRIMP *enters, in black suit, string tie, punching buttons on calculator.*)

BENJAMIN SCRIMP: Twenty-five thousand forty dollars, forty-one, forty-two. *(Shakes head)* Not enough. I must have more, more, more money.

4TH CAROLER: That's our character, Benjamin Scrimp. He started working at the tender age of eight with a small paper route.

5TH CAROLER: Now, at age fourteen, he is a thousandaire with an interest-bearing account, blue-chip stocks, and bonds. He's the class treasurer and the only junior high school student who is incorporated.

3RD CAROLER: But nobody loves Benjamin Scrimp.

CAROLERS *(Together)*: Nobody. (PAPER BOY, *in ragged jeans and jacket, enters, holds hand out to* BENJAMIN.)

PAPER BOY: Please, oh, please, Benjamin Scrimp. Advance me a few small coins on my paper route salary. My poor old mother is sick and I want to buy her some daisies.

BENJAMIN: I won't give you a plugged nickel. If you want daisies, pick them yourself. (PAPER BOY *exits, weeping.*)

CAROLERS (*Together*): Boo. Hiss. For shame, Benjamin Scrimp. (BENJAMIN *crosses to exit, muttering.*)

BENJAMIN: Twenty-five thousand forty-four, forty-five, forty-six . . . (*Exits*)

6TH CAROLER: We take you now to the gymnasium of the Charles Dickens Junior High School, where the Christmas committee is planning the annual Christmas party. (CAROLERS *sing "Deck the Halls" as they exit. Curtain opens.* NOTE: CAROLERS *sit on floor downstage if play is given in gymnasium.*)

* * * * *

SETTING: *Bare gym with basketball hoop up center. Stepstool is up left; small table down right center.*

AT RISE: PENNY, LORA, KIM, MIKE, *and* RALPH *are onstage.* PENNY *stands on stepstool.* LORA, *clipboard in hand, stands up right.* KIM *sits on floor, center, gazing at ceiling.* MIKE, *tape measure in hand, kneels down left.* RALPH *stands down right, checklist in hand.* BENJAMIN *sits at table, head bent over calculator, checkbook and pen in front of him.*

RALPH: Two hundred hot dogs, thirty pounds of hamburger, fifty pounds of Christmas candy, and twelve gallons of punch. What a bash!

BENJAMIN: It'll cost an arm and a leg.

PENNY: Don't worry, it isn't your arm and leg, Benjamin. It's the student body's money.

LORA: Get with it, Benjamin. There've been Christmas parties in this gym for over thirty years.

KIM (*Coyly*): Benjamin, I'm thinking of hanging some mistletoe right up there. (*Points up*) Will you stand under the mistletoe with me tonight? (*All laugh and applaud.*)

BENJAMIN: I have no time for such silliness. (*Continues working at calculator*)

MIKE: I've measured this corner for the twenty-foot Christmas tree. Who's going to help us put it up?

PENNY: Who's going to help hang the banner behind the basketball hoop?

LORA: And who's going to hang those hundreds of stars from the ceiling?

RALPH (*Cupping hands around mouth*): H-E-L-P! (TINY TOM, *a very tall boy in basketball uniform, runs on, dribbling basketball. He pauses center, casually flips ball through hoop.*)

TINY TOM (*Grinning*): Did you call for someone tall?

PENNY: It's Tiny Tom!

LORA: Always friendly, kind and helpful.

TINY TOM (*Modestly*): How can I help you?

KIM: You can help us put up the decorations, Tiny Tom.

LORA: They'll be here any minute.

RALPH (*To* BENJAMIN): Do you have the check ready, Benjamin?

BENJAMIN: I have the check, but I warn you, I'll sign it under protest.

TINY TOM: Some folks have a talent for basketball. Some folks have a gift for music. But you, Benjamin Scrimp, have a positive genius for meanness.

BENJAMIN: Thank you, Tiny Tom. (*Wryly*) I practice a lot. (PETER *enters with dolly, piled high with boxes.*)

PETER (*As he wheels dolly center*): Special delivery. Christmas goods for Charles Dickens Junior High School.

KIM: Hooray! We're all set for the party.

PETER: Hold it. I need a check from you for the full amount of the shipment.

RALPH: The check, please, Benjamin. (BENJAMIN *crosses to* PETER *with checkbook and pen.*)

BENJAMIN: How much is this ridiculous Christmas nonsense going to cost?

PETER (*Taking slip from jacket pocket*): The whole thing comes to four hundred twenty-nine dollars and seven cents.

BENJAMIN: Four hundred twenty-nine dollars and seven cents? This must be some joke!

MIKE: What's so funny about it?

BENJAMIN: We haven't got it, that's what's so funny. The entire balance for the student activities account is two hundred dollars even.

LORA (*To* PETER): Will you take our check for two hundred dollars, and put the rest on account? We'll have more money from the student fees in January.

PETER (*Shaking his head*): Sorry. My instructions are to get the full amount due, or take this load back.

KIM (*Upset*): This is awful! I'd contribute, but I spent all my money on Christmas presents.

RALPH: Same here.

MIKE: I could give you seven cents.

PENNY: Doesn't anybody have any money we could borrow? (*All shake heads, then turn slowly to* BENJAMIN.)

RALPH: Benjamin Scrimp! What about you?

BENJAMIN: Don't look at me! I never borrow, and I never lend.

PENNY: Oh, please—

BENJAMIN (*Angrily*): No, no, a thousand times no!

PETER: Sorry, kids. These Christmas trimmings go back to the warehouse. (*Turns to exit*)

TINY TOM: Wait! (PETER *turns back.*) Benjamin Scrimp, I'm going down on my knees to you. (*He leaps into air, landing on knee, then crumples in pain.*) Oh! Ow! Ooh! My knee! (*All gather around, except* BENJAMIN.)

MIKE: Call the First Aid Squad.

RALPH: Who's got a bandage?

KIM (*To* BENJAMIN): *Now* look what you've done, Benjamin Scrimp.

PENNY (*Crossing to* PETER): Please don't spoil our Christmas party. For Tiny Tom's sake.

PETER: Aw-w-w, you're making me feel like a rat.

BENJAMIN: Rats are smart. Take it all away.

PETER: Listen, I have to make a couple of deliveries across town. I'll stop back here in one hour. If you can raise the entire amount by then, I'll leave the stuff for the party.

TINY TOM (*Sitting up*): Thanks a lot. (PETER *pushes dolly off.*)

PENNY: How will we ever get the money in an hour?

TINY TOM: There's only one way. I'm due to play an exhibition game in fifteen minutes. (*Proudly*) I will see to it that the proceeds are turned over for the Christmas celebration. (*Groaning suddenly*) Ooh!

LORA: Your knee is all swollen—it looks horrible!

TINY TOM (*Bravely*): Don't worry, I'll play the game. (*Heroically*)

Get me an ace bandage and a basketball! (*All applaud, except* BENJAMIN.)

KIM: It's your fault, Benjamin Scrimp, you miserly money-grubber.

ALL (*Sarcastically*): Merry Christmas, Benjamin Scrimp. (*Curtains close.* BENJAMIN *steps in front of curtain. "God Rest Ye Merry, Gentlemen" plays softly in background.*)

BENJAMIN (*To audience*): Merry Christmas, eh? Well, let me tell you about Christmas. It's the time of year when there are blizzards, people get the flu, and everybody sends those dumb Christmas cards with overweight Santa Clauses grinning foolishly, and sappy verses to wish you holiday cheer. (*With a sneer*) You can bet your bottom dollar none of those cards says: "Please find check enclosed." (*Scornfully*) Christmas. Bah, humbug! When you open a package, there's a crummy hand-knit tie with dropped stitches from your Aunt Minnie. Why couldn't she send you cash? Happy holidays, my foot! People want to shake your hand, and when you put your hand out, they ask you for a handout. But you never catch them greasing *your* palm with silver. (*Strongly*) People overeat, overspend and overdo, all in the name of "fun." Fun! Does fun put bucks in your bank? Does fun add one blue chip to your stock portfolio? Who cares if there's no Christmas party this year? The students should thank me for putting a stop to this ridiculous, expensive *nonsense*. (*Sound of thunderclap is heard. Lights go off, then come up on* GHOST OF CHRISTMAS PRESENT, *dressed like a flashy rock star.*)

CHRISTMAS PRESENT (*Ominously*): Benjamin Scrimp?

BENJAMIN (*Frightened*): Yes? Who are you?

CHRISTMAS PRESENT: Hey, Merry Christmas, dude. I am the Ghost of Christmas Present.

BENJAMIN: You must have the wrong Benjamin Scrimp. I never give Christmas presents, and I never take Christmas presents.

CHRISTMAS PRESENT: Oh, you're the right man, all right. No, I'm not Christmas present, as in *gift*. I am Christmas Present, as in *now*. Get it? I was sent by The Boss to give you another chance.

BENJAMIN: Another chance? For what?

CHRISTMAS PRESENT (*Pointing up*): You know, pal, at this very instant up there a lot of ex-people with wings are voting.

BENJAMIN: Voting for what?

CHRISTMAS PRESENT: They're voting on whether or not you are fit to be a member of the human race. (*Shakes head*) I've got to tell you, it looks like a hung jury. If it were up to me, I'd vote *no way*. But The Boss says, "Give the guy another chance." So— away we go! (*Leads* BENJAMIN *right*)

BENJAMIN: Where are we going?

CHRISTMAS PRESENT: That's for me to know and you to find out. (*Lights flash. "God Rest Ye Merry, Gentlemen" is heard.* CAROLERS *sing first verse as curtains open and lights come up on gym.* BENJAMIN *and* GHOST OF CHRISTMAS PRESENT *watch.* TINY TOM, *swathed in bandages, sits on a cot.* DOCTOR *is kneeling beside him. He is listening to* TINY TOM'S *heart with stethoscope.* RALPH, MIKE, PENNY, LORA, *and* KIM *stand around cot.*)

RALPH (*To* DOCTOR): Will he be all right, Doctor?

DOCTOR (*Shaking head*): He should never have played that exhibition game. His knee has several fractures.

MIKE: He was so brave. Too bad the game brought in only ten dollars and ninety-eight cents.

PENNY (*Discouraged*): It was all in vain. We still don't have enough for the Christmas party.

KIM: Will he be able to play basketball again?

DOCTOR (*Rising, walking downstage*): Sh-h-h. I don't want him to hear this. (*All group around* DOCTOR, *eagerly.*) Tiny Tom has a complex complicated compound compression of his entire skeleton. I'm afraid he's lost his—lost his—

OTHERS (*Together*): Lost his *what?*

DOCTOR: He's lost his tallness. (*Others gasp.*) Tiny Tom is now truly tiny. He has shrunk to four feet eight inches. (*Sighs deeply*) He'll never play basketball again.

MIKE: Oh, no! (*Points accusingly at* BENJAMIN) Benjamin Scrimp, you did this! (*Lights down, curtain closes. In front of curtain,* BENJAMIN *cringes, as* CHRISTMAS PRESENT *exits.*)

BENJAMIN: I'm sorry, Tiny Tom—as sorry as a miserly money-grubber can be. You were the only one who had a good word for me. You said I had a genius for meanness. (*Lights flash on and off. Just as "Jingle Bells" is heard* GHOST OF CHRISTMAS PAST *enters. He is dressed in red and green striped "zoot" suit, and twirls long watch chain around finger.*)

CHRISTMAS PAST (*Heartily*): Greetings, cat. Let's celebrate. (*Music fades out.*)

BENJAMIN: Another ghost? Where did you come from, the woodwork?

CHRISTMAS PAST: Don't you recognize the zoot suit with the reet pleat? I'm the Ghost of Christmas Past. Ho, ho, ho! Hey nonny nonny and a hot-cha-cha!

BENJAMIN (*Sourly*): Hot-cha-cha yourself. If I had my way, I'd abolish Christmas, past, present, and future.

CHRISTMAS PAST: Now, now. Get hep to the jive. I'm going to show you a scene from those quaint old days before MTV, before heavy metal, and before acid-washed jeans. Come on, cat. It's 1955. Let's go. (*They cross right, as curtains open to boogie-woogie "Jingle Bells." Banner proclaiming,* CHRISTMAS SOCK HOP, 1955, *is on wall of gym. Decorated Christmas tree is down left, and there are benches upstage. There is a bandstand and old-fashioned stand microphone right.* BANDLEADER *and* BAND *wear tuxedos. They play jitterbug number—or pantomime playing to recorded music—as* DANCERS *applaud and cheer, then sit on benches.* DEBBIE ANN JEAN MARIE SMITH *enters, dressed as bobby-soxer. She wears frilly apron. She carries tray of coffee cups which she passes to* DANCERS.)

BANDLEADER (*Tapping baton; to* DANCERS): Is everybody happy?

DANCERS (*Together*): You bet!

BANDLEADER: Merry Christmas, everybody!

DANCERS (*Together*): Merry Christmas!

BENJAMIN (*Grimacing*): Disgusting!

BANDLEADER: We have a real treat for our sock hop, guys and gals. The number-one crooner of Charles Dickens Junior High is here to sing for us. (*Extending arm*) Mr. Swell Guy himself, Frankie Bing Scrimp! (DANCERS *applaud. Girls scream.* DEBBIE *puts down tray, claps wildly and looks adoringly at* FRANKIE BING SCRIMP. *He enters, wearing white "zoot" suit, and grabs mike.*)

BENJAMIN (*Amazed*): Frankie Bing Scrimp! That's my father!

CHRISTMAS PAST: That's right, Jack. I remember him well. Now, *he* knew how to enjoy a Christmas party. . . . (*Music to "White Christmas" is heard.* FRANKIE BING *croons song. Girls scream, boys applaud.*)

DEBBIE (*Walking center*): Ooh, Frankie Bing, I'm going to faint. (FRANKIE BING, *still clutching mike, runs to* DEBBIE, *supporting her with one arm.*)

FRANKIE: A girl who swoons! A fainting girl. What a compliment. You must be a *swell* girl. (*Suavely*) What's your name, swell girl?

DEBBIE: Debbie Ann Jean Marie Smith.

FRANKIE: That's a swell name.

BENJAMIN: Debbie Ann Jean Marie Smith? That's my mother. (FRANKIE *and* DEBBIE *hold pose.*)

CHRISTMAS PAST: You're on the beam, Jack. She knew how to have a good time, too.

BENJAMIN: Do you call swooning and screaming a good time?

CHRISTMAS PAST: No doubt about it. Swooning and screaming were major forms of teenage fun back in 1955.

FRANKIE: Debbie Ann Jean Marie Smith, how would you like to be my Christmas present?

DEBBIE (*Clasping hands*): Oh, gosh, golly gee. That would be (*Sighs*) swell. (*Band strikes up "White Christmas."* FRANKIE *and* DEBBIE *dance a few bars, then are joined by* DANCERS *as curtains close.* BENJAMIN *and* CHRISTMAS PAST *cross down right in front of curtain.*)

CHRISTMAS PAST: Do you still want to abolish Christmas Past? If you do, you'll abolish yourself right out of the scene.

BENJAMIN (*Pleading*): No, no. Keep your old Christmases. Have all the fun you want. Just leave me out of it!

CHRISTMAS PAST (*Shaking head*): You're hopeless. There's only one last chance for you. Look! (*He points off right, then exits.* BENJAMIN *looks right, as* GHOST OF CHRISTMAS FUTURE *enters wearing astronaut helmet. He remains silent, pantomiming through following speech. He points accusingly at* BENJAMIN.)

BENJAMIN: Go away. I've had enough ghosts. And don't point at me. You're giving me the willies. (GHOST *points to curtain, then pulls* BENJAMIN *toward center.*) Let go. Your hand is clammy. (GHOST *tugs again.*) All right, all right, I'll come with you. (*Curtain opens. Gym is bare except for banner upstage reading,* CHRISTMAS REUNION, CLASS OF 199-. *An elderly* LORA, *in granny costume with white wig, stands center, holding clipboard.* RALPH *and* MIKE, *dressed as elderly men, enter down.* PENNY *and* KIM, *in outfits similar to* LORA's, *enter up right.*)

LORA: Welcome, everyone! (*Gesturing*) Register right here. Do you remember me? Lora?

KIM (*Hugging* LORA): Lora, dear. How could I *ever* forget you?

PENNY: My goodness! Here are Ralph and Mike! They haven't aged a minute.

RALPH: You look might spry, yourself, Penny.

MIKE: Does anybody want to see pictures of my grandchildren?

LORA (*Brushing him aside*): Now, we all have grandchildren. We're here to reminisce about us. (*Looking around*) Where's our Tiny Tom?

RALPH (*Shaking head*): Poor old Tiny Tom. He's permanently muscle-bound.

BENJAMIN: Muscle-bound? (*Putting hands to head*) Oh, no. Tell me it isn't so, Ghost of the Future. (GHOST *shakes head.*)

MIKE: He would have been the best basketball player the school ever had. If only he hadn't hurt his knee.

PENNY: He wouldn't have if that Benjamin Scrimp had lent us the money for the Christmas party.

KIM: Benjamin Scrimp. I haven't thought of him in years.

BENJAMIN (*Aside*): Not even one thought? That's terrible.

KIM: Whatever happened to him? Not that I care!

BENJAMIN: Oh, please, care. I want you to care.

RALPH: I don't know. Whatever happened to him, I hope the punishment fit his crime.

MIKE: I heard that somebody up there (*Points up*) recalled him.

BENJAMIN: *Recalled* me? Like a defective car?

MIKE: Yes, he had a defective spirit and didn't deserve to be part of the human race.

RALPH: He wasn't human. He was transistorized.

PENNY: He had a calculator for a heart.

ALL (*As curtains close; together*): Benjamin Scrimp? Bah, humbug! (*Curtains close.* GHOST OF CHRISTMAS FUTURE *and* BENJAMIN *remain in front of curtain.* BENJAMIN *wipes eyes with handkerchief, turns to face* GHOST.)

BENJAMIN (*Pleading*): Oh, please! Don't recall me! Look, I'm having fun. (*Grins*) I'm smiling. See? (*Singing*) I'm singing. (*Does clumsy shuffle*) I'm dancing. (GHOST *shakes head and exits*) Don't leave me! (*Starts to follow* GHOST, *then with conviction*) There may still be enough time. I'll make it up to Tiny Tom and the others—I will! (*Curtains open.* LORA, PENNY, KIM, MIKE *and* RALPH, *dressed in modern school clothes, are grouped around* TINY TOM, *who holds knee, grimacing.*)

TINY TOM (*Nobly*): I'll do it. I'll play the game. Get me an ace bandage and a basketball. (*All applaud, as* BENJAMIN *joins the group.*)

KIM (*To* BENJAMIN): It's all your fault, Benjamin Scrimp, you miserly money-grubber.

ALL (*Sarcastically; together*): Merry Christmas, Benjamin Scrimp! (PETER *enters with dolly*)

PETER: I'm back with your Christmas shipment. Do you have enough to pay for all of it?

PENNY (*Pointing at* BENJAMIN): Ask Mr. Moneybags here.

PETER: Well?

BENJAMIN (*Pretending reluctance*): I don't know. It's a lot of money. (*All groan.*) It's really against my principles. (*All groan louder.*) However—(*He whips out checkbook and pen, scribbles on check with a flourish; suddenly cheerful*) here's your check, in *full!* (*Smiling*) And a little extra for your trouble. Merry Christmas!

PETER (*Surprised*): Say, thanks! (*Puts boxes on floor*) And a Merry Christmas to you.

BENJAMIN (*Crossing to* TINY TOM, *patting him on shoulder*): You don't have to play that exhibition game, Tiny Tom. I'll see to it that you stay tall enough to reach those baskets. (*Turns*) Ralph, Mike, would you take our Tiny Tom to the nurse's office? (RALPH *and* MIKE *help* TINY *off.*)

TINY TOM (*As he exits*): It's a miracle. Bless you, Benjamin Scrimp.

BENJAMIN: O.K., let's open these boxes, and get ready for the party!

LORA (*To* PENNY): He's gone bananas, but I like him now. (BENJAMIN *pulls* KIM *down center.*)

BENJAMIN: Where do we hang the mistletoe, Kim?

KIM (*Surprised*): Well, up *there,* Benjamin. (*Points up*)

BENJAMIN: Up *where?* (*Stands close to* KIM)

KIM (*Pointing*): *There.* (BENJAMIN *hugs her.*) Well! Welcome back to the human race, Benjamin Scrimp!

PENNY: Merry Christmas, Benjamin Scrimp!

BENJAMIN (*To girls*): Merry Christmas. (*To audience*) Merry Christmas, one and all. And bless you, Tiny Tom! (*Curtains close, as* CAROLERS *sing "We Wish You a Merry Christmas."*)

THE END

The Christmas Nutcracker

Based on a story by *E. T. A. Hoffman*
Adapted by *Adele Thane*

An exciting adaptation of a Christmas classic . . .

Characters

MARCHEN, *10*
FRITZ, *her brother, 12*
JUDGE SILBERHAUS
FRAU SILBERHAUS
DOCTOR DROSSELMEYER
LORD CHANCELLOR
ROYAL ASTROLOGER
ROYAL MATHEMATICIAN
KING PUDGY PODGY
KITCHEN MAID
PRINCESS PIRLIPAT
THE MOUSE KING
NICHOLAS NUTCRACKER
CLOCK, *offstage voice*

TIME: *Christmas Eve.*
SETTING: *Drawing room of Judge Silberhaus' home in old Ger-*

man village. Large Christmas tree, lighted and decorated with tinsel, candy canes, and nuts in small paper baskets, stands right. Doll, toy soldiers, and other wrapped gifts are under it, as well as a nutcracker in the shape of a man, with movable jaws. Fireplace is left, with armchair near hearth. There is a grandfather clock in alcove in back wall.

AT RISE: JUDGE *and* FRAU SILBERHAUS *stand center, and* DOCTOR DROSSELMEYER *sits in armchair. He wears glasses and has gray beard and hair.* JUDGE *holds Swiss music box, which plays.* MARCHEN *and* FRITZ *run in.*

FRAU SILBERHAUS: Merry Christmas, children! (MARCHEN *and* FRITZ *run to Christmas tree.*)

MARCHEN (*Picking up doll*): A new doll! How beautiful she is!

FRITZ (*Examining soldiers*): Soldiers in bright red coats! Just what I wanted!

FRAU SILBERHAUS: Children, you haven't said Merry Christmas to Dr. Drosselmeyer.

FRITZ (*As he sets up soldiers in a line*): Merry Christmas, Dr. Drosselmeyer.

MARCHEN (*Going to* DROSSELMEYER, *who rises to greet her*): Merry Christmas, Dr. Drosselmeyer.

DROSSELMEYER: Merry Christmas, my dear.

FRAU SILBERHAUS: I'll go see if the other guests have arrived. (*Exits*)

MARCHEN (*Pointing to nutcracker*): What is that?

DROSSELMEYER: That is a nutcracker. (*Crosses to tree. He walks slowly and is slightly bent over.*)

MARCHEN (*Following him*): A nutcracker?

DROSSELMEYER (*Picking up nutcracker*): Yes. Just watch. (*Takes walnut from tree or bowl on table*) You put a nut in his mouth, like this, and then—(*He pretends to crack nut.*) Crack! The strong jaws of the nutcracker will break the nut open.

MARCHEN (*Eagerly*): May I have him?

DROSSELMEYER: Well, I gave him to the whole family, but since he pleases you so much, I shall place him in your care.

MARCHEN (*Taking nutcracker*): Oh, thank you! (*Turns*) Fritz, look at my nutcracker!

FRITZ: Let's see if he can crack this nut. (*Takes large nut from tree*)

MARCHEN (*Handing nutcracker to* FRITZ): Do be careful! (FRITZ *places nut in nutcracker's mouth and cracks it with great force.*)

FRITZ (*Looking closely at nutcracker*): This nutcracker has broken. The nut must have been too big for it. I didn't mean to break it.

JUDGE (*Sternly*): Fritz! You must be more careful with things!

MARCHEN (*Upset*): Give him back this instant! (MARCHEN *snatches nutcracker from him.*) Oh, my poor nutcracker! Fritz, you've broken his jaw!

FRITZ: He's not a good nutcracker anyway. His jaws are too fragile to crack nuts.

MARCHEN (*Angrily*): You're mean, Fritz!

FRAU SILBERHAUS (*Entering up left*): Come, everyone. It's time for dinner.

FRITZ: Good! I'm starved! (*He runs out.*)

JUDGE (*Severely*): Fritz, such manners! (*He follows* FRITZ *off, shaking his head disapprovingly.*)

FRAU SILBERHAUS: Doctor, Marchen—are you coming?

MARCHEN: In a minute, Mama. I want to put a bandage on nutcracker's jaw. (*She sits in armchair.*)

FRAU SILBERHAUS: Very well, dear, but don't be long.

DROSSELMEYER: I'll wait for Marchen.

FRAU SILBERHAUS (*Smiling*): Very well. (*She exits.*)

MARCHEN: Poor little nutcracker! Does your jaw hurt dreadfully? (*Takes handkerchief from pocket*) I'll tie it up with my handkerchief. (*She proceeds to do so.*)

DROSSELMEYER: I'll tell you a story about nutcracker after dinner.

MARCHEN: Oh, couldn't you begin the story now and finish it after dinner?

DROSSELMEYER: We mustn't keep your family waiting.

MARCHEN: Just a *little* beginning—*please?*

DROSSELMEYER: I have a better idea. I'll tell the story while we're eating dinner. I should like everyone to hear it—especially Fritz. Then, perhaps, he will think more kindly of nutcracker.

MARCHEN: Yes, yes! But please, begin *now!* (MARCHEN *rises from chair. DROSSELMEYER puts his arm around her shoulders, and they walk slowly toward alcove. Lights dim, except on grand-father clock.*)

DROSSELMEYER: Many years ago, when I was a young man, there lived a king named Pudgy Podgy. (MARCHEN *giggles.*) In the king's throne room there stood a wonderful clock that never had to be wound and didn't strike the hours of the day. (*They stop before grandfather clock.*)

MARCHEN: How did people know what time it was?

DROSSELMEYER (*Smiling*): They knew, all right. You see, I invented that clock and gave it to the king. It *spoke* the hours and the day and the month. No one had to count the time at all. They just had to listen.

VOICE OF CLOCK (*Offstage or behind clock*): Three o'clock in the afternoon on the first day of April. Three o'clock in the afternoon on the first day of April. (DROSSELMEYER *and* MARCHEN *listen, then exit. After a brief pause, lights come up full, as* LORD CHANCELLOR *enters hurriedly down right, wearing long wig and robe.*)

CHANCELLOR (*Over his shoulder*): Come, come, Royal Astrologer! The king wants to see us. (ROYAL ASTROLOGER *enters. He wears long robe and large pointed hat with suns, moons, and stars on it, and holding telescope up to eye.*)

ASTROLOGER: Here I am.

CHANCELLOR (*Sharply*): Put down that telescope! There are no stars out now. It's only three o'clock in the afternoon. We must get the Royal Mathematician and go to the king. (*He starts to cross left.*)

ASTROLOGER (*Following him*): How is the king today?

CHANCELLOR: Happy as a lark. Hurry, now. (*Calls off*) Mathematician! The king wishes to see you. (ROYAL MATHEMATICIAN, *wearing robe with numbers and equations on it, hurries on, holding notebook and pencil.*)

MATHEMATICIAN: How *is* King Podgy today? Stodgy?

CHANCELLOR: No, he's happy as a lark. (KING PUDGY PODGY *enters, singing merry tune and dancing jig. He wears royal*

robes, stuffed with a pillow to make him plump, and crown. His
cheeks are painted red.)

CHANCELLOR, MATHEMATICIAN, *and* ASTROLOGER (*Ad lib*): Good
day, King Pudgy Podgy! You seem so happy today! It's nice to
see you dancing and singing. (*Etc.*)

KING (*Reciting and dancing*):
The happiest king in all the world
Is good King Pudgy Podgy,
Who used to be so very glum
And oh! so very stodgy.
But now he has declared it treason
To be sad for any reason,
And it's clearly out of season
To be sad. So be glad! Oh, be glad, oh!
(*With a flourish*) I'm as happy as a lark!

ASTROLOGER: How happy is a lark is a lark is a lark—(CHANCEL-
LOR *quickly pulls* ASTROLOGER'S *hat down over his head.*)

MATHEMATICIAN: Shall I add up some numbers for you, Your
Majesty?

KING: No! Where's the Royal Astrologer?

MATHEMATICIAN (*Pointing to him*): Talking through his hat,
Your Majesty.

KING: Unhat him! I want to ask him a question. (MATHEMATI-
CIAN *lifts up* ASTROLOGER'S *hat.*) Astrologer, did you or did you
not say that the stars would be favorable for sausage-making
today?

ASTROLOGER: I did, Your Majesty.

KING (*Exuberantly*): Then I shall eat sausage after sausage after
sausage in honor of the Princess Pirlipat's twelfth birthday.
(*He tosses crown into the air.*) To fair Pirlipat!

CHANCELLOR, MATHEMATICIAN, *and* ASTROLOGER (*Together*): To
fair Pirlipat! (CHANCELLOR *tosses his slipper into air,* MATHE-
MATICIAN *his notebook, and* ASTROLOGER *his hat.*)

KING (*Proudly*): Did you know that she was born with perfect
teeth and could crack nuts with them at the age of one month?

CHANCELLOR: I remember, sire. The Princess bit me at the chris-
tening! (KITCHEN MAID *enters up left, out of breath.*)

MAID (*Wailing*): Oh, Your Majesty!

KING (*Annoyed*): Yes, what is it?

MAID: I don't know how to tell you.

CHANCELLOR: Speak up!

MAID: It happened just after the sizzling aroma of sausage had spread through the palace.

KING: Yes, yes! Go on. I'm getting hungrier by the moment.

MAID (*Speaking rapidly*): An army of mice invaded the kitchen. We all had to fight them off.

KING: Heavens! What a narrow squeak! I was afraid they'd eaten my sausages.

MAID (*Wringing her hands*): They did, Your Majesty.

KING (*In panic*): All of the sausages are gone?

MAID (*Nodding*): Not a grease spot left.

KING (*Wailing*): Oh-h-h! (*He staggers and faints into arms of* ASTROLOGER.)

CHANCELLOR (*To* MAID): Now you've done it! And he was so happy! (CHANCELLOR *and* MATHEMATICIAN *lead* KING *to armchair.* PRINCESS PIRLIPAT *enters.*)

MAID (*Curtsying*): Goodness! The Princess Pirlipat! (*She scurries out.*)

PRINCESS (*Alarmed*): What has happened to Papa?

CHANCELLOR: He has had a sudden shock, Your Highness.

PRINCESS: Has he heard about the sausages?

KING (*Suddenly coming to; in a rage*): Heard about it! (*He stands.*) *Heard* about it! Oh-h-h! Send for Dr. Drosselmeyer at once! *He* will know what to do!

PRINCESS: Dr. Drosselmeyer is already here, Papa.

KING (*Amazed*): He is? My, that was quick!

PRINCESS: He came to bring me a birthday present.

KING: Fetch him! Fetch him at once!

PRINCESS: Yes, Papa. (*She goes up right and calls off.*) Dr. Drosselmeyer! (DROSSELMEYER *enters. He no longer has beard and his hair is dark. He walks with sprightly step.*)

DROSSELMEYER (*Bowing*): What is your pleasure, sire?

KING: Pleasure! I have no pleasure. My sausages have been eaten up.

DROSSELMEYER: I know, Your Majesty. I was in the kitchen when it happened.

KING: You were? Why didn't you do something about it?

DROSSELMEYER: I did, sire. I set my special traps and caught all the mice—except one. . . .

KING: Which one?

DROSSELMEYER: The Mouse King. He alone escaped.

ALL (*Crying out together*): The Mouse King! (*Blackout. Thunder and lightning.* MOUSE KING *suddenly appears, wearing a tiny gold crown. A green spotlight shines on him.*)

MOUSE KING (*In loud, shrill voice*):
Pudgy Podgy, you are due for a fall!
You've killed my subjects, killed them all!
I'll have my revenge, and it won't be small!
Pudgy Podgy, you are due for a fall!
(*Thunder and lightning. Blackout.* PRINCESS *screams, then faints.* MOUSE KING *exits. Lights come up full.*)

KING (*Turning in circles*): Where did he go? Where is he?

DROSSELMEYER (*Kneeling beside* PRINCESS): Your Majesty, the Princess Pirlipat—

KING (*Desperately*): Is she dead?

DROSSELMEYER: No—worse than that.

KING: *Worse?*

DROSSELMEYER: The Mouse King has bitten her. Look! (*He raises* PRINCESS' *head. She wears a grotesque mask, similar to the face of the nutcracker.*)

KING: Pirlipat! Why do you look like this?

DROSSELMEYER: It is the revenge of the Mouse King. He has put her under a spell.

KING (*To* CHANCELLOR *and* MATHEMATICIAN): Take her to her room. (*Wails loudly*) Oh, my beautiful daughter! (CHANCELLOR *and* MATHEMATICIAN *carry* PRINCESS *off.* KING *turns furiously to* DROSSELMEYER.) It's all your fault, Dr. Drosselmeyer! If you don't restore the Princess to her former beauty, I shall deal with you severely. (ASTROLOGER *has been peering through his telescope.*)

ASTROLOGER (*To* KING): Sire, I believe I know the quickest way to restore the Princess's beauty. I see it written in the stars.

KING (*Impatiently*): Yes, yes, what do the stars say?

ASTROLOGER: There is a certain nut called the Krakatu.

KING: Krakatu?

ASTROLOGER: The shell is so hard that even a cannon can pass over it without breaking it. The stars say that this nut must be cracked in the presence of the Princess by a young man who has never shaved and always wears boots.

KING: Yes, yes, go on!

ASTROLOGER: This young man must present the nut to the Princess with his eyes closed, and with his eyes still closed, take seven steps backward without stumbling. (*Ominously*) Such is the prophecy of the stars.

KING (*To* DROSSELMEYER): Doctor, you must find this Krakatu nut and the young man, and bring them both to the palace.

DROSSELMEYER (*Worried*): But what if I should fail?

KING: You must *not* fail! (*Blackout. Thunder and lightning. MOUSE KING appears again in green spotlight.*)

MOUSE KING:
You may search throughout the land,
The Krakatu is not at hand.

KING (*To* DROSSELMEYER): Be off, Doctor, before the Mouse King defeats us again! (DROSSELMEYER *hurries out.*)

MOUSE KING:
He may search throughout the land,
The Krakatu is not at hand.
(*Thunder and lightning. Blackout. There is a brief pause, during which music from "The Nutcracker Suite" may be played. As the music fades, spotlight comes up on grandfather clock.*)

VOICE OF CLOCK: Three o'clock in the afternoon on the twenty-fourth day of December. Three o'clock in the afternoon on the twenty-fourth day of December. (*Lights come up full, revealing* ASTROLOGER *standing right, peering through telescope. At left,* MATHEMATICIAN *is busily adding figures in large notebook.* KING *enters and goes to* ASTROLOGER.)

KING: Do you see Dr. Drosselmeyer up there anywhere?

ASTROLOGER: No, sire.

KING: Oh, woe is me!

MATHEMATICIAN (*Coming over*): How does the Princess look to-day, Your Majesty?

KING: Uglier than ever. She does nothing but crack nuts with her teeth.

MATHEMATICIAN: Sh-h-h! Here she comes.

KING (*Turning away*): I can't look at her.

MATHEMATICIAN: Neither can I. (*Pulls hat down over his face. PRINCESS enters, eating a nut.*)

KING (*Without looking at her*): Sit down, my dear. (*She sits in armchair, puts nut in her mouth, and pretends to crack and eat it.*) Dear me. My poor Princess.

CHANCELLOR (*Running in up right*): Your Majesty, Dr. Drosselmeyer is back! (DROSSELMEYER *enters.*)

KING (*Embracing* DROSSELMEYER): Returned at last! (*He turns to* PRINCESS.) Pirlipat, my dear Dr. Drosselmeyer has come back with a cure for you. (*Princess cracks another nut and eats it.* KING *shakes head.*) Did you find the Krakatu nut, Dr. Drosselmeyer?

DROSSELMEYER: Yes, sire, I found it.

KING: What about the young man?

DROSSELMEYER: He is without.

KING (*Alarmed*): Without boots?

DROSSELMEYER: No, Your Majesty—he *waits* without.

KING (*Relieved*): Oh! Have him brought in at once.

CHANCELLOR (*To* MATHEMATICIAN): Bring the young man in. (MATHEMATICIAN *exits up right.*)

KING: Where did you find the nut?

DROSSELMEYER: I searched everywhere—in the mountains, in the forest, by the ocean. I finally found it in a jungle in the tropics. (MATHEMATICIAN *ushers in* NICHOLAS NUTCRACKER, *a boy of twelve or thirteen wearing shiny boots and sword.*) This is the young man, Your Majesty—Nicholas Nutcracker.

KING (*Looking* NICHOLAS *up and down*): Hm-m. Does he fit all the qualifications?

NICHOLAS: I do, Your Majesty. I have never shaved, and I always wear boots.

KING: Even in bed?

NICHOLAS (*Nodding*): Even in bed.

KING: Remarkable! Anything else?

NICHOLAS: I have good strong teeth. I can crack the hardest nuts.

KING: Nicholas Nutcracker, I promise you a chest of gold if you succeed in making my daughter beautiful again. (*To* DROSSELMEYER) Where is the Krakatu nut?

DROSSELMEYER (*Taking nut from pocket and giving it to* NICHOLAS): Right here, Your Majesty.

KING: Begin, then—begin! (NICHOLAS *puts Krakatu nut in his mouth, places one hand on top of his head, the other on his chin, and pushes slowly. Others, except* PRINCESS, *do this with him in pantomime. There is a loud cracking noise.*) He has cracked it!

DROSSELMEYER: Now, Nicholas, close your eyes and give the nut to the Princess.

NICHOLAS (*Closing his eyes*): Your Highness. (*He bows and hands nut to* PRINCESS, *who puts it into her mouth, eats it slowly. The others imitate her.*)

DROSSELMEYER: She has eaten the Krakatu nut. (*Blackout. Thunder and lightning.*)

ALL (*Ad lib*): Oh, no! What's happening? (*Etc. After a moment, lights come up.* PRINCESS *is still in chair, but mask has been removed.*)

KING (*Overjoyed, leaping about*): She's beautiful again! The spell of the Mouse King is broken! Nicholas, my boy! (*He rushes to* NICHOLAS, *who has not moved.*)

DROSSELMEYER (*Grabbing* KING): Wait a minute, Your Majesty! There's more to be done. Nicholas must walk backward seven steps.

KING: Of course! Seven careful steps, my boy.

CHANCELLOR: Don't stumble.

MATHEMATICIAN: Don't trip.

ASTROLOGER: Seven steps, Nicholas. (NICHOLAS *starts walking backward. All count, raising their voices on each successive step.*)

ALL (*Together*): One. Two. Three. Four. (NICHOLAS *starts to sway.*)

DROSSELMEYER: Easy, Nicholas.

KING: No one breathe. I'll have the head of the first man who breathes. (NICHOLAS *takes another step.*) You are breathing, Astrologer.

ASTROLOGER: I can't help it. (NICHOLAS *takes sixth step.*)

ALL: Six. (NICHOLAS *is about to take seventh step when there are flashes of lightning and a great crash of thunder. Blackout.* MOUSE KING *appears in green spotlight.*)

MOUSE KING: Hah! Who dares defy the power of the Mouse King's magic?

ALL (*Together*): The Mouse King!

MOUSE KING: Now you, Nicholas Nutcracker, shall wear the nutcracker face—until some lady, young and fair, says she loves you for yourself, sincerely. (*Thunder and lightning. Blackout. Lights come up.* PRINCESS *cowers and grabs* KING *by the arm.* NICHOLAS *lies on floor.*)

CHANCELLOR: Nicholas has fallen!

DROSSELMEYER: The Mouse King upset him just as he was about to take the seventh step.

ASTROLOGER: Look at him! It's the curse of the Mouse King! (NICHOLAS *stands. He is wearing ugly mask* PRINCESS *wore before.*)

DROSSELMEYER (*To* PRINCESS): Princess, help Nicholas. Say you love him. Break the spell of the Mouse King.

PRINCESS (*Coldly*): That hideous creature is not the young man who gave me the nut. Turn him out of the court! (*She flounces out haughtily.*)

KING (*Running after her*): Pirlipat! My dear! Come back! Help the young man! (KING *exits, followed by* DROSSELMEYER, CHANCELLOR, MATHEMATICIAN, *and* ASTROLOGER. NICHOLAS *stands alone.*)

NICHOLAS (*Boldly*): Watch out, Mouse King! I swear that some day your life shall pay for this face! (*He pulls out his sword. Blackout, during which* NICHOLAS *exits. Music. After a pause, lights come up, revealing* JUDGE *and* FRAU SILBERHAUS, MARCHEN, *and* FRITZ *seated around fireplace.* DROSSELMEYER, *with gray beard and hair, stands center in the militant attitude of* NICHOLAS *at end of preceding scene.* MARCHEN *holds nutcracker.*)

DROSSELMEYER (*Repeating* NICHOLAS' *closing speech*): Watch out,

Mouse King! I swear that some day your life shall pay for this face! (*He breaks pose, smiles.*) That is the story of the nutcracker.

FRAU SILBERHAUS: What a fine story! (*She stands.*) But now it's time we were all in bed. Come, Fritz, Marchen. (FRITZ *exits, stretching and yawning, with* FRAU SILBERHAUS.)

JUDGE (*To* DROSSELMEYER): You are to have your old room, Doctor. Good night and Merry Christmas. (*He exits up right.*)

MARCHEN: Dr. Drosselmeyer?

DROSSELMEYER: Yes, Marchen?

MARCHEN: That wasn't *really* the end of the story, was it? There ought to be more about the nutcracker and the Mouse King.

DROSSELMEYER: There *is* more, my dear. But I can't tell you about it, because it hasn't happened yet.

MARCHEN (*Puzzled*): It hasn't happened?

DROSSELMEYER (*Smiling*): No, not yet. Good night, Marchen.

MARCHEN: Good night! (DROSSELMEYER *exits up right.* MARCHEN *speaks to nutcracker.*) Poor nutcracker! I wouldn't have done as the Princess did. I wouldn't have deserted you, because I really love you for yourself, sincerely. (*She puts nutcracker under tree, out of sight.*) Good night, dear nutcracker. (*Suddenly she is startled by a shrill laugh.*) Who's there? (*Laugh is repeated.*) Who is laughing? (MOUSE KING *appears and advances into room.*)

MOUSE KING: Do you think you can protect the nutcracker from my vengeance?

MARCHEN (*Frightened*): Go away, Mouse King!

MOUSE KING: I'll give *you* an ugly face, too!

MARCHEN: Nutcracker, help! Save me!

MOUSE KING: He can't save you. He is only a toy!

MARCHEN (*Desperately*): Nutcracker! Nutcracker! (NICHOLAS *leaps from behind Christmas tree. He wears white bandage around bottom of his nutcracker mask.*)

NICHOLAS: Stand back, Marchen! This will be a fight to the finish!

MARCHEN: Oh, my brave nutcracker! You must defeat the wicked Mouse King! (NICHOLAS *and* MOUSE KING *square off with drawn swords.* MARCHEN *watches anxiously. They fight back and forth, then exit, still fighting. A loud squeak is heard, then a moment later,* NICHOLAS *enters, holding sword in one hand,* MOUSE KING'S *crown in the other. His nutcracker mask is gone.* MARCHEN *runs to him.*) Oh, Nutcracker! You've won!

NICHOLAS: Please accept this trophy of victory from one who would serve you until death. (*With a flourish, he presents crown to* MARCHEN.)

MARCHEN (*Taking it with curtsy*): Thank you. Oh, thank you!

NICHOLAS: And now, dear Marchen, if you will excuse me, I must go to my people.

MARCHEN (*Curiously*): Who are your people?

NICHOLAS: The toys. I am their king. (*He exits right.* MARCHEN *looks after him wistfully.* DROSSELMEYER *appears in alcove.*)

DROSSELMEYER: Marchen! Why aren't you in bed yet?

MARCHEN: Nutcracker and the Mouse King had a duel, and Nutcracker won! Look! Here is the Mouse King's crown.

DROSSELMEYER: This is a magic crown, Marchen. If you put it on, you will be Queen of the Toys. (*He sets crown on* MARCHEN'S *head.*)

MARCHEN: Is the story all told now?

DROSSELMEYER: Yes, my dear.

MARCHEN: But you weren't here to tell it. You don't think it was a dream, do you?

DROSSELMEYER: Who can say? Children dream wonderful things on Christmas Eve. Come. It's time for you to go to bed. (DROSSELMEYER *puts his arm around* MARCHEN, *and they walk out slowly. Lights dim to single spotlight on clock.*)

VOICE OF CLOCK (*Offstage*): Twelve o'clock midnight on the twenty-fourth of December. Twelve o'clock midnight on the twenty-fourth of December. Merry Christmas! (*Curtain*)

THE END

The Left-Over Reindeer

by Helen Louise Miller

The sale of a house hinges on some strange conditions. . . .

Characters

MR. MARBORO, *elderly homeowner*
MR. SYLVESTER
MRS. SYLVESTER
MANDY ⎱
SARAH ⎰ *their daughters*
FAITH, *Irish nursemaid*
ROBBIE
SANDY, *Mr. Marboro as a boy*
FATHER MARBORO
MRS. WINTERS, *housekeeper*
ST. NICHOLAS
JING ⎱
JANG ⎰ *his helpers*
CASEY, *gardener*
OFFSTAGE VOICES, *extras*

TIME: *The present.*
SETTING: *Living room of Mr. Marboro's home.*

144

AT RISE: MR. *and* MRS. SYLVESTER, MANDY, SARAH, *and* MR. MARBORO *stand near fireplace.*

MR. SYLVESTER (*To* MR. MARBORO): I think we can draw up the papers now, Mr. Marboro. Everything seems to be in good condition.

MANDY: I love this house, Mom. Do you think Sarah and I could use the sitting room for a playroom?

MRS. SYLVESTER: I don't see why not, Mandy.

MR. MARBORO: You know, my brother Robbie and I used that very room when we were children. I'm glad young people will be living here again.

MRS. SYLVESTER (*Happily*): And we can move in just in time for Christmas. Finally, we'll be able to have a nice big tree.

MR. MARBORO: You might even want to cut your own tree. There are plenty of pines in the woods.

MRS. SYLVESTER (*Looking out window*): The grounds are so lovely. But we'll have to get rid of that monstrosity of a deer under the oak tree. (MR. SYLVESTER *joins her.*)

MR. SYLVESTER (*Laughing*): But, Penny, it's a real antique!

MRS. SYLVESTER: Then let an antique dealer come and get it.

MR. MARBORO (*Clearing throat*): Excuse me, folks, but perhaps I should tell you about the well. (SYLVESTERS *turn to face* MR. MARBORO.) Last summer some of the neighbors came down with a stomach bug, and they blamed the water supply. The lake water sometimes seeps into the wells in these parts, you know.

MRS. SYLVESTER: How awful. (*To* MR. SYLVESTER) We couldn't risk that, Jack.

MR. MARBORO: And then, I should mention the bats.

ALL: The what?

MR. MARBORO (*Matter-of-factly*): Bats. They won't bother you in winter, but in the summer, they do venture out of these old fireplaces.

MRS. SYLVESTER: Bats! I hate bats!

MR. MARBORO: And then, there's the water in the cellar. . . .

MR. SYLVESTER (*Annoyed*): Mr. Marboro, you told me a while ago that the cellar is as dry as a bone!

MR. MARBORO: Well, it is mostly, but . . . well, we had quite a flood down there a few years ago.

MRS. SYLVESTER: Goodness! I had no idea there were so many things wrong with the house. I'm not sure we should buy it after all.

MR. SYLVESTER: I'm feeling somewhat doubtful, too. But (*Looks at* MR. MARBORO) I'm also wondering what made you change your tune.

MR. MARBORO: Change my tune?

MR. SYLVESTER: Yes. Only a short while ago you were singing its praises. Now you're telling us all the things that are wrong with it. Don't you want to sell it?

MR. MARBORO: Of course I want to sell. This house is too big for me, too much responsibility. But . . .

MR. SYLVESTER: But what? You don't want *us* to buy the house, is that it?

MR. MARBORO (*Awkwardly*): Well, I *did* want you to buy the house until Mrs. Sylvester spoke about getting rid of the deer.

MRS. SYLVESTER: What does that have to do with buying the house?

MR. MARBORO: This may sound very strange to you, but I couldn't sell the house to anyone who would remove the deer from the lawn.

MRS. SYLVESTER (*Laughing*): You can't be serious!

MR. MARBORO: I told you it would sound peculiar, but that's how it is.

MR. SYLVESTER: You mean you'd let that cast-iron deer stand between you and the sale of this house?

MR. MARBORO (*Firmly*): That's right.

MANDY: It must be a very special deer.

MR. MARBORO: Yes, it is. In fact, it's *so* special that I'd do almost anything to keep it there. I never dreamed anyone would want to remove it, or I don't believe I would even have put the house up for sale.

MR. SYLVESTER: Are you sure you're not letting sentiment run away with you?

MR. MARBORO: I'm not a particularly sentimental man, Mr. Sylvester, but . . . well, that deer goes deeper than sentiment.

To me and to the people of this village it symbolizes Christmas.

MR. SYLVESTER: I can see you're serious about this.

MR. MARBORO: Very serious. And I'm sure you would be too if you knew the whole story.

SARAH: What *is* the whole story, Mr. Marboro?

MR. MARBORO: Do you really want to know?

MRS. SYLVESTER: We love the house, Mr. Marboro, and we might even learn to love the deer, if you'd tell us why it means so much to you. (*All move outside curtain to apron of stage. Curtains close.* MR. *and* MRS. SYLVESTER *sit on chairs; children sit on floor.* MR. MARBORO *remains standing.*)

MR. MARBORO: You see, my father was not a sentimental man. In fact, he always insisted that my brother and I see the practical side of things. Robbie and I accepted his rule, except when it came to Christmas. Then it was hard. You see, there were no stockings, no tree, no letter to Santa . . .

MANDY (*Shocked*): That's terrible!

SARAH: Didn't you ever write and tell Santa what you wanted for Christmas?

MR. MARBORO: Never . . . never, that is, until the Christmas I was six, because up to that time St. Nicholas did not exist for us.

SARAH: Didn't you believe in him at all?

MR. MARBORO: I didn't believe in him, because I'd never heard of him!

MANDY: Never heard of St. Nick!

MR. MARBORO: In fact, it was right in this room that I first heard of St. Nicholas. It was the winter that Faith, our dear Irish nursemaid, came to stay with us. On this particular Christmas Eve, she sat here and read me the story of *A Visit from St. Nicholas*. (*Curtains open on same setting, except for addition of two cots with spreads.* FAITH *sits on cot, reading to* SANDY, *who is perched on stool at her feet.*)

FAITH:
"The moon on the breast of the new-fallen snow
Gave the lustre of mid-day to objects below,
When what to my wondering eyes should appear
But a miniature sleigh and eight tiny reindeer,

With a little old driver, so lively and quick,
I knew in a moment, it must be St. Nick."

SANDY: Faith, who is St. Nick?

FAITH: Sandy, you know as well as I do who St. Nick is.

SANDY: No, I don't. I never heard of him.

FAITH (*Surprised*): But surely every child has heard of St. Nicholas!

SANDY: Well, I never have. Tell me about him, please.

FAITH: Well, listen to the story, and you'll find out all you want to know about the jolly old Saint who brings good children the presents they want most on Christmas Eve.

SANDY: Father brings Robbie and me our presents on Christmas Eve. But they aren't always the things we want most. Last year I wanted a sled, and Robbie wanted a train, but we got socks and overcoats instead.

FAITH: Socks and overcoats are very useful and lots of little boys would be grateful for them. You and Robbie can be thankful you were never cold and hungry.

SANDY: We *are* thankful, but what about St. Nicholas? How does he know what children want for Christmas, and how does he get into their houses?

FAITH: He comes in his sleigh, over the rooftops, and down the chimney.

SANDY: How can a sleigh get up on the rooftops?

FAITH: Begorra, you're as full of questions as a plum pudding is full of plums! The sleigh is driven by eight tiny reindeer, and if you listen to the story, you'll learn their names! (*Reads*)
"More rapid than eagles his coursers they came,
And he whistled and shouted and called them by name!
Now, Dasher! Now, Dancer! Now, Prancer and Vixen!
On, Comet! On, Cupid! On, Donder and Blitzen!
To the top of the porch! To the top of the wall!
Now, dash away! Dash away! Dash away all!"

SANDY: What splendid names! I must try to remember them. But what happens next?

FAITH: Why, the reindeer keep right on going, of course, and the next thing you know, they're on the roof! Listen. (*Reads*)
"And then in a twinkling I heard on the roof,

The prancing and pawing of each little hoof!
As I drew in my head and was turning around,
Down the chimney St. Nicholas came with a bound.
He was dressed all in fur from his head to his foot,
And his clothes were all tarnished with ashes and soot!"

SANDY: Oh, dear! Now he'll have to go to the dry cleaner's!

FAITH: Not St. Nicholas. Now, don't interrupt. Here comes the best part! (*Reads*)
"A bundle of toys he had flung on his back,
And he looked like a peddler just opening his pack."

SANDY (*Jumping up and down*): Oh, I want to see him, Faith. Will he come here? Will he?

FAITH: I'm sure he will, Sandy. Old St. Nicholas would never forget such good little boys as you and Robbie. (ROBBIE *enters in time to hear* FAITH'*s last speech.*)

ROBBIE (*In disapproval*): Shame on you, Faith O'Flanagan, for filling Sandy's head with such foolishness! Father would be angry if he knew.

SANDY: But he won't know, Robbie. I'll never tell. It's the most wonderful story! Sit down and listen.

ROBBIE: I won't, and neither will you. Only silly children believe in St. Nicholas.

SANDY: Oh, be quiet. I want to hear the rest. Go ahead, Faith.

FAITH (*Hesitating*): I wouldn't want to do anything to displease your father. If Master Robbie thinks—

SANDY: Oh, Robbie's just an old meanie! Father won't care.

ROBBIE: Don't be too sure of that, Sandy. You know how strict Father is about the truth.

FAITH: But it's true enough, Master Robbie. It's all here in black and white. It tells just how he looks. (*Reads*)
"His eyes—how they twinkled! His dimples how merry!
His cheeks were like roses, his nose like a cherry!
His droll little mouth was drawn up like a bow,
And the beard on his chin was as white as the snow.
The stump of a pipe he held tight in his teeth,
And the smoke, it encircled his head like a wreath.
He had a broad face, and a little round belly,
That shook when he laughed like a bowl full of jelly."

SANDY (*Laughing*): That's funny! Robbie, wouldn't you love to see him?

ROBBIE (*Almost laughing*): Yes, it might be fun . . . but there's no use thinking that St. Nick would ever come here.

SANDY: Why not?

ROBBIE: Because Father would never permit it. So put the book away, Faith, before he catches you reading it to us.

SANDY: No, Faith! Read the rest.

FAITH: It can't do any harm to finish the story now that I've started it. And you might as well listen, too, Master Robbie. (ROBBIE *stands closer to* FAITH *as she reads.*)

"He spoke not a word, but went straight to his work,

And filled all the stockings; then turned with a jerk,

And laying his finger aside of his nose,

And giving a nod, up the chimney he rose:

He sprang to his sleigh, to his team gave a whistle,

And away they all flew, like the down of a thistle.

But I heard him exclaim, ere he drove out of sight:

'Happy Christmas to all, and to all a good night!' "

(FATHER MARBORO *enters during above speech and stands glowering at* FAITH *and boys. As soon as she finishes, he bellows.*)

FATHER: And that means "Good night" and "Goodbye" to you, Faith!

BOYS (*In alarm*): Father!

FAITH (*Rising*): Mr. Marboro! I'm sorry, sir!

FATHER: Faith, you have disobeyed my orders. It was distinctly understood that we do not fill the boys' heads with fairy tales and falsehoods. You will pack your things at once!

ROBBIE: But tomorrow is Christmas!

FATHER: My calendar says December 25th. I will not have my orders disobeyed.

SANDY: Father, Faith was only reading us a beautiful story.

FATHER: I am the best judge of which stories are to be read to you boys. Faith will leave within the hour, and I want both of you boys in bed before she goes.

ROBBIE: But it isn't even suppertime!

FATHER: You knew as well as Faith that such stories are forbidden in this house. You and Sandy will be able to think more clearly on empty stomachs.

SANDY (*Clinging to* FAITH): Faith, don't go!

ROBBIE: I'm sorry, Faith. We'll miss you terribly.

FAITH: I've done my best, Master Robbie. Now come along, both of you, and I'll tuck you into bed before I leave.

FATHER: Just go right along, Faith. The boys can take care of themselves. Please send Mrs. Winters to me at once. (*To boys*) I'll see you settled for the night.

FAITH: Very well, sir. And please believe me, I am very sorry.

SANDY (*Sobbing*): Now St. Nicholas will never come! He'll never stop at this bad house. Never, never, never! (*Boys and* FAITH *exit.*)

FATHER: Poor little fellows! Perhaps their mother would have been able to handle this St. Nicholas problem in a different way. (*Grimly*) As it is, I must see that they know the truth from the very start.

MRS. WINTERS (*Entering*): You sent for me, sir?

FATHER: Yes, Mrs. Winters. I must ask you to keep an eye on the boys tonight. Their nursemaid is leaving.

MRS. WINTERS (*Surprised*): Faith is leaving? But why? She is so fond of the boys.

FATHER (*Abruptly*): I found her services were no longer necessary.

MRS. WINTERS: I see. (*Pause*) Are there any special orders for tomorrow, sir?

FATHER: Just the usual meals, served at the regular time. And please remind the gardener to check on the main gates. I don't want carolers trampling over the grounds.

MRS. WINTERS: Yes, sir. And I hope you have a very merry . . . I mean . . . I hope you have a very satisfactory holiday, sir.

FATHER: Thank you, Mrs. Winters. And please see that Faith receives her wages till the end of the week.

MRS. WINTERS: Yes, sir. (MRS. WINTERS *exits as* SANDY *and* ROBBIE *re-enter in bathrobes.* FATHER *turns back spread on each cot. Boys climb in, pull up spreads.*)

FATHER: I—er—I feel very sorry about sending Faith away, children, but after her conduct this evening, it would be impossible to keep her. Now, if you are *very* hungry, I will ask Mrs. Winters to bring you a glass of milk.

BOYS (*In small voices*): No thank you, Father.

FATHER: Good night, then. I will see you in the morning.

BOYS: Good night, Father. (FATHER *exits. Lights dim.*)

SANDY: I wish we had a father who believed in St. Nicholas.

ROBBIE: Well, we don't, and there's nothing we can do about it, so be quiet, and go to sleep.

SANDY (*After a brief pause*): Dasher, Dancer, Prancer, Vixen, Comet, Cupid, Donder . . . what was the other reindeer's name, Robbie?

ROBBIE (*Crossly*): How should I know?

SANDY: Blitzen! That was it! Blitzen. (*Repeats names*)

ROBBIE: Sandy, if you don't stop muttering, I'll call Father.

SANDY: But don't you want to learn all you can about St. Nick and his reindeer?

ROBBIE: No, and if you know what's good for you, you'll stop thinking about him. (*Pause, then* SANDY *jumps excitedly out of bed*)

SANDY: I know what I'll do! I'll write a letter to St. Nicholas.

ROBBIE: You wouldn't dare!

SANDY: I would so, and I'm daring right now. (*Runs to table, gets paper and pencil and begins to write*)

ROBBIE (*Joining* SANDY *at table*): You hardly know how to write, and you can't spell.

SANDY: I can spell well enough for this. (*As he writes*) Dear St. Nick: Please, please, come to see us. We don't care about the presents. But we would like to know you have been here, just so we could prove to our Father that you really are real.

ROBBIE: Aw, that's no good. And the spelling is so bad, he'd never be able to read it.

SANDY: St. Nicholas is smart at reading letters.

ROBBIE: Where are you going to put it so Father won't see it?

SANDY: On my pillow.

ROBBIE (*Disgusted*): If it will make you feel any better. Just remember to stick it under the pillow when Father comes in tomorrow morning. Now, get back to bed, before you catch cold. (*Boys go back to bed.* SANDY *puts letter on pillow.*)

SANDY: Do you really think St. Nick will come?

ROBBIE: Not unless we go to sleep. He never comes when children are awake.

SANDY: Then I'll go to sleep as fast as I can. I'll just say the reindeer names over and over to myself till I can't say them any more.

ROBBIE: What did I ever do to get such a brother! (SANDY *keeps reciting reindeer names in monotone, lights grow dimmer, and his voice trails off. Blackout.*)

* * * * *

(*There is a short pause; then clock chimes twelve. A few seconds later there is a sound of sleighbells, which gets louder, then stops.*)

ST. NICK (*Offstage*): Whoa! Whoa! (*There are scrambling noises, then spotlight comes up on fireplace, revealing* JING, JANG, *and* ST. NICK *creeping into room.*)

JING: I'm sure we've never been here before, St. Nicholas.

JANG: The Marboro name is not on our list. I'm sure of that.

ST. NICK: Of course it's not on our list. And you're quite right— we've never been here before. What's more, we wouldn't be here now, if it weren't for Dancer and his temperamental hoof.

JING: Is his hoof really as bad as he says?

ST. NICK: I don't know. Every year when we pass this house, he suddenly goes lame, and starts pulling in this direction. That's why I thought we should just land here and let him rest a bit. It also gives us a chance to come inside and get warm.

JING: Too bad we couldn't have picked some place where we had toys to deliver.

JANG: But why don't we have toys to deliver here? (*Points to beds*) Aren't these children good?

ST. NICK: Oh, they *are* good children; don't come any better. But their father doesn't believe in me, and won't let his children mention my name or listen to my stories. So what can we do? We certainly can't go against a father's wishes.

SANDY (*In his sleep*): On, Dancer! On, Prancer! On, Cupid and Vixen!

JANG: Why, he's saying the names of the reindeer! He *must* know something about you.

ST. NICK (*Leaning over* SANDY's *bed and discovering note*): Bless my whiskers! Here's a note the little fellow has written to me. (*Reads note aloud*) Well, well, well! What are we going to do about this?

JING: Can't we leave some toys?

ST. NICK: We have none to spare. Every single thing in my pack is a special order.

JANG: But, St. Nicholas, you can't disappoint him. You'll have to leave *something* he can show his father.

JING: I've got it! We'll leave Dancer.

ST. NICK (*In amazement*): Leave Dancer? *Where?*

JING: Right where he is . . . up on the roof! That way he can rest his hoof, and these children will have absolute proof that you have visited this house. And we can pick Dancer up tomorrow night.

JANG: But what would people think? What would they say when they find a reindeer on the roof?

ST. NICK (*Beginning to laugh*): Jing, you're a genius! A positive genius! If it's proof these children are after, they'll have it and then some! I'd give a pretty penny to see their father's face when he wakes up and discovers Dancer on his rooftop! Ho! Ho! Ho! I haven't had such a good laugh in centuries!

JING: Sh! Be careful, or you'll wake the children.

ST. NICK: We mustn't do that, must we? Well, come along and help me give this man Marboro the shock and surprise of his unbelieving life. (ST. NICK, JING, *and* JANG *exit. Curtain closes.*)

* * * * *

MANDY (*Excitedly*): Mr. Marboro, tell us what happened in the morning!

SARAH: Was Dancer really there?

MR. MARBORO: He was there, all right.

MRS. SYLVESTER: And what did your father do?

MR. MARBORO (*Chuckling*): You never saw a man so upset as my father was that Christmas morning.

MR. SYLVESTER: I can well understand that! And I can't wait to hear how it all turned out.

MR. MARBORO: Well, Robbie and I were awakened by the sound of voices outside our window shouting something about a reindeer. Before we could make out what they were saying, Father came tearing into the room, shouting for Casey, the gardener, and threatening to have half the county arrested for trespassing.

* * * * *

(*Curtains open on Mr. Marboro's living room.*)

FATHER (*Shouting*): Confound that Casey! He left the gates open last night, and the carolers are on our south lawn.

OFFSTAGE VOICES: Look! There's a reindeer on the roof!

SANDY *and* ROBBIE (*Ad lib*): What's that? What are they saying about a reindeer? (*Etc.* CASEY *enters*)

FATHER (*Sternly*): Casey! Perhaps you have an explanation for all this?

CASEY (*Baffled*): Me, sir? (*Shakes head*) It's beyond me, sir. I never expected to see such a sight as that reindeer pokin' his head around the chimney.

SANDY (*Gleefully*): There *is* a reindeer out there! Oh, Robbie, St. Nicholas was here. He really was!

ROBBIE: How did it get there, Casey?

CASEY: I can't tell you, my boy. 'Tis a mystery we'll never be able to solve. Fact is, I'm sort of shook up from seeing it myself.

FATHER: Will you stop talking nonsense about a reindeer, and answer my questions? How did those people get in here? Did you or did you not leave the gate open?

CASEY (*Sheepishly*): I guess I did leave it open for the carolers, Mr. Marboro. I—I know you told me to lock it, but I thought it might be nice for Sandy and Robbie to hear the Christmas carols. (*Shaking his head*) But I can't account for the deer being up on the roof. (*More shouting is heard offstage.*)

SANDY: Come on, Robbie, let's go see the reindeer.

FATHER (*Sternly*): You boys will not set foot outside this house without my permission. Now, go get dressed. Casey, you and I will settle this foolishness as soon as I chase those carolers off my lawn. Reindeer, indeed! (CASEY *and* FATHER *exit.*)

ROBBIE: Come on, Sandy, let's get dressed.

SANDY: In a minute. I want to see what's going on. (*Runs to window*) Oh, Robbie, there's a whole crowd of children on the lawn. And there's Mr. Wiggins, the choirmaster.

ROBBIE: Is there really a reindeer?

SANDY: I can't see from here. Look! There goes Father! (ROBBIE *goes to window.* MRS. WINTERS *enters.*)

MRS. WINTERS (*Excited*): Boys! Hurry and get dressed, so you can go out and see the reindeer.

ROBBIE: Is he really there, Mrs. Winters?

MRS. WINTERS: He's there, all right. And such excitement! The whole village is outside.

SANDY (*Excitedly, pointing*): Look! The reindeer! There he goes!

ROBBIE: He's jumped down off the roof. Now he's running straight into the crowd.

MRS. WINTERS: Mercy! He'll kill somebody.

SANDY: No, he won't. St. Nick's reindeer never hurt anyone, and besides, he's lame. See? He's limping.

ROBBIE: Look! He's going straight up to Father. (*After a pause: in disbelief*) I can't believe it! Father's even patting him.

SANDY (*Excitedly*): Now he's looking at the reindeer's foot.

MRS. WINTERS (*Amazed*): I can't believe it, but he's throwing his arms around the critter's neck!

SANDY: Robbie! Father is hugging the reindeer!

ROBBIE (*Running to exit*): Come on. Let's go. (*Sandy starts to follow.*)

MRS. WINTERS: Put on some warm clothes! (*They exit.* MRS. WINTERS *shakes her head.*) They say seeing is believing, but the sight of that man on his knees, with his arms around that reindeer, is too much for me! (CASEY *enters.*)

CASEY (*Sitting; in disbelief*): I never saw the like, Mrs. Winters. I guess I'll lose my job as soon as he comes in here, but it's been worth it, seeing him talking to that reindeer, just like something out of a storybook. (FATHER *enters, in a daze.*)

FATHER: Ah, good morning, Mrs. Winters. Where are the boys?

MRS. WINTERS: They went to get dressed, sir. I'll get them at once.

FATHER: Yes, do. I don't want them to miss a minute of this. (MRS. WINTERS *exits.*) Well, Casey, this will be a day to remember.

CASEY (*Surprised*): Yes, sir. And I'm sorry, sir, about the gate.

FATHER: Forget it, Casey. I have more on my mind today than gates or carolers or a front lawn. (*Walks to* SANDY's *bed and notices letter on pillow*) I just don't see how it happened. (*Picks up letter and reads it*) Hm-m-m. Maybe this is a partial explanation. (*Chuckling*) Well, if it was proof I needed, it was proof I got in full measure. (*Boys enter.*)

SANDY: Father, may we go see the reindeer?

ROBBIE: You really touched him, didn't you, Father? We saw you pat him and throw your arms around him.

SANDY: And he really *is* St. Nick's reindeer, Father. He really is!

ROBBIE: Hush, Sandy.

FATHER: It's all right, Robbie. Sandy is right. Dancer really is one of St. Nick's reindeer.

SANDY: Dancer! You know his name?

FATHER: I should. I gave him his name. You see, when I was just a little lad, no bigger than you, Sandy, I believed in St. Nicholas, even though believing was not always easy. We lived in a very small house in the woods, and there were never any presents on Christmas morning. Year after year, I was disappointed, but then, the Christmas Day I was seven, I got Dancer.

SANDY: A reindeer in your stocking?

FATHER: Not in my stocking, but in our farmyard. There he was, a tiny, shivering little fawn with the same big brown eyes he has today.

ROBBIE: You mean he's the *very same* reindeer?

FATHER (*Nodding*): I know it *seems* impossible, but Dancer himself has brought me the proof. You see, we had a wonderful day together, that little fawn and I. We frolicked in the snow, we raced and leaped over fences and had the time of our lives. And all day long, I was thanking St. Nicholas for the wonderful present. When night came, I built a little compound for Dancer near the barn. We said goodnight to each other and two or three times I crept out of bed and looked out the window to make sure he was still there. In the morning, I raced outside before breakfast, but he was gone. During the night, he had leaped over the fence . . . and in the morning, the hunters got him.

BOYS (*Despairing*): Oh, no!

FATHER: I found his tracks in the snow, and the drops of blood trailing off into the forest, but I never found Dancer. And I never believed in St. Nicholas again. It was too cruel to give a present and then take it away.

SANDY: But it wasn't St. Nick's fault, Father.

FATHER: I guess I was too upset to think straight. But one thing I decided: No child of mine would ever be subjected to such disappointment. I know better now . . . the biggest hurt of all is not to believe.

ROBBIE: But how do you know it is the same reindeer, Father?

FATHER: I'd know Dancer anywhere. Besides, he told me who he is.

ROBBIE: You mean he *talked* to you?

FATHER: Dancer and I always understood each other. And then, there is his hoof.

SANDY: What's wrong with it?

FATHER: He has an old scar from the wound those hunters gave him so long ago. Oh, yes, it's Dancer, all right . . . and we three are going to have a wonderful day together. A day we'll never forget!

SANDY: Oh, Father, I wish Faith could come, too. Just to see that St. Nicholas was really here.

FATHER: I'm sorry about Faith, son, I truly am . . . but . . .

CASEY: Beg pardon, sir, but my wife and I took Faith in with us for the night. I think you'll find her right outside with the rest of the deer watchers.

FATHER (*Happily*): Then we'll have her back again, if she'll let us. And she can read *St. Nicholas* from morning to night, on one condition.

ROBBIE: What's that, Father?

FATHER (*Smiling*): That I may listen, too. (*Curtain; players exit.*)

* * * * *

(*Curtains open on Marboro living room.*)

MR. MARBORO: That was the beginning of the merriest Christmas we ever had. That night, when Father tucked us in, he told us Dancer would not be with us in the morning, that he had to join the other reindeer in St. Nicholas's stable. At first, we were heartbroken, but Father explained that Dancer would come again. (*Group moves center, into living room.*)

MANDY: And did he?

MR. MARBORO: Yes . . . and no. When Robbie and I went out to play the next morning, there on the lawn, right where Dancer had landed the day before, was a life-size statue of the left-over reindeer, a constant reminder of Dancer and his Christmas promise.

MR. SYLVESTER: That's a wonderful story, Mr. Marboro, and I can see why we must leave the statue just where it is.

MRS. SYLVESTER: We wouldn't move it for the world.

MR. SYLVESTER: And we'll put it in writing!

MR. MARBORO: Oh, I'm sure your word is enough, Mr. Sylvester.

MR. SYLVESTER: Thank you, but I feel we should have something more enduring than that.

MANDY: I know! We could put up a plaque at the base of the statue.

SARAH (*Musing*): And it could say:

ALL (*Together; facing audience*):
All honor to Dancer, and long may he stand,
The reindeer most cherished and loved in the land.

MANDY:
So touch not an antler, and harm not a hoof,

SARAH:
Of this marvelous creature once left on our roof.

MRS. SYLVESTER:
We know it is blessed to give and receive,

MR. MARBORO:

But better than all—is the power to believe.

MR. SYLVESTER:

So all who believe in St. Nick and his cheer,

ALL:

Believe in the tale of this Left-Over Deer!

THE END

The Twelve Days of Christmas

by Doris G. Wright

A dramatization of a famous holiday song . . .

Characters

KING
QUEEN
JESTER
HERALD
LADY ELSPETH
COURTIERS
PAGES
MAIDS
THREE LADIES-IN-WAITING
SEVEN SWANS
EIGHT MILKMAIDS
NINE LADIES
TEN LORDS
ELEVEN PIPERS
TWELVE DRUMMERS
CHORUS

BEFORE RISE: KING *enters, holding clipboard and pen. He paces the floor, looks at paper, shakes his head and scratches something out, then sighs deeply.* JESTER *peers in, then enters unnoticed and sits on floor in corner.* KING *continues his pacing and* JESTER *chuckles.* KING *turns, startled.*

KING: Knave, why do you presume to laugh when I, your king, is so greatly troubled?

JESTER: Sire, I have a riddle which perchance may divert the King's mind. When is a door not a door?

KING (*Impatiently*): Any idiot knows that—when it is ajar.

JESTER (*Crestfallen*): Alas. (*Brightly*) I have one that I'll wager you do not know. What's black within, red without, and has four corners, round about? (KING *stops pacing and frowns, then turns on* JESTER *angrily.*)

KING: Why should I try to guess your silly riddles when I have a far more difficult one to solve? . . . Tell me the answer, then.

JESTER: Sire, it is a chimney.

KING (*Scornfully*): A chimney, of course. I'm tired of your silly riddles. Now you solve *my* riddle.

JESTER (*Delightedly*): Certainly, Sire.

KING: Come here and I will make it known to you. The Yule season approacheth—(JESTER *rises, crosses to* KING.)

JESTER (*Interrupting*): A time to make merry, to eat (*Rubs his stomach*), and to receive gifts!

KING (*Assertively*): The Yule season approacheth when every heart *is,* or *should be* joyous. I wish to give my Queen, the fair Lynette, a gift worthy of her. But she has jewels, silken gowns without number, a harp of gold to play when she wearies of your foolish jokes. (*Sighs*) What is there in all my kingdom that is not already hers?

JESTER: Sire, leave this matter to me. I shall think upon it.

KING: Mind now, the gift must be worthy of the Queen.

JESTER: And if I succeed, how shall I be rewarded?

KING: Have I ever yet not paid you what you deserve?

JESTER: Nay, Sire, not even a lashing when I needed it.

KING: Go, then, and if the Queen is pleased, your reward shall be handsome. But delay not, for in but a few days the merrymaking begins. (*They exit together.*)

* * *

TIME: *A few days later.*

SETTING: *Throne room.*

AT RISE: KING *and* QUEEN *are seated on thrones at one side,* JESTER *on steps to throne.* LADY ELSPETH *and* THREE LADIES-IN-WAITING *sit in chairs around room.* CHORUS *stands at rear.* HERALD *enters, blows a fanfare on his trumpet.*

HERALD: His Majesty the King hath proclaimed twelve days of rejoicing, when all in his kingdom shall feast and give and receive gifts to celebrate the Yule season. Let joy be unrestrained. (*Goes to one side.*)

CHORUS (*Singing*):

On the first day of Christmas,

My true love sent to me,

A partridge in a pear tree.

(COURTIER *enters, carrying a partridge in a pear tree, bows to* QUEEN *and presents it to her.*)

QUEEN: Truly, my Lord, this sweet bird is most welcome. When I hear his cheery note, I will forget the snow and the chill of winter winds.

HERALD (*Coming forward*): The second day of Christmas. (*Goes to one side*)

CHORUS (*Singing*):

On the second day of Christmas,

My true love sent to me,

Two turtledoves,

And a partridge in a pear tree.

(TWO COURTIERS *enter, each with a turtledove, which they present to* QUEEN.)

QUEEN (*Smiling at* KING): The cooing of the doves will be music to my ears.

KING: Yes, my love. (JESTER *clears his throat significantly, looking pointedly at* KING, *who ignores him.*)

HERALD (*Coming forward*): The third day of Christmas . . .

CHORUS (*Singing*):

On the third day of Christmas,

My true love sent to me,

Three French hens,

Two turtledoves,

And a partridge in a pear tree.

(THREE COURTIERS *enter, each with a fat hen with a ribbon around its neck. They present hens to* QUEEN, *then go to stand at rear.*)

QUEEN: These hens, while not so graceful as the doves and the partridge, shall be no less welcome, as each day they shall lay an egg. *One* shall be for my breakfast . . .

KING: And two for mine!

JESTER (*Leaping up; frowning*): Hath the King forgotten his promise of reward—

KING (*Interrupting*): On second thought, the third egg shall go to the Jester. He is a good-natured soul, even though he is a knave. (JESTER *sinks down onto steps.*)

HERALD: The fourth day of Christmas . . .

CHORUS (*Singing*):

On the fourth day of Christmas,

My true love sent to me,

Four calling birds,

(*Repeat to end of song.* TWO MAIDS *and* TWO PAGES *enter, each with a blackbird.*)

LADY ELSPETH: Before my lady e'er dreamed of being a queen, we roamed the fields, two happy girls together, and in the spring the blackbirds' song did tell of golden weather.

QUEEN: 'Tis true, Lady Elspeth, and my heart is filled with joy at their sweet notes. Ne'er have I received such gifts as these. My Lord hath outdone himself. (KING *smiles at her.* JESTER *rises.*)

JESTER: But, Your Majesty, I—(KING *whispers in* JESTER'S *ear and pushes him away.*)

CHORUS (*Singing*):

On the fifth day of Christmas,

My true love sent to me,

Five golden rings,

(*Repeat to end of song.* FIVE MAIDS *enter, each rolling a gold hoop.* QUEEN, *delighted, descends from throne.*)

QUEEN: Maids, I pray thee, may I join in thy sport? (1ST MAID *gives hoop to* QUEEN, *who rolls it about stage, along with other* MAIDS. QUEEN *returns hoop to* 1ST MAID *and returns to throne.*)

For the moment I quite forgot that as Queen, I must conduct myself with appropriate dignity.

KING (*Anxiously*): Do you so miss those carefree days of your youth?

QUEEN: Nay, my Lord. But even the happiest queen likes to throw off the cloak of dignity at times, to be a girl again.

HERALD: The sixth day of Christmas . . .

CHORUS (*Singing*):
On the sixth day of Christmas,
My true love sent to me,
Six geese a-laying,
(*Repeat to end of song.* SIX COURTIERS *enter, each carrying a goose.*)

JESTER (*Springing up and turning a cartwheel*): With six geese a-laying, the cooks can make omelettes, custards, cakes, sweet pastries, pies, meringues . . .

KING: Greedy fool! Thou dost forget thyself.

JESTER: Sire, it is thou who dost forget that I am to receive a reward for—

KING: Silence! Did I not promise thee a new-laid hen's egg for thy breakfast every morning?

JESTER: Yea, but one small egg is small reward for all my hard work.

KING: Thou shalt have thy share of all these delicacies and a handsome reward as well, only be not so forward in claiming it.

HERALD: The seventh day of Christmas . . .

CHORUS (*Singing*):
On the seventh day of Christmas,
My true love sent to me,
Seven swans a-swimming,
(*Repeat to end of song.* SEVEN SWANS *enter with swimming motion and stand before* QUEEN.)

ALL (*Ad lib*): Oh, how lovely! How beautiful! (*Etc.*)

HERALD: The eighth day of Christmas . . .

CHORUS (*Singing*):
On the eighth day of Christmas,
My true love sent to me,

Eight maids a-milking,
(*Repeat to end of song.* EIGHT MILKMAIDS *enter, each with a pail and stool. They curtsy to* QUEEN *and stand at rear.*)
JESTER: Now we will have milk punch, creamy eggnog—
KING: Hold thy tongue, glutton! Thinkest thou of nothing but thy stomach?
JESTER: Yea, Sire, of my reward.
HERALD: The ninth day of Christmas . . .
CHORUS (*Singing*):
    On the ninth day of Christmas,
    My true love sent to me,
    Nine ladies dancing,
(*Repeat to end of song.* NINE LADIES *enter and dance onto steps to recorded music from offstage.* JESTER *jumps beside them, imitating them.*)
KING (*To* JESTER): At last, something other than food stirs thy knavish heart!
HERALD: The tenth day of Christmas . . .
CHORUS (*Singing*):
    On the tenth day of Christmas,
    My true love sent to me,
    Ten lords a-leaping,
(*Repeat to end of song.* TEN LORDS *leap on and dance with* NINE LADIES.)
HERALD: The eleventh day of Christmas . . .
CHORUS (*Singing*):
    On the eleventh day of Christmas,
    My true love sent to me,
    Eleven pipers piping,
(*Repeat to end of song.* ELEVEN PIPERS, *each playing a recorder, enter and parade around stage, stopping at rear.*)
HERALD: The Twelfth day of Christmas . . .
CHORUS (*Singing*):
    On the twelfth day of Christmas,
    My true love sent to me,
    Twelve drummers drumming,
(*Repeat to end of song.* TWELVE DRUMMERS *enter, beating drums as they march about stage, then line up at rear.*)

KING (*Rising*): It is plain to all that not only is my Queen pleased with her gifts, but that they have given pleasure to all. It is now time to reward him who hath assembled them, so now I bestow this purse and robe upon the Jester, who shall no longer be a jester but shall become one of my wise counselors. His first duty shall be to find a new court jester. (JESTER, *completely taken by surprise, leaps up.* KING *gives him leather purse, then takes robe from throne and places it on* JESTER's *shoulders.* JESTER *takes a few steps, then trips and falls. All laugh.* JESTER *tries again to walk with dignity, then trips, and all laugh louder.* JESTER *turns to* KING, *and throwing off robe, dons his jester's cap again.*)

JESTER: Sire, thy praise and the gratitude of thy fair Queen are full reward for my labors. 'Twould be a burden for me to be serious and wise, so long have I cut capers. I cannot change. If it please your majesty, I'll keep the purse and claim the fresh-laid egg for breakfast, but return this cloak to you and be a jester 'til I die. (*Curtains close slowly, as entire cast sings verse of "The Twelve Days of Christmas." Song may also be sung in front of curtain.*)

THE END

Randy, the Red-Horned Rainmoose

by Rick Kilcup

What happens when Rudolph's nose is on the blink. . . .

Characters

RANDY THE RAINMOOSE
SANTA
RUDOLPH
HUSTLE ⎫
BUSTLE ⎬ *Santa's messy elves*
FRED ⎭
WEATHER ELF
TISSUE ELF
DASHER ⎫
DANCER │
PRANCER │
VIXEN │
COMET │
CUPID ⎬ *singing reindeer*
DONDER │
BLITZEN │
RALPH │
MATILDA ⎭

TIME: *Christmas Eve.*

SETTING: *Santa's workshop. At center, there is a workbench covered with tools, boxes, and wrapping paper. Large can of "Sleigh Wax" and tool chest are on floor at rear. Toys, boxes, long sheets of paper are scattered about stage.*

AT RISE: RANDY THE RAINMOOSE *is sweeping floor.*

RANDY (*Singing to the tune of "Row Your Boat"*):
Scrub, scrub, scrub, and sweep,
Polish every day.
When will all this hard work end
So I can stop and play?
(*Stops sweeping, leans on broom and mops brow; to audience*)
Hi, I'm Randy, the rainmoose. I used to live in the rain forest, where it rains so much that moss grows even on antlers. (*Points to his antlers*) Then one day, I saw an ad for a job that promised excitement and a chance to work with Santa and Rudolph. (*Starts sweeping*) I was so tired of the constant rain that I took the job. Unfortunately, I didn't read the fine print. What Santa needed was a cleaner-upper! So now it's (*Sings*)
Scrub, scrub, scrub, and sweep,
Polish every day.
When will all this hard work end
So I can stop and play?
The job's not that bad—don't get me wrong. I like working with Santa, and Rudolph's my all-time hero. It's those pesky elves, Hustle, Bustle, and Fred that get me down. They're so messy! Every time I get the place cleaned up, they mess it up again! (HUSTLE, BUSTLE, *and* FRED *enter.* FRED *carries clipboard; others, stacks of computer paper.*) Oh, no! Here they are!

FRED: All right, Hustle and Bustle. It's almost time for Santa to take off, so we'd better go over our preflight checklist.

HUSTLE *and* BUSTLE: Right, Fred! (FRED *calls out items, and others tear off sheets of paper as they answer, then throw them on floor.*)

FRED: All wooden toy boxes painted?

HUSTLE *and* BUSTLE: Check.

FRED: Wind-up toys wound up?

HUSTLE *and* BUSTLE: Yes.

FRED: Packages wrapped and labeled?

HUSTLE *and* BUSTLE: Right.

FRED: So far, so good!

HUSTLE (*Pointing*): Why, here's Randy. (*Moves to him*) Hi, Randy. What's the matter? You sure look down in the dumps.

BUSTLE (*Patting* RANDY *on back*): Cheer up! You shouldn't be so gloomy on Christmas Eve!

FRED: That's right—smile! (*Looks around*) Uh—I hate to mention it, Randy, but this place is a mess.

RANDY (*Exasperated*): Well, I've been trying to . . .

FRED (*Interrupting*): By the way, Randy, don't forget to wax the sleigh and brush the reindeer. (RANDY *shakes his head angrily.*)

HUSTLE (*Suddenly*): The reindeer! We forgot to put them through their warm-up exercises!

BUSTLE: Oh, no! We'd better get to it, Hustle. We can't have the reindeer getting pulled muscles.

FRED: Let's go! (*Elves run off.*)

RANDY (*To audience*): See what I mean about those messy elves? Maybe I should just pack up my galoshes and umbrella and head back to the rain forest. (*Begins to pick up papers.* SANTA *and* RUDOLPH *enter.* TISSUE ELF *follows, pulling wagon with wastebasket and boxes of tissue.*) Hi, Santa! Hi Rudolph!

SANTA: Randy, I want you to know I think you're doing a great job. Without you, those messy elves would never get anything done!

RANDY: Thanks, Santa! (*To audience*) On second thought, I don't think I'll pack after all.

RUDOLPH: A—choo! The sleigh's almost loaded, Santa. (*Takes tissue from wagon, blows nose, then throws tissue into wastebasket*) A—choo!

SANTA: Bless you, Rudolph! (*Concerned*) Is your cold getting worse?

RUDOLPH: I'm afraid so. My nose is all stuffed up, and my throat's sore. (*Coughs into tissue, throws it into basket.*)

TISSUE ELF (*Shaking empty tissue box*): Rudolph's used seven boxes of tissue already today, Santa!

SANTA (*Worried*): I sure hope you're not too sick to lead my sleigh tonight, Rudolph.

RUDOLPH: Don't worry, I'll make it. . . . A—choo! . . . somehow.

SANTA: Let's hope for clear weather—then you won't need to lead the sleigh, and you can stay home in bed! (WEATHER ELF *enters, wearing Hawaiian shirt, sunglasses, shorts, sandals, straw hat. He carries clipboard and can of soda. Beach towel is draped over his shoulder; bottle of suntan lotion sticks out of his pocket.*) Speaking of weather, here's the Weather Elf with the latest report.

WEATHER ELF: I've got good news, Santa! (*Checks clipboard*) The skies are clear, and the air is warm all around the world. Should be a perfect night for your flight.

SANTA: Great! (RUDOLPH *sneezes.*)

WEATHER ELF: Gosh, Rudolph, you sound awful, and you look even worse! Santa, you'd better take his temperature while I go check the radar.

SANTA: Good idea. Come on, Rudolph, let's go find a thermometer. (*All exit except* RANDY.)

RANDY (*Picking up can of sleigh wax*): I'd better go wax the sleigh and brush the reindeer. (HUSTLE, BUSTLE, *and* FRED *enter, followed by* DASHER, DANCER, PRANCER, VIXEN, COMET, CUPID, DONDER, BLITZEN, RALPH, *and* MATILDA.)

FRED (*Trying to keep reindeer in line*): All right, you reindeer, keep those knees up! (*Reindeer form line facing front;* RALPH *and* MATILDA, *at end of line, are out of step.*)

BUSTLE: All right, let's get going! (*Elves lead Reindeer through warm-ups—toe touches, jumping jacks, etc.—while singing to tune of "Jingle Bells."*)

Let's warm up!
Let's warm up!
Soon it's time to fly!
Oh, what fun it is to soar
With Santa in the sky!

Run in place,
Stretch and twist.
Soon it's time to go.

Oh, what fun it is to fly
With Santa—ho, ho, ho!

HUSTLE: Now for swooping and soaring practice.

RANDY (*Panicking*): No! No! Not swooping and soaring!

BUSTLE: Ready, set, go! (*Reindeer swoop and soar around set, knocking items off table and making a mess.* RANDY *looks frustrated.* RALPH *and* MATILDA *are still not in step.*)

FRED: O.K., hold it! (*All stop.*) Great job! Now, let's head back to the stables for a hearty meal of hayburgers, oatshakes, and candy cane juice before takeoff! (*Reindeer cheer, jog off as names are called.*) On Dasher and Dancer, on Prancer and Vixen!

HUSTLE: Now Comet and Cupid, now Donder and Blitzen!

BUSTLE: On Ralph and Matilda! (RALPH *and* MATILDA *don't move.*) Hey, come on, you two! (*They jump to attention and begin to jog off in wrong direction, then turn around and clumsily follow other reindeer off.*)

RANDY: Ralph and Matilda? I've never heard of those two reindeer.

BUSTLE: They're new—extra help hired for the holiday rush.

FRED (*Looking around*): You know, Randy, this place is still a wreck! Get with it, will you? (*Elves exit.*)

RANDY: Well, here I go again. (*Begins cleaning up, as* SANTA, RUDOLPH, *and* TISSUE ELF *enter.* RUDOLPH *holds ice pack on his head.*)

RUDOLPH: Santa, my throat feels terrible, and I'm starting to lose my voice.

SANTA: Oh, Rudolph, if you lose your voice and the weather turns bad, we'll be in big trouble! Thanks to your nose, you're the only one who can see through bad weather to lead the sleigh, and if you can't shout directions to the other reindeer, they might take a wrong turn! We could get stuck in a tree or tangled up in some telephone wires! Let's hope the weather stays clear so you won't have to shout. (WEATHER ELF *rushes in, looking worried. He wears raincoat, rain hat, and galoshes. He carries clipboard and umbrella.*)

WEATHER ELF: Here's the latest forecast! (*Waves clipboard*)

There's a storm front moving in! Heavy rain is headed our way!

SANTA: Oh, dear, Rudolph! You'll have to shout after all!

RUDOLPH (*Hoarsely*): I'll do my best, boss, but even if I don't lose my voice, I'm not sure I can fly and sneeze at the same time. A—choo! (*Grabs tissue*)

SANTA (*Shaking his head*): Things are going from bad to worse. Come on, Rudolph, we'd better hook up the sleigh's windshield wipers.

WEATHER ELF: I'm off to the weather center, Santa. I'll let you know if there's any change in the forecast. (WEATHER ELF *hurries off.* SANTA *and* RUDOLPH *exit, looking grim.* RANDY *picks up papers and stacks them on workbench.*)

RANDY: If Rudolph does lose his voice, how can Santa deliver the presents? Christmas could be in big trouble! (*Looks around*) Well, the workshop's all cleaned up—again. Now, where's that big can of sleigh wax? (*Looks around, picks up can of wax*) Ah, here it is. (HUSTLE, BUSTLE, *and* FRED *enter.* Fred *holds clipboard, others carry computer paper.*)

FRED: Is Santa's rain gear packed?

HUSTLE *and* BUSTLE: Check!

FRED: Reindeer rain hats ready to go?

HUSTLE *and* BUSTLE: You've got it!

FRED: Lists of naughty and nice kids packed?

HUSTLE *and* BUSTLE (*Looking at papers, then at each other, in shock*): Oh, no!

HUSTLE: Where can those lists be? We had them this morning.

BUSTLE (*Snapping fingers*): I know! We left them on the workbench! (*Points to neatly arranged table*)

FRED: We'd better find them, and fast! (*They dig through neatly stacked papers, throwing them around.*)

HUSTLE (*Holding up long sheets of paper*): Here they are!

BUSTLE: Whew! That was a close call!

FRED (*Shaking finger at* RANDY): Randy, if we'd lost those lists, it would have been your fault. You stacked all our papers so neatly, it's hard to find anything. Come on, Hustle and Bustle! Let's get these things loaded. (*They exit.*)

RANDY (*Starting to pick up papers again*): Sometimes I wonder why I even bother! (*Coughing is heard offstage.* SANTA, RUDOLPH, *and* TISSUE ELF *enter.*)

TISSUE ELF: It's pouring out there, Santa. (RUDOLPH *grabs tissue, blows his nose.*) That's twelve boxes, boss. (WEATHER ELF *enters, wearing snow boots, ski jacket, ski cap, mittens, and earmuffs. He carries clipboard.*)

WEATHER ELF: Santa, I've got some good news and some bad news: The good news is that the rain is going to stop before takeoff.

SANTA (*Happily*): That's great!

WEATHER ELF: The bad news is that there's a new storm blowing in. A real blizzard with lots of snow and fog. (*Shakes his head*) The way I see it, there's no avoiding this one! (*Rushes out*)

SANTA (*Discouraged*): This is terrible! Rudolph, your voice just has to last!

RUDOLPH (*In faltering voice*): Maybe some cough drops would help. (*Coughs, then tries to talk, but no words come out. He points to his mouth in panic.*)

TISSUE ELF: His voice is gone! Christmas is doomed!

RANDY: I wish I could do something to help!

SANTA (*Pleading*): Speak to me, Rudolph! (*Elves enter.*) Say something, anything!

FRED: What's the matter, Santa?

SANTA: Rudolph has lost his voice. He won't be able to guide my sleigh tonight!

HUSTLE: Don't worry, Santa! We'll have him fixed up in no time! (HUSTLE, BUSTLE, *and* FRED *rush over to* RUDOLPH.)

SANTA (*Doubtfully*): Are you sure you know what you're doing?

BUSTLE: Sure! If we can build walking, talking dolls and homework machines, we can fix a reindeer voice. (FRED *pulls sheet, three white smocks, and three sets of white gloves from under table.*)

FRED: Here, Santa. (*Hands* SANTA *sheet*) Lay Rudolph down on the workbench and cover him with this sheet while Doctors Hustle, Bustle, and (*Points to himself*) Fred get ready to see the patient. (SANTA *helps* RUDOLPH *to table;* RUDOLPH *lies down, and* SANTA *covers him with sheet. Elves put on smocks and gloves.*)

SANTA: Well, I hope this works. Takeoff is in two hours!

FRED: Don't worry. We'll have Rudolph's voice back in no time. Bustle, bring the doctor's kit!

BUSTLE: Right, Fred. (*Grabs tool kit, sets it on table with loud clank*)

TISSUE ELF (*Worriedly*): That's not a doctor's kit—it's a tool kit!

HUSTLE: It sure is. We elves always come prepared.

TISSUE ELF (*Concerned*): Santa, are you sure these elves know what they're doing?

SANTA: Let's hope so. Christmas is at stake!

FRED: Now, Rudolph, this isn't going to hurt much . . . er . . . I mean . . . Oh, never mind. (RUDOLPH *looks upset.*) Open wide. (*As* RUDOLPH *opens his mouth,* FRED *pantomimes using screwdriver as tongue depressor.*) That's right. Now say "ah." (*No sound*) Say "ah!" (*No sound; angrily*) How do you expect me to help you if you won't even say "ah"?

HUSTLE: Uh, Fred. He can't say "ah"—he can't say anything!

FRED (*Embarrassed*): Oh, yeah.

BUSTLE: Here, let me take a look. (*Pulls flashlight and pliers from kit, peers down* RUDOLPH'S *throat*) I've got it! His battery is worn out! (*Pulls battery from kit*) I'll just plop in a new one and his voice will be good as new. (*He looks for a place to insert battery.*) Where do you put this in, anyway?

HUSTLE (*Exasperated*): Bustle! Rudolph's not a toy! He doesn't use batteries.

BUSTLE (*Embarrassed*): Oh, that's right.

HUSTLE: Give me that flashlight! (*Looks down* RUDOLPH'S *throat, feels his forehead; in serious tone*) Well, Santa, I've got the cure for Rudolph.

ALL (*Eagerly; ad lib*): You do? Great! What is it? (*Etc.*)

HUSTLE: Have him drink plenty of fluids; give him two aspirin, and put him in bed for a good night's sleep. Call me in the morning. His voice should be fine by then.

TISSUE ELF (*Exasperated*): But we need him to lead the sleigh tonight!

SANTA (*Gravely*): I think Hustle's advice is the best so far. Fred, take that sheet off Rudolph. (*To* RUDOLPH) Let's go get you a big glass of orange juice and two aspirin. (FRED *removes sheet from* RUDOLPH *and tosses it onto* RANDY's *antlers.*)

FRED: Here, Randy, fold up this sheet. (RANDY *struggles, pulls off sheet, revealing bright red antlers. See Production Notes.*)

SANTA (*Surprised*): Hey, where's that red glow coming from?

HUSTLE (*Pointing*): Look! It's coming from Randy's antlers!

FRED: Randy! What's happened to your horns?

RANDY (*Shocked*): I don't know. They've always been covered with moss, so I never knew they glowed! I guess the moss came off when I pulled the sheet off my head.

BUSTLE (*Excitedly*): Santa, Randy's the answer to your problems. He and his flashy antlers can guide your sleigh!

ALL (*Ad lib*): Great idea! Hurrah! Christmas is saved! (*Etc.*)

SANTA: How about it, Randy? Will you light the way and save Christmas?

RANDY: I'd love to, but I can't fly.

FRED: No problem. (*Reaches into tool kit and pulls out can*) One little dose of Momma Elf's Magical, Multi-Purpose Oven Cleaner and Reindeer Flying Elixir, and you'll be able to loop the loop in no time!

RANDY: I've always wanted to fly, but there's one other problem.

SANTA: What's that?

RANDY: I still have a lot of work to do. The sleigh hasn't been waxed, and the workshop's a mess . . . again.

SANTA: Don't worry about that, Randy. I've got the perfect replacements for you (*Looks at Elves*)—three of them!

BUSTLE: Oh, no! I hate sleigh waxing and workshop cleaning!

FRED: Santa, couldn't we discuss this?

SANTA (*Emphatically*): Absolutely not!

TISSUE ELF: Congratulations, Randy! You saved Christmas! Three cheers for Randy, the red-horned rainmoose! (*As* TISSUE ELF, HUSTLE, BUSTLE, FRED, *and* SANTA *give three cheers,* REINDEER *and* WEATHER ELF *enter.*)

ALL (*Singing to the tune of "Rudolph the Red-Nosed Reindeer"*):
Randy, the red-horned rainmoose,
Has two very shiny horns.

And until Santa saw them,
He was really quite forlorn.

Then that foggy Christmas Eve,
Santa came to say:
"Randy with your horns so bright,
How'd you like to fly tonight?"

Then how we reindeer loved him
As we shouted out—all right!
Randy, the red-horned rainmoose,
You will lead us through the night!

RANDY: (*To audience*) Merry Christmoose to all and to all a good night!

THE END

I Have a Dream

by Aileen Fisher

Martin Luther King's stirring call for equal rights . . .

Characters

JEFF
SUSAN
GRANDFATHER
SAMUEL
OTHER AUDIENCE MEMBERS
M.C.
BUS DRIVER
MRS. ROSA PARKS
BUS PASSENGERS
POLICE OFFICER
MARTIN LUTHER KING
BLACK MEN AND WOMEN
DALTON
COREY
CHORUS, *6 or more male and female*
STAGEHANDS
MARCHERS
LOUDSPEAKER VOICE

BEFORE RISE: *Music of "We Shall Overcome" is played in background as several audience members enter from back of auditorium and go to front rows to take seats. JEFF and SUSAN enter, carrying on conversation.*

JEFF: Until we studied about Martin Luther King in school, I never realized what a difference he made to this country.

SUSAN (*Nodding*): He was a great man. I'm glad the school is honoring his birthday with this program. (*Looks around for seats*) Jeff, here are two good seats together. (*They sit. GRANDFATHER and SAMUEL enter at back of auditorium, start walking toward front.*)

SAMUEL: Where do you want to sit, Grandpa?

GRANDFATHER: Thanks to Martin Luther King, Samuel, we can sit any place we please. We black folks couldn't always do that.

SAMUEL: I know. We were considered second-class citizens, weren't we? When I hear you and Grandma talk about it, I wonder why it was like that.

GRANDFATHER: That's what Martin Luther King was always wondering—and asking. And he did something about it—something that changed the whole country. He reminded everyone that people in the United States should all have the same chance. That's what the Constitution says—"with liberty and justice for all."

SAMUEL (*Pointing to two seats*): Let's sit right here, Grandpa. (*Lights dim.*) The program's about to begin.

* * * * *

SETTING: *Stage is bare. M.C.'s stand is at one side of stage. At the other side are two rows of chairs, angled so that they face the audience. A large sign reading* RESERVED FOR WHITES *is placed near the chairs in front. Chairs at the back have sign reading* COLORED SECTION. *A single chair for Bus Driver is placed in front of the two rows. On the backdrop is a large picture of Martin Luther King. If available, slides of Martin Luther King and activities in which he was engaged may be flashed on the backdrop from a projector throughout the play.*

AT RISE: *Spotlight goes up on M.C.'s stand. M.C. enters and addresses audience.*

M.C.: We are gathered here today to celebrate the birthday of a great American—Martin Luther King—who made a lasting impression on our history in his short life of 39 years. Actually, his career as a leader in the freedom movement didn't begin until he was 26 years old. Before that his life ran smoothly enough. He went to college, received a doctorate in theology, married, and became pastor of a Baptist church in Montgomery, Alabama. But on a December night in 1955, something happened that changed the direction of his life. Picture a crowded bus in the city of Montgomery, carrying passengers home after a busy day. (BUS DRIVER *enters, sits in single chair. BUS* PASSENGERS *enter and sit in chairs—white passengers in front section, blacks in back section. Spotlight goes up on chairs. BUS* DRIVER *pantomimes driving for a few moments, then stops. More* PASSENGERS *enter, pay fare to* DRIVER, *and take seats.* MRS. ROSA PARKS, *a black woman carrying heavy bags, enters, pays fare to* DRIVER, *then looks wearily at the chairs—mostly filled except for one in front section. She sits there.*)

PASSENGER (*Angrily; to* ROSA): You'll have to move to the back of the bus, lady. (*Rosa doesn't move.*) Can't you read? (*Points to* RESERVED FOR WHITES *sign*) These seats are for whites only. (DRIVER *looks around, gets up, and goes over to* ROSA.)

DRIVER: Lady, these seats are reserved. Go to the back of the bus where you belong. (ROSA *doesn't move or speak.*)

OTHER WHITE PASSENGERS (*Ad lib*): She won't move! Doesn't she know she can't sit in the front of the bus? (*Etc.*)

DRIVER (*Angrily*): All right, lady. You asked for it. (*Steps to center stage, calls off*) Officer! Officer, would you come here, please? (OFFICER *enters.*)

OFFICER: What seems to be the problem?

DRIVER (*Pointing to* ROSA): This lady is the problem. She won't move to the back of the bus.

OFFICER (*To* ROSA): You won't move, eh? (*Grabs her arm, pulls her out of chair*) Then you're under arrest. (*He drags* ROSA *off. Light goes out on chairs.* DRIVER *and* PASSENGERS *exit;* STAGE-HANDS *remove chairs and signs. Spotlight goes up on* M.C.)

M.C.: For years black people in Alabama and other southern

states had been treated as if they had no rights. If they complained, they were put in jail. White people made the rules, and black people were expected to follow them. But the arrest of Mrs. Parks aroused the black community in Montgomery to join together and do something. They turned to their pastor, Martin Luther King, for help. (MARTIN LUTHER KING, COREY, DALTON, *and several* BLACK MEN *and* WOMEN *enter, stand center stage.*)

1ST MAN: Reverend King, we have to fight against this injustice.

1ST WOMAN: What happened to Rosa Parks is a disgrace. We've all suffered enough from white people's laws.

COREY: Let's take action—now! Not next week or next year!

OTHERS (*Ad lib; angrily*): Yes, that's right! Let's fight! (*Etc.*)

KING (*Holding up hand for silence*): I agree the time has come to act. But we must do it peacefully, not with meanness and violence. Excited talk blocks common sense, and the only way for us to fight unjust laws is to unite against them. We have to fight injustice with words and nonviolent action instead of clubs or guns.

DALTON: Reverend King, I have an idea. What if we all boycott the buses—walk to our jobs and have our children walk to school, instead of riding in the back of the bus.

2ND WOMAN: But my job is five miles away! I can't walk that far twice a day!

KING: Dalton has a good idea. (*To* 2ND WOMAN) You could find a ride with someone who has a car. Anything but ride the bus. If we all unite to boycott the buses, then maybe the white men who make the laws will change those laws!

OTHERS (*Ad lib*): Maybe a boycott could work! Yes, let's try it. (*Etc.*)

KING: But always remember the boycott must be orderly, and peaceful. No threats, no fighting, no violence. We're not doing this out of hatred of the white men, but to make them see that our cause is just.

COREY: That's right, Reverend King. We're tired of being mistreated, tired of being kicked about. It's time to act, but in a peaceful way! When will the boycott start?

KING: Tomorrow morning! Let's spread the news to our brothers and sisters, and remember to impress upon them the importance of nonviolence. "He who lives by the sword shall perish by the sword." (KING *and others exit. Spotlight goes up on* M.C.)

M.C.: The very next day, December 5, 1955, the boycott began. Bus after bus clattered down the street with no black passengers. Bus after bus, day after day, for months—until finally, the law was changed and blacks could sit anywhere on a bus, not only in Montgomery, Alabama, but in other cities and states as well. (MARTIN LUTHER KING *enters and crosses to center stage. Spotlight comes up on him.*)

KING: At last the words of our Declaration of Independence are beginning to have some meaning! "We hold these truths to be self-evident—that all men are created equal; that they are endowed by their Creator with certain inalienable rights; that among these are life, liberty, and the pursuit of happiness."

M.C.: Other words, bold words, mighty words, were written into the preamble to the Constitution of the United States:

KING: "We the people of the United States, in order to form a more perfect Union, establish justice, insure domestic tranquillity, provide for the common defense, promote the general welfare, and secure the blessings of liberty to ourselves and our posterity. . . ." (KING *exits. Spot up on* M.C.)

M.C.: Martin Luther King's work for liberty had just begun. In many states, particularly in the South, white children and black children were not permitted to go to the same school; black children could not play in public parks. Many restaurants had signs in their windows: COLORED NOT WELCOME. One by one, Martin Luther King tackled the issues, driven on by his dreams of justice, and more and more black people looked to him for leadership. Meanwhile, Reverend King was put in jail again and again for his uncompromising stand on equality. His house was bombed. Still, his faith never wavered. (CHORUS *crosses backstage, singing first stanza of "We Shall Overcome."*)

CHORUS: We shall overcome
We shall overcome

We shall overcome some day.
Oh, deep in my heart
I do believe
We shall overcome some day.

M.C.: Then came August, 1963, one hundred years after Abraham Lincoln issued his Emancipation Proclamation freeing the slaves. With the blessing of Martin Luther King, more than 200,000 people, black and white, took part in a "march for jobs and freedom" and gathered at the Lincoln Memorial in Washington, D.C., where Dr. King gave his famous "I Have a Dream" speech. It was carried in newspapers all over the country. (KING *enters, crosses center. Spotlight goes up on him.*)

KING: I have a dream that my four little children will one day live in a nation where they will not be judged by the color of their skin but by the content of their character.

I have a dream today.

I have a dream that one day the state of Alabama will be transformed into a situation where little black boys and black girls will be able to join hands with little white boys and white girls and walk together as sisters and brothers.

I have a dream today. . . .

And if America is to be a great nation this must become true. So let freedom ring from the prodigious hilltops of New Hampshire! . . .

Let freedom ring from every hill and mole hill of Mississippi. From every mountainside, let freedom ring.

When we let freedom ring, when we let it ring from every village and every hamlet, from every state and every city, we will be able to speed up that day when all of God's children, black men and white men, Jews and Gentiles, Protestants and Catholics, will be able to join hands and sing that old Negro spiritual, "Free at last! Free at last! Thank God almighty, we are free at last!" (*Exits*)

M.C.: Martin Luther King's success in promoting nonviolence as a solution to racial problems was recognized by the world in 1964, when he received the Nobel Peace Prize. He was only 35 years old, the youngest person ever to receive the prize. All over the world people watched on television as he accepted the award of $54,000. He donated it all to the civil rights movement. (KING *enters; spotlight goes up on him.*)

KING: On behalf of all men who love peace and brotherhood, I accept this award . . . with an abiding faith in America and an audacious faith in the future of mankind . . . and a profound recognition that nonviolence is the answer to the crucial political and moral question of our time. Though 22 million of our black brothers and sisters in the United States are still fighting for full freedom and justice in nonviolent ways, I have faith that eventually they will achieve their goal, and that the long night of racial injustice will be over. I still believe that we shall overcome. (*Exits;* CHORUS *sings offstage*)

CHORUS: We'll walk hand in hand
We'll walk hand in hand
We'll walk hand in hand some day.
Oh, deep in my heart
I do believe
We'll walk hand in hand some day.

M.C.: The climax of Martin Luther King's career came in the spring of 1965, with the 54-mile march from Selma, Alabama, to Montgomery, the state's capital. It was a march to dramatize the "right to vote" problem. Although the 15th Amendment, ratified almost 100 years before the Selma march, gave blacks in this country the right to vote, blacks in some states still couldn't vote, because they were not allowed to register. This was an injustice that Martin Luther King was determined to fight. He faced bitter opposition in Alabama.

Hundreds of marchers, of every faith and race, started on the walk from Selma under a sweltering spring sun. But they had gone only a few blocks when they were met at a bridge by a living blockade of state troopers wearing helmets and swinging billy clubs. They carried canisters of tear gas. The marchers knelt down before the troopers, who pressed ahead swinging their clubs with abandon and spraying the air with gas. Dr. King saw that there was nothing to do but to retreat.

Two weeks later he tried again, this time leading 8,000

black and white supporters on the long march to the state capital. Meanwhile, a federal court order was issued to protect the marchers, and National Guard troops were on hand in case of trouble. Five days later the long march ended at the capitol building in Montgomery, where 25,000 people had gathered to welcome Reverend King and his fellow marchers. (MARTIN LUTHER KING *and* MARCHERS *enter, gather at center.*)

KING: We are on the move! And we are not about to go back. We will go on, with faith in nonviolent action, for our cause is humane and just. It will not take long, because the arm of the universe bends toward justice. . . .

MARCHERS (*Ad lib*): We will go on! (*Etc.*)

M.C.: As a champion of peace, Martin Luther King opposed the war in Vietnam. He spoke out against it with anxiety and sorrow.

KING: We must work for peace by peaceful means. War is madness, and this madness must cease. Those who love peace must organize as effectively as those who love war. (*Exits with* MARCHERS)

M.C.: For his outspoken views on this and many other national problems, Martin Luther King was continually in danger for his life. His family, too, suffered from threats, and several times the King home was bombed. In April, 1968, he went to Memphis to address striking sanitation workers. As usual his message was for peace, justice, and equality. No one was prepared for the violence that erupted. While Dr. King was speaking to a friend from the balcony of his motel, a shot rang out. Dr. King slumped to the floor. . . .

LOUDSPEAKER: Special news bulletin from Memphis, Tennessee! Martin Luther King has just been assassinated! Who the assassin is, no one knows at this point. We will supply more details as they come in. . . .

M.C.: Martin Luther King died just an hour after the shooting, a martyr to the cause of equality and peace. He was not yet forty years old. (*Music of "We Shall Overcome" is heard softly offstage.*) Yes, Martin Luther King had a dream, a dream for the future that will bring hope to the oppressed wherever they are,

a dream to overcome injustice with fairness and equality. For as Reverend King said, the arm of the universe bends toward justice. (*Music of "We Shall Overcome" swells as curtain falls.*)
THE END

Young Harriet Tubman

by Mary Satchell

A courageous slave makes a difficult decision. . . .

Characters

ARAMINTA ROSS, *young slave girl*
BEN ⎫
⎬ *her parents*
HARRIET ⎭
JIM, *16, runaway slave*
MARTHA, *Jim's sister*

TIME: *1834; late evening during Christmas season.*
SETTING: *The Ross family's one-room log cabin on Edward Brodas' plantation near Bucktown, Maryland. Wooden bed with pillow, brightly colored patchwork quilt, and worn blanket, is against wall right. Small bundle is hidden under bed. Large, open fireplace with huge pot hanging over low-burning fire is upstage. Rough-hewn table, benches are center; a candle burns low on table. A window is in the rear wall beside the fireplace. A working door is left.*
AT RISE: ARAMINTA ROSS *enters, quickly crosses to bed, and kneels beside it. She pulls bundle from under bed and rises. There is soft knocking at door, which startles her. She hides*

187

bundle under bed again, then moves cautiously left as knock-ing grows louder.

ARAMINTA (*Guardedly*): Who's there?

JIM (*Offstage, behind door*): It's Jim. (*Urgently*) Let me in, Minty. (ARAMINTA *opens door and* JIM *enters quickly.*)

ARAMINTA (*Closing door*): What are you doing here? Our plan was to meet at midnight. We've got at least two more hours till then. (*Peers at* JIM) Has something happened?

JIM (*Hesitating*): No. Nothing could make me change my mind. (*Nervously crosses to table*)

ARAMINTA (*Suspiciously*): Why are you looking like that?

JIM (*Defensively*): Like *what?* (*Before she can answer*) There you go again, Minty. You're always jumping ahead of everybody and heading the wrong way.

ARAMINTA (*Moving toward* JIM): Jim, I know something's wrong, so you might as well tell me what it is. If we're going to run away to freedom together, we'll have to learn to trust each other—starting now. (JIM *sinks onto bench and sighs.*)

JIM: Minty, I've been thinking about this all week long. If anything happened to you, it would be my fault.

ARAMINTA (*Exasperated*): Jim, nothing's going to happen, except that we'll escape to Philadelphia and be free. I'll find work. You won't have to take care of me after we cross the freedom line. We can go our separate ways then. (*Studies* JIM's *face for a moment*)

JIM (*Morosely*): Minty, I can't take you with me.

ARAMINTA (*Fiercely*): What? But you promised!

JIM (*Taking her arm*): You're too young!

ARAMINTA (*Pulling away angrily*): You went back on your word . . . and after I trusted you!

JIM (*Plaintively*): But what about your ma and pa? How will they feel if anything goes wrong? (*Rising*) You know what happens when runaway slaves are caught. And what with your older sisters being sold down South the first of this year, it would kill Aunt Harriet and Uncle Ben to lose you, too.

ARAMINTA (*Coldly*): I thought you were my friend. I showed you Papa's secret fishing place and where he set his hunting traps.

JIM (*Taking a step toward her*): Minty.

ARAMINTA (*Backing away*): Stay away from me! You broke your promise!

JIM (*Persistently*): Minty, you've got to understand. You're young yet, and it may be some years before you have to leave your folks. But this could be my last chance to get away. Old Jake heard that I may be sold down Virginia way right after Christmas. (*Desperately*) We've got only a few more days before Christmas is over.

ARAMINTA (*With concern*): Did Old Jake really say that? (*Trying to be reassuring*) Nobody listens to Jake and his talk. Most of the time he's wrong—you know that.

JIM (*In a low voice*): I'll need some time before the master finds out I'm gone. I know you're angry, and you think I've betrayed you, but you've got to help me get away by keeping our plan to yourself.

ARAMINTA (*Turning away*): So you won't let me go with you.

JIM (*Pleading*): Please, Minty. There's no one else I can trust. Martha will tell Ma if she finds out. And you know they wouldn't let me go. (*Determined*) Minty, I won't be a slave forever.

ARAMINTA (*Slowly facing* JIM): I can't refuse to help anybody wanting to be free. Everyone's got a right to be free.

JIM (*Smiling in relief*): I knew you'd understand. (*Sounds of laughter off*)

ARAMINTA (*Moving to window to peek behind curtain*): They're busy celebrating. Nobody's going to sleep till long after midnight. (*Returns to table*)

JIM: I've already spread the word that I'm sick. (*Lowering his voice*) Said I ate too much, and I was going to lie down in one of the cabins here.

ARAMINTA: That was a good idea. Folks will think you didn't feel like walking all the way back to the farm.

JIM: I'll hide in the woods behind the church. When the time's right, I'll make my move. You'll know when I'm leaving, Minty. Listen for three hoots of the old night owl.

ARAMINTA: You'll need help finding your way North.

JIM: Zeke Hunn promised to take me to his friends on the Eastern shore. They'll help me get to Philadelphia.

ARAMINTA (*Surprised*): Ezekiel Hunn? Is he the Quaker who lives right outside of town?

JIM (*Nodding*): He's a conductor for the underground railroad.

ARAMINTA (*Frowning*): What's the underground railroad?

JIM: It's a secret route the Quakers and their friends use to help runaways get to freedom.

ARAMINTA (*Astonished*): A secret way to freedom?

JIM (*Quickly*): You've got to be careful that nobody else finds out.

ARAMINTA: You know I'd never tell a soul, Jim. (*Moves to get bundle under bed*) Here, you'll need this. (*Hands it to* JIM) It's some food I packed myself for the road. If Master Brodas or anyone else starts asking questions, I'll tell them you're sick with a bellyache, and I don't know which cabin you're sleeping in.

JIM: Thanks, Minty. It'll take some time for them to search every cabin.

ARAMINTA (*Seriously*): Don't worry about me, Jim. We'll meet someday in Philadelphia. I promise you that. (*Door opens, startling* ARAMINTA *and* JIM. MARTHA *enters, looking at* JIM *in surprise.*)

MARTHA: Jim, what are you doing here? Everybody's talking about how you ate too much and got sick.

ARAMINTA (*Hurriedly*): Evening, Martha. I was just giving Jim his Christmas gift.

JIM (*Putting bundle on table; nervously*): That's right, Sister. This is my Christmas gift.

MARTHA (*Suspiciously*): You don't look sick to me. Why did you make up a story like that? (JIM *starts to speak, but* ARAMINTA *interrupts.*)

ARAMINTA (*In commanding tone*): Keep quiet, Jim. You don't have to explain anything to Martha.

MARTHA: Minty, I'm his sister. I care about him. (*Glances from* JIM *to* ARAMINTA) If you two are planning something that may get you in trouble . . .

JIM: Sister, you've got no right to accuse us of anything. (*Angrily*) Anyway, you can't tell me what to do. I'm older than you.

MARTHA (*Becoming distraught*): I *know* something's wrong. I just know it! Minty's always getting herself in trouble. She's forever talking about running away and being free. Jim, I'm scared you'll find yourself in trouble, too, if you follow her. (*Paces restlessly*) I had a dream about you a few nights ago. I saw you running along a dark road—all by yourself. And there were people running behind, trying to catch you. (MARTHA *begins to cry and stops pacing; urgently.*) Jim, your life was in danger!

JIM (*Softening*): Sister, don't worry. I'll be all right.

MARTHA (*Sharply*): It's true, then. Minty's trying to get you to run away with her. Is that it? Tell me the truth!

ARAMINTA (*Harshly*): *I'll* tell you the truth, Martha. It won't matter because you can't change your brother's mind now. Jim and I had plans to go North, but he's decided to go alone.

MARTHA (*Frantically*): No! You can't go! You'll break Mama's heart. She'll be worried sick about you.

ARAMINTA: What if Jim's sold away from here the way my sisters were? (*Softly*) I still ache for them.

JIM (*Determined; moving to door*): I have to go, or I'll miss Zeke and his wagon.

MARTHA (*Tearfully*): Oh, Jim, will we ever see each other again? (*Jim stops, puts his arm around* MARTHA.)

ARAMINTA (*Urgently; opening door*): Hurry, Jim. You can't miss Zeke's wagon. It's up to you to lead the way to freedom.

JIM (*Pulling away from* MARTHA): I'll be on the road in a little while, Minty. Remember my signal—the sound of an old hoot owl. (MARTHA *sits crying at table as* JIM *exits.* ARAMINTA *looks out window.*)

ARAMINTA (*To herself*): Good luck, Jim. You've just got to make it to freedom.

MARTHA (*Rising*): And what if he can't make it to freedom? What then? (*Moves to door*) I'm going to tell Aunt Harriet and Uncle Ben what you've done. They'll stop you before you get yourself sold away from them.

ARAMINTA (*Determined*): No matter what you do, Martha, I will be free some day. (MARTHA *gives her an angry look before rushing out door.* ARAMINTA *continues after door is shut.*) I *will* be free, and I'll help others to be free. (*Sound of Christmas song and children playing, offstage.* ARAMINTA *sits at table and covers her face with her hands until song ends. After a brief silence, low, distinct sound of three hoots of an owl is heard.* ARAMINTA *raises her head, rushes to look out window.* BEN *enters quietly; his face is grave.* ARAMINTA *stays at window;* BEN *crosses to stand near table.*)

BEN (*Calmly*): Minty?

ARAMINTA (*Turning in surprise*): Papa!

BEN: Why didn't you tell us what you were planning to do? I thought we were close enough so that you trusted me. (ARAMINTA *doesn't move or speak.* BEN *touches her shoulder.*) Don't you know that you can always come to me?

ARAMINTA (*Earnestly*): Papa, would you really let me go?

BEN (*Bowing head*): That's a hard question, Minty.

ARAMINTA (*Matter-of-factly*): I know Mama wouldn't let me. (*Both move to table.*) She'd just yell at me, and probably lock me up.

BEN: Your mama loves you just as much as I do, Minty.

ARAMINTA (*Voice rising*): Why doesn't she act like it? Mama never listens. (*Sinks on bench*) I don't think she even tries to understand.

BEN (*Sitting across from* ARAMINTA): You and your mama are too much alike. But people can have their differences and still love each other.

ARAMINTA: I'll miss you after I go North, Papa.

BEN (*Nodding*): Martha told us what happened tonight. Has Jim left already?

ARAMINTA: Yes.

BEN (*Smiling*): I'm glad he got away. He'll make it. Jim's smart like you.

ARAMINTA (*Rising*): Papa, I always thought Jim was my friend till he wouldn't let me go with him tonight.

BEN: You can't blame Jim. He did the best thing for now. You're still very young and have a lot to learn yet.

ARAMINTA: I've already learned that I'm a slave and my life is not my own.

BEN (*Sadly*): You learned your lesson well, child. (ARAMINTA *rises, stands with her back to door.* HARRIET *enters;* ARAMINTA *is unaware of her presence.*)

ARAMINTA: Papa, I don't mean to hurt you and Mama, but—
(*Determined*) I can hardly think of anything except being free.

HARRIET (*Forcefully*): That's just the problem, Minty. You never
think of anything except what you want. (ARAMINTA *whirls
around in surprise, faces* HARRIET.) You should think of other
people's hurts, for once.

BEN (*Rising*): Minty and I talked things out, Harriet. Our
daughter's got a might strong will, but she's only saying aloud
what the rest of us feel.

ARAMINTA: Mama, you'll miss me for a while after I'm gone, but
you'll get over it.

HARRIET (*Incredulously*): How can a mother get over losing her
children? What does it matter if they're sold away from her, or
if they run away of their own free will? You never get over
losing your loved ones.

ARAMINTA: I cried every day after Master Brodas sold away my
sisters. Even now, I cry when I think about them. (*Bitterly*) I
never saw you shed a tear, Mama.

HARRIET: Minty, have you forgotten that your sisters are my own
daughters? You have cried the loud, angry tears of a child; but
I've cried silently and alone in my heart. (*Touches her heart*)
The hurt runs deep and the tears stay hidden inside me.

ARAMINTA (*Contritely*): I'm sorry, Mama. I thought you didn't
care.

HARRIET: If you could look behind my eyes, Minty, you'd see my
tears. (ARAMINTA *rushes to* HARRIET, *and they embrace.
Sounds of laughter are heard offstage;* HARRIET's *mood becomes lighter.*) Oh, Minty, I almost forgot. I told Martha you'd
help pass out sweets to the little ones. They're so excited.
Christmas is the only time they get to be happy.

ARAMINTA (*Frowning*): I'll never have anything else to do with
Martha.

BEN (*Gently*): Minty, what have I told you about carrying anger
inside you?

ARAMINTA: You said I should forgive, Papa.

HARRIET: Carrying hate makes a person weak in mind and
spirit. Forgiveness brings strength. (*Touches* ARAMINTA's
cheek) Minty, you'll need great strength to live your life as a

free person. Someday, you'll use that strength and will of yours to take others to freedom.

ARAMINTA (*Happily*): Mama, you *do* understand!

HARRIET: I've always understood your need to be free. We all want freedom, but you have the kind of courage that comes to very few people.

BEN (*Gravely; looking out window*): Jim's sure to be missed before morning. I hope he'll have the chance to get a good way down the road. (HARRIET *starts to unfold quilt.*) What are you doing, Harriet?

HARRIET (*Determined*): I mean to give Jim the time he needs. (*Arranges quilt and pillow to resemble a person sleeping*) If anyone comes looking for him, we'll say he's lying down in our cabin awhile. Just in case anybody looks through the window or door, they'll see Jim sleeping like a baby.

ARAMINTA (*Gleefully*): They'll think your quilt is Jim!

HARRIET: Let's hope and pray it'll work out that way. (*Beckons*) Come on, Minty, and help me here. (*She and* ARAMINTA *hurriedly shape quilt and pillow as* BEN *watches.*)

BEN (*Doubtfully*): Master Brodas may decide to come in and have a close look there. Harriet, you know what will happen if it's found out we helped Jim escape.

HARRIET (*Pausing to look at* BEN): If Minty's willing to risk her life to help Jim, so am I.

BEN (*Smiling*): I am, too. (HARRIET *and* ARAMINTA *cover quilt with blanket. Singing of Christmas carol begins again, offstage.*) We should join the party now. I won't go too far away from the cabin so I can keep an eye on everyone who comes near. (*All move toward door;* ARAMINTA *pauses to douse candle.*) No, Minty. Better let it burn. We want our Jim to be seen with no trouble.

ARAMINTA: All right, Papa, but before we go, I want to tell you and Mama something.

HARRIET: What is it, Minty?

ARAMINTA: I'm going to change my name.

HARRIET: But, why? What's wrong with being Araminta Ross?

ARAMINTA (*Earnestly*): I want to be named after a brave and kind person.

BEN (*Puzzled*): Who's that?

ARAMINTA: I want to be called Harriet, after you, Mama.

HARRIET (*Hugging* ARAMINTA): Oh, Minty, you've made me very proud. Prouder than I ever thought I'd feel in my lifetime. That would be a great honor, but you know it's against the law for a slave child to be given her mother's name.

BEN: You'll be our Harriet here at home with the family.

HARRIET (*Proudly*): And after you're free, you can take your new name for all to know.

ARAMINTA (*Seriously*): I'll take you and Papa to freedom someday. We'll go North and live together. (*Enthusiastically*) Papa, you can hunt and fish, and do exactly as you please. Mama, you can sit and rock in your chair all day, (*Points to bed*) or make another quilt like that one you love so much.

BEN (*Joking*): Two Harriets in the family? What a problem that's going to be! (*All laugh.* BEN *opens door; sound of Christmas singing grows louder.*) Merry Christmas!

ARAMINTA (*Laughing*): Merry Christmas, Papa! (*All exit. Curtain*)

THE END

A Man Like Lincoln

by Jane McGowan

Father and son resolve their differences in the tradition of The Great Emancipator. . . .

Characters

ERIC GIFFORD, *candidate for governor*
MRS. SHIRLEY SULLIVAN, *his secretary*
STACEY, *her daughter*
CRAIG GIFFORD, *Mr. Gifford's son*
JILL HANKS
PAULA O'DONNELL
RICKY NOLAN
DEAN BUDNICK
LARRY LAZLO, *campaign manager*

TIME: *The present.*
SETTING: *The law office of Eric Gifford.*
AT RISE: MRS. SHIRLEY SULLIVAN *works at desk, as* MR. GIFFORD *talks on telephone.*
MR. GIFFORD: O.K., Larry, I'll do it if you say so, but I'm warning you, I'm no TV personality. (*Pause*) Sure, I trust you. You're a fine campaign manager, but I can't for the life of me see how

my appearance on a Lincoln's Birthday show is going to do anything for the campaign. (*Pause*) My image? Now, listen, Larry, enough is enough. If I'm going to be Governor of this state, I'm going in on my own merit—not on Lincoln's coat-tails! (*Pause*) No, nothing's wrong with Lincoln, and I admit I quote him a lot, but I'm no more like Lincoln than any other small-town lawyer. (*Pause*) The fact that I collect Lincoln lore is no grounds for a comparison. That slogan you cooked up— "A Man Like Lincoln"—it's downright presumptuous. Next thing you know, you'll want me to grow a beard! (*Pause. Using a milder tone*) No, I'm not angry, but take it easy, O.K.? (*Pause*) I'll see you this afternoon. (*Hangs up; to* SHIRLEY) I just can't see myself on a Lincoln's Birthday show, Shirley.

MRS. SULLIVAN: You'll be great!

MR. GIFFORD: Larry Lazlo is such a publicity hound! Did you see all that baloney in the morning paper?

MRS. SULLIVAN: I don't think it's baloney. All it says is that this state could use a man like Lincoln in the Governor's mansion. And if you don't mind my saying so, you are like Lincoln in many ways.

MR. GIFFORD (*Wryly*): Oh, sure. I was born in a log cabin, I split rails, tended a country store, and read my way through Blackstone all by myself.

MRS. SULLIVAN: You can laugh, Mr. Gifford, but you *are* honest, and you stick to your principles.

MR. GIFFORD: I should hope so. By the way, Shirley, is Stacey coming in this morning?

MRS. SULLIVAN: She should be here any minute. I have a note on my calendar that she's having a meeting of the history club here. I hope she cleared it with you.

MR. GIFFORD: Yes, she did. I'm always happy to have the kids go through my Lincoln library collection.

MRS. SULLIVAN: Working here has done a lot for Stacey, Mr. Gifford. We both appreciate it.

MR. GIFFORD: She's done a fine job here, and she's been a great help in the campaign.

MRS. SULLIVAN: Is there anything special you want her to do today?

MR. GIFFORD: You might ask her to dig out some material on Lincoln's Cooper Union speech. Since I've agreed to be on that program, I might as well show the audience my copy of the Cooper Union and compare Lincoln's views on the federal government's power versus states' rights with current opinions.

MRS. SULLIVAN: O.K. I'll have Stacey do that first thing.

MR. GIFFORD (*Consulting watch*): Ooops! It's later than I thought. I have an appointment with Judge Morgan. By the way, if you see Craig, tell him to call me if he hears anything on college applications. (*Shakes head*) I'm worried about that boy.

MRS. SULLIVAN: He's not in any trouble, is he?

MR. GIFFORD: Not that I know of, but something's eating him lately. He's just not himself.

MRS. SULLIVAN: It's probably this uncertainty about college. Stacey was a nervous wreck before she finally got her acceptance at State.

MR. GIFFORD: Maybe I'm too anxious to change my shingle to *Gifford and Gifford* some day. Craig has the makings of a good lawyer, and I want to see him get into the right school.

MRS. SULLIVAN: But he has so many talents: music, painting . . .

MR. GIFFORD: Oh, I know he has a lot of interests, but he's never considered anything else but law, and for that, he needs a good, solid foundation. I guess I'm just a worrywart. It's tough being a single parent.

MRS. SULLIVAN: You're doing a wonderful job, Mr. Gifford.

MR. GIFFORD (*Shrugging*): I'm not so sure of that. I've never had the time to get mixed up in the P.T.A. or visit the schools, or do half of the things that so many parents seem to do. (*Suddenly*) Gosh, I just remembered tomorrow's Craig's birthday, and I haven't got anything for him. Well, I'll have to stop at Simpson's and get him a shirt or a sweater. I'll be back before lunch.

MRS. SULLIVAN: O.K. (MR. GIFFORD *exits.*) Poor man! He really does have his hands full! Well, I might as well work on this deposition. (*Opens folder, reads papers.* STACEY *enters*)

STACEY: Hi, Mom. Sorry I'm late, but the traffic was murder! I stopped to get those Japanese brushes Craig has been dying for. His birthday's tomorrow.

MRS. SULLIVAN: Yes, I know. Mr. Gifford was talking about getting Craig a shirt or sweater.

STACEY: Oh, no! Not again! Couldn't you drop a hint to show Mr. Gifford that what Craig really wants is an easel and a set of water colors?

MRS. SULLIVAN (*Sighing*): With this campaign he doesn't know whether he's coming or going.

STACEY (*Sharply*): Well, he'd better start a "Father and Son Campaign" soon, if you ask me.

MRS. SULLIVAN: Stacey! You know Craig's father is devoted to him.

STACEY (*Sharply*): Maybe he needs less devotion and more understanding.

MRS. SULLIVAN (*Smiling*): And I suppose *you* understand Craig.

STACEY: At least I understand he's tearing himself apart trying to make himself into something he isn't. Take college, for example. Craig doesn't stand a chance of being accepted at any of those schools his father picked out. What's more, he doesn't even want to go to any of them. He wants to go to art school.

MRS. SULLIVAN (*Surprised*): Art school? Then why didn't he apply?

STACEY: Because he just wouldn't do anything to disappoint his father. All he's ever heard is law, law, law, so he's trying to force himself in that direction. Somebody's going to get hurt.

MRS. SULLIVAN (*Exasperated*): Oh, Stacey, aren't you being a bit overdramatic?

STACEY: Ask Mr. Ames, the guidance counselor, if you don't believe me. If Mr. Gifford would take time to talk with him, I think it would help.

MRS. SULLIVAN (*Musing*): If you think it's so important, we can try to set up an appointment.

STACEY: Don't bother. Mr. Ames is going to try to catch Mr. Gifford when he comes to the school to speak at our Lincoln's Birthday program—Craig promised that his dad would give the main address.

MRS. SULLIVAN (*Alarmed*): But that's at 7:30, and Mr. Gifford didn't say anything about it. In fact, he's going on TV at that time.

STACEY (*Upset*): That's impossible! We're counting on him.

MRS. SULLIVAN: Larry Lazlo thinks this TV appearance is very important to his campaign.

STACEY: The campaign isn't nearly as important as Craig. Mom, I have to do something about this.

MRS. SULLIVAN (*Sighing*): There's nothing you can do, dear. Now, Mr. Gifford wants you to get out all his material on Lincoln's address at Cooper Union. He wants to show his original copy and do a commentary on federal vs. state government.

STACEY: The Cooper Union speech! That means going through stacks of books.

MRS. SULLIVAN: I'm sorry, Stacey, but that's what he wants. (*Looks at watch*) Well, I'm off. I have to stop at the courthouse (*Picks up folder*), and there's some material Mr. Gifford wants from the Law Library and the Historical Society. If there's an important call, you can give Judge Morgan's number. Otherwise, take a message. Mr. Gifford will be back before lunch. 'Bye, dear. (*Exits*)

STACEY (*To herself*): I still can't understand why Craig's father would turn him down. (*At files*) Let's see. Lincoln—autographs, biographies, candidacy, Cooper. Here it is—Cooper Union, New York City, February 27, 1860. See *The Lincoln Papers,* edited by David C. Mearns. See *Lincoln's Sons* by Ruth Painter Randall. Now, what would a book about Lincoln's sons have to do with a political speech? Maybe I can dig up a new angle. (*She looks through books in bookcase. CRAIG enters.*)

CRAIG: Hi, Stacey. Do you know where my father is?

STACEY (*Startled*): Craig! You scared the life out of me. Your dad's with Judge Morgan right now, but more important than that is where your father will be at 7:30 on February 12th.

CRAIG (*Uncomfortably*): Oh, boy! I knew you'd call me on that. I know you'll be angry, but, well . . . (*Quickly*) I didn't actually ask my father to speak because I can't afford to have him anywhere near the high school. You know as well as I do that Mr. Ames would corner him right away—and spill the beans!

STACEY: What beans are there to spill?

CRAIG: Plenty. Mr. Ames knows I've been rejected by all the big-name colleges.

STACEY (*Sympathetically*): Oh, Craig, I'm sorry to hear that. But since your father knows the worst, what can Mr. Ames tell him?

CRAIG: That's just it. My father doesn't know. I haven't told him.

STACEY: But he'll have to know sooner or later. You can't keep a thing like that to yourself.

CRAIG: I can't keep *anything* to myself these days. Everywhere my dad goes, everything he does—there's a reporter on the spot. I'm not just an ordinary guy with a college problem: I'm news. Can't you just see the headline—"Candidate's Son Rejected By Major Colleges."

STACEY: Come on, Craig. You're exaggerating.

CRAIG (*Sighing*): I wish I thought so.

STACEY: What are you going to do?

CRAIG: Tell Dad as soon as I get the chance. I know I should have told him in the first place, but each time I heard from one school, I kept hoping for better news the next time.

STACEY: You really are in a mess—and so are we. Where are we going to get a speaker on such short notice?

CRAIG: Beats me! (JILL, PAULA, RICKY *and* DEAN *enter.*) Ah! Here's the committee . . . maybe they'll have some ideas.

RICKY: Ideas about what?

STACEY: Craig has just been telling me we'll have to get another speaker for Parents' Night.

DEAN: What happened? I thought we were going to have the "Man Like Lincoln."

STACEY: Craig's father is scheduled for a TV program that night.

PAULA: You're kidding! How did that happen?

CRAIG (*Unhappily*): I'm afraid I blew it, Paula. I never asked Dad to speak. I've been turned down by every college on my list, and I didn't want him to hear about it from Mr. Ames.

JILL: Gosh, Craig, I'm sorry.

PAULA: What about art school?

CRAIG: That's out. Dad's always had his heart set on my being a lawyer.

RICKY: But you have real artistic talent. Look at your work on the yearbook.

STACEY: And all the poster contests you've won.

DEAN: I'll bet Mr. Ames could sell your dad on the idea of applying to art school.

CRAIG (*Upset*): I don't want to talk about it. Let's drop the whole subject.

JILL: I know this is hard for you, Craig. But we still need a speaker—so we have to talk about it.

RICKY: Jill's right, Craig. This is everyone's problem, now. And I say your dad's still the best man for the job. You know, he really is like Lincoln in a lot of ways.

STACEY: Speaking of Lincoln, I could use help in digging up material for Mr. Gifford—I need information on the Cooper Union speech. (*Pointing*) That whole folder is full of references, but I hardly know where to begin.

CRAIG: That's a great speech. It's what really won him the nomination in 1860. (*Group moves to table to look at books.*)

STACEY: There's some material in these two books and plenty more in the others. (*She picks up file, consults it, and pulls more books from shelves.*)

DEAN (*Looking at books*): This is a long speech—pages and pages.

STACEY: See if you can organize the points he made on the powers of the federal government versus states' rights. (DEAN *nods and begins to read.*)

PAULA (*Holding up book*): Here's a book that's new to me— *Lincoln's Sons*, by Ruth Painter Randall.

STACEY: I doubt if you'll find very much about the Cooper Union speech in that.

PAULA (*Leafing through book*): It's listed twice in the index.

RICKY (*Leafing through volume*): This book is called *The Lincoln Papers*—they're the papers that belonged to his son, Robert.

PAULA: Hey, listen to this. (*Reads from book*) "Years afterward Robert often said with a smile that he was mainly responsible for his father's first nomination for President—that if he had not flunked his examinations at Harvard, and if his father had not in consequence been so much worried about him that he wanted to come East to see him, it might not have happened. For both Robert and Mr. Lincoln that flunking proved remarkably beneficial."

CRAIG: Hey, let me see that. (*Looks over* PAULA's *shoulder*)

DEAN: You mean Abraham Lincoln's son flunked out of Harvard? (*Group gathers around* PAULA.)

PAULA: Wait a minute. Let me go back to the beginning of the chapter.

RICKY: There's something about it in *this* book. I don't think it means he flunked out of Harvard. It means he couldn't get in. Listen. (*Reads*) "I resolved to enter Harvard College, imagining that there would be no trouble in doing so, in which idea, it is unnecessary to say, I was very much mistaken." Then it goes on to say that when Robert took his college exams he flunked fifteen out of sixteen subjects!

DEAN: Now, there's a record that's hard to beat.

JILL: What did he do?

PAULA: Here it says: (*Reads*) "On being examined I had the honor to receive a fabulous number of conditions which precluded my admission. However, I was resolved not to retire beaten, so, acting under the advice of President Walker, I entered the well-known Academy of Exeter, New Hampshire."

CRAIG: Wow! And all this time his father was on the verge of being nominated for the Presidency of the United States!

PAULA: That's not all. (*Reads*) "I went to Exeter hoping to enter the class preparing to enter college, the next July, as Sophomores. The worthy Principal, Dr. Soule, soon convinced me of the vanity of my aspirations, and I was obliged to enter the Subfreshman Class."

JILL: *Subfreshman!* That's pretty low.

STACEY: How does this fit in with the Cooper Union speech?

PAULA: Well, according to this, his parents were worried about him.

DEAN: No wonder.

PAULA: Lincoln apparently wanted to visit Robert but didn't have the money. Then Robert got a letter saying some men in New York had asked Lincoln to speak to them and had offered the money for the trip.

STACEY: And that speech turned out to be the Cooper Union address.

PAULA: And two days later he went to Exeter, visited his son, and made practically the same speech at the school.

CRAIG: You mean he wasn't ashamed of his son's record?

PAULA: I guess not. According to this, they had a fine visit and everything was great.

CRAIG: But what about the reporters? The press was rough, even in those days.

JILL: Well, it certainly didn't hurt his chances or damage his campaign.

STACEY: This is a terrific story, but I'm not sure it's what Mr. Gifford needs.

CRAIG: Maybe not, Stacey, but it's something *I* need. Lincoln wasn't ashamed of a son who flunked fifteen out of sixteen subjects. He went halfway across the country just to visit Robert, to see how he was doing. And all this in the midst of a Presidential campaign.

STACEY: Craig, do you really think your father is "A Man Like Lincoln"?

CRAIG: You know I do, Stacey.

STACEY: Then haven't you sold him short by not being honest with him?

CRAIG: I never thought of it that way. I wish now I had asked him to speak at our meeting.

DEAN: It's not too late.

CRAIG: But he's already made this TV commitment.

STACEY: The contract hasn't been mailed yet. He hasn't even signed it. (LARRY LAZLO *enters carrying briefcase.*)

MR. LAZLO: Does anybody here know where I could find a good lawyer?

CRAIG: Hi, Mr. Lazlo. Dad had an appointment with Judge Morgan this morning. These are some of my friends—Stacey Sullivan, Jill Hanks, Paula O'Donnell, Ricky Nolan, and Dean Budnick. (*To others*) This is my father's campaign manager, Mr. Lazlo.

MR. LAZLO: Nice to meet you. I'm anxious to get hold of your father before lunch. Are you expecting him back in the office?

STACEY: He's supposed to be back before lunch.

MR. LAZLO: Good. I think I'll wait, if you don't mind.

CRAIG: No problem. Have a seat. (*He points to a chair by table.* MR. LAZLO *sits down.*)

DEAN: We should be going. If you have any news for us, Craig, let us know.

PAULA: We can wait a few days to have the program printed.

CRAIG: I'll call you this afternoon.

RICKY: Here's my rough draft of the program, Stacey. (*Hands her program*) We'll leave it with you, and you can make any changes.

STACEY: Thanks, Ricky.

JILL: Good luck, Craig. Nice to have met you, Mr. Lazlo. (*Committee ad libs goodbyes and exit.*)

STACEY: Well, I guess I'd better get to work. (*Sits at table with books and makes notes*)

MR. LAZLO: Glad to see you have such nice friends, Craig. I hope you realize you'll be in the limelight when your dad's campaign really gets rolling. A candidate's personal life is always important.

CRAIG: I realize that.

MR. LAZLO: Your father's a good man, Craig, but a tough one to handle, politically speaking. I had a rough time signing him up for a TV appearance.

CRAIG: Is it so important to his campaign?

MR. LAZLO: Everything's important to his campaign, Craig. We've got to keep his image before the public, and see that he meets the right people, makes the right contacts with the right organizations. (MR. GIFFORD *enters.*)

MR. GIFFORD: Hello, everyone! Looks as if we have a full house. Larry, what's on your mind that won't keep till after lunch?

MR. LAZLO: Just wanted to make sure everything's in order with the TV contract, Eric, and I have some new press releases for you to O.K.

MR. GIFFORD: Save those releases for a bit, Larry. I can't bear to look at them on an empty stomach. Well, Craig? Got any news for me?

CRAIG: Yes and no, Dad. I have news, but I'm afraid it's not what you want to hear.

MR. GIFFORD: Did you hear from one of the schools?

CRAIG: I heard from all of them, Dad. I didn't get in anywhere.

MR. GIFFORD (*Disappointed*): Oh, Craig. That *is* bad news. But how did you find out—did they all come at once?

CRAIG (*Giving him letters from his pocket*): Not exactly, Dad. The last one came this morning. I know I should have told you the minute the first one came, but I kept hoping for better news, and, well . . . I just couldn't bear to disappoint you.

MR. GIFFORD: So that's why you've been going around with such a long face. You should know by this time, son, I can take a few disappointments.

STACEY: Excuse me, sir. I have some references on the Cooper Union speech. (*Handing him sheaf of papers*) It might not be exactly what you wanted, but . . .

MR. GIFFORD (*Absently*): I'm sure it's fine, Stacey. (*Glancing at papers*) Wait a minute. I think you made a mistake. This seems to be some sort of program. "Parents' Night: A Lincoln's Birthday Get-Together at Hamilton High School." Say, what is this . . . "Keynote Speaker, Attorney Eric C. Gifford"?

CRAIG: Look, Dad, Stacey didn't make a mistake. I did. I promised the committee I'd ask you to make the keynote address, but I lost my nerve.

MR. GIFFORD: You lost your nerve? How hard is it to ask me to do something for you and your school?

CRAIG: It's hard to explain, Dad, but, I just didn't want you to come to school.

MR. GIFFORD (*Upset*): You mean you're ashamed of me?

CRAIG: Gosh, no, Dad—it's the other way around. I didn't want you to be ashamed of me. I didn't want Mr. Ames to corner you and tell you what a flop I am.

MR. GIFFORD: Just what sort of flop are you?

CRAIG: Those rejection letters should tell you. Mr. Ames has told me all along to apply to art schools instead.

MR. GIFFORD: Art school! But I thought you wanted to be a lawyer!

CRAIG: I thought *you* wanted me to be a lawyer, Dad.

MR. GIFFORD (*To* MR. LAZLO): Larry, something tells me we should schedule another time to talk. I'm taking my son out to lunch.

MR. LAZLO: I'll call you tonight, Eric. And don't forget that contract.

MR. GIFFORD: I've already forgotten it, Larry. Haven't you heard? I'm going to be the keynote speaker at Hamilton High.

MR. LAZLO (*Incredulous*): But what about your campaign?

MR. GIFFORD: Look, Larry, I appreciate what you're trying to do for my campaign. But, I must defer to Abe Lincoln this time.

MR. LAZLO: What does Abe Lincoln have to do with your campaign?

MR. GIFFORD: You seemed to think he had a lot to do with it when you called me "A Man Like Lincoln."

MR. LAZLO: It's a great slogan, Eric, even if you don't like it.

MR. GIFFORD: But I *do* like it, Larry. I like it so much that I'm going to do my best to *be* like Lincoln. Tell me—what do you know about his Cooper Union address?

MR. LAZLO (*Shrugging*): It won him the Presidential nomination.

MR. GIFFORD: But do you know why he agreed to travel all the way from Springfield, Illinois, to New York City to make that speech?

MR. LAZLO (*Exasperated*): What is this? An exam in American history?

MR. GIFFORD: Not exactly. But you can find the answer in these notes Stacey took for me. The main reason Lincoln ever agreed to make that journey was the two-hundred-dollar fee attached to the invitation. He needed the money to get to see his son at prep school in New Hampshire.

MR. LAZLO: What are you getting at?

MR. GIFFORD: I'm getting at the fact that my own son's school is within walking distance of my office, and I haven't been inside it for over a year. I'm getting at the fact that Robert Lincoln had a problem very much like Craig's, and he had his father's support in solving it. A man who seeks to be like Lincoln has to do more than follow his example as an honest man, an able politician, and a good lawyer. He must also learn to be a good father. And that's what I'm going to do, Larry, campaign or no campaign. Do you get the message?

MR. LAZLO (*Nodding*): Loud and clear, Eric. I'll call WCAV and give them your regrets.

CRAIG: Dad, I don't know what to say.

MR. GIFFORD: We have lots to talk about, Craig, and I hope you'll find me a good listener. (*Puts arm around* CRAIG)

MR. LAZLO: Well, get along, then, you two. If you don't mind, I'll stick around here and brush up on my history—I'm sure Stacey can show me where to start. (STACEY *laughs and picks up some books.*)

CRAIG: Let's get going, Dad. I can't wait to have lunch with "A Man Like Lincoln." (*Curtain*)

THE END

The Perfect Tribute

by *Mary Raymond Shipman Andrews*
Adapted by *Glenhall Taylor*

A dramatic episode that reveals Abraham Lincoln's character. . . .

Characters

ABRAHAM LINCOLN
WARRINGTON BLAIR, *15*
CARTER BLAIR, *his brother, mid-twenties*
SENTRY
NURSE
HOSPITAL PATIENTS, *4 extras*

SCENE 1

TIME: *The late afternoon of November 20, 1863—the day after President Lincoln delivered the Gettysburg Address.*
SETTING: *A street in Washington, D.C.*
BEFORE RISE: *A city street. There are a streetlamp and a hitching post at right. As the house lights are dimmed, a spot light comes up right. ABRAHAM LINCOLN enters, deep in thought, and steps into circle of spotlight. WARRINGTON BLAIR enters left, running. He trips and stumbles against LINCOLN, who grabs hold of the boy.*

WARRINGTON (*Blurting it out*): Do you want the whole street? Can't a gentleman from the South walk about in Washington without—without—(*Suddenly breaks into sobs.* LINCOLN *leans down and tenderly puts hand on his shoulders.*)

LINCOLN (*Gently*): Young man—the only one who's interfering with your walking about in Washington is you. (WARRINGTON *stops sobbing, looks up at* LINCOLN. *Wipes his eyes on back of his hand.* LINCOLN *straightens up, smiles.*) There, young man—that's better. . . . Now, tell me—what's wrong?

WARRINGTON (*Angrily*): Wrong? Everything's wrong! This war! All the killing! The way the North is ruining our homes—our plantations—our—our everything! (*Takes deep breath*)

LINCOLN (*Patiently*): What else is bothering you? (WARRINGTON *is silent for a moment then looks up at* LINCOLN.)

WARRINGTON (*Desperately*): I'm looking for a lawyer. I don't know where to find one and I need one right away!

LINCOLN (*Kindly*): What do you want with a lawyer?

WARRINGTON (*Trying to control his tears*): I—I want him to draw a will. My brother—(*Pauses*) They say he's dying!

LINCOLN (*Concerned*): Dying?

WARRINGTON (*Bravely*): Of course, I don't believe it. He can't be dying—he just can't! (*Pauses*) Anyway—my brother wants to make a will. . . .

LINCOLN: I see. Where is your brother?

WARRINGTON: He's in the prison hospital. (*Points off left*) He's a captain in the Confederate Army. He was wounded at Gettysburg.

LINCOLN (*Gently*): I used to practice law myself—in a small way, that is. If you'd like, I'll be glad to draw the will for him.

WARRINGTON (*With pride*): We can pay, mind you—we're not paupers. My brother is Carter Hampton Blair, of Georgia. I'm Warrington Blair. We're the Hampton Court Blairs, you know.

LINCOLN (*Smiling indulgently*): Oh.

WARRINGTON (*Quickly*): You see, my brother is engaged to marry Miss Sally Maxfield. They would have been married already, if he hadn't been wounded and taken prisoner. So he wants to leave her everything he has. There's quite a lot of money, and that ought to go to Carter's wife. That's what Miss Sally is—

just about—and if he dies and doesn't make a will, the money will come to me and my sister Nellie.

LINCOLN: So you're worrying for fear you'll inherit some money? (WARRINGTON *nods; then tugging* LINCOLN's *arm he pulls him left.*)

WARRINGTON: I'm sorry I was so rude. Thank you for coming with me. (*He starts to walk faster.*) We'd better hurry. And don't worry about us getting into the prison. They all know me, there. (*They exit, left. Blackout*)

* * * * *

TIME: *A short time later.*

SETTING: *A small hospital room, dimly lighted. There are two barred windows on rear wall.*

AT RISE: *Upstage, there are four cots occupied by* HOSPITAL PA-TIENTS. *Downstage left, in a spotlighted area,* CARTER BLAIR *lies on cot, propped up on his pillow. Next to cot stand a chair and a table. On table are basin, towel and lamp, a Bible, folded newspaper, ink bottle, pen, and sheaf of paper. Union Army* SENTRY *stands right, holding rifle.* NURSE *enters left, and goes to* CARTER's *cot, dampens the towel, wipes his brow with it.* WARRINGTON *enters right.*

WARRINGTON (*To* SENTRY): It's all right, sir. (*Points over his shoulder*) He's with me.

SENTRY: Yes, Master Blair. (WARRINGTON *hurries toward* CARTER's *cot.* SENTRY *looks off, does a double take as* LINCOLN *enters. He smiles, and gives* SENTRY *a casual salute.* NURSE *sees* LINCOLN *and gapes, then exits left.* LINCOLN *joins* WARRINGTON.)

CARTER: Good boy, Warry. You've brought me a lawyer, eh? (WARRINGTON *nods, as* LINCOLN *extends his hand to* CARTER.) Thank you for coming. (*Suddenly winces in pain, then forces a smile*) Whoo! That nearly blew me away! We'd better get on with the legal work before one of those little breezes carries me too far. (*Gesturing feebly*) There's pen and paper on the table, Mr.—ah—(*Hesitates*) I'm sorry—my brother didn't tell me your name.

LINCOLN: Your brother and I met only informally. (*Smiling*) As a matter of fact, he charged into me like a young bull calf.

(WARRINGTON *laughs embarrassedly.*) My name is Lincoln.
(CARTER *looks at him thoughtfully but does not recognize him.*)

CARTER: Lincoln, eh? That's a good name, from your point of
view. I take it you *are* a Northerner?

LINCOLN (*With amusement*): I'm on that side of the fence, yes. If
you like, you may call me a Yankee.

CARTER: On the contrary, Mr. Lincoln. If I may, I'd like to call you
a friend.

LINCOLN (*Extending his hand*): Friend it is.

CARTER (*Taking his hand; ironically*): 'Til death do us part.
(*Briskly*) We'd better get on with the will.

LINCOLN (*Sitting*): Very well, Captain Blair. When your mind's
relieved about your estate, you'll be able to rest easier and get
well faster. (CARTER *smiles.*)

CARTER: It should be a simple will, Mr. Lincoln. All that needs to
be stated is that I leave everything I own to Miss Sally Maxfield.

LINCOLN (*Smiling*): You're right, Captain Blair—that *is* all that
needs to be stated. But if everyone were to write it down like
that, I'm afraid we lawyers would do precious little business.
I'll put it in proper legal terms so some other lawyer won't be
able to dispute it. For example, instead of saying, "you leave
everything you own," we'll say "all your worldly possessions."
(*As* LINCOLN *writes hurriedly,* CARTER *and* WARRINGTON *whisper together.* LINCOLN *finishes writing then hands paper to*
CARTER.) You'd better read this over carefully to make certain
I've stated it the way you want it. (CARTER *takes paper and
reads it.*)

CARTER (*As he reads*): It's just fine, Mr. Lincoln. Our family's
lawyer might have made it a lot longer, but he certainly
couldn't improve upon it. (LINCOLN *picks up the Bible, places
the will on it, dips pen into ink, then hands both to* CARTER.)

LINCOLN: Then, it's all ready for your signature. (*Holds Bible as*
CARTER *writes*) Using the Good Book as a writing desk seems
most appropriate on an occasion like this. (LINCOLN *puts Bible,
pen and paper on table, then stands.* CARTER *puts out his
hand.*)

CARTER: Please, don't go yet, sir. (*Winces as if in pain, recovers and smiles*) You see—I've never before come to like a stranger so well upon such short acquaintance. And I would like to talk a little—if you don't mind. Or are you too busy?

LINCOLN: It's not the lawyers who are the busy men these days— it's the soldiers. (*Takes watch from pocket and looks at it*) I do have a meeting to attend later on, but it will be my pleasure to stay with you a little while longer. (*Pockets watch. Stage grows dim except for spotlight on cot.* LINCOLN *sits.* NURSE *re-enters, right, crosses to table by* CARTER's *cot, "lights" kerosene lamp— flashlight may be inside lamp—and exits right.*)

CARTER: I want to talk to you about your namesake—that man Lincoln. By the way, is he related to you?

LINCOLN (*Dryly*): Well, yes, there is a kind of connection.

CARTER: You know, I'm Southern right to the core. I believe with all my heart in the cause I've fought for. (*Squeezes his brother's shoulder*) But that President of yours—even though he may be a misguided devil himself—is a man of principle. Did you read that speech of his in yesterday's paper?

LINCOLN (*Expressionless*): No, I didn't.

CARTER: You haven't read it? And your name's Lincoln? . . . My sister Nellie was at Gettysburg yesterday. She *heard* it. Nellie said that after it was over not a sound came from the audience.

LINCOLN: I wonder why.

CARTER: According to my sister, applauding that speech would have been sacrilege—like applauding in church. I think that silence is the most perfect tribute that could be paid any orator. That speech will live, sir. (*Gestures*) Warry—hand me that newspaper Nellie left here this morning. I want to read that speech to Mr. Lincoln. (WARRINGTON *starts to hand* CARTER *newspaper, then hesitates.*)

WARRINGTON: Let me read it, Carter—I don't want you to tire yourself. (*Smiling,* CARTER *nods, then drops his head back on pillow.* WARRINGTON *reads without enthusiasm.*) "Fourscore and seven years ago our fathers brought forth on this continent a new nation conceived in liberty and dedicated to the proposition that all men are created equal." (*He looks up.* LINCOLN *and his brother nod.*) "Now we are engaged in a great

civil war, testing whether that nation, or any nation so conceived and so dedicated, can long endure. We are met on a
great battlefield of that war. We have come to dedicate a por-
tion of that field as a final resting-place for those who here
gave their lives that that nation might live." (*He frowns at his
brother, but realizing* CARTER *is unperturbed, he continues.*) "It
is altogether fitting and proper that we should do this. But, in
a larger sense, we cannot dedicate, we cannot consecrate, we
cannot hallow, this ground. The brave men, living and dead,
who struggled here have consecrated it far above our poor
power to add or detract." (*Spotlight narrows so that only* WAR-
RINGTON *and* CARTER *are lighted.* LINCOLN *remains seated in
the darkened area. Reading more meaningfully*) "The world
will little note nor long remember what we say here, but it can
never forget what they did here. It is for us the living rather to
be dedicated here to the unfinished work which they who
fought here have thus so far nobly advanced." (*As the boy
continues,* LINCOLN *rises, but does not enter spotlight. He
stands erect, looking up.*) "It is rather for us to be here dedicated to the great task remaining before us—that from these
honored dead we take increased devotion to that cause for
which they gave the last full measure of devotion—that we
here highly resolve that these dead shall not have died in vain,
that this nation under God shall have a new birth of freedom,
and that government of the people, by the people, for the
people shall not perish from the earth." (WARRINGTON *solemnly lowers newspaper, folds it, and returns it to table.*)

CARTER (*Deeply moved*): That is a wonderful speech. Other men
have spoken stirring words for the North and South before,
but never with the love of both breathing through them. Only
a great man could be partisan without bitterness. Such a man
is not just a Northerner or a Southerner—but an American.
(CARTER *looks at* LINCOLN *eagerly.*) Do you agree with me?

LINCOLN (*After a pause; modestly*): I believe it is a good
speech. . . . I had heard, though, that President Lincoln felt he
had disappointed those who were assembled at Gettysburg.
(*Smiles and puts his hand on* WARRINGTON'S *shoulder*)

CARTER: What Lincoln said is all wrong from my point of view, but it doesn't alter my opinion of the man and his words. I'd like to put my hand in his before I die, and tell him I know that what we're fighting for—both North and South—is the right of our country as it is given each of us to see it. (*He breathes with difficulty.*)

WARRINGTON (*Frightened*): Carter!

CARTER (*Putting his hand on boy's arm reassuringly*): When a man gets close to death, all bitterness leaves him. That speech has made me feel love for my country—and satisfaction in giving my life for it. (*His voice becomes weaker.*) My only wish—and now it's too late for it to be granted—is that I might put my hand in Abraham Lincoln's. (*His voice stops short. He sits, suddenly, as if in pain, grasps* LINCOLN's *hand.* LINCOLN *bends over him.* WARRINGTON *embraces* CARTER. LINCOLN *puts his free hand over* CARTER's *and lowers his head. Spotlight dims to blackout, as the curtain slowly falls.*)

THE END

Looking for Lincoln

by Deborah Newman

Abe Lincoln is launched on his political career. . . .

Characters

ABE LINCOLN
MRS. GREENE
SAM HILL, *storekeeper*
BILL
JACK
CALEB
MRS. ALLEN
MRS. LUKINS
SUSAN
JANE
MENTOR GRAHAM, *schoolmaster*
JOHN STUART, *lawyer*

TIME: *April, 1834.*
SETTING: *A store in New Salem, Illinois. Over door up center is sign reading,* GENERAL STORE—SAM HILL, PROP. *Counter at left has display of vegetables, seed, furs, cheeses, and bolts of material. Counter at right has sign reading* POST OFFICE, NEW

SALEM, ILLINOIS—A. LINCOLN, POSTMASTER. *Guns and tools hang on the walls. Down right is rocking chair. Several wooden kegs may be placed around the store.*

AT RISE: ABE LINCOLN *is standing at counter, right, reading a book. He makes note on a piece of paper, then turns page.* MRS. GREENE *enters.*

MRS. GREENE: Good morning, Abe. What are you studying now?

ABE: Morning, Sally. (*Closes book*) I'm studying law. (*Modestly*) I'm kind of figuring on being a lawyer some day.

MRS. GREENE: Law! Lands sakes, Abe, you're going to wear yourself out with all this studying.

ABE (*Chuckling*): Oh, I reckon I won't do that. Well, Sally, what can I do for you?

MRS. GREENE (*Holding up letter*): I want to send a letter to my cousin.

ABE (*Bowing*): Postmaster Lincoln, at your service. (*Takes letter*) Boston? That's quite a way from here—maybe a thousand miles. I reckon your cousin will have to pay twenty-five cents to get this letter. (*As he writes on envelope*) Postage, twenty-five cents. Some day soon we'll have postage stamps in this country. (*Puts letter under counter*) I'll see your letter goes out on the next mail stage.

MRS. GREENE: Thank you, Abe. (*She starts to exit.*)

ABE: Hold on a minute, Sally. (*He gets a letter from under counter, picks up hat, puts letter in hat, and then puts hat on.*) I'll walk with you a way. A letter came for Mrs. Short, and I know she's been looking for word from her brother. I might as well take the letter out to her.

MRS. GREENE: That's right nice of you, Abe. (ABE *and* MRS. GREENE *exit left.* SAM HILL *enters, goes to counter at right and starts to arrange bolts of material.* BILL, JACK, *and* CALEB *enter, carrying poles with fish hanging from the ends.*)

SAM: Howdy, boys.

BILL, JACK, *and* CALEB (*Ad lib*): Howdy, Mr. Hill. How are you? Good to see you. (*Etc.*)

JACK (*Holding up pole*): Look what we've caught—catfish and sunfish.

CALEB: The river's full of them.

BILL: We're looking for Abe—we want him to come fishing with us. Where is he?

SAM: It's hard to tell. He might be out delivering some letters. Abe always likes to see folks get their mail right away.

JACK: We'll never find him if he's out delivering mail.

SAM: Why, it won't take you any time at all to walk around New Salem and find Abe. (*Shakes his head*) New Salem's one of the smallest towns in Illinois now.

BILL: Come on, boys, let's go look for Abe. It's more fun to fish when he goes with us—he always tells us jokes.

JACK: Mr. Hill, if Abe comes in, would you tell him we're looking for him?

SAM (*Nodding*): I'll do that. (BOYS *exit.* SAM *cuts himself a slice of cheese, as* MRS. ALLEN *and* MRS. LUKINS *enter.*)

MRS. ALLEN: Good morning, Sam.

SAM: Morning, ladies. I have some fine bacon, and dandy calico for a new summer dress. (*He points to bolts of material.*) Just think how pretty you'd look in a dress made from this.

MRS. ALLEN (*Fingering material*): I always did fancy lots of flowers on a dress. But we didn't come in to buy anything today, Sam.

MRS. LUKINS: We're looking for Abe Lincoln.

SAM (*Shaking his head*): Looking for Abe Lincoln! Everyone's always looking for Lincoln. You'd think I was his pappy, instead of a storekeeper, the way everyone keeps asking me, "Where's Abe?" "Where's Abe?" Well, I don't know where Abe is. (*He takes cloth from under counter and wipes counter as they talk.*)

MRS. LUKINS: Sam, this is important. John Allen just came back from Springfield, and he says the government's going to close the post office here in New Salem.

MRS. ALLEN: They said we don't need a post office because so many people are moving away.

SAM (*Sighing*): New Salem sure isn't as big as it used to be.

MRS. LUKINS (*Concerned*): But what's Abe going to do then? He needs his job as postmaster.

MRS. ALLEN: Poor Abe. (*She counts on her fingers as she speaks.*)

First he loses his job because Offutt's store goes out of business. Then he tries to be elected to the legislature—and loses. Then his own store goes under, and he owes money to everyone. And now, just when he's doing nicely as postmaster, the government may take that away from him, too.

SAM (*Nodding*): You're right. This would be bad for Abe.

MRS. LUKINS: We want to find Abe to tell him we'll all help him. Goodness knows, he helps all of us. (SUSAN, *carrying a man's shirt, and* JANE, *carrying a jug of maple syrup, enter.*)

SUSAN: Good morning, Mr. Hill. We're looking for Abe Lincoln.

SAM (*Shaking his head*): Everyone's looking for Lincoln.

JANE: Mammy sent us over with some maple syrup and a new shirt for Abe. She made the shirt to thank him for cutting all our firewood when Pappy was sick.

MRS. ALLEN: Isn't that just like Abe!

SUSAN: Abe's the best wood chopper I ever saw.

MRS. LUKINS: I reckon Abe's the strongest man in New Salem. Why, when he's chopping wood, you'd think three men were working, he goes so fast.

SUSAN (*Holding up shirt*): Ma made the shirt sleeves extra long. Abe's arms are longer than most.

MRS. ALLEN (*Smiling*): Abe's clothes always do seem a mite small for him. (*To* SAM) Sam, if Abe comes in, will you tell him we're looking for him?

SAM: I'll do that. (MRS. ALLEN *and* MRS. LUKINS *exit.* SAM *addresses* JANE *and* SUSAN.) Girls, why don't you leave your presents here? I'll see that Abe gets them.

SUSAN *and* JANE (*Ad lib*): Much obliged, Mr. Hill. We'll leave them here on the counter. (*Etc.* SUSAN *and* JANE *put shirt, jug on counter, then exit.* SAM *sits in rocking chair, yawns, then falls asleep, snoring loudly.* MENTOR GRAHAM *enters with* JOHN STUART.)

GRAHAM (*Shaking* SAM *by shoulder*): Ahem! Sam! Sam, could you wake up for just a minute?

SAM (*Opening eyes*): Hm-m? Oh, howdy, Mentor. (*Apologetically*) I think I have a touch of spring fever. How's the school teaching going? Do your pupils have spring fever?

GRAHAM: Oh, I reckon some do. (*Shakes head*) Not Abe, though. He's my prize student, the smartest one I've ever had. I'm glad to help him study at night.

SAM (*Getting up*): What can I do for you? Getting ready to plant your garden? We just got in some seed.

GRAHAM: No, thank you, Sam, I don't need any seed right now. As a matter of fact—

SAM (*Nodding*): I know. You're looking for Abe.

GRAHAM (*Smiling*): That's right. This is John Stuart from Springfield, a friend of Abe's. (*To* STUART) John, this is Sam Hill.

STUART: Hello, Mr. Hill.

SAM: Pleased to meet you, Mr. Stuart.

GRAHAM (*To* SAM): Do you have any idea where Abe is?

SAM: Mentor, I'll tell you something. I need to come to your schoolroom to get some learning. Seven people have come in this morning, all of them asking the same question: Where is Abe Lincoln? That's what everyone wants to know. Everyone's looking for Lincoln.

STUART (*Nodding*): I came all the way from Springfield to talk to Abe. I want to see if he'll run as a candidate for assemblyman. Illinois needs men like him.

SAM (*Nodding*): You'll never find a better man than Abe Lincoln, Mr. Stuart. I can tell you that. (*Screams are heard offstage.* SUSAN *and* JANE *run in, shouting excitedly.*)

SUSAN: Sam, save us!

JANE (*Hysterically*): There's a wolf running around New Salem. (*Wolf howls are heard offstage.*)

SUSAN: We'll all be killed! (*Girls huddle together.* GRAHAM *and* STUART *go to comfort them.*)

SAM (*Grabbing gun*): Don't you worry, girls. I'll get the critter. (*As he starts to exit,* ABE *enters, holding* JACK, CALEB, *and* BILL *firmly and pulling them into store.*)

ABE: Sam, put the gun down. Here's your wolf. (JACK *starts to pull away, but* ABE *grabs him.*) Jack, why don't you tell us about the wolf in New Salem?

JACK: Aw, Abe, it was just a joke.

BILL: We wanted to give the girls a scare.

CALEB: We didn't think anyone would believe us. (MRS. ALLEN, MRS. LUKINS, *and* MRS. GREENE *enter.*)

MRS. GREENE: What's all the shrieking about? We could hear the girls clear down the street.

ABE: It was a joke, ladies. These young turks have a funny sense of humor, that's all. I don't think they'll play that joke again . . . (*Shakes* JACK *by shoulder*) right, boys?

JACK: We won't, Abe. Promise.

STUART (*Stepping forward and holding out hand*): Hello, Abe. It's good to see you.

ABE (*Surprised and pleased*): John Stuart! (*They shake hands.*) Well, I'm sure glad to see you. What brings you all the way to New Salem?

STUART (*Seriously*): Abe, I want you to run as a candidate for assemblyman again.

ABE (*Shaking his head*): I'm afraid you have the wrong man, John. You know I lost the last time I ran.

STUART: But almost everyone in New Salem voted for you.

SAM: We sure did. And now—why, Abe, I reckon you're the most popular man in town. All morning long folks have been coming in here asking for you.

ABE (*Hesitantly*): I'd like to be an assemblyman, but I'm happy here in New Salem, being postmaster, and studying.

MRS. ALLEN: Listen, Abe, you may not be postmaster much longer. They say the government's going to shut down the post office here.

ABE (*Disturbed*): Is that true, John?

STUART (*Nodding*): I've heard talk about it. Abe, New Salem's a small town, and getting smaller. You can do bigger things than being postmaster. You can go to the state capital—and then maybe to Washington.

SUSAN: Washington! That's where the President lives.

JANE: Wouldn't it be wonderful if Abe got to be President some day?

MRS. ALLEN (*Confidently*): I wouldn't be surprised if Abe *did* get to be President of the whole United States some day.

ABE: Whoa! Hold on, everyone. This talk's running faster than a prairie hen. I'm still trying to make up my mind about an election in New Salem. (*Shakes head*) John, I don't know. Wouldn't folks want to vote for an educated man instead of me? I've had less than one year of regular schooling.

GRAHAM: If you keep on studying the way you have, Abe, you'll know more than any lawyer around.

SUSAN: If I could vote, I'd vote for you, Abe.

ABE (*Smiling*): Thank you, Susan.

CALEB: When I'm a man, I'll vote for you, Abe.

ABE: Thanks, Caleb.

GRAHAM (*Urgently*): Abe, you have to run. We're all behind you.

ABE (*Thoughtfully, after a pause*): Well, it looks as though I have no choice. With all of my good friends here voting for me, I guess I'll just have to run for assemblyman.

BILL: Hurrah for Abe!

OTHERS (*Ad lib*): Good for you, Abe! You'll have my vote! (*Etc.*)

STUART (*Clapping* ABE *on back*): I'm glad we were able to convince you. I have a feeling that more than just the good people in New Salem will be voting for Abraham Lincoln some day. (*All crowd around* ABE *and ad lib congratulations as curtains close.*)

THE END

What Rhymes with Cupid?

by Anne Coulter Martens

Plans for a Valentine's Day celebration
set romance in right direction. . . .

Characters

MISS FENMORE, *store manager*
JANEY, *clerk*
LESTER, *verse writer*
PAULETTE, *his dream girl*
STANTON, *free spender*
MRS. HIGBY
WHELAN, *police officer*

TIME: *Just before Valentine's Day.*
SETTING: *Higby's Greeting Card Store. There are racks of cards left and right, tables, several chairs, and a counter with telephone on it. Exits lead to street, storeroom, and Miss Fenmore's office. Store is decorated with balloons, large bow and arrow, and target with heart at center.*
AT RISE: MISS FENMORE *is putting greeting cards in rack.* JANEY *is standing on stool fastening large sign reading* LET US PLAN YOUR PARTY *on wall.*
JANEY: Do I have the sign straight, Miss Fenmore?

MISS FENMORE: Yes—looks good, Janey. (*Phone rings.* MISS FENMORE *answers it.*) Good afternoon. Higby's Greeting Cards. . . . (*Surprised*) Mrs. Higby? . . . Yes, of course, we have everything you'll need. . . . Fine. We'll be glad to help you make all the plans. Goodbye. (*Hangs up*)

JANEY (*Getting down from stool*): Was that *the* Mrs. Higby?

MISS FENMORE (*Nodding*): *The* Mrs. Higby. She's having a party for a teen group she sponsors, and she wants us to plan it for her.

JANEY: I suppose she'll need valentine tablecloths, napkins, plates—the works. (*She moves stool to adjust string of balloons.*) Great decorations, don't you think?

MISS FENMORE (*Preoccupied*): Yes, Janey, they're very nice. I'd better check in the storeroom for some samples to show Mrs. Higby when she comes in. (*Moves toward rear exit.* LESTER *enters, carrying small portfolio.*)

JANEY (*Getting down from stool*): Hi, Lester. Come to buy a valentine for your girl?

LESTER (*Surprised*): Why, Janey, I didn't know you worked here.

JANEY: Part-time—after school. (*To* MISS FENMORE) Miss Fenmore, this is Lester Graham. He's in my math class.

MISS FENMORE: Hello, Lester. Anything we can do to help you?

LESTER: Maybe. (*Diffidently*) I need some money in a hurry, and I've . . . well . . . I've been writing some greeting card verses. (*Indicates portfolio*) For Valentine's Day. . . .

MISS FENMORE: I'm afraid you've come to the wrong place. All of Higby's greeting card verses are bought at the main office.

LESTER: Oh, I see.

JANEY: Anyway, you're much too late for Valentine's Day. Most of the cards are planned six months in advance.

MISS FENMORE: Sorry. (*Exits*)

LESTER (*Sighing*): It was just an idea that hit me. (*Sits in chair*) Kind of a stupid one, I guess.

JANEY: Maybe not, if you're good at that kind of thing. Mr. Higby might buy now for next year.

LESTER (*Brightening*): Do you think so? Would I get paid very much?

JANEY: You wouldn't get rich, but money's money.

LESTER: The thing is, Paulette wants a bracelet we saw in a jeweler's window, and it costs more than I can save by Valentine's Day.

JANEY: Paulette? I thought she was dating Stanton now.

LESTER (*Firmly*): Absolutely not! Anyway, if I give her the bracelet, she won't even look in his direction.

JANEY: I see. Do you have some of the verses with you?

LESTER (*Opening his portfolio*): Just rough drafts. (*Takes out some papers*) They'll need polishing.

JANEY: Read them anyway.

LESTER (*Reading from a paper*):
"Tell me honest, tell me true,
Do I have a chance with you?"
And inside it says—

JANEY: Be my valentine.

LESTER: How did you guess?

JANEY: They all say that.

LESTER: Here's another one. (*Reads*) "Good grief! Stop thief!"
And inside—

JANEY: A picture of a girl running away with a heart. (*Pointing to card on rack*) We have one very much like that.

LESTER (*Crestfallen*): Oh. In this one I tried a little humor. (*Reads*)
"My wallet is mini,
My love is maxi;
Will you ride on my bike
Instead of a taxi?"
(*Looks at her doubtfully*) Does it grab you?

JANEY: Want the truth?

LESTER: I guess so.

JANEY: The answer is . . . no.

LESTER: I was afraid it lacked a certain something.

JANEY: You do much better with math problems, Lester.

LESTER: How about this one? (*Reads*)
"You're so pretty, valentine,
Please have pity, valentine."
And inside it says, "Don't string me along." A picture of a girl with a piece of real string tied to a heart.

JANEY (*Gently*): Lester, maybe you should try another holiday. Remember, six months in advance.

LESTER: But that would be . . . August. Nothing ever happens in August.

JANEY: People have birthdays and anniversaries all year, you know.

LESTER: Right. August . . . August. (*Picks up his pen*) I'll tell you when I have something. (MISS FENMORE *enters, carrying table-cloth, napkins and plates; puts them on counter.*)

MISS FENMORE: Mrs. Higby may want balloons, and perhaps some big wall decorations, Janey.

JANEY: We have these large hearts. (*Crosses to card rack and holds up large cardboard heart*)

MISS FENMORE: Fine.

LESTER (*Reading*):
"August is hot and August is muggy,
Forget your birthday? I must be buggy!"

JANEY (*Shaking her head*): Sorry, Lester.

LESTER: Maybe I'd better give up. (*Sighs*) And lose Paulette.

JANEY: Just keep trying.

LESTER: All I seem to think of are valentine rhymes. (*He writes again.* MRS. HIGBY *breezes in importantly.*)

MRS. HIGBY: Good afternoon. I'm Eleanora Higby.

MISS FENMORE: Oh, hello, Mrs. Higby. What a pleasure. We're all ready to help plan your party. (*Gestures*) As you see, we have many pretty things for Valentine's Day.

MRS. HIGBY (*Glancing about*): About what I expected.

LESTER (*Aloud, to himself*): Celebrate . . . congratulate . . . (MRS. HIGBY *points to him.*)

MRS. HIGBY: Does he work here?

JANEY: Oh, no. Lester is trying to write some verses for your husband's greeting card company.

MRS. HIGBY: How ridiculous! (*Laughs*) My husband buys only from professional writers.

LESTER: If you'd just look at some of these . . . (MRS. HIGBY *turns her back.*)

JANEY (*Quickly*): Please, Lester.

MISS FENMORE (*Brightly*): How large a party are you planning, Mrs. Higby?

MRS. HIGBY: About fifty young people. (*With enthusiasm*) I want it to be different, spectacular! A party they'll remember. Something on the order of . . . well, you know how a big cake is wheeled in, and then a girl pops out of it? Maybe the Queen of Hearts. But, no, not the Queen of Hearts.

LESTER (*Aloud, to himself*): What rhymes with Cupid . . . stupid. (*Shakes head*) Not too good.

MRS. HIGBY: Why, that's perfect! Cupid, of course!

MISS FENMORE: I don't follow you, Mrs. Higby.

MRS. HIGBY: It would be the climax of the evening. I can just see it . . . a beautifully decorated cake wheeled in—cardboard, of course. Could you do that?

MISS FENMORE: I'm sure we could.

MRS. HIGBY: And then at a signal, up pops Cupid with his bow, to shoot an arrow high in the air!

MISS FENMORE (*Grimly*): I can almost see it myself. But—

MRS. HIGBY: No buts. I've given you the idea; you do the planning.

JANEY: It might be a little hard to get someone to play Cupid.

MRS. HIGBY: Not when he hears there'll be a substantial fee. (*Airily*) I have an errand to do now—when I come back, have a demonstration ready for me. (*Sails out*)

MISS FENMORE (*Annoyed*): Just like that! "Have a demonstration ready for me."

JANEY: She's the boss's wife.

MISS FENMORE: I don't need reminding. (*Sighs*) Now, let's see. . . . For a table, we can use a large cardboard carton, open top and bottom. . . .

JANEY: Covered with a couple of our Valentine tablecloths!

MISS FENMORE: A cardboard cake with a paper top—

JANEY: Painted to look like icing—

MISS FENMORE: With Cupid inside! (*Worried*) But who? (*Slowly, she and* JANEY *turn to look at* LESTER.)

LESTER (*Noticing them*): What are you staring at?

MISS FENMORE *and* JANEY: You!

LESTER (*Jumping up*): Oh, no, I'm not wearing any Cupid outfit!

JANEY: We could use plenty of crepe paper and some big red hearts . . .

MISS FENMORE: Little wings, don't you think?

JANEY: Yes, and this bow and arrow from the wall. (*Gets on stool and takes them down*) Please, Lester.

MISS FENMORE: No one at Mrs. Higby's would recognize you. Just think of yourself as an actor on an assignment.

JANEY: On a *paid* assignment.

LESTER (*Weakening*): Paid . . . hm-m . . . I could buy Paulette that bracelet. Better than anything Stanton would give her. Do you think that would make her pay more attention to me than to him?

JANEY: Could be.

LESTER: Then I'll do it!

MISS FENMORE: You'll find everything you need in the storeroom. (*Points*)

JANEY: You might want to cover the white crepe paper with a few of these big hearts. (*Gives him some large hearts*) Here's the bow and arrow. (*Gives them to him.* PAULETTE *enters, followed by* STANTON.)

PAULETTE: Lester! What are you doing here?

LESTER (*Moonstruck*): Paulette!

PAULETTE: Stanton insisted on buying me the prettiest valentine he can find. (*Coyly, to* STANTON) Go ahead. I won't peek!

STANTON (*Giving her a little hug*): You'd better not, baby. (*Goes to card rack, starts to look through cards*)

LESTER (*Unhappily*): Excuse me. (*Exits*)

JANEY: Me, too. (*Exits through opposite door*)

PAULETTE: It's so nice to be surprised. (*Sits at table and takes scarf from around her neck, putting it on back of chair.* WHELAN *enters.* MISS FENMORE *approaches him.*)

MISS FENMORE: Good afternoon, officer. May I help you?

WHELAN: My wife's been hinting that Valentine's Day is coming up. Guess I'd better buy her a card.

MISS FENMORE: Then you've come to the right place. We have some very nice "to my wife" cards on this side of the rack. (*Takes him to rack*) Do you want a sweet one or a funny one?

WHELAN: A joke card? And get her mad at me? I'd better go for a sweet one. (*Looks at some cards.* PAULETTE *gets up and walks around, looking at decorations.*)

PAULETTE: Stanton, I'm not peeking. (*Picks up something from floor*)

STANTON: What did you find?

PAULETTE: Just a pin. (*Looks at it, then goes to stare at string of balloons speculatively*) Stanton . . . (*Behind* MISS FENMORE's *back, points pin at balloons*) Wouldn't it be fun . . . ?

STANTON: No. (*Choosing a very large valentine; to* MISS FEN-MORE) I'll take this one. (*Gives money to her*)

MISS FENMORE: She's a lucky girl. (*Puts valentine in bag*)

PAULETTE: He's going to get me some red roses, too, aren't you, Stanton? And a big box of chocolates?

STANTON: You'll have to wait and see.

PAULETTE: He's so very, very generous. He'd do anything for me, wouldn't you, Stanton?

STANTON (*Taking her arm*): Cut it out, Paulette. Let's go. (*They exit.*)

WHELAN (*Glancing at his watch*): This is taking longer than I thought. Time for me to call in at the station.

MISS FENMORE: Then come back later, when you can take your time.

WHELAN: I'll do that. See you later. (*Exits.* LESTER *peeks in, embarrassed.*)

LESTER: Ps-st! (*She turns.*) Now?

MISS FENMORE: There's no one here but me. (*LESTER enters dressed as Cupid. Over his chest and back, two large hearts hang from ribbons around his neck. Pair of small wings is attached to back of heart. He carries bow and arrow, and still wears socks and shoes.*)

MISS FENMORE: You look great!

LESTER (*Gaining courage, prancing around*): Do you really think so?

MISS FENMORE: But does Cupid wear shoes and socks?

LESTER: Should I take them off?

MISS FENMORE: It won't matter, because most of you will be inside the box.

LESTER: I don't mind this as much as I thought I would. (*Playfully aims arrow at her*)

MISS FENMORE (*In mock alarm*): Don't shoot! (JANEY *enters, pulling decorated cardboard carton, with a cake on top.* LESTER *aims arrow at her.*)

JANEY (*Laughing*): I surrender! (*Indicating her creation*) How do you like it?

MISS FENMORE (*Looking at it*): Not bad at all, Janey!

JANEY: I even painted some rosebuds on top.

LESTER (*Looking*): Is the top just paper?

JANEY: Yes. You won't have any trouble popping out of it.

LESTER: Do we give the demonstration when Mrs. Higby comes?

JANEY: Yes. I'll fix a much better-looking cake later.

LESTER: O.K. How do I get into it?

MISS FENMORE: Bend down. (*He does*) We'll put the box over you. (*She and* JANEY *lift carton and lower it over him*) There! Can you hear me, Lester?

LESTER (*From box*): Loud and clear.

MISS FENMORE: We'll have to decide on a signal.

JANEY: How about "Happy Valentine's Day"?

MISS FENMORE: Fine. When you hear that, Lester, pop out and shoot your arrow.

LESTER (*From box*): Well, hurry. I'm getting claustrophobia!

JANEY: Relax, Lester! (MRS. HIGBY *enters.*) Here's Mrs. Higby now.

MRS. HIGBY: Ah, I see you have a model all ready—a crude one, of course.

MISS FENMORE: We'll improve it later.

MRS. HIGBY: Good. I'm just fascinated with this idea of mine.

MISS FENMORE: Very original, Mrs. Higby.

JANEY (*Loudly*): Happy Valentine's Day! (LESTER *pops up, breaking through paper.* MRS. HIGBY *gives a pleased gasp of surprise.* LESTER *aims arrow just as she moves into his line of fire. He pretends to release arrow as she screams and quickly holds an arrow to her chest.* NOTE: *Arrow may be concealed in her pocket.*)

MRS. HIGBY: He shot me! I'm dying! (*She sways, then sinks to the floor.*)

LESTER: Oh, what have I done? (*Climbs out of carton*)

MISS FENMORE (*Bending over* MRS. HIGBY): You'll be all right, Mrs. Higby. Calm down.

MRS. HIGBY: Call an ambulance! Oh, my poor heart! (MISS FENMORE *and* JANEY *help her to her feet. She points at* LESTER.) He did this on purpose!

LESTER: I did not!

MRS. HIGBY: All because I laughed at his greeting card verses. (PAULETTE *and* STANTON *appear at entrance.* LESTER *ducks behind counter.*)

PAULETTE (*As they walk to center*): I forgot my scarf. (*She picks it up.*)

STANTON (*To* PAULETTE): Paulette, I can't do it. (*Others are too busy with* MRS. HIGBY *to notice them.*)

PAULETTE: You're chicken? (*Taking pin from him*) Give me the pin. (*She tiptoes to balloons, quickly punctures three or four of them, then dashes out with* STANTON. *At the popping sound,* MRS. HIGBY *screams again and* LESTER *comes from behind counter.*)

MRS. HIGBY: Now he's trying to gun me down! (WHELAN *enters.*) Officer, thank heaven you're here. (*Points to* LESTER) Arrest him! He hates me!

WHELAN (*Pointing to* LESTER): Him?

MISS FENMORE (*Putting an arm around her*): Come, lie down in my office, Mrs. Higby. (*Leads* MRS. HIGBY *off*)

JANEY (*Upset*): Officer, this is all a mistake.

WHELAN: He shot at her, didn't he?

JANEY: Yes, but . . . I mean . . .

WHELAN: That's hunting out of season with a bow and arrow!

LESTER: It's not what you think! (*Edges toward door*)

WHELAN: We'll see about that. (*Starts for* LESTER. JANEY *bends down as if to pick up something. In his haste,* WHELAN *trips over her.* LESTER *runs out.*) Oops! (*Stops to help* JANEY *to her feet*)

JANEY: Oh, I'm so sorry, officer.

WHELAN: Forget it. Let me go after him! (*Hurries out*)

JANEY: This is awful! (LESTER *hurries in at other entrance. This time he is wearing* JANEY's *coat and has a scarf over his head.*)

LESTER: I found your coat back there.

JANEY: You'd better get out of here fast! (WHELAN *enters.*) Uh-oh. (JANEY *steers* LESTER *to upstage side of card rack as if he is a customer and speaks brightly.*) What kind of card are you looking for, miss?

LESTER (*In falsetto*): Do you have any that say "A valentine for my aunt"?

JANEY: We sure do. Just look them over.

WHELAN (*To* JANEY): Where did he go?

JANEY (*Innocently*): Your guess is as good as mine, officer.

WHELAN: Wait till I get my hands on him, upsetting that poor woman! (*He whirls around, looking at doors.*)

JANEY: You might look outside.

WHELAN: I did, but he was too fast for me. I'll call in an all-points alert. (MISS FENMORE *enters.*) I still haven't bought that valentine for my wife.

MISS FENMORE: There are some on this side that are very pretty. (*Indicates rack where* LESTER *is standing, then takes second look and covers her mouth in dismay*)

WHELAN (*Moving to* LESTER's *side of rack*): Did you find one for your aunt?

LESTER (*In falsetto*): They're a little too fancy for her.

WHELAN: That's the kind my wife likes. (LESTER *inches away from* WHELAN *as* WHELAN *reaches rack.*)

LESTER: Guess I'll have a look some place else. (*Starts toward exit*)

WHELAN (*Looking after him*): Wait a minute. (*Moves between* LESTER *and exit*) Your shoes and socks look kind of familiar. . . . Miss, would you mind taking off your coat?

LESTER (*In his own voice*): I beg your pardon! (*Runs out.* WHELAN *starts after him, and* MISS FENMORE *delays him by pushing small stool in his way. He falls over it.*)

WHELAN: Ouch!

MISS FENMORE: I'm so sorry, officer.

WHELAN: Never mind. (*Hurries out*)

JANEY: Is Mrs. Higby all right?

MRS. FENMORE: She's fine—but furious. (LESTER *hurries in.*)

LESTER: What do I do now? (JANEY *goes to look out door.*)

JANEY: Too many people out there. There's only one safe place. (*She signals to* MISS FENMORE, *and they lift cake box.*) Back under here! (LESTER *gets under box, and they lower it, as* WHELAN *re-enters.*)

WHELAN: He got away again! Did you see him come in here?

JANEY: I wasn't watching the door all the time. (WHELAN *stands near cake table, looking around, then relaxes, resting his arm on corner of table.*)

WHELAN: Funny thing about me, I have a sort of sixth sense about fugitives.

JANEY: What do you mean?

WHELAN: I can always tell when they're close. Bloodhound Whelan, they call me on the force. (*Lifts his arm from table*)

MISS FENMORE (*Nervously*): That's a wonderful skill to have in your business. (LESTER *moves under carton, trying to get it nearer to door.*)

WHELAN: Yes, ma'am, I've got a nose like a real bloodhound. (*Without looking, starts to rest his arm on table again and reacts with surprise*) That table! It was right here a minute ago.

JANEY: You must have moved a little, officer.

WHELAN: Oh . . . well, maybe I did. My wife's been telling me I ought to get glasses.

MISS FENMORE: Right. After all, how could a table move?

WHELAN: It couldn't, unless there's someone under it. (*Snaps his fingers*) He's in the cake! (*Thundering*) Come out of there— now! (*Table moves a little, then is still.*) I'll give you till the count of three. One . . . two . . . three! (LESTER *pops out of cake, still wearing* JANEY's *coat and scarf.*)

LESTER (*Holding hands up*): I give up. (*Climbs out and takes off coat and scarf as* MRS. HIGBY *enters.*)

WHELAN: About this arrest, ma'am—

MRS. HIGBY (*Still angry*): I should insist that you lock him up! But, no, my husband wouldn't like the publicity. So I won't press charges.

WHELAN: Whatever you say, ma'am.

MRS. HIGBY: Thank you for your cooperation, officer.

WHELAN (*Studying* LESTER): Can't say he looks *too* vicious. (*Exits*)

MRS. HIGBY (*To* MISS FENMORE): But don't think I'll forget this! I'll tell my husband that this party-planning idea of yours is a complete failure, and you've proved yourself an incompetent store manager!

MISS FENMORE (*Dismayed*): I have?

MRS. HIGBY: Yes, by hiring *him* (*Points to* LESTER) when you should have known he'd want to get back at me for not liking his rhymes. (*Nose in air, she moves toward exit, then turns abruptly.*) My handbag!

MISS FENMORE: It's in my office. I'll get it. (*Exits*)

LESTER: Mrs. Higby . . . (*She stands stiffly, not turning.*) Please listen to me. I didn't have any grudge against you for not liking my verses. Janey had already told me they weren't very good. And I didn't aim that arrow at you. You moved just as I let it fly.

MRS. HIGBY (*Considering*): Well . . . maybe I did.

LESTER: As for what you thought were gun shots—look! (*Picks up deflated balloons*)

MRS. HIGBY: I guess my actions were a bit hasty. . . .

LESTER: So were mine. (*He goes to storeroom, as* MISS FENMORE *enters with handbag.*)

MRS. HIGBY (*Enthusiastically*): Listen, I have a marvelous idea! We'll do the party skit just as it happened, with the same boy as Cupid!

MISS FENMORE: You've changed your mind?

MRS. HIGBY: Yes! I'm beginning to see how funny it was. This will really *make* my party! Cupid pops up, shoots an arrow at somebody, she collapses. . . .

JANEY (*Getting into the mood*): Then the police officer chases him and almost arrests him for bow-and-arrow hunting out of season. . . .

MISS FENMORE: Just the way it happened. (*Gives* MRS. HIGBY *the handbag*)

MRS. HIGBY: But as hostess, I can't be shot, so . . . (*Suddenly, to* JANEY) Would you play the part, Janey?

JANEY: I'd love it!

MRS. HIGBY: Maybe I can hire that nice police officer for the chase. Oh, I'm quite creative! (LESTER *enters, in his own clothes.*) At the end of the skit, just before Cupid is arrested, the girl he shot can beg for his freedom and give him a big kiss. Will you do that, Janey?

JANEY (*Reluctantly*): Well . . .

LESTER: I'd like that part, Janey.

JANEY (*Shyly*): O.K., Lester.

MRS. HIGBY (*Picking up* LESTER's *portfolio*): Is it all right if I show your verses to my husband? There's always a chance . . .

LESTER (*Eagerly*): I'd really appreciate it, Mrs. Higby.

MRS. HIGBY: I'll be in touch with you all. (*Starts to exit, as* WHELAN *enters. She gives him a friendly pat on the arm, then exits.*)

WHELAN: Everything O.K. here?

MISS FENMORE: Very much so.

WHELAN: I still don't have a valentine for my wife.

MISS FENMORE: Will you let me select it? (*Picks out card*) This one's perfect. (*Puts it in bag*) On the house!

WHELAN: Thank you very much. (WHELAN *exits.*)

LESTER (*To* JANEY): Know something? As a Cupid I was really stupid. (*Goes to look at cards on rack*)

JANEY (*Joining him*): Why? (MISS FENMORE *quietly exits.*)

LESTER: Trying to impress the wrong girl when the right one was here beside me.

JANEY (*Surprised*): Oh!

LESTER (*Picking up a valentine*): This says exactly what I mean. (*Gives it to her*)

JANEY (*Reading it*): "Will you be my Valentine?" (*She selects a card and hands it to him.*)

LESTER (*Reading card*): All it says is "Yes!"

JANEY: That's enough—we don't need any fancy rhymes.

LESTER: Maybe as a Cupid I'm not so stupid after all. (*They smile at each other as curtain closes.*)

THE END

The Kingdom of Hearts

by Georgiana Lieder Lahr

What could have happened to the Queen's Valentine's Day tarts? . . .

Characters

KING OF HEARTS
QUEEN OF HEARTS
KNAVE OF HEARTS
SIX MAIDS OF HEARTS
ROYAL COURT HERALD
JACK FROST
KING WINTER
SIX SNOW BUNTINGS
CHILDREN, *extras*

TIME: *Early afternoon, Valentine's Day.*
SETTING: *The Royal Court Room of* KING *and* QUEEN OF HEARTS, *Two thrones stand center.*
AT RISE: KING *and* QUEEN OF HEARTS *are seated on thrones.* KNAVE OF HEARTS *stands left of King's throne.* MAIDS OF HEARTS *stand right of Queen's throne.*
KING: Will the Herald of the Royal Court of Hearts please enter and read my proclamation for Valentine's Day! (*Sound of*

236

trumpet fanfare is heard from offstage, and HERALD *enters left. He approaches thrones and unrolls large parchment scroll.*)

HERALD: Your Royal Highness, King of Hearts! (HERALD *bows low before* KING.) Your Royal Highness, Queen of Hearts! (HERALD *bows low before* QUEEN, *and then to* MAIDS.) I shall now read the Royal Proclamation. (*Reads*) "On this Valentine's Day there are three problems facing our Royal Kingdom of Hearts: Problem One: The tarts which the Queen of Hearts baked this morning for our Valentine's Day party have disappeared!"

OTHERS (*Ad lib*): Disappeared? No! It can't be.

HERALD (*Reading*): "Problem Two: As yet this Royal Court has not found the person who is to receive the 'Royal Award of the Loving Heart' for this year. This award must be made today, or the entire Royal Court of Hearts may never meet again."

OTHERS (*Ad lib; sadly*): Never meet again! We can't believe that! That must not happen!

HERALD (*Reading*): "Problem Three: Last of all, we have no entertainment for our Valentine's Day party. And a party without entertainment is no party at all."

OTHERS (*Ad lib*): Oh, dear! No party at all! Ah, no! (*Etc.*)

HERALD (*Reading*): "Signed King Richard of the Royal Court of Hearts, this fourteenth day of February." (*Bows to court*)

KING: Do not be sad, my loyal subjects. I am sure that we shall find a way to solve our problems. We always have.

QUEEN: We have always found the answers we need.

KING: Let us begin with the disappearance of the tarts. Does anyone know anything about the theft?

1ST MAID: This morning, when I was in the Royal Kitchen, helping to clean up after all the baking the Queen of Hearts and the Maids of Hearts had done for the Valentine Party, I saw a familiar face peering in the kitchen window.

2ND MAID: So did I. It was a boy, and he looked just like the Knave of Hearts. (*She points to* KNAVE OF HEARTS.)

OTHERS: The Knave of Hearts!

KING: What? (*To* KNAVE) Tell us, Knave of Hearts, why you were out there in the snow, when your place is in the Royal Court of Hearts on Valentine's Day?

KNAVE: I was looking at the big pan of delicious-looking tarts.

QUEEN: Why in the world were you doing that?

KNAVE: I was planning to take them.

QUEEN: You were going to take them?

KING (*Angrily*): And then, I suppose you were going to eat them all up, just like a greedy boy!

KNAVE (*Protesting*): Oh, no! I was going to give them away.

KING: A likely story, one I cannot possibly believe. I shall tolerate no thieves in the Royal Kingdom of Hearts! (*To* HERALD) Escort the Knave of Hearts to the dungeon at once. (HERALD *takes* KNAVE *roughly by the arm and starts to lead him out.*)

KNAVE (*Struggling to get free*): But, Your Majesty, please listen to me! You have not heard my whole story.

KING: I have heard enough. Herald, take him to the dungeon— now! Now!

OTHERS (*Ad lib*): The King has spoken. Take him away! Out with him!

KNAVE: But, Your Majesty, listen to me! I am not really guilty. (*Music is heard from offstage, and* JACK FROST *enters left. He carries white paintbox and silver paintbrush.*)

JACK FROST: Stop! Stop! The Knave of Hearts is innocent. I know it, for I am Jack Frost, and I travel everywhere in this land of ice and snow. I know everything that happens here. The Knave of Hearts is innocent.

KNAVE: He speaks the truth. I am innocent. Please believe me!

JACK FROST: I know all about your tarts!

OTHERS (*Ad lib; happily*): Jack Frost knows everything! Hooray for Jack Frost. (*Etc.*)

KING: Then please tell us.

JACK FROST: This morning I saw the Knave of Hearts steal into the Royal Kitchen and take the tray of tarts. Then he fed the tarts to some hungry snow buntings outside who could not find food. How the birds enjoyed that delicious feast! They had not eaten anything for days, and they were starving.

KING: Are there any witnesses besides you, Jack Frost? This Royal Court needs evidence.

JACK FROST: Yes, indeed. King Winter also saw everything that happened. I'll call him here now, and he will tell you the same story. (JACK FROST *claps hands three times.* KING WINTER *enters.*)

KING WINTER: Your Majesty, every word that Jack Frost has told you about the Knave of Hearts and the tarts is true.

OTHERS (*Ad lib; happily*): Every word is true! Wonderful! Hooray! (*Etc.*)

KING WINTER: And for more witnesses, here are the snow buntings. (SNOW BUNTINGS *enter and "fly" to center, singing "Frosty the Snowman."*) I shall let the snow buntings speak for themselves.

1ST SNOW BUNTING (*To* QUEEN): Your tarts were delicious, Queen of Hearts, and we snow buntings ate every last crumb.

2ND SNOW BUNTING: We were truly starving when the Knave of Hearts came and fed us.

3RD SNOW BUNTING: He told us he had read the note that you, the Queen of Hearts, had placed next to the tray of tarts. It read, "These tarts were baked with love and must be given with love."

4TH SNOW BUNTING: And the Knave of Hearts gave those tarts to us with love.

5TH SNOW BUNTING: Those tarts really saved our lives.

QUEEN (*To* SNOW BUNTINGS): I am very happy that the Knave of Hearts gave those tarts to you.

KING (*To* HERALD, *who is still holding* KNAVE OF HEARTS *by arm*): Release the prisoner at once! He is forgiven. (*To* KNAVE) Come, take your rightful place at my side, knave. (KNAVE *bows and returns to his place beside* KING.)

OTHERS (*Clapping and shouting; together*): The Knave of Hearts is forgiven! All is well in the Kingdom of Hearts.

KING: And now we have solved our first problem, the disappearance of the tray of tarts. Now for Problem Two! Who is to receive the "Award of the Loving Heart" this year?

OTHERS (*Ad lib; happily*): The Knave of Hearts! The Knave of Hearts! The award belongs to him. (*Etc.*)

KING: So be it! (*To* KNAVE) Please approach the royal throne. (KNAVE *approaches throne, bowing first to* KING *and then to* QUEEN.) I name you, Knave of Hearts, the winner of this year's "Loving Heart Award." (KING *takes large red heart from under throne and pins it on* KNAVE's *chest.*) And here, also, is a silver loving cup, which will be inscribed with your name. (KING *hands loving cup to* KNAVE.)

KNAVE (*Holding loving cup high, and proudly patting the large red heart on his chest*): Thank you, royal King and Queen of Hearts. (*To the court*) Thank you one and all!

KING: And now there is just one more problem to be solved. What shall we do for entertainment at our Valentine's Day party?

KING WINTER: I can help you, for I peek through so many windows that I know almost everything that is going on in the Kingdom of Hearts.

KING: What have you seen?

KING WINTER: Yesterday I saw a group of children in a school room, practicing songs for their school celebration. The music would be just right for your Valentine's Day entertainment. Shall I bring the children here?

QUEEN: Yes, please bring the children here at once.

KING WINTER: Just three claps of my hands, and the children will be here. (*He claps three times. A group of happy* CHILDREN *enter and gather center stage.*)

KING: Welcome to the Kingdom, children. The King and Queen of Hearts and their Royal Court would like you to sing at our Valentine Party today. Will you sing for us?

CHILDREN (*Ad lib*): Yes, yes. With pleasure! Of course! (*Etc.*)

QUEEN: Please sing for us now, so that we may begin our Valentine's Day party.

1ST CHILD: We have a Valentine's song for you. We hope you will like it. (CHILDREN *sing appropriate "heart" or Valentine's Day song. Live or recorded accompaniment may be played. Royal Court applauds the* CHILDREN *when they finish singing.*)

KING: What a happy Valentine's Day this has turned out to be! (*If desired, the entire cast may join in with another song as curtains close.*)

THE END

Express to Valley Forge

by Earl J. Dias

A courageous patriot saves the day for George Washington's army. . . .

Characters

GRANDMA HEATHER
KATHLEEN, *maid at Heather Inn*
DEBORAH HEATHER
MR. HEATHER
MRS. HEATHER
ELIJAH HARRIS, *stagecoach driver*

SCENE 1

TIME: *Late afternoon in January, 1777.*
SETTING: *The kitchen of Heather Inn in Chester County, Pennsylvania, about five miles from Valley Forge.*
AT RISE: GRANDMA HEATHER *sits in rocking chair, knitting.* KATHLEEN *is taking cups, saucers, plates and cutlery from cabinet as she sets the table. She keeps blowing on her hands.*
KATHLEEN: By all the saints, 'tis cold! This Pennsylvania is a bitter land, if you ask me. Snow and ice and hail and sleet— 'tis enough to chill the devil himself.
GRANDMA: Now don't be complaining, Kathleen. After all, you've

241

been here only a month. Wait till the spring when everything is fresh and green, and the summer when a cool breeze from the Schuylkill River fans us. (*She motions to footstool at her feet.*) Come sit, sit here, Kathleen. (KATHLEEN *crosses to* GRANDMA *and sits on stool.*) Are you really so unhappy here?

KATHLEEN (*Quickly*): Oh, no, ma'am, I wouldn't want to be givin' the wrong impression. Sure, you and Mr. and Mrs. Heather, and that sweet colleen, Deborah, have been kindness itself to me.

GRANDMA: And remember, you're to be a bonded servant only for a year. Then you'll be free to do as you wish.

KATHLEEN: Like as not, I'll choose to stay here at the Heather Inn. 'Tis only that at times I miss the green grass and the peat bogs of Ireland.

GRANDMA (*Understandingly*): Of course you do. I felt the same way when I came from England long ago, before you were born. (*Smiles*) And now, let me hear your lessons.

KATHLEEN: As you will, ma'am. But I do notice that Mr. and Mrs. Heather do not approve of what you're teaching me. Nor does Elijah Harris, the stagecoach driver.

GRANDMA (*Snippily*): That's because they're afraid to change as the world changes. They close their eyes to what's going on about them. Now, recite to me. (*Puts down her knitting*) What is freedom, child?

KATHLEEN (*Reciting patly, by rote*): Freedom is the right to think and act as you believe, provided you do not hamper the freedom of others in doing so.

GRANDMA (*Pleased*): Splendid, child, splendid! And, now, who is the chief fighter for freedom?

KATHLEEN (*Chuckling*): General George Washington, ma'am— who is camped with his men, not ten miles from here at Valley Forge.

GRANDMA (*Nodding*): And against whom is he fighting?

KATHLEEN: The Lobster Backs, ma'am, or the redcoats, or the British—give 'em what name you wish.

GRANDMA: Don't tempt me, child. And who will win the fight?

KATHLEEN (*Chuckling*): General George Washington, without a doubt. (DEBORAH HEATHER *enters. She is an attractive girl of*

17, very warmly dressed. GRANDMA *and* KATHLEEN *do not see her as she hangs her cloak on hook near door.*)

GRANDMA: And who is the greatest man in the land?

KATHLEEN (*Laughing merrily*): By the good saints, ma'am, the answers to your questions are all the same. Sure, and a parrot could answer them.

DEBORAH (*Loudly*): General George Washington. (KATHLEEN *leaps to her feet, startled.* GRANDMA *begins knitting again hurriedly.* DEBORAH *laughs as she comes over to rocker and hugs* GRANDMA) It's only me, Grandma.

KATHLEEN (*Returning to setting the table*): Faith, Miss Deborah, but you gave us a start.

GRANDMA: Where have you been, Deborah? (DEBORAH *goes to table, where she sits down with a sigh.*)

DEBORAH: Out in our stable. Blacksmith Hawkins is mending the wheel of Elijah's stagecoach. Elijah had to stop here to get it done.

GRANDMA: Any passengers? Anybody who travels in such bitter weather either has rocks where his brains ought to be or is up to no good.

DEBORAH (*Smiling*): Don't be so suspicious, Grandma.

GRANDMA: I know what I've seen. The country round about is teeming with spies and nosey critters who look as though they'd slit your throat with pleasure.

DEBORAH: There is just one passenger, and he looks harmless enough. A mild-mannered man with a wen on his nose.

GRANDMA: I never did trust people with wens.

KATHLEEN (*Lightly*): And has Elijah proposed to you again, Miss Deborah? The man must have a dry throat from asking you so often!

DEBORAH (*Laughing*): He proposes every time I see him—and in the same words. I think he learned to speak by rote—like an actor in a play.

KATHLEEN: He's a handsome enough man.

GRANDMA (*Snappily*): But too old for Deborah—May and December don't suit each other. Besides, I don't like his ideas. He has too many friends among the Lobster Backs.

DEBORAH: I nearly forgot, Kathleen. Elijah wants a cup of tea. Will you take it to him in the stable?

KATHLEEN: That I will, Miss Deborah. (KATHLEEN *takes her cloak from a hook, puts it on, takes a cup to fireplace and fills it with tea.*) The poor man will be needin' something hot out in this cold. (KATHLEEN *exits.* DEBORAH *rises from chair and comes down to sit on footstool.*)

DEBORAH: Have you ever known a colder winter, Grandma? Abner Hawkins says that General Washington and his men are well-nigh freezing to death at Valley Forge.

GRANDMA: And you've had no word from Nathan Merriman?

DEBORAH (*Sadly*): None at all. Though I know he's still on General Washington's staff.

GRANDMA: And your heart's there with him, isn't it, child?

DEBORAH (*Rising from footstool, crosses to bench, sits and warms her hands at fireplace*): It is. But the war looks so hopeless. Elijah says over half of Washington's army has deserted. (*Sadly*) Sometimes I think that I'll never see Nathan again— that he's sacrificing himself for a losing cause.

GRANDMA (*Getting to her feet and crossing over to put an arm around* DEBORAH's *shoulder*): Don't speak that way, child. Causes aren't lost so easily. General Washington knows what he's doing. (MR. *and* MRS. HEATHER, *wearing heavy coats, enter.*)

MR. HEATHER (*Grumpily*): General Washington! General Washington! That's your tune from morn till night, Mother.

GRANDMA (*Returning to rocker*): And a good tune, too.

MRS. HEATHER: A haughty Virginia squire who has brought nothing but death and destruction to Pennsylvania. The sooner he is defeated, the better!

MR. HEATHER: Right! Then some of us will be able to sleep in peace.

GRANDMA (*Angrily*): But not in freedom. You can lick King George's boots if your tongue's long enough. I won't!

MR. HEATHER (*Impatiently*): Now, Mother, we've spoken enough of this before. In heaven's name, at least let's have some peace under this roof. (*To* DEBORAH) I saw Elijah in the stable. Why aren't you with him?

GRANDMA (*Sharply*): She doesn't want to be—that's why.

MRS. HEATHER (*Shaking her head*): Still mooning over that young scamp Nathan Merriman, who left his good farm to fight for Washington and his rabble.

DEBORAH: He isn't a scamp. He's doing what he thinks right.

MR. HEATHER: Elijah is a good, sound man who would make you a respectable, hardworking husband.

GRANDMA: Hmmph! He's too friendly with the British for my liking.

MR. HEATHER: That's enough, Mother. As for you, Deborah, you'd do well to think kindly on Elijah's proposal. There are many maids in Pennsylvania who would be happy to have him.

MRS. HEATHER (*Rather tenderly*): And, after all, marriage might help drive a lot of silly notions out of your head. And you, Mother, forget about George Washington!

MR. HEATHER: Come, Martha, we'd best rest a bit before supper. The walk from the village was tiring. (MR. *and* MRS. HEATHER *exit.*)

GRANDMA (*Sighing*): To think that a son of mine would talk like such a clothhead.

DEBORAH (*Coming to center; thoughtfully*): Mother and Father are just sick of war and confusion. I suppose we can't blame them for that.

GRANDMA: And how do you think Washington and his men feel in the snowdrifts at Valley Forge with hardly a bite to eat?

DEBORAH: I know, Grandma. But sometimes it seems as though the bloodshed will never end, and that Nathan—

GRANDMA: And that Nathan will never return? (*Gently*) But he will, child. He will. (KATHLEEN *bursts into room.*)

KATHLEEN (*Wildly excited*): Oh, the saints protect us! I've heard the most terrible thing!

DEBORAH: What is it, Kathleen?

KATHLEEN (*Getting her breath*): Well, ma'am, when I took the tea to Elijah, he was deep in talk with a stranger.

DEBORAH: That must have been the stage passenger.

KATHLEEN: They stopped talking when they saw me but it seemed to me they looked a bit guilty. I'd heard them mention the name of General Washington, though.

GRANDMA: Aha!

KATHLEEN: So Elijah drank his tea, and, I left—or, at least, he thought so. But I crept behind the stable and listened—there's many a crack in the wall—and I heard the most terrible thing. You wouldn't believe—(ELIJAH HARRIS *enters. He is a tall, heavy, broad-shouldered man of forty, good-looking enough but rather pompous and with an air of false heartiness.*)

ELIJAH (*Going to fireplace to warm his hands*): Wouldn't believe what, my lass? (KATHLEEN, *in confusion, removes her cloak and hangs it on peg.* ELIJAH *laughs heartily.*) You look as though you'd seen a ghost or Satan himself.

GRANDMA: Get Elijah another cup of tea, please, Kathleen.

ELIJAH: Tea warms the bones on a day as bitter cold as this. (KATHLEEN *goes to fireplace, pours tea from kettle into a cup, and hands it to* ELIJAH.) Your hand's shaking, lass. (*Both* DEBORAH *and* GRANDMA *cast exasperated looks at each other as* ELIJAH *drinks his tea.* ELIJAH *sits on bench in front of fireplace.*)

DEBORAH (*Innocently*): Where is your passenger, Elijah?

ELIJAH: He has walked over to the Blake farm. He knows old Blake and wants to chat with him. (*Chuckling*)

DEBORAH: Is the wheel repaired?

ELIJAH: Right as rain, and the horses are hitched up. We'll leave when the passenger returns—in an hour or so. There's no particular hurry. I'm so far behind my schedule now that time no longer matters. (KATHLEEN *stands in corner, pointing frantically at* ELIJAH *and then at door.* GRANDMA *and* DEBORAH *nod understandingly.*)

DEBORAH: Elijah, do you remember the artist fellow who stayed here in October?

ELIJAH (*Still sipping tea*): Aye, a thin rail of a man with eyes that seemed to pop out of his head.

DEBORAH: He painted my portrait while he was here—a miniature he called it.

ELIJAH: Did he now?

DEBORAH (*Coquettishly*): Would you like the picture, Elijah?

GRANDMA: What in the world are—

DEBORAH (*Warningly*): Now, Grandma! Would you like it, Elijah? (ELIJAH *places his tea cup on the bench, rises, comes to* DEBORAH, *places his arm about her waist, and draws her to him.*)

ELIJAH: Why, of course I'd like it, Deborah. Are your feelings softening toward old Elijah? Does this mean that you and I—

DEBORAH (*Skillfully freeing herself*): It might, Elijah.

ELIJAH (*Grinning broadly*): Go fetch the picture.

DEBORAH: It's upstairs in Mother's and Father's sitting room. Why don't you get it, Elijah? Mother and Father will be glad to give it to you, for they think highly of you, as you know.

ELIJAH (*Preening*): Do they now?

DEBORAH: They think that you'd turn any girl's head. (ELIJAH *grins broadly.*) And (*Very coquettishly*) I think they're right. (ELIJAH *attempts to kiss her, but she dodges him.*) Tell them I said you were to have the miniature.

ELIJAH: And one kiss to seal the bargain?

DEBORAH (*Fluttering her eyes*): Later, Elijah.

ELIJAH (*Going toward door, still grinning*): Later, then! (*He blows her a kiss and exits.*)

GRANDMA: The snake in the grass!

KATHLEEN: I thought he'd never go! I must be quick: Elijah and the stranger said that tomorrow night a messenger will be ridin' from Valley Forge with the campaign plans for the spring. He'll be ridin' to Philadelphia to deliver them to the leaders of the Continental Congress. The stranger, with Elijah's help, will waylay the messenger, get the plans, and turn them over to the British. And the messenger—

GRANDMA (*Impatiently*): Out with it, child.

KATHLEEN: And the messenger is likely to be killed. (*Tearful*) And the messenger is Nathan Merriman.

DEBORAH (*Gasping*): Nathan! Oh! But how did they know all this?

KATHLEEN: From what I gathered, 'tis Elijah himself who nosed out the information.

GRANDMA: The mealy-mouthed windbag!

DEBORAH: I must do something! (*Her face suddenly lightens, and she rushes to window.*) The stage is all ready to go.

KATHLEEN: Oh, Miss Deborah, you're not thinkin' of—

GRANDMA (*Jumping spryly from rocker*): Of course she is! And I'd like to see Elijah's face when he finds out!

DEBORAH (*Putting on her cloak*): I'll drive the coach to Valley Forge and warn Nathan!

GRANDMA: That's the spirit!

KATHLEEN: But the weather's so bitter. . . .

GRANDMA (*Chuckling*): Not so bitter as Elijah, blast him, will be.

DEBORAH (*Going to door*): If only Elijah stays up there until I'm away.

GRANDMA (*Going purposefully to door*): He'll stay there if I have to sit on him—depend on it. (*Pauses at door*) And give my love to General Washington. (DEBORAH *exits.* GRANDMA *exits after her.* KATHLEEN *goes to window and looks out intently. The sound of hoofbeats is heard.*)

KATHLEEN: She's off, thank heaven, and may the Saints guide her on her way.

* * * * *

SCENE 2

TIME: *Five hours later.*

SETTING: *The same.*

AT RISE: *Mr. and* MRS. HEATHER *are seated at table.* GRANDMA *sits in rocker, knitting.* KATHLEEN *sits on bench,* ELIJAH *is pacing up and down nervously. All seem jittery except* GRANDMA.

ELIJAH: Five hours now since the minx left! I don't understand how a young woman who is supposed to be well brought up and modest could do such a thing.

GRANDMA: Deborah's not a minx, Elijah. You'll favor me by keeping such thoughts to yourself.

MR. HEATHER: Yes, Elijah. I'll not have my daughter slandered. She may be headstrong and willful at times, but—

MRS. HEATHER: As she has a right to be. I was myself at her age.

GRANDMA (*Pleased*): Well, you're both beginning to sound almost human—for a change.

ELIJAH (*Sarcastically*): Headstrong and willful, indeed. The girl steals my stage—and she'll probably ruin the horses—and I'm supposed to smile at her little whim as being merely the folly of youth. (*Thoughtfully*) It seems to me that she was unusually pleasant to me this afternoon—I should have been suspicious. The minx—

GRANDMA (*Sharply*): No more of that, Elijah.

ELIJAH (*Angrily*): And have I no right to complain? How can I explain all this later? My passenger is angry beyond belief; he has stalked off calling down curses on my head! To be tricked thus by a girl! (GRANDMA *cackles merrily, and* ELIJAH *gives her an irate look.*) I'll be a laughing stock! (*He goes to fireplace*) And what earthly reason she'd have to drive the coach is beyond me.

GRANDMA (*Ironically*): Perhaps that great brain of yours just isn't working well tonight, Elijah.

ME. HEATHER (*Suspiciously*): I surmise that you know more about all of this than you're telling, Mother.

GRANDMA: I? Why, son, I'm as innocent as a new-born sparrow.

MRS. HEATHER: Will you bring me some tea, Kathleen, please?

KATHLEEN (*Rising from bench*): Yes, ma'am. (*She takes cup from cabinet, fills it from kettle, and brings it to table. To* MR. HEATHER) Would you be wantin' some, sir?

MR. HEATHER: No, Kathleen, thank you. (KATHLEEN *returns to bench.* ELIJAH *eyes her suspiciously.*)

ELIJAH: And I'll wager that this lass knows a thing or two.

KATHLEEN (*Innocently*): Me, sir?

ELIJAH: Aye, you've been strangely quiet all the night.

KATHLEEN (*Primly*): 'Tis a servant's place to be seen and not heard, sir. (ELIJAH *goes to window and peers out.*)

ELIJAH: No sign of her yet. Where can she have gone?

MRS. HEATHER: You may as well sit and be comfortable, Elijah. She'll be here when she arrives—not before. All we can do is wait.

ELIJAH: And to think I asked so willful a creature to be my wife, thinking she was a quiet, modest young woman who would grace my hearth.

GRANDMA: She never said yes that I know of.

MR. HEATHER: Let's not stir up more trouble, Mother. Elijah is beside himself with worry. Such criticism of Deborah is not gentlemanly, Elijah. She may have good reason for what she does.

ELIJAH: Reason! To steal my stage from under my nose! (*Sound of hoof beats is heard in the distance.* ELIJAH *rushes to door and throws it open.* KATHLEEN *and* MR. *and* MRS. HEATHER *go to window and look out.* GRANDMA *remains in rocker, knitting and smiling to herself.* ELIJAH *exits.*)

KATHLEEN (*Excitedly*): It's Miss Deborah, all right! Heaven be praised! Elijah seems to be tellin' her a thing or two, and she's laughin'—

GRANDMA: Good! (DEBORAH *enters, breathless and red-cheeked.* ELIJAH *follows her in.*)

ELIJAH (*Angrily*): And now, miss, we'd like you to explain all this!

MRS. HEATHER (*Going solicitously to* DEBORAH): Are you all right, child?

DEBORAH (*Laughing*): Yes, Mother, of course.

MR. HEATHER: Now Deborah, you do owe us all an explanation. What made you do such a thing?

ELIJAH (*Sarcastically*): Aye, Miss Heather, what whim—

DEBORAH (*Slyly*): I'm no longer Miss Heather, Elijah.

MRS. HEATHER: What do you mean, Deborah?

DEBORAH (*Proudly*): I am now Mrs. Nathan Merriman.

MR. HEATHER (*Astonished*): Mrs. Nathan Merriman!

KATHLEEN: What a lovely surprise!

ELIJAH: Lovely surprise! Do you mean that you stole my stage only to go to your own wedding?

DEBORAH (*Laughing*): Borrowed, Elijah—not stole. I did, indeed. Nathan and I were married at Valley Forge by Parson Ames, who is there with the troops.

MR. HEATHER: You drove to Valley Forge on this bitter night?

DEBORAH: I did, Father.

ELIJAH (*Taking his coat from hook and putting it on*): So it's Mrs. Nathan Merriman, is it? (*He reaches into coat pocket, takes miniature from it, and places on table.*) I won't be needing this miniature of your lovely self, then. (*With sly malice*) As for your marriage, it might not be a long one.

DEBORAH (*Coldly*): Indeed?

ELIJAH: Indeed! I know a thing or two concerning Nathan Merriman.

MRS. HEATHER: What do you mean, Elijah?

ELIJAH (*Going to door*): Time will tell. And, Mistress Deborah, it's only my regard for your father and mother that prevents me from prosecuting you for stealing my coach.

DEBORAH (*Lightly*): Thank you, sir.

ELIJAH (*Opening door*): Aye, I know a thing or two about Nathan Merriman. (*Sharply*) Good night. (*Exits*)

GRANDMA (*Chuckling*): And I know a thing or two or three or four about you.

MRS. HEATHER (*Shrugging shoulders*): This is all a mystery to me. If you wanted Nathan enough to steal a stage and drive ten miles to him, there's nothing left to say. (DEBORAH *hugs her mother affectionately.*)

DEBORAH: I know I've done the right thing, Mother. Don't you worry.

MR. HEATHER: At least you're back safe. (*Sternly*) I may have more to say about this in the morning.

GRANDMA (*Smiling*): I'm sure you will.

MR. HEATHER (*Yawning*): But now it's time all of us were in bed. Come, Martha. (MR. *and* MRS. HEATHER *exit.* DEBORAH *rushes to* GRANDMA, *as does* KATHLEEN. GRANDMA *hugs* DEBORAH.)

GRANDMA: Bravely done, child. Is everything safe now for Nathan?

DEBORAH: Yes, Grandma. The plans will be delivered, but Elijah will never know it.

KATHLEEN: Congratulations, Miss Deborah, on your marriage.

DEBORAH: Isn't it wonderful, Kathleen! I'm so happy. Nathan said there was no sense in wasting a good opportunity with Parson Ames on hand.

GRANDMA: Did you see General Washington?

DEBORAH: Indeed, I did. He attended the wedding ceremony. He's so kind. He called me his little apple-cheeked patriot and said that my ride tonight might prove as important as Mr. Paul Revere's two years ago. (*Sadly*) But oh, Grandma, the men are suffering so at Valley Forge. The General tries to keep cheerful, and keep up the spirits of his men.

GRANDMA: Of course.

DEBORAH: I told the General all about you, Grandma. (*She reaches into her cloak.*) And he gave me this letter for you. (DEBORAH *hands the letter to* GRANDMA, *who opens it with trembling fingers.*)

GRANDMA (*Amazed*): A letter for me from the General?

DEBORAH: Yes, Grandma.

KATHLEEN: Now will wonders never cease! Oh, do read it to us, ma'am!

GRANDMA (*Her voice shaking*): "My dear Grandma—"

KATHLEEN: Grandma, indeed. Why, how human the General is!

GRANDMA: "Your granddaughter, a brave girl, has made it known to me what a loyal and steadfast admirer I have in you. Although I am unworthy of such admiration, please believe that it is faith such as yours that gives me strength to go on in the arduous tasks that I consider to be my duty and privilege. So long as such loyal spirits as yours light the way through the darkness, our cause will not be lost, and freedom will be won. Your obedient and grateful servant, George Washington." (GRANDMA *wipes the tears from her eyes.*)

KATHLEEN: 'Tis beautiful, that's what it is!

DEBORAH: It's a lovely letter, Grandma.

GRANDMA: He has made a foolish old woman very happy. (*She wipes her eyes again, recovers herself, and then smiles broadly.*) Kathleen, sit here. (*Points to footstool*) It's not too late for our lessons. (KATHLEEN *sits.* DEBORAH *remains standing beside rocker.*) Now, what is freedom, child?

KATHLEEN (*Smiling happily*): Freedom, ma'am, is the right to think and act as you believe, provided that you do not hamper the freedom of others in doing so.

GRANDMA (*Also smiling*): And who is the greatest fighter for freedom?

KATHLEEN: General George Washington, bless him!

GRANDMA: And now—and I want you to answer too, Deborah— who is the finest man in the land?

KATHLEEN *and* DEBORAH: General George Washington! (*All laugh happily.* KATHLEEN *rises from footstool, and both she and* DEBORAH *hug* GRANDMA.)

THE END

Prelude to Victory

by Graham Du Bois

A suspected spy in the American Revolution surprises patriots and redcoats. . . .

Characters

GRANNY WITHERS
SARAH WITHERS ⎫
CLARA JOHNSON ⎭ *her daughters*
ROBERT WITHERS, *her husband*
DICK JOHNSON, *Clara's husband*
TOMMY, *Johnsons' son*
LIEUTENANT PIEL, *Hessian officer*
GENERAL GEORGE WASHINGTON

TIME: *Christmas night, 1776.*
SETTING: *Living room of a house in Trenton, New Jersey. Door up center, and window, up right center, open on street. Coat rack is up left center. Table with chairs is down center. Door left center leads to bedroom; door up right center leads to kitchen. Down right center is open fireplace, before which is an armchair.*
AT RISE: CLARA JOHNSON *is standing at window.* GRANNY WITHERS *and* SARAH WITHERS *sit at table.*

254

SARAH: Clara, there's no use standing there.

CLARA: I suppose not. (*Sighs*) What a fool I was to let Tommy go out on a night like this! (*Turns away from window, disappointed*) How could I expect him to find his father? (*Sits at table*)

GRANNY: You were a goose to believe your husband—or any of Washington's men—could get through this town tonight. The streets are full of Hessians.

CLARA: I know, Mother, but Dick promised to spend at least part of Christmas night with us.

GRANNY: The more fool he was to make a promise he couldn't keep. Doesn't he know there's a price on his head?

CLARA: He knows that well enough, but he thought with the Hessians reveling tonight, he might get through.

GRANNY: Well, you should have let your father go when he offered, instead of sending Tommy out.

SARAH: Father could hardly stand against this raging blizzard. And he looked especially tired tonight.

GRANNY: Well, Dick certainly won't get here tonight, so we might as well all go to bed and get some sleep.

CLARA: I can't go to bed until Tommy gets home—and besides, how can anyone sleep tonight, with all those carousing Hessians about? (*Rises and goes to window*) There's not a patriot's home in Trenton that's safe tonight. (TOMMY *enters center.* CLARA *turns and, relieved, rushes to hug him.*) Tommy! I'm so glad you're home! Did you find out anything?

TOMMY (*Hanging coat and cap on rack*): No, but I saw Grandpa.

SARAH: That's impossible! He's in bed.

TOMMY (*Crossing to fireplace*): He wasn't in bed when I saw him. He was talking to the Hessians. (*Warms hands at fire*)

GRANNY (*Sharply*): This is no time for jokes, Tommy.

TOMMY (*Insistently*): But I *did* see him, Granny.

CLARA: I'll look in Father's room and see. (*Exits left*)

SARAH (*Ironically; to* TOMMY): And I suppose that in all this snow, Grandpa was swapping stories with those bloodthirsty hirelings?

TOMMY: No, he was just standing there on King Street, near the tavern.

SARAH: Did you speak to him?

TOMMY: Of course!

GRANNY: What did he say?

TOMMY: He acted funny. He didn't even look at me. He made believe he was deaf, the way he always does when he doesn't want to hear something. (CLARA re-enters, upset.)

CLARA: He's not there. His bed hasn't been touched, and the window was half open. I closed and fastened it. (Sits at table)

SARAH (To TOMMY): Are you sure it was really Grandfather you saw?

TOMMY (Angrily): I guess I know my own grandfather when I see him! The light from the tavern was shining right on him. I was so close to him that when I ducked behind the fence, I could even hear what they were saying.

GRANNY: What were they saying?

TOMMY: Well, first I heard the Hessians thank Grandfather for the basket he gave them.

SARAH: What basket? What was in it?

TOMMY: I couldn't see everything with all the snow, but there was a turkey and some apples in it, and . . .

SARAH (Breaking in): That's one mystery solved.

CLARA: What do you mean?

SARAH: Our apple barrel was getting pretty low, and the potatoes weren't lasting as long as usual. And the big gobbler I've been fattening—he was missing this morning. (Angrily) To think that my own father would take food out of the mouths of his family to feed those barbarians!

GRANNY: You talk as if we were starving, Sarah. Don't take it so seriously.

CLARA (Slowly): I'm afraid it is serious, Mother. It's a very serious matter to give aid and comfort to the enemy.

GRANNY (Tensely): Tommy, tell us what you heard.

TOMMY: I heard one Hessian colonel ask Grandpa about General Washington's army.

SARAH (Upset): That's terrible! What did he tell them?

TOMMY: I couldn't catch it all, but whatever he said must have pleased that Colonel, 'cause he laughed, slapped Grandpa on the back, and said, "That miserable rabble's too weak to whip a regiment of children."

CLARA: And then what happened?

TOMMY: I sneezed, and I was afraid they'd catch me, so I ran home as fast as I could.

CLARA (*Sighing*): You must be very tired, Tommy. You'd best go to bed now. We'll wait up for Grandpa.

TOMMY (*Yawning*): I do feel pretty sleepy. Good night. (*Exits left*)

CLARA (*To* SARAH): What do you make of all this? You know it's not the first time Father's been seen with those Hessians. The neighbors are beginning to talk.

GRANNY (*Tartly*): Meddlesome busybodies!

SARAH (*Sighing*): I'm afraid Father has some misguided notion about being generous to those miserable Hessians.

CLARA: I'm afraid it's not so simple. I wish it were only kindness that makes him carry on this way.

GRANNY (*Sharply*): What's on your mind, Clara? Out with it! I've had enough of your insinuations. You think your father's some kind of spy, or traitor, is that it?

CLARA: I wouldn't put it just that way, Mother. But after all, Father was born in England, and—

GRANNY (*Angrily*): And because of that you think he would betray the country he came to of his own free will? Well, let me tell you this: There's no more devoted patriot in America than your father!

SARAH: Maybe you are a bit hasty, Clara. Father is getting old and perhaps he talks too much, but there's no evil motive behind what he does.

CLARA: I'm not so sure.

SARAH (*Angrily*): What do you mean?

CLARA: He never liked Dick, you know.

GRANNY: What has that to do with it?

CLARA: Father never wanted me to marry Dick. I think that if he could deliver Dick into the hands of the Hessians, he would jump at the chance. Don't you suppose he would persuade himself that it was his duty to the King?

GRANNY: He recognizes no king except his conscience. He serves no country except these colonies. (*Suddenly; listening*) I think I heard the gate shut.

SARAH: I guess it's just blowing in the wind.

CLARA: No; there's somebody on the porch. (*Stamping of feet is heard.*) Could it be Dick? (*Rises nervously; doorknob turns.*)

GRANNY: Maybe it's your father. (*There is a knock on door.*)

CLARA (*Crossing to door*): I'll see who it is.

SARAH: Be careful! (CLARA *unbolts door, opens it a crack, and peeps out.*)

CLARA (*Startled*): Father! (ROBERT WITHERS *enters. He is covered with snow, obviously cold and weary.*) Where in the world have you been on a night like this? (*Closes door and bolts it*)

WITHERS (*Stamping his feet and rubbing his hands together*): Haven't seen this much snow in years. (*Takes off coat and hat and hangs them on rack*)

GRANNY: What were you doing out there, Robert? (WITHERS *crosses to armchair near fire and sits.*)

CLARA (*Before he can answer*): Have you seen Dick? Do you know where he is?

WITHERS (*Cupping ear with hand*): What say?

CLARA (*Shouting*): Dick, I said. Dick!

WITHERS: No, I'm not sick. Never felt better in my life.

SARAH: Father's just being stubborn. He can hear as well as I. (*To* WITHERS) I'd like to know about that basket.

WITHERS (*Cupping ear*): How's that?

SARAH (*Shouting*): What became of the basket?

WITHERS: Ask it? Ask what?

SARAH: What happened to that turkey?

WITHERS: Can't hear you. Speak louder.

SARAH (*Shouting*): Didn't you give a turkey to the Hessians?

WITHERS: No, no, the Hessians don't come from Turkey; they come from Germany.

SARAH: This is maddening. Every time he has been with the Hessians he pretends he can't hear. (*Rises and goes to* WITHERS) Father, it's very late. Don't you think you'd better go to bed?

WITHERS: Go to bed yourself. I'm staying up.

SARAH: What for?

WITHERS: I'm expecting a guest.

GRANNY: A guest at this hour? Don't you realize it's after midnight?

WITHERS (*Cupping his ear*): What's that you're saying?

SARAH (*Shaking her head*): It's no use. He'll tell us only what he wants to tell us. (*Goes back to chair*)

WITHERS: Why don't you women go to bed? This isn't the time to be a-setting around gabbing.

GRANNY (*To* SARAH *and* CLARA): We might as well.

CLARA: Not I! This may be a trap for Dick.

SARAH: I won't budge. We can't afford to lose any more food. (*Knocking at door*)

WITHERS (*Rising*): That must be my guest now. (*To* CLARA) I have a surprise for *you*. (*Knocking on door is repeated.* WITHERS *crosses to door.*)

LIEUTENANT PIEL (*From off*): Open in the name of the King.

SARAH (*Rising, terrified*): It's the Hessians!

WITHERS (*Calling through door*): What's the password?

CLARA (*Alarmed*): Father's asking the Hessians for a password! I guess what the neighbors are saying is true: He's working for the Redcoats. (*Knocking is repeated.*)

PIEL (*From off*): Open this door at once in the name of the King.

WITHERS: First, the password.

PIEL (*From off*): "Gunpowder."

WITHERS (*Unbolting door*): "Gunpowder," it is. (*Opens door, and* PIEL *enters*) Lieutenant Piel, this is an unexpected pleasure. Will you take your coat off and hang it over on the rack? (*Points to rack.* PIEL *hangs hat and coat on rack.*) Let me introduce you to my wife (*Points to* GRANNY) and to my daughters. (*Points to* CLARA *and* SARAH)

GRANNY: Good day. (CLARA *and* SARAH *nod coldly, and* PIEL *bows stiffly.*) Now, Lieutenant, have a chair. (PIEL *sits in chair near* WITHERS.)

PIEL: Thank you. I have only a minute. I bring you a message from Colonel Rahl.

WITHERS (*Looking nervously at women*): Shall the ladies withdraw?

PIEL: No; I prefer that they remain. What I have to say should be a warning to them. . . . We have just captured one of Washington's men. (*Women eye one another nervously.*)

WITHERS: You have? How did he get across the river? It's filled with blocks of ice. And all the bridges are carefully guarded.

PIEL: It's of no consequence how he crossed. What is important is the information we got from him.

WITHERS: Made him talk, did you?

PIEL: We certainly did. It was from him that we learned Captain Johnson planned to visit this house tonight.

WITHERS: What? Why, that would be madness.

PIEL (*Leaning toward* WITHERS): Can we have your assurance that he has not already arrived?

WITHERS: You can.

PIEL: We know that we can trust you, Mr. Withers. But the Colonel told me he had talked with you on the street only a short while ago. Isn't it possible that Johnson could have come in your absence—that he is here now?

WITHERS: Not likely. (*Rises and walks to door left*) I'll look through the house.

PIEL: Good. And in the meanwhile I have a word for these ladies. (WITHERS *exits left.*) I hope you realize the danger you run by sheltering a spy. If he should come here, you must report at once to headquarters. (*Noise is heard at door.*) What's that? (*Rises*) There's somebody fumbling with that lock. (*Crosses to door and opens it*) Come in, whoever you are. (DICK, *disguised as a peddler, enters. He wears spectacles and a wig and carries a wooden tray suspended by straps from his shoulders. In the tray are packages of needles, pins, spools of thread, etc.*)

DICK (*Obviously perturbed at seeing* PIEL *but quickly regaining his composure*): Can you spare a poor man food and shelter? It's bitter cold, and I am half starved. (*To women*) Pins? Needles? Thread?

PIEL: Who is this man?

CLARA: I don't know.

SARAH: I never saw him before; but we can't turn him out in this storm. We have soup on the stove in the kitchen.

DICK: Bless you, lady. (*Showing his wares*) I'll give you a present. Help yourself to a pack of needles or a spool of thread.

SARAH: No, poor fellow. You must keep what you have.

PIEL (*Suspiciously, to* DICK): Where did you come from, and what are you doing here?

DICK: I'm just a poor man trying to make an honest living selling odds and ends. I was caught in the storm. I live out on the Princeton road.

PIEL: You seem pretty at home here—enough at least to fumble with that lock. (*Sarcastically*) Do you have a key, too?

DICK: No. I guess my hand was so cold I couldn't knock, and so I just turned the knob. (*To* CLARA) I can't take anything without paying for it. (*Hands her a spool of thread*) Won't you please take this thread?

CLARA (*Taking thread and looking closely at him*): Thank you. And now if you'll come to the kitchen, I'll give you a bowl of soup. (*Walk toward kitchen door*)

PIEL: Stay where you are! (*To* CLARA) I'll keep an eye on this man until I know who he is. If he's hungry, I'll go to the kitchen with him. I'll search him there. As soon as Mr. Withers returns he may be able to identify him. If not, I'll have him locked up for investigation. (*Leads* DICK *off*)

CLARA (*Crossing to chair and sitting*): Father mustn't see him.

SARAH (*Puzzled*): Why not? I don't believe Father knows him, and even if he does—

CLARA: Didn't you recognize him through that disguise?

SARAH: What do you mean?

CLARA (*Impatiently*): That peddler is Dick!

SARAH (*Incredulous*): Are you sure?

CLARA: Don't you think I'd recognize my own husband? And when he gave me the spool of thread, he pressed my hand. (*Puts thread on table*) It was a signal for help—I know it!

GRANNY: What can three defenseless women do to help him?

CLARA (*Desperately*): Mother, we can't leave him to the mercy of the Hessians! You know what that would mean—death as a spy! (*Rising*) There's only one way to save him.

SARAH: And what is that?

CLARA (*Slowly*): Father must not identify him.

GRANNY (*Angrily*): I tell you, Clara, you will be sorry some day for judging your father so harshly.

CLARA: I'm not taking any chances with Dick's life at stake. I'm going to beg Father . . . (*Starts toward door left*)

GRANNY (*Interrupting*): Wait, Clara. (CLARA *pauses at door.*) If that man knows you've been talking to Father, he will suspect all of us. You'll be doing Dick more harm than good. (WITHERS *enters.*)

WITHERS: Not a sign of him. I've searched every nook and cranny in the house. (*Suddenly*) Why, where's Lieutenant Piel? (PIEL *enters, as* WITHERS *speaks.*)

PIEL: Here I am, Mr. Withers. (DICK *enters.*)

DICK (*Seeing* WITHERS): Fine needles, sir? Want any pins or thread? Here's some strong enough to hang General Washington.

PIEL: Be quiet! (*To* WITHERS) Do you recognize this peddler? (WITHERS *crosses room and studies* DICK *briefly.*)

WITHERS (*Laughing*): Recognize him? I should say I do!

PIEL: Who is he, then?

CLARA (*Rising, anxiously*): Father!

WITHERS: Why, that's poor old Isaac Selden. A bit befuddled, to be sure, but as harmless as a kitten. I reckon you've scared the poor soul half to death.

PIEL (*Pompously*): Well, I have to take every precaution. The colonel will hold me responsible.

WITHERS: I thought everyone around knew Ike. He's always hanging around the soldiers trying to sell them needles or pins. It's a good thing I was here, Lieutenant, or you'd have locked him up, and they'd all certainly have had a good laugh on you.

PIEL (*Sheepishly*): I figured all along the poor old chap was probably harmless, but I had to be sure.

WITHERS: Quite right. In these times, people have to be suspicious even of their own kin. (*Glances knowingly at* CLARA)

PIEL: I'll be getting back to headquarters. Keep your eyes open, and if you have any word of Johnson, notify us at once.

WITHERS: I can assure you, Lieutenant, that he'll not be in this town very long before you will know it.

PIEL: Good. (*Takes coat and hat from rack and puts them on*) I'll bid you good night. (*Bows stiffly to women and exits*)

WITHERS (*Crossing to window*): He's making tracks to headquarters in a hurry. (*Turns, addresses* CLARA) Well, Clara, here's the surprise I promised you.

CLARA (*Going to* DICK *and embracing him*): Oh, Dick, I was weak with fright.

DICK: Everything will be all right, Clara. (*He removes wig, spectacles, and tray, and sits near* WITHERS.) That was certainly a close call. I could almost feel a noose about my neck. (*To* WITHERS) I owe my life to you, Mr. Withers.

WITHERS: It was nothing, Dick. Just a little quick thinking. . . . So—tell us the news. How are things going?

DICK: Like clockwork so far. The information you brought us this morning was the determining factor. General Washington decided to strike at once.

SARAH (*Puzzled*): I don't understand.

CLARA: You mean to say that Father has been serving *our* cause?

DICK: He certainly has, and serving it so well that the success of this whole venture depends on him.

GRANNY: What venture?

DICK: General Washington is planning to cross the Delaware.

CLARA (*In disbelief*): In this storm?

DICK (*Nodding*): At this very moment. Any time now you may hear his guns in the streets.

SARAH: But the river is a mass of floating ice. His boats will be smashed to pieces.

DICK (*Proudly*): The General will get through somehow. He always does. And Mr. Withers and I are waiting here to guide the troops as soon as we hear the first shots.

WOMEN (*Ad lib*): Guide the troops? Where? (*Etc. Suddenly, stamping of feet is heard, then pounding on door.*)

SARAH: Who can that be now?

PIEL (*Off*): Let me in! Open this door!

CLARA: Quick! It's Lieutenant Piel again! (*Urgently*) Father! Dick! Get into the bedroom. I'll try to hold him off as long as possible. (DICK *takes wig, glasses, and tray and exits, followed by* WITHERS. *Knocking on door is repeated.*)

PIEL (*Off*): Open this door! In the King's name, I say, let me in.

CLARA: Let us all keep our heads about us, and pray that General Washington will not be too late. (*Crosses to door and opens it*) Why, come in, Lieutenant Piel. It didn't take you long to get back from headquarters.

PIEL (*Agitated*): I never got to headquarters. (*Angrily*) I met Colonel Rahl, and he told me that your father has been duping us for months. I know he's in this house, and he can't escape my men. We have the place surrounded. You might as well give him up, or else I'll have to search the house. (CLARA *walks slowly back to her chair, sits.*)

CLARA (*Calmly*): You are most welcome to search the house, Lieutenant. (*Others sit.*)

PIEL (*Crossing to door left*): I'll start with the bedroom. (*As he opens door,* WITHERS, *disguised as peddler, enters.*) You're still here, old man?

WITHERS: Fine pins, sharp needles, strong thread. Won't you buy something from poor old Ike?

PIEL: Out of here, you wretch, before I kick you out! (PIEL *exits left*; WITHERS *exits center.*)

CLARA (*Relieved*): Thank heavens Dick got away, but how can Father escape?

PIEL (*Coming back into doorway and speaking to someone behind him*): You'd better come along now. The game's up. No use your looking out the window. I have two men stationed just outside it.

CLARA (*Rising and walking toward* PIEL): My father's an old man. You can't arrest him.

PIEL: It's not your father I've taken. I have a bigger prize—a man we've been after for months. Colonel Rahl will be delighted. Come on, Captain Johnson. (*Enters, followed by* DICK)

CLARA (*Amazed*): Dick! Why, only a moment ago I saw you—

DICK (*Shaking his head to silence her*): Never mind, dear. Remember what I told you: we shan't have long to wait.

PIEL: No, Captain; I promise you a speedy trial and prompt justice. (*Sound of firing in the distance*) What's that?

DICK: I suspect, Lieutenant, that our troops will be having a little celebration of their own.

PIEL (*Scornfully*): A few miserable scouts, I suppose. Our outposts will deal with them in a hurry. (*Sound of firing gets closer.* CLARA *runs to window and looks out.*)

CLARA: Dick! Washington has crossed the river. His men are swarming through the streets. They are driving the Hessians before them.

DICK (*To* PIEL): It looks as though our positions have been reversed, Lieutenant: you are now my prisoner.

PIEL: Not so fast, Captain. You forget that our regiments are made up of men long trained in the art of war.

DICK (*Grabbing* PIEL's *arm*): And you don't know that General Washington has thrown a cordon around the house. You have no chance of escaping. (WASHINGTON *enters, followed by* WITHERS, *still disguised as peddler.*)

CLARA: General Washington!

WASHINGTON (*Bowing*): My compliments, madam, and my congratulations to you and your husband and your father here. (*Lays hand on* WITHERS' *arm*)

WITHERS (*Cupping his ear toward* CLARA): What's that? I can't hear you. Speak louder!

CLARA: Father! You mean—

WITHERS (*Removing wig and spectacles*): Kind of surprised, aren't you, Clara? Well, you aren't half as surprised as the Lieutenant over there. Had to get out of here somehow, you know. Dick insisted I put on the disguise, and the Lieutenant literally kicked me out. Very obliging of him.

DICK (*Leading* PIEL *to* WASHINGTON): General Washington, I have taken this prisoner. Lieutenant Piel.

WASHINGTON: Captain, please escort the Lieutenant to the rear. I shall deal with him later.

DICK: At once, sir. (*Salutes and exits with* PIEL)

CLARA: Won't you sit down, General?

WASHINGTON: No, thank you. I cannot stay. We must press on. Greater battles lie ahead. This is but a prelude to victory. (*Turns and exits, as curtain falls*)

THE END

Attic Treasure

by Jean Gould

George Washington sets a good example for a modern young boy. . . .

Characters

TOD
TIM
BILLY
MRS. TAYLOR
JIMMY, *Billy's friend*

SETTING: *The attic of the Taylor home.*

AT RISE: TOD, TIM *and* BILLY *are just entering the attic.*

TOD: I'm glad you thought of this, Tim. There's no place to play that's as nice as an attic on a rainy Saturday.

TIM: I know; attics are so cozy when it's raining.

BILLY: They smell dusty, and full of secrets.

TOD (*Laughing*): Well, I don't think we'll find any secrets here. We've explored this attic a hundred times.

TIM (*Who has been looking around, and now starts upstage, stopping in front of a little trunk resting against the rear wall*): I don't know about that! Here's a little old trunk I never saw before.

266

TOD (*Coming close to investigate,* BILLY *following*): Hey! I never saw it before, either.

BILLY: Neither did I!

TOD: Gosh, it looks old; wonder where it came from?

BILLY: Maybe it's a pirate's chest.

TIM: Sure, some pirate came in and left it here since the last time we came up, just like that.

BILLY: Well, you can't tell. Maybe the trunk was here all the time, only we never noticed it before.

TIM: We couldn't have missed it, silly.

TOD (*Who has been searching around, pointing to a key hanging on the wall above the trunk*): Hey, fellas, look at this key! I'll bet it fits the trunk!

TIM: Let's try it!

TOD (*Taking down the key and inserting it in the lock*): Perfect . . . the lid's opening!

TIM and BILLY: Oh, boy! (TOD *throws open the lid of the trunk, and the three boys bend over the contents.*)

TOD: Well, what . . .

BILLY: I smell moth balls. (TOD *takes out tissue paper wrappings, then a three-cornered hat, a pair of black breeches with buckles and a white shirt with long cuffs and a frill in front. Finally he pulls out a faded blue coat with gold epaulettes. The boys stare at each other.*)

TOD (*Trying on the hat and coat*): This looks like a George Washington costume.

TIM: I wonder whose it was?

BILLY: I'll ask Mother. (*Calling downstairs*) Mother, mother! Come see what we found.

MRS. TAYLOR (*Entering from right after a moment*): What is it, boys?

TOD: We just found this old George Washington costume. Did Dad wear it to a costume party?

MRS. TAYLOR (*Shaking her head, smiling*): That isn't a costume, Tod. It's a uniform that belonged to your great-great-great grandfather who lived in George Washington's day; he was with our first President at Valley Forge.

Boys (*Ad lib*): He was? Wow! (*Etc.* TIM *and* BILLY *touch the epaulettes curiously, reverently.*)

BILLY: How did it get here all of a sudden?

MRS. TAYLOR: Grandma sent the trunk here last week. I meant to show it to you boys when you came home from school, but I've been so busy I forgot about it. You'd better take those things off now, Tod.

TOD: O.K.

MRS. TAYLOR (*Helping him remove the coat*): We must put the clothes back right away. They are very valuable because they are so old. Your father and I thought we would give them to the Smithsonian in Washington, where all kinds of keepsakes in American history are stored. (*Begins putting the things back in the trunk*)

BILLY (*Wonderingly*): Did our great-great-great grandfather really know George Washington?

MRS. TAYLOR (*Smiling*): That's right, Billy.

BILLY: Did George Washington really chop down the cherry tree, and then tell his father about it, like the story?

MRS. TAYLOR: We don't know. George Washington was a very honest man; and the story of the cherry tree is probably a legend or story told to show us that he always spoke the truth, even when he knew he might be punished. Now, boys, you'd better find something else to play with. I don't want anything to happen to these. (*Shuts and locks the lid, replacing the key*) They're our treasure!

TIM: The rain's almost stopped anyhow. Let's see if we can get the team together for a little practice, Tod.

TOD: Good idea.

BILLY: I'm going to find Jimmy. Maybe he'll come back here.

MRS. TAYLOR: We'll all go down together. (*All exit right. A minute or two later* BILLY *enters with* JIMMY.)

BILLY: Bet you can't guess what we've got in our attic, Jimmy.

JIMMY: What is it? What have you got up here?

BILLY (*Impressively*): An old, old uniform my great-great-great grandfather wore when he was with George Washington at Valley Forge.

JIMMY (*Skeptically*): Sure, Billy.

BILLY: Honest. He really was there. Mother told us Grandma sent the trunk with the uniform last week.

JIMMY: Let's see the uniform!

BILLY (*Excited*): Sure, I'll show it to you! Come on. (*He runs to the trunk at rear, takes down the key and opens the trunk, pulling the uniform out quickly.*) There! What did I tell you?

JIMMY (*Impressed, examining the coat*): That's neat, all right. Look at the brass buttons! Look at the shoulders! Try it on, Billy.

BILLY (*Forgetting what his mother has said*): O.K. You try on the hat. (*They put on the things; the coat falls nearly to* BILLY'S *ankles.*)

JIMMY: Let's pretend we're at Valley Forge! We're cold and hungry.

BILLY: Yes, let's! (*Wrapping his arms around his chest, clapping his hands against his shoulders*) Brrr! I'm freezing to death! If we only had more firewood.

JIMMY: If we only had more food! I'm starving to death. All the men are!

BILLY: I will go out and try to find some food! (*He starts to run, but trips and falls.*) Oops! (*He sits up, rubbing his knee, notices that one of the coattails has torn.*) Oh . . . I ripped the coat! (*Suddenly remembering, putting his hand over his mouth*) Oh-oh, I just remembered!

JIMMY: What?

BILLY: Mother said we shouldn't play with the clothes. They're valuable. She was so careful putting them away. Ohh! What'll we do?

JIMMY (*Examining the tear*): Let's see. (*Hopefully*) It's only a little teeny tear. Maybe it will never be noticed. (*They put the things away very carefully, lock the trunk and hang up the key.*)

BILLY: I don't feel like playing in the attic any more, do you?

JIMMY: No . . . I think I'd better go home.

BILLY: Let's go outside. (*They exit. Shortly after* MRS. TAYLOR *enters.*)

MRS. TAYLOR: Guess I might as well get those things off to the Smithsonian right away. Then nothing can happen to them. (*Takes down the key, opens the trunk, lifts out the uniform and notices the ripped coattail.*) What? I didn't see this before. (*Goes to exit right and calls*) Tod! Tim! Billy!

TOD (*Offstage*): What is it, Mother?

MRS. TAYLOR: Come up to the attic a moment, please. All of you. (*After a moment, the boys enter,* BILLY *slowly following his older brothers.*)

TOD: Mom, the team is downstairs.

MRS. TAYLOR: Well, they'll have to wait. (*Holding up the coattail*) Just look at this! (TOD *and* TIM *bend over it,* BILLY *hangs back.*) I may have caught it on the trunk lid when I put the coat away, but I don't remember anything like that happening.

TOD: I don't either.

MRS. TAYLOR: Do any of you know anything about it?

TOD *and* TIM (*Shaking their heads*): No, Mother. (BILLY *is silent.*)

MRS. TAYLOR (*Turning to him*): Billy?

BILLY (*Starts to shake his head, too, but hesitates, then steps in front of* TOD *and* TIM): I tore the coat, Mother.

MRS. TAYLOR (*Amazed*): You did? But how, Billy?

BILLY (*Blurting it out*): Jimmy and I were playing "Valley Forge"—I forgot what you told us. I tripped . . . over the curtain rod . . . and . . . (*He stops, watching his mother's face.*)

MRS. TAYLOR (*Thoughtfully*): I'm sorry you and Jimmy were so careless, Billy. But I'd be a lot sorrier if you hadn't told me how this happened.

BILLY (*Surprised*): Gee, you're not angry?

MRS. TAYLOR (*Smiling*): Now go back and play while I see if I can mend it! (TOD *and* TIM *exit.* BILLY, *about to follow, smiles at* MRS. TAYLOR.)

BILLY: Thanks, Mother. I guess George Washington had the right idea. I'd feel pretty bad if I hadn't told the truth about that coat!

MRS. TAYLOR (*Returning his smile*): So would I!

THE END

Cinder-Riley

by *Claire Boiko*

Cinderella in Ireland gives a hilarious twist to this old favorite. . . .

Characters

LEPRECHAUN
CINDER-RILEY
THE STEPMOTHER
AGGIE ⎫ *stepsisters*
MAGGIE ⎭
FAIRY GODMOTHER
JACK O'CLOCK
DANCERS
STAGE HANDS

BEFORE RISE: *Music of a lively Irish jig is heard. While music plays,* LEPRECHAUN, *carrying a stick, pokes his head through curtain opening. Turns his head to one side, then to the other, then leaps out and sits cross-legged on apron of stage. Music stops.*

LEPRECHAUN: Well now, it's a fine audience ye are! We have a grand play for you to watch this day. 'Tis the old Hibernian legend, "Prince Cinder-Riley," or "The Lost Brogan." Our ac-

271

tors are guaranteed to make you split your sides with laughter one minute, and cry your way through three handkerchiefs the next! But first, we'll need your cooperation. In order to make the play begin, we'll need some loud clapping. This clears the air for the actors. Now, would you mind applauding, please? (*He taps his stock, and all applaud. Curtains open.*)

* * *

SETTING: *Stage is bare. Backdrop is hung with drawing of large knives, forks, spoons and skillets.*

AT RISE: TWO STAGE HANDS *carry in large screen, which they set at center. They walk behind screen, so they are not seen and remain there. Table covered with cloth reaching to floor is "walked" on-stage by* FAIRY GODMOTHER *and* STAGE HAND, *who are hidden beneath it, giving magical effect of a walking table. On table are pile of papers, quill pen, and inkstand.*

LEPRECHAUN (*Holding up hand to stop applause*): Sure, that was fine! Now, just applaud a bit more, and our actors will come out and begin the play. Ready? Let's clap for the Princess Cinder-Riley, her wicked stepmother, and her two disgustin' stepsisters. (*He taps stick again. All applaud.* STEPMOTHER, AGGIE, *and* MAGGIE *enter, noses in the air. They are followed by* CINDER-RILEY, *who wears long gown, crown, and silver slippers.* CINDER-RILEY *is crying.*)

STEPMOTHER: Now, Princess Cinder-Riley, it's no good cryin' at all, at all! You must keep to the schedule. Riding lesson at two o'clock. Music lesson at three. Etiquette lesson at four. Dancing lesson at five. And at six, the royal state banquet with the Duke of Downderrydown, the Earl of Earlyrise and your betrothed, the King of West Muffinland!

CINDER-RILEY: Must I, Stepmother? Oh, please don't make me marry the King of West Muffinland! He has turned-up toes and a wart on his nose, and he's as dull as dishwater!

AGGIE *and* MAGGIE (*Linking arms and dancing around mockingly*): Ha! Ha! Cinder-Riley's going to marry the King of West Muffinland!

AGGIE: With turned-up toes!

MAGGIE: And a wart on his nose!

AGGIE *and* MAGGIE (*Together*): And as dull as dishwater!

STEPMOTHER: Now, don't carry on so, Cinder-Riley. After all, you are a princess, and princesses must marry kings. I shall see to it that you do! Now, you must send out a proclamation that your stepsister Aggie shall marry the Duke of Downderrydown.

AGGIE: The Duke of Downderrydown—ah! He's so handsome!

STEPMOTHER: And your stepsister Maggie shall marry the Earl of Earlyrise.

MAGGIE: The Earl of Earlyrise—ah! He's so rich!

STEPMOTHER: And speaking of proclamations, here are thirty-three dozen more matters of proclamation to be signed before sundown. (*She points to papers on table.*) Come, girls, we must rest ourselves for the royal banquet this evening. Princess Cinder-Riley, I'd advise you to hustle your bustle if you wish to be finished before the sun goes down! (STEPMOTHER *exits.* AGGIE *and* MAGGIE *follow, noses in the air.* LEPRECHAUN *bounces to side and shouts "Boo," encouraging audience to do likewise. As* CINDER-RILEY *comes downstage, he puts finger to lips, shushing audience.*)

CINDER-RILEY: Alas! Alack! Sure, and woe is me! (*She sobs.* LEPRECHAUN *takes out large red hanky and pantomimes wiping away tears.*) I do not love the King of West Muffinland. Nay! Nay! A thousand times nay! I love handsome Jack O'Clock. But oh, bitter fortune, Jack O'Clock is only a kitchen boy. Would that I were a simple scullery maid. I would give all my satins, all my jewels, yes, my very crown itself, just to be a kitchen maid. For this is the night of the Pantry Frolic. All the lads and colleens who work in the kitchen will be dancing and singing. And Jack O'Clock, my own true love, will be crowned Prince of the Potatoes! I cannot be there. Oh, my heart is breaking!

FAIRY GODMOTHER (*Poking head out from under tablecloth*): Pssst! Cinder-Riley! (CINDER-RILEY *looks around, startled, sees* FAIRY GODMOTHER.)

CINDER-RILEY: My goodness! Who might you be? (GODMOTHER *steps out, dressed in kitchen outfit and carrying a broom and reticule.*)

GODMOTHER: Sure, I'm your fairy godmother, I am, I am. I've come to help you out of your miserable plight. Dry your tears, me pretty. We must be quick.

CINDER-RILEY: But, fairy godmother, I have thirty-three dozen matters of proclamation to sign before the sun goes down!

GODMOTHER: Pish posh! That's a simple thing for a fairy to fix. Here, now—just write your name in the air, whilst I wave me wand. (CINDER-RILEY *writes her name in air.* FAIRY GOD-MOTHER *waves broom as she chants.*)
Dimple-dee, dample-dee, dumple-dee dined
Proclamations—be ye signed!
(CINDER-RILEY *claps hands in amazement as she looks at papers.*)

CINDER-RILEY: Oh, how *marvelous!* They're all signed! 'Tis a miracle, to be sure!

GODMOTHER: Tonight you shall be a simple kitchen maid. First, you need a raggedy dress . . . aha! Me magic shears. (*Takes huge pair of shears from reticule, snips at* CINDER-RILEY'S *dress, turning it into a short gown with a ragged hem*) Now, a mob cap. (*She takes off her cap. Underneath it, she wears another cap*) And a sweet little apron. (*Takes off her own apron. There is another apron beneath it.*) Now you are all ready to go to the Pantry Frolic! (CINDER-RILEY *takes off crown, puts it on table. She puts on cap and apron, looks down at feet.*)

CINDER-RILEY: Ah—but my shoes!

GODMOTHER: Sure, I almost forgot. You need some nice comfortable brogans. You could never dance the night in those slippers. (*She takes off her own shoes. Underneath she wears another pair.* CINDER-RILEY *takes off her slippers, puts them on table, and puts on brogans.*) There is only one more thing, Cinder-Riley. You must be home at midnight. Are you ready now?

CINDER-RILEY: Indeed I am, Fairy Godmother. You've made me so happy!

GODMOTHER (*Waving broom*):
Rimple-dee, rample-dee, rumple-dee row
Bring us the Pantry Frolic now!

(STAGE HANDS *behind screen move it off so that it looks as though it is moving by itself.* STAGE HAND *under table moves it off. Music of Irish jig is heard.* DANCERS *enter, clapping hands to music and dancing a jig. When music stops,* JACK O'CLOCK *enters, dressed in tatters, with a crown of potatoes.* CINDER-RILEY *and* GODMOTHER *stand to one side, watching.*)

DANCERS:

Here's Jack O'Clock, let's give him a cheer,

He's the Potato Prince without a peer!

Hip, hip, Potato! Hip, hip, Potato!

  Hip, hip, Potato Prince!

(LEPRECHAUN *cheers and leads audience in cheers and applause for* JACK O'CLOCK. DANCERS *shout in unison.*) Lead us in a jig, Jack!

JACK: That I will! (*Piano begins jig,* DANCERS *freeze in pose.* JACK *spots* CINDER-RILEY, *holds up hand. Piano changes to "When Irish Eyes Are Smiling," which is played sentimentally throughout remainder of scene between* JACK *and* CINDER-RILEY.) Wait! Here's a colleen the like of whom I've never seen. She's as lovely as a May morning. 'Tis herself I shall dance with and none other. Come, me little flower. (GODMOTHER *exits, as* JACK O'CLOCK *and* CINDER-RILEY *dance together. At end of dance,* JACK *goes downstage, speaks in aside to audience.*) Me heart! Me heart is not in its rightful place! Sure, it's been stolen! Stolen by the maid with the raggedy dress. Dare I speak me deepest feelings to her? (LEPRECHAUN *nods eagerly.* CINDER-RILEY *crosses to other side, speaks in aside to audience, as she holds her hand on her heart.*)

CINDER-RILEY: My heart! My heart is beating like the drums in a marching band! Ah! He's so manly! Dare I speak my mind to him? (LEPRECHAUN *nods and takes* CINDER-RILEY *by hand; goes center, beckons to* JACK, *who joins them. He joins their hands, then holds his finger to his lips for silence.*)

JACK: Oh, lovely kitchen maid!

CINDER-RILEY: Oh, Jack! (*They strike a pose.* LEPRECHAUN *beams and claps hands, motioning audience to applaud, also. Chime sounds twelve times.*) Oh, dear! 'Tis midnight. I must go! (*On stroke of twelve, screen and table are walked back on again.*

GODMOTHER *is beneath table.* DANCERS *go behind screen.* CINDER-RILEY *leaves one shoe on stage, as she runs back near screen.* JACK *picks up shoe, scratches head, goes behind screen with shoe.* STEPMOTHER, AGGIE, *and* MAGGIE *enter, noses in air.*)

STEPMOTHER (*Horrified*): Princess Cinder-Riley, where in the great rollin' world were you this evening?

AGGIE: We looked hither and yon for you!

MAGGIE: And the King of West Muffinland was so angry, he popped three gold buttons off his coat!

STEPMOTHER: Cinder-Riley! What are you doing in that dreadful rag? Take off that apron! (*She snatches apron off* CINDER-RILEY.)

AGGIE: Put on your crown! (*Takes cap off* CINDER-RILEY'S *head and thrusts crown on*)

MAGGIE: Put on your slippers! (*Tosses slippers to* CINDER-RILEY, *who puts them on, hiding other brogan behind table*)

STEPMOTHER: And throw my cloak over that tattered dress! (*Puts cloak around* CINDER-RILEY'S *shoulders*) Foolish girl! You must prepare to marry the King of West Muffinland immediately!

CINDER-RILEY: Oh, no! Please! Wait! The marriage cannot be official unless there is a proclamation.

STEPMOTHER: I took care of the proclamation. It was in this great pile. You signed it yourself.

AGGIE *and* MAGGIE (*Together*): So there!

CINDER-RILEY: Oh, woe! Alas! 'Tis true. Oh, I shall fade away and die.

STEPMOTHER: Come, Cinder-Riley. (*Starts to lead her off.* JACK *comes out in front of screen, puts his hands up and shouts.*)

JACK: Wait! (*They turn and stare.* STEPMOTHER *eyes him icily.* CINDER-RILEY *sighs longingly.* LEPRECHAUN *signals for cheers, and fanfare is sounded.* JACK *bows.*) I beg your pardon, me ladies and Your Royal Highness, but I have a boon to ask ye.

CINDER-RILEY (*Aside*): Handsome Jack O'Clock. My own true love! (*To* JACK) Speak, young man, I command you.

JACK: I have in me hand a darlin' little brogan which a fair lass, the pride of my life, wore to the Pantry Frolic. And I swore to meself that I would not rest until I tried it on the foot of every maid in the kingdom.

AGGIE (*Giggling*): Oh, isn't he a fine lad! Let him try it on my foot! (JACK *puts brogan on* AGGIE's *foot. Toe of shoe is slit, so that her stocking, stuffed with cotton, protrudes visibly.*)

MAGGIE: You silly colleen! Your foot is the size of an elephant's! Here, young man—try my dainty foot! (JACK *puts shoe on her. The same thing happens.*)

JACK (*Sadly*): Well, I suppose that is that! Your ladyship is the last girl in the kingdom—except of course you, Your Highness. I suppose I shall never find my lost kitchen maid. (*He turns to go.*)

CINDER-RILEY: Wait! Try the shoe on my foot.

JACK: But, Your Highness!

CINDER-RILEY: Please.

JACK: Very well, but I hardly think the shoe could belong to Your Royal Highness. (*He slips shoe on* CINDER-RILEY. DANCERS *come from behind screen and cheer.*)

DANCERS (*Cheering*): Hip, hip, Potato Prince! (LEPRECHAUN *leaps up and down and leads cheers. All show astonishment, as* GODMOTHER *comes out from under table, slips cloak off* CINDER-RILEY, *and replaces the cap and apron.*)

JACK: Princess Cinder-Riley! You are me lost love!

STEPMOTHER: Lost love? The likes of you, Jack O'Clock, speakin' about the Princess Cinder-Riley as your lost love! What impudent nonsense! The princess is promised to the King of West Muffinland. It is officially proclaimed! (GODMOTHER *waves broom over papers.*)

GODMOTHER (*Stepping up and curtsying*): Begging your pardon, madam, but if you will examine this proclamation (*Picks up paper and waves it*) you will find that she is promised to someone quite different.

STEPMOTHER (*Snatching paper angrily*): Indeed! Let me read it! Why, I wrote the proclamation myself. I certainly should know what I have written! (*Righteously*) Ahem! (*Reads*) "Hear ye! Hear ye! The Princess Cinder-Riley is hereby promised in marriage to the Prince of Potatoes, Jack O'Clock." (*She stares at paper, astonished.*) All is lost!

GODMOTHER: And 'tis signed by the Princess' own hand. That makes it official. (LEPRECHAUN *cheers in pantomime.*)

STEPMOTHER: But what shall I tell the King of West Muffinland?

GODMOTHER: Dear me, the good King still needs a wife, does he not? (*Snaps fingers*) Ah! The very thing. Another proclamation. (*Hands one to* STEPMOTHER *with a flourish*)

STEPMOTHER: Ahem! (*Reading*) "To Whom It May Concern." (AGGIE *and* MAGGIE *peer over her shoulder to see better as she reads*) "The King of West Muffinland shall be married this morn to her ladyship, the former regent of the realm, stepmother of Princess Cinder-Riley." (*She screams.*) Oh, *no!*

AGGIE: And 'tis signed by Cinder-Riley's own hand!

MAGGIE: That makes it official!

STEPMOTHER (*Throwing up hands*): Oh, no! Oh, woe! He has turned-up toes and a wart on his nose.

AGGIE *and* MAGGIE (*Together*): And he's dull as dishwater!

STEPMOTHER: Help me, daughters, I am about to faint! (*She faints in their arms. They drag her offstage.*)

JACK: Come, Cinder-Riley, let us prepare for our joyous weddin'. Oh, happy day! (*"Wedding March" music is played, as they strike pose.*)

CINDER-RILEY: Yes, dear Jack. And you shall be my prince regent and the king of my heart, forever!

GODMOTHER: Faith, now, I've done a full day's work. I've banished the wicked stepmother and the disgustin' stepsisters; I've joined the lovers; and I've even found a wife for the King of West Muffinland. (*She strikes pose, as* LEPRECHAUN *steps up and shakes her hand. All form tableau, as* LEPRECHAUN *motions for applause. Fast jig is played. Curtains close.* LEPRECHAUN *turns his head from right to left, then waves goodbye and disappears.*)

THE END

Bunnies and Bonnets

by Jane McGowan

Easter egg "magic" saves a television Holiday Special. . . .

Characters

MISS AMBROSE, *receptionist*
MRS. MURPHY
FLOPSY ⎫
MOPSY ⎬ *her daughters, tap dancers*
COTTONTAIL ⎭
MRS. ROSS
PETER, *her son, a trumpeter*
MR. FULTON
OSWALD THE RABBIT, *his son, a one-man band*
MISS BLOSSOM, *dancing teacher*
THE BUNNY BALLET, *dancers*
THE WHITE RABBIT ⎫
ALICE ⎬ *mind readers*
MR. HUNTER, *a TV producer*
EASTER BUNNY

SETTING: *Waiting room in TV studio. Desk is left; benches are at rear.*
AT RISE: MRS. MURPHY *is talking to* MISS AMBROSE, *who sits at*

desk. MRS. MURPHY, FLOPSY, MOPSY, *and* COTTONTAIL *sit to-gether on bench.* PETER, *holding huge carrot, and* MRS. ROSS *sit on another bench.*

MRS. MURPHY (*Impatiently, to* MISS AMBROSE): Will you please tell Mr. Hunter that the Bunnyland Tappers are here? They're billed as Flopsy, Mopsy, and Cottontail.

MISS AMBROSE: I'm sorry, but Mr. Hunter is still out.

MRS. MURPHY: But you said he'd be back at two. We've already waited more than an hour.

MISS AMBROSE: I'm sorry, but I have no way of knowing how long he'll be delayed.

FLOPSY: Can't we go home now, Mamma? I'm tired.

MOPSY: I'm hungry.

COTTONTAIL: Me too! (*Raises one foot*) And these tap shoes hurt my feet! I don't want to be on TV, anyway.

MRS. MURPHY: Don't be silly! Everybody wants to be on television! (*Pats her lap*) Put your foot up here in my lap. I'll loosen that strap for you. (COTTONTAIL *raises foot.* MRS. MURPHY *fixes strap.*)

COTTONTAIL: It still hurts! (*Scowls*)

MRS. MURPHY: Now, I don't want to hear any more complaints from you three. Mr. Hunter, the producer, will be here any minute and I want him to see nice big smiles. (*To* MRS. ROSS) I always think a smile is half of the battle, don't you?

MRS. ROSS: Of course, but Peter just sits and scowls.

PETER: I don't feel like smiling. My baseball team has a game this afternoon and they need me to pitch.

MRS. ROSS: But Mr. Hunter needs a trumpet player for his Easter Bunny TV special.

PETER: I wish I'd never learned to play that dumb old trumpet! It's wrecking my sports career.

MRS. ROSS (*To* MRS. MURPHY): He does play a mean trumpet, when he wants to.

MRS. MURPHY (*Politely*): I'm sure he does.

MRS. ROSS (*Eagerly*): Best of all, his trumpet fits inside that (*Points*) artificial carrot. (MR. FULTON *enters, carrying guitar case.*)

Mr. Fulton (*Calling over shoulder*): Come on, Oswald. This is the place. (*To* Miss Ambrose) Is Mr. Hunter in? (*Puts guitar case in front of bench*)

Miss Ambrose: No, he isn't, but you're welcome to sit down and wait. (Oswald, *dressed in rabbit suit and carrying bass drum, enters.*)

Oswald (*Whining*): This bass drum weighs a ton!

Mr. Fulton: Put it down, Oswald, and get organized. (*To* Mrs. Ross, *proudly*) Oswald is a one-man band. (Oswald *puts drum on floor, opens guitar case, puts guitar on bench next to* Mr. Fulton.) Oswald, where's your harmonica?

Oswald: In my pocket, Dad. (*Pats pocket*) Don't worry! I have everything. (*He sits next to guitar.* Miss Blossom *enters with* Bunny Ballet.)

Miss Blossom (*Flustered*): Oh, dear! I hope we're not late. (*To* Miss Ambrose) Will you please tell Mr. Hunter that Miss Blossom and the Bunny Ballet are here?

Miss Ambrose: I'll tell him as soon as he comes in.

Miss Blossom (*Disappointed*): He's not here? (*Sighs*) Very well. (*Herds children to bench*) Come, children, sit down, and be careful! Don't crush your costumes. (*They sit*) Now remember, the very instant Mr. Hunter appears, I want you to be on your toes.

Bunnies (*Together*): Yes, Miss Blossom. (White Rabbit *enters with* Alice.)

White Rabbit (*Looking at watch*): What did I tell you? I knew we'd be late!

Alice: We're not late!

White Rabbit (*Waving arm*): But look how many people are ahead of us. I should have known better than to wait for you.

Alice: And how far do you think you'd get without me? (*To* Miss Ambrose) Good afternoon. I'm Alice Fenway, and this is my brother. We'd like to see Mr. Hunter about a mind-reading act for the Easter Bunny Special.

Miss Ambrose (*Tiredly*): I'm sorry, Miss Fenway, but Mr. Hunter isn't back from lunch.

Alice: When are you expecting him?

MISS AMBROSE (*Embarrassed*): I really don't know. Something important must have come up. (*Looking at door*) Oh, thank goodness! I think he's here now! (MR. HUNTER *enters, carrying a briefcase.*)

ALL (*Springing to their feet*): Mr. Hunter! Mr. Hunter!

MR. FULTON: Quick, Oswald! Go into your act! (OSWALD *whips out harmonica and begins to play it simultaneously with guitar, while pressing foot pedal on drum.*)

MR. HUNTER (*Drawing back; annoyed*): What is this? Who are these people, Miss Ambrose?

MISS AMBROSE: They've come for the Easter Bunny Special.

MR. HUNTER: The what?

MISS AMBROSE: The Easter Bunny Special. You sent out the notices last week.

MR. HUNTER (*Exasperated*): But there isn't going to be an Easter Bunny Special! (MRS. MURPHY *rushes forward.* FLOPSY, MOPSY, *and* COTTONTAIL *trail after.*)

MRS. MURPHY (*To* FLOPSY, MOPSY, *and* COTTONTAIL): Come on, children, let's give Mr. Hunter a great big smile, and on the count of three, sing! One, two, three! (*They start to sing "Peter Cottontail."* MRS. ROSS *takes trumpet from case.*)

MRS. ROSS (*Thrusting trumpet into* PETER's *hands*): Here, Peter! Now blow good and loud. (*All start performing their acts at once.* ALICE *and* WHITE RABBIT *rush over to* MR. HUNTER.)

ALICE: Think of any number, Mr. Hunter, from one to fifty, and my brother will tell you what it is.

MR. HUNTER (*Loudly, hands on ears*): Quiet! Quiet, everyone! Miss Ambrose, get these people out of here! (PETER *and* OSWALD *continue to play instruments.*)

MISS AMBROSE (*Standing*): Please, everyone, do be quiet!

MR. HUNTER (*Yelling at the top of his lungs*): Qui-et! (*There is complete silence.* MR. HUNTER *clears his throat.*) Thank you. I appreciate the fine talent you've all brought here today, but there has been a terrible mistake. The Easter show this year is a *Bonnet* show, not a *Bunny* show, as you apparently have been informed. It's *bonnets* we need, not bunnies!

ALL (*Together*): What!

MRS. MURPHY: But Mr. Hunter, that's impossible! The agency distinctly said an Easter *Bunny* Special.

FLOPSY (*Tugging at* MRS. MURPHY's *sleeve*): Aren't we going to be on television now, Mamma?

PETER: Hurray! Now I can get home in time for the game. (*He starts for door at right.* MRS. ROSS *grabs him by jacket.*)

MISS BLOSSOM: This is an outrage! After I dragged the children clear across town for these tryouts!

MR. HUNTER (*Shrugging*): I assure you it's just as distressing for me as it is for you, but our sponsor has decreed an Easter *bonnet* production this year, and his word is law. (*Turns*) Miss Ambrose, I must have a conference with the staff. I am not to be disturbed. (*Exits left*)

MRS. MURPHY: I've never heard of such a thing! He can't do this to us.

MISS AMBROSE (*Sitting*): Well, folks, you heard what Mr. Hunter said. He needs bonnets, not bunnies. (EASTER BUNNY *enters, carrying basket of Easter eggs.*)

EASTER BUNNY (*Cheerily*): Happy Easter, everybody! (*All stare at him glumly.*)

MISS AMBROSE (*Wearily*): Excuse me, but there's no call for rabbits today. The show has been canceled.

EASTER BUNNY (*Upset*): That's impossible! No one can cancel Easter.

MISS AMBROSE (*Impatiently*): I'm not talking about canceling Easter. But we just don't need any rabbit acts for our special. (*Raising her voice*) We don't need any rabbit actors, singers, dancers, magicians, or mind readers. (*Turns away*)

EASTER BUNNY (*Protesting*): But I'm not any of those things.

MISS AMBROSE: Then who are you?

EASTER BUNNY: I'm the Easter Bunny. (*All laugh*)

MISS AMBROSE (*Sharply*): Well, Mr. Easter Bunny, I'm sorry to tell you, there's nothing for you here.

EASTER BUNNY: I wasn't expecting anything.

MISS AMBROSE (*Puzzled*): Then why did you come?

EASTER BUNNY (*Holding up basket*): To give out my magic Easter eggs. Isn't your name Miss Ambrose? I think I have one here for you. (*Looking in basket*) Yes, indeed, here it is . . . *Annabel Ambrose,* in pink icing. (*Takes egg out and hands it to her with a flourish*)

MISS AMBROSE (*Confused*): Well, thank you very much.

EASTER BUNNY (*Peering into basket*): Now, if you'll just call Mr. Hunter, I'll give him this big egg with the yellow roses.

MISS AMBROSE: Oh, I couldn't possibly disturb him. He's in conference.

EASTER BUNNY: Well, I'll give it to him later. Now, let me see! (*Looks in basket*) Here's one for Mamma Murphy, and three lovely ones for Flopsy, Mopsy and Cottontail! (*Distributes eggs*)

WHITE RABBIT (*Puzzled, to* ALICE): Say, what is this? Another mind-reading act?

ALICE: I wonder how he knows their names.

EASTER BUNNY (*Smiling*): It's my business. (*Takes another egg from basket and hands it to her*) Here's your egg, Alice, with your name in blue.

ALICE (*Astonished*): Thank you.

EASTER BUNNY (*To* WHITE RABBIT): And as for you, I've kept your color scheme pink and white, to match your handsome suit. (*Hands egg to* WHITE RABBIT; *members of* BUNNY BALLET *burst into tears.* EASTER BUNNY *stares at them.*) Bless my whiskers! What are they crying about? I have eggs for them, too.

MISS BLOSSOM: They're not crying about eggs. They're crying because they're not going to be on television.

EASTER BUNNY: Why not?

MRS. MURPHY (*Shaking her head*): We thought Mr. Hunter was doing an Easter Bunny Special, but it turns out he's doing an Easter *Bonnet* Show instead.

EASTER BUNNY: That's too bad. But I'm sure things will straighten themselves out.

PETER (*To* EASTER BUNNY): What is your act, anyway?

EASTER BUNNY: It's no act at all. I'm the Easter Bunny. It's my job just to distribute Easter eggs, and to make people happy.

MISS AMBROSE (*Gloomily*): Well, you can't make anyone here happy.

EASTER BUNNY: Everyone will be happy once they feel the magic in these eggs. Here, children, come and get your eggs. (*Hands eggs to* BUNNY BALLET) These are for you, and this one is for Peter. (*Gives egg to* PETER) Now this one is for a fellow named Oswald. Oswald Rabbit.

OSWALD (*Stepping forward*): That's for me. Thanks. You know, I believe you really are the Easter Bunny.

EASTER BUNNY (*Patting* OSWALD's *shoulder*): Thanks. I'm glad to hear it. Now, for the grown-ups. (*Hands eggs to* MRS. ROSS, MR. FULTON, *and* MISS BLOSSOM. *To* MISS AMBROSE) Could you call Mr. Hunter now, so I can give him his Easter egg?

MISS AMBROSE: I told you before—I can't disturb him for that. Why, he'd be furious with me.

EASTER BUNNY: I see. Well, suppose you all take a few minutes to relax. Just hold your eggs tightly, close your eyes, and wish. (*They hesitate*) Come on, give it a try. Once you've done it, you'll all feel much better. (*All close eyes and begin to smile.*)

ALICE: I'm feeling happier already.

EASTER BUNNY: Sure you are! (*To others*) Tell me . . . how do you feel?

FLOPSY, MOPSY, *and* COTTONTAIL (*Together*): We feel happy, too.

FLOPSY: I'm not tired anymore.

MOPSY: I'm not hungry anymore.

COTTONTAIL: And my tap shoes don't hurt one single bit. (*Does a few dance steps*) I could dance all day!

EASTER BUNNY: How about you, Mrs. Murphy? Do you feel any better?

MRS. MURPHY: Somehow, I don't feel quite so angry. (MRS. ROSS *nods vigorously.*)

MRS. ROSS: I guess we should forgive Mr. Hunter—even big TV producers can make mistakes.

PETER (*Eagerly*): Say, Mom, if we get a chance to be on TV, I'll play baseball some other time.

1ST BUNNY (*Pointing to others in* BUNNY BALLET): We feel great, Mr. Easter Bunny. When do we dance?

MISS BLOSSOM: I won't mind all this one bit if we just get a chance to make other children happy on Easter.

EASTER BUNNY: That's the spirit, Miss Blossom.

WHITE RABBIT: You know, Alice, you'll be the hit of our act. The children will just love you.

ALICE (*Pleased*): Now I *know* these are magic Easter eggs! You always said *you* were the main attraction of our act!

WHITE RABBIT: I know, but I guess I was a little conceited.

ALICE: It doesn't matter, as long as the children have a good time.

EASTER BUNNY: Wonderful! You're really getting the Easter spirit. How about you, Miss Ambrose?

MISS AMBROSE (*Standing*): I feel terrific! And I really would like Mr. Hunter to have his egg. It would do him a world of good!

EASTER BUNNY: Then call him!

ALICE: Yes, please call him, Miss Ambrose. Let's see what happens when he holds his Easter egg!

MISS AMBROSE: But remember . . . he wants *bonnets,* not bunnies.

EASTER BUNNY: But it's bunnies that he has, Miss Ambrose, and I'm sure we can make him learn to like us in short order.

MISS AMBROSE: O.K. Here goes! (*Pushes button and speaks into phone*) Excuse me for interrupting, Mr. Hunter, but you're needed out here—it's sort of an emergency. (*Pauses*) Thank you. (*Hanging up phone*) He'll be right out. (MR. HUNTER *rushes onto stage.*)

MR. HUNTER (*Frantically*): What's the trouble? (*All smile at him.*) Where's the emergency? (*Annoyed*) I told you I was not to be disturbed, Miss Ambrose. We're calling all over town trying to get Easter bonnets and models for them. (*Looks around*) I thought I told you to get rid of all these bunny characters!

MISS AMBROSE (*Stubbornly*): Just a minute, sir. I told you someone wanted to see you.

EASTER BUNNY (*Stepping forward*): I'm the one who wants to see you, Mr. Hunter! I brought you your Easter egg. (*Takes egg from basket, holds it out*)

MR. HUNTER (*Sputtering with rage*): Why, this is ridiculous! Preposterous! (*Pushes egg away*) Leave here at once!

EASTER BUNNY (*Putting hand on* MR. HUNTER's *shoulder*): Please, Mr. Hunter. Remember your blood pressure.

MR. HUNTER (*Pulling away*): What do you know about my blood pressure?

EASTER BUNNY: I know it's reaching the boiling point, sir, and if you'll just calm down a minute, I'm sure I can help you.

MR. HUNTER: How could you possibly help me?

EASTER BUNNY: Well, am I right in assuming that you're worried about your sponsor?

MR. HUNTER (*Sighing*): That's putting it mildly.

EASTER BUNNY: Would an Easter bonnet help you out of your difficulty?

MR. HUNTER (*Bitterly*): Ha! Try to find one at this stage of the game!

EASTER BUNNY: Mr. Hunter, you've heard of a magician taking a rabbit out of a hat, haven't you?

MR. HUNTER: Of course.

EASTER BUNNY: But have you ever heard of taking a hat out of a rabbit?

MR. HUNTER (*Impatiently*): What is this nonsense?

EASTER BUNNY: Watch closely, Mr. Hunter. (*Holds egg out again*) Take this Easter egg—it's the last one I have. (MR. HUNTER *takes egg reluctantly.* EASTER BUNNY *turns his empty basket upside down, to show that it is actually a wide-brimmed straw hat, the ties of which have been used as a handle. It is beautifully trimmed with flowers.*)

MR. HUNTER (*Staring*): A hat! A beautiful Easter bonnet.

EASTER BUNNY: Of course, and here is your model, Miss Blossom. (*Puts bonnet on* MISS BLOSSOM's *head*) There! Isn't that lovely!

MR. HUNTER: It's fantastic! Just what we need! (*Takes* MISS BLOSSOM's *arm, pulls her toward door*) Come with me, my dear Miss Blossom. We'll take some photos of you right away.

EASTER BUNNY: Just a moment, Mr. Hunter. There's something else you have to do. (MR. HUNTER *stops, turns around.*) You have to make a wish on your Easter egg.

MR. HUNTER (*Shaking head*): Don't be ridiculous!

MISS BLOSSOM: But you'll really have to, Mr. Hunter. Close your eyes, hold onto your egg, and make a wish. (*Stubbornly*) I won't budge out of this room until you do.

MR. HUNTER (*Slapping hand to forehead*): Another temperamental star! Well, O.K. (*Closes his eyes briefly, then opens them*) There! Are you satisfied?

MISS BLOSSOM: Not entirely, Mr. Hunter. Keep them closed a little bit longer. (MR. HUNTER *closes his eyes.*)

MR. HUNTER: Mm-m. (*Opens his eyes and smiles*) Hey, I feel great—in fact, I've never felt better in my life! (*Looking around*) Wow! These are cute costumes! In fact, they're the cutest bunny costumes I've ever seen.

MISS BLOSSOM: Good for you, Mr. Hunter. You're feeling the magic of Easter.

MR. HUNTER: Yes, if only I hadn't promised our sponsor I'd do a show on bonnets. (*Pauses, then brightly*) I'll bet our viewers would love all these rabbits. (*To* FLOPSY) Who are you supposed to be?

FLOPSY: We're Flopsy, Mopsy, and Cottontail. We're tap dancers.

BUNNY BALLET (*Together*): We dance, too! We're the Bunny Ballet.

MR. HUNTER (*To* OSWALD): And who are you?

OSWALD: I'm Oswald and I'm a one-man band.

MR. HUNTER (*Excitedly*): And here are the White Rabbit and Alice in Wonderland! Why, kids would love seeing their favorite bunny characters on Easter morning.

MISS AMBROSE: Will you sign them up, Mr. Hunter?

MR. HUNTER: I sure will! (*Others cheer.*) But what about the sponsor? He's expecting *bonnets*.

MISS AMBROSE: Well, give him this bonnet (*Pointing to* MISS BLOSSOM's *bonnet*), and fill in the rest of the time with bunny acts.

MR. HUNTER: You know, Miss Ambrose, I think you've solved my problem. I have the bonnet *and* the bunnies.

MISS AMBROSE: That's right. Just what the TV audience would want for Easter.

MR. HUNTER: Give 'em what they want, I always say. That's the secret of television.

EASTER BUNNY: I wouldn't know about that, sir, but I think you're pretty close to the secret of a happy Easter. (*Bows*) And now, good day to you, one and all. (*Starts for door at right*)

ALL (*Together*): Wait, wait! (EASTER BUNNY *pauses.*)

MISS AMBROSE: Don't go, please. I'm sure Mr. Hunter could use you in his show.

EASTER BUNNY: Sorry, Miss Ambrose, but being the Easter Rabbit is a full-time job! (*Waves and exits*)

MR. HUNTER: Say, who was he? Haven't I seen him somewhere before?

MISS AMBROSE: He *said* he was the Easter Bunny, and you know, I really think he was telling the truth. (*All may sing an Easter song as curtains close.*)

THE END

A Man Called Appleseed

by Betty Holmes Cochran

Johnny's seeds of friendship bear fruit. . . .

Characters

SARAH DILLON
POLLY DILLON
TOMMY DILLON
MELODY
JOHNNY APPLESEED
OWL'S WING

TIME: *1814.*

SETTING: *Interior of cabin on the frontier.*

AT RISE: SARAH *is putting supplies into basket on table.* MELODY *sits nearby.*

SARAH: We are so happy that you have come to live with us, Melody. Luke wanted to welcome you, too.

MELODY (*Nervously*): Are you all alone? Where is Luke?

SARAH: He had to go to the settlement for supplies. Your bed is in the loft, if you'd like to rest.

MELODY: So this is your home.

SARAH: You sound disappointed.

MELODY (*Apologetically*): Sarah, I'm sorry. You and Luke are my only relatives, and it's kind of you to take me in. It's just so different here. Don't you find it lonely and scary with so few people around?

SARAH: Not at all. I'm too busy to think much about it. (*Puts arm around* MELODY) But I understand. It's new and strange to you now, but you'll soon grow to like it here.

MELODY: I'm frightened. Here we are, two women and two children in the wilds, with nothing between us and danger but that door.

SARAH (*Comforting her*): You're just tired from your long journey in the wagon train.

MELODY: It was so bumpy. I'm black and blue from the jolting, and I haven't slept in weeks. The endless forests and the fear of fighting Indians!

SARAH (*Returning to basket*): Didn't you see any Indians on the way?

MELODY: No, but I could sense them watching us from the shadows. And a wild-looking man kept popping out of the woods all along the trail.

SARAH: What did he look like?

MELODY: His suit was made of flour sacks, and he was barefoot. And on his head, as I live and breathe, there sat a saucepan, handle and all.

SARAH (*Laughing*): No wonder you had no trouble with Indians. Johnny Appleseed is more protection than a regiment of soldiers.

MELODY (*Surprised*): You know this ragged old man?

SARAH: Of course. Johnny Appleseed is a friend to all of us.

MELODY: Appleseed! Mercy, his name is ridiculous as his looks.

SARAH: His real name is John Chapman, but few people know that. (*Firmly*) Never make fun of him again, Melody. Just be thankful for the man called Johnny Appleseed. (POLLY *enters, followed by* TOMMY, *carrying wood.*)

POLLY: Appleseed! Is Johnny coming here, Mother?

TOMMY (*Excited*): Is he, Mother?

SARAH: He may be. Melody saw Johnny on the way out here.

TOMMY (*Putting wood by fireplace*): I hope so. I want to show him the little trees he helped us plant.

POLLY: He said he'd come back if we took good care of them, and we have.

MELODY (*Scornfully*): How silly to plant trees! Everyone else on the frontier cuts them down.

POLLY: But these are apple trees!

TOMMY: Someday we'll have pies and jelly made from our own apples! (SARAH *is tying on her bonnet.*)

MELODY: Sarah, why are you putting on that bonnet? Where are you going?

SARAH: The Keefer baby is sick, and they need my help. (*To* POLLY) Polly, will you see to supper? Measure the cornmeal carefully, and add some beans to the stew. I'll be back as soon as I can. (*To* TOMMY) Tom, don't let the fire go out. (*Picks up basket and starts out left*)

MELODY: Sarah Dillon! Aren't you afraid? Wolves, bears, and who knows what other dangers are out there in that forest!

SARAH: I'll be perfectly safe. I must go. Goodbye, children. (SARAH *exits.*)

MELODY: Wait, Sarah! Don't leave me! I'm coming with you. (*Exits*)

TOMMY (*Shaking his head*): Melody's afraid of her own shadow.

POLLY: Everything here is new to her, that's all. (*Looking out window*) Look at the sky. It's going to storm.

TOMMY (*Looking*): Those clouds are black! The wind is rising, too.

POLLY (*Uneasily*): I heard Father tell Mother something before he left to get supplies. (*Wind and low thunder are heard.*)

TOMMY: What did he say?

POLLY: Some Indians are camped just over the ridge, and Father said if we didn't need supplies so badly, he wouldn't leave. (*Fearful*) I wish he hadn't gone.

TOMMY (*Pointing to gun*): There's Father's gun, if we need it.

POLLY: Guns scare me more than anything! (*Bravely*) Forget what I said. Fix the fire, and I'll get supper ready. (*Crosses to table*) Where's the water bucket? (*Looking into bucket*) Oh, dear. It's only half full.

TOMMY (*Stirring fire*): Give it to me. I'll go down to the creek and get some water.

POLLY: No. It's too dark.

TOMMY (*Impatiently*): Don't be silly. Give me the bucket.

POLLY: No. We have enough water, really we do. (*Suddenly*) I heard something just then!

TOMMY: It's just the wind—isn't it?

POLLY: No, listen. (*Pauses*) There it is again. Could it be Father?

TOMMY (*Getting gun*): No. We would have heard the horses. (*Sound of whistle is heard.*) That's an Indian's signal! They may break in. (*Points gun at door*) Get ready. (POLLY *stands by door with bucket raised. Door flies open and* JOHNNY APPLESEED *bursts in. He wears loose sacking suit with rope belt, has saucepan on his head, carries hoe and sack.*)

POLLY (*Relieved*): It's Johnny! Johnny Appleseed!

TOMMY (*Putting gun back*): Phew! Are we glad to see you!

JOHNNY: It's me, all right. (*Hugs* POLLY) You grow faster than my apple trees, Polly. And as pretty as a blossom, too. Let me unpack. (*Pauses*) My kitchen. (*Puts hat on hearth*) My servant. (*Leans hoe against wall. Starts taking things from sack*) The seeds that are my treasure. (*Puts papers and pouch on table*) Now then, Tommy, why the gun? Are you going duck hunting?

POLLY (*Ashamed*): We thought we heard Indians.

JOHNNY: Indians, eh? See here, Tom, it's all right to use guns to get your food, but don't point them at your friends. (*Pounding on door is heard.*)

POLLY (*Opening door*): Melody!

MELODY (*Entering and heading for fire*): I had to come back! I was too cold. (*Sees* JOHNNY) Goodness, it's that man again!

JOHNNY (*Shaking her limp hand*): Evening, ma'am.

TOMMY (*To* JOHNNY): Melody is our cousin. She has come to live with us, Johnny.

JOHNNY: Welcome to the frontier, Miss Melody.

MELODY (*Sharply*): I don't feel welcome out here. I'm cold and hungry.

POLLY: I forgot the cornbread! (*Goes to table and starts stirring in bowl, puts skillet on hearth. She sets table during following dialogue.*)

JOHNNY (*Reaching into pocket*): Maybe I have something to add to the feast. (*Pulls out apples*)

TOMMY: Apples!

JOHNNY: One for Polly—and one for Miss Melody. (*Hands them apples*)

TOMMY: I hope this storm won't hurt our apple trees.

JOHNNY: Don't fear Mother Nature's storms, Tom. Human beings cause more damage than nature. I've seen signs of trouble all along the trail—even here.

TOMMY: Here at our house?

JOHNNY: You met me at the door with a gun. What if I had been an Indian?

TOMMY: I'd have been mighty scared.

JOHNNY: Of what? Indians are different from us, but that's not necessarily bad. I've learned many things from them, and so can you.

POLLY: How can we make friends with them? They don't like us.

JOHNNY: Treat them as your friends, and they'll like you. They just don't understand your ways. Some people don't understand mine, you know. Wearing a cooking pot on your head is crazy, they say, but (*Smiles*) I have a rainproof hat and my hands are free.

TOMMY: But, sometimes the Indians steal our livestock.

JOHNNY: Only when they're hungry. Why not make friends by giving them some food?

MELODY: You may be right, but I've heard frightening stories about them.

JOHNNY: There are both good and bad Indians *and* settlers. My, this table looks fit for a party. So it is! A "welcome, Melody" party. Somebody start up a song.

TOMMY: We don't know any songs.

MELODY: I can teach you lots of them.

JOHNNY: Of course you can. That's what you will be, a teacher! How about "Skip to My Lou" for a starter?

MELODY (*Singing "Skip to My Lou" slowly*):
    Fly in the buttermilk, shoo, fly, shoo!

JOHNNY (*Joining in*):
    Fly in the buttermilk, shoo, fly, shoo!

JOHNNY *and* MELODY (*Singing together*):

Fly in the buttermilk, shoo, fly shoo!

Skip to my lou, my darling.

JOHNNY (*Motioning to* POLLY *and* TOM): Come on, you two! Sing out! (*They skip about, singing, until sound of thunder is heard.*)

TOMMY: Phew, that was close!

POLLY: Pull up the chairs, Tom. (TOM *pulls four chairs around fire.*) Isn't this fun? Johnny, I hope you'll stay with us a long, long time.

JOHNNY: That's nice to hear, Polly, but I can't. In the winter I go to the cider mills for my seeds. By planting time I'm ahead of the settlers where towns will be someday. In between I watch over the orchards I've already set out. (*Heavy crash is heard from offstage, followed by a cry.*)

POLLY (*As all jump and listen*): What was that? An animal?

JOHNNY (*Rushing to door*): No. That was a human cry. (*Rushes off, followed by* TOMMY)

MELODY (*Fearfully*): Why did I ever leave home?

POLLY (*Looking out door*): Some branches were blown down from the big tree right outside the house.

MELODY: Can you see anything else?

POLLY: Tommy and Johnny are carrying someone! (JOHNNY *and* TOMMY *enter, supporting* OWL'S WING. *They help him sit on bench.*)

MELODY (*Frightened*): It's an Indian!

JOHNNY: Yes, this is Owl's Wing. I know his father well.

TOMMY: He's alive, isn't he?

JOHNNY (*Examining boy*): Yes, thank heaven. No bones broken, either. That falling branch just knocked him out.

MELODY: Look! What's in his hand?

POLLY (*Upset*): It's Mother's bonnet! (*Picks it up*)

TOMMY: Why would he have her bonnet?

MELODY: Something terrible must have happened to Sarah!

JOHNNY: Slow down, Miss Melody. We don't know what happened yet.

MELODY (*Angrily*): You're more concerned about this boy than Sarah! Oh, what has he done to her?

JOHNNY: I've no time to waste, ma'am. A spark of misunderstanding can cause a large fire. Just trust me. Tom, take good care of Owl's Wing. The peace of the entire frontier may depend on your treatment of him. (*Exits*)

MELODY (*Indignantly*): Take care of him, indeed! What about your mother, Tommy? You keep an eye on that Indian. No telling what he'll do. (*Exits rear*)

POLLY (*Going to* OWL'S WING): He doesn't look mean. Don't listen to Melody!

TOMMY: I'll do what Johnny said, but I'm not taking any chances.

POLLY (*Sighing*): Our supper will be ruined! Oh, dear, if Mother. . . . (*Resolutely*) Mother won't like having good food go to waste. The stew can go back near the fire, and the cornbread can be wrapped up. (*Clears table*)

TOMMY: Let me have a piece first.

POLLY: Taste the stew. (OWL'S WING *moves, unnoticed by* POLLY *and* TOMMY.)

TOMMY (*Dipping spoon into stew*): Mm! (*Abruptly*) Did Owl's Wing move just then?

POLLY (*Turning*): I think he's still unconscious.

TOMMY: I hope he stays that way. What'll he do when he wakes up?

POLLY: What would you do if you woke up with a wounded head in a strange house? (*Moves dishes to hearth.* TOMMY *puts wood on fire, as* OWL'S WING *slowly stands unnoticed by them.*)

TOMMY: I'd be scared out of my wits.

POLLY: We'll need water to wash these dishes.

TOMMY: The storm's over. Give me the bucket, and I'll go fill it. (OWL'S WING *silently moves toward* TOMMY, *stands with folded arms.*)

POLLY (*Seeing him*): Tommy! (*Points at* OWL'S WING)

TOMMY: What's the matter? (*Turns, then jumps back, startled*) Oh! (*Quickly*) Don't be frightened. We are your friends.

OWL'S WING (*Scornfully*): Friends who hit me? (*Indicates head*) Took me captive?

POLLY: No, you're wrong! It was a tree that fell on you in the storm. Don't you remember?

TOMMY: Johnny Appleseed found you, and we brought you here because you were hurt.

OWL'S WING (*Picking up apple*): I see that Johnny has been here. This is his sign.

TOMMY: Where is my mother?

OWL'S WING: White squaw run through forest crying like screech owl. Hair like cornsilk.

POLLY: That was Melody. (*Picks up* SARAH's *bonnet*) Mother wore this bonnet.

OWL'S WING: Saw only one squaw.

TOMMY: You must know something about Mother. We found her bonnet in your hand.

OWL'S WING (*Angrily*): Saw no mother!

TOMMY (*Flaring up*): I don't believe you, Owl's Wing.

OWL'S WING: You gave me shelter. You are my friend. Friends speak only true words to friends.

TOMMY: You're right. I'm sorry. It's just that I'm worried about Mother. (*Pause*) You must be hungry. Why don't you eat the apple?

POLLY: I'll divide my apple with you, Tommy. (*To* OWL'S WING) Owl's Wing, may I use your knife to cut it? (OWL'S WING *takes knife from belt, as* MELODY *enters.*)

MELODY: Polly! Watch out! He has a knife!

POLLY: Melody, be quiet! You don't understand!

MELODY (*Rushing to* OWL'S WING): Drop that knife, I tell you! What have you done with Sarah?

POLLY (*Trying to restrain* MELODY): Stop, Melody, he's a friend.

MELODY (*Raising arm to strike* OWL'S WING): How did you get Sarah's bonnet? Tell me, or get out of this house! Where is Sarah Dillon? (*Door bursts open, and* SARAH *and* JOHNNY *enter. Others freeze.*)

JOHNNY: What in tarnation is going on?

POLLY (*Running to* SARAH): Oh, Mother, you're safe!

MELODY (*Backing away from* OWL'S WING): Sarah! Thank goodness, you're safe.

TOMMY (*To* SARAH): Owl's Wing was only going to cut an apple with his knife, but Melody thought because he had your bonnet you were hurt.

SARAH: My bonnet? It blew off as I ran in the storm. (*To* OWL'S WING) Johnny tells me that we have an injured guest. Let me have a look at you, young man. (*Inspects* OWL'S WING) A bad bump, a few bruises. Nothing serious.

MELODY (*Ashamed*): But I accused him unfairly. (*Sinks weakly onto bench*)

TOMMY (*Angrily*): Yes, and you could have started a lot of trouble.

JOHNNY: It was a mixup, but it's blown over now, like the storm. Owl's Wing, you must be moving on. Your father will worry about you.

SARAH: Don't leave us so soon, John.

JOHNNY: I'll have a look at your trees first. (*Gets pouch of seeds and hoe; to* POLLY *and* TOM) When they bear fruit, do you promise to give some of the fruit away every year?

TOMMY: Of course.

POLLY: But whom shall we give it to?

JOHNNY: It doesn't matter. Just give it in friendship.

OWL'S WING (*To* POLLY *and* TOMMY): Friends, I go now. I will not forget. (MELODY *rises and goes to* OWL'S WING.)

MELODY: Owl's Wing, I'm sorry. I misjudged you. Please forgive me. (*Extends hand. There is a pause as* OWL'S WING *looks at it.*)

OWL'S WING (*Taking beads from neck, putting them into her hand*): In friendship. Like apple. (*Waves farewell and starts to exit*)

POLLY: Wait, Owl's Wing. Tommy and I will walk part way with you. (TOMMY, POLLY *and* OWL'S WING *exit.*)

MELODY (*Looking at beads*): How beautiful! Imagine that he would be friendly to me after the way I acted! (*To* JOHNNY) Mr. Appleseed, I'm so ashamed.

JOHNNY: Don't fret over past mistakes, Miss Melody. You can't see ahead of you if you're looking backward. You won't forget Owl's Wing. Don't forget me, either. Think of the gift you have to give—learning! Now, that beats beads or apples! (*Smiles*) Goodbye! (*Waves and exits*)

SARAH (*At door*): Goodbye, John Chapman. (*Closes door*) That wonderful man.

MELODY (*Thoughtfully*): I've been wrong about so many things. But maybe if I start all over—(*Sees* JOHNNY's *papers on table*) Look. He forgot his papers. (*Picks them up*)

SARAH: He didn't forget them, Melody. That's what he calls his news from heaven. You see, Johnny Appleseed plants ideas as well as seeds.

MELODY: Know what, Sarah? Some that he gave me have just begun to grow. (*Curtain*)

THE END

Conversation Piece

by Jessie Nicholson

"Choice" gifts for Mother's Day . . .

Characters

MR. HOLMES
MRS. HOLMES
ROGER, *15* ⎫
SALLY, *16* ⎬ *their children*
CHRIS, *11* ⎪
PENNY, *10* ⎭
HILDA SWENSEN, *housekeeper*
DELIVERY PERSON
MESSENGER

SCENE 1

TIME: *Day before Mother's Day.*
SETTING: *The Holmes living room. Mantel of fireplace, at rear, has pair of candlesticks on it. Sofa, several easy chairs, and telephone on table are center. Bookshelves, lamps, paintings, etc., complete furnishings. Exit left leads outside; exit right, to rest of house. There is a closet down left.*
AT RISE: *MR. HOLMES sits in easy chair, reading paper. MRS. HOLMES, humming, dusts mantel with feather duster. She stands back and looks thoughtfully at mantel.*

MRS. HOLMES: I wonder how a big Chippendale-period tray would look—or would a painting of a New England barn be better?

MR. HOLMES (*Looking up from paper*): What's that, Alice?

MRS. HOLMES: I'm just trying to decide what would look best over the mantel.

MR. HOLMES (*Chuckling*): You've been trying to decide that for five years, ever since we moved into this house.

MRS. HOLMES: But I want just the right thing. It's the most important spot in the living room—a sort of focal point.

MR. HOLMES (*Dryly*): How about that stuffed eagle Uncle Albert sent us from Alaska? I'll bet that would catch people's eyes!

MRS. HOLMES: Don't be absurd!

MR. HOLMES: Well, don't say I didn't try. (*Looks around*) By the way, where is everybody? The house is unusually quiet.

MRS. HOLMES: Penny and Chris went on some mysterious errand, and Roger and Sally are being equally secretive. As for Hilda, I let her have the day off to visit her sister.

MR. HOLMES (*Casually*): Tomorrow's Mother's Day, you know. I expect they have big plans. I see in the paper they're having an auction at Finney's. I guess I'll just drop over and watch the fun for an hour or so.

MRS. HOLMES: Well, don't get carried away, dear. The attic is full of your auction "bargains."

MR. HOLMES (*Defensively*): Alice, antiques are as good as money in the bank. They grow more valuable every year.

MRS. HOLMES: As long as you're going to the auction, I think I'll go shopping. Just wait till I get my purse.

MR. HOLMES (*Quickly*): You'd better take your own car, Alice. You may want to get home before I do. Why don't we meet in town for lunch?

MRS. HOLMES (*Shrugging*): Fine with me, dear. (*She exits right. Doorbell rings.* MR. HOLMES *goes to door, opens it.* DELIVERY PERSON *enters carrying a bulky, oddly shaped package.*)

DELIVERY PERSON: Package for Mr. Roger Holmes.

MR. HOLMES: Mr. *Roger* Holmes? Are you sure it's for Roger Holmes?

DELIVERY PERSON: Yes, sir—Mr. Roger Holmes. (MR. HOLMES

signs receipt, takes package, and lugs it into room, as ROGER *enters left, out of breath.* DELIVERY PERSON *exits.*)

ROGER: Gosh, Dad, be careful how you handle that! Here, let me take it. (*He struggles to put package into closet, emerges a moment later, closing door behind him.*)

MR. HOLMES: What on earth is that, may I ask?

ROGER: It's a Mother's Day present. Was I ever lucky!

MR. HOLMES (*Skeptically*): Maybe *you* were, but will your mother be?

ROGER: It can't miss. Mom's been looking for something to put over the mantel for ages.

MR. HOLMES (*Wryly*): You aren't going to make me wait to find out what it is, are you? The suspense would be too much. (ROGER *whispers in his father's ear, then draws back and watches him expectantly.*)

ROGER: Isn't that cool? I bought it for half price, too, at a sporting goods store—they were going to throw it out! Can you imagine that? (MR. HOLMES *hides a grin.*)

MR. HOLMES: Well, I must say it is original! (MRS. HOLMES *enters, carrying purse.*)

MRS. HOLMES: Oh, Roger, you're home. Your dad and I are going out for a while. There's lunch for you and Sally in the refrigerator. Chris and Penny are over at Amy's.

MR. HOLMES: Roger, if you're looking for something to do while we're gone, you might clean the garage.

ROGER: O.K., Dad, I will—*if* I'm looking for something to do. (MR. *and* MRS. HOLMES *exit.* ROGER *looks toward closet, rubs his hands together gleefully.*) Is Mom ever going to be surprised! I just can't wait to see her expression when she opens my present. Wonder what Sally's going to get her? She was so secretive about it. Well, two can play that game. (*He exits, right. A moment later* SALLY *enters left, carrying large, flat package. She goes into closet, draws back quickly, after leaving her package in closet.*)

SALLY: I wonder what that weird package is in there. Probably some kind of Mother's Day surprise. Well, my present for Mom is *perfect.* (*Stands back and looks at mantel*) It'll look great over the mantel. (*Phone rings, and she answers it.*) Hello. . . .

Roger Holmes? Sorry, he's not home right now. May I take a message? . . . His picture will be in the paper tonight? You're kidding! What for? . . . The most originality in the selection of a Mother's Day present? (*Miffed*) Well, I like that! No one surveyed me, and I bought Mom a great present—not some kind of a monster! . . . Oh, never mind what I mean. Goodbye! (*Slams phone down.* ROGER *enters, eating sandwich.*)

ROGER: Was that phone call for me, Sally?

SALLY (*Crossly*): Yes, it was. I didn't know you were home. It was a reporter from the *Bugle*. He said you were going to have your picture in the paper tonight, because you bought the most original Mother's Day present.

ROGER (*Groaning*): Oh, no, not tonight—he told me it would be in Sunday's paper! I can't have Mom seeing what she's going to get before Mother's Day. It's a surprise!

SALLY (*Coldly*): Some surprise. If it's that weird thing in the closet, it may ease the shock if she *does* know what it is.

ROGER (*Outraged*): You didn't unwrap it!

SALLY: Of course not! I wouldn't touch it with a ten-foot pole. Not after it poked me!

ROGER (*Disgusted*): Don't be silly. It's not alive!

SALLY: Well, it poked me.

ROGER (*Grimly*): My advice to you, then, is to keep out of the closet, or the next thing you know it'll be chasing you! But all kidding aside, we have to take that page with my picture out of the paper tonight before Mom sees it. You'll help me, won't you?

SALLY (*Sighing*): Oh, I suppose so. But I'm only doing it out of pity for Mother.

ROGER: Thanks, Sally. You're a real pal. Come on out to the kitchen. Mom left us some lunch. (*They exit right. Shortly,* CHRIS *and* PENNY *enter left.* CHRIS *carries package, wrapped in plain brown paper, which he puts on table.*)

PENNY: Hurry up, Chris. This is our big chance to see how it looks on the mantel. (*She and* CHRIS *unwrap package, to reveal large piece of driftwood. They put it on mantel and stand back, looking at it critically.*)

CHRIS (*Dubiously*): You know, it would have looked better with that bird sitting on it, the way it was at the flower shop.

PENNY: But that would have cost more money than we had. Let's go up to the attic and see if we can find something else to decorate it. (*They exit right, taking driftwood with them.* MR. HOLMES, *dragging large bearskin rug, enters right. He spreads it out on floor.*)

MR. HOLMES (*Pleased*): What a buy! Alice will love this. She always wanted a bearskin rug in front of the fireplace—I think. I'd better put it in the closet before anyone shows up. (*As he drags rug into closet, doorbell rings. He quickly pulls closet door shut from inside.* SALLY *enters, goes to door, opens it to* HILDA.)

SALLY (*Surprised*): Hilda! I thought you'd gone to visit your sister.

HILDA: I forgot to take the birthday cake I'd made for her—I left it in the refrigerator.

SALLY (*Dismayed*): Birthday cake—for your sister? Oh, no, Roger and I thought, that is, he thought—

HILDA (*In exasperation*): Don't tell me you and Roger cut into my prize chocolate ripple cake made with six eggs and a half a pound of butter and smothered in whipped cream!

SALLY: We—we not only cut into it, we demolished it! (*Upset*) I'm really sorry, Hilda.

HILDA (*Sighing heavily*): I might have known. (*Pats* SALLY *on shoulder*) Never mind, Sally, it wasn't your fault. I'll just have to make another one and take it over later. I might as well get right to it. (*She takes off jacket and heads for closet.*)

SALLY (*Hastily*): Let me hang your jacket for you, Hilda.

HILDA: Nonsense! I'm not old enough to be waited on yet. (*She tries to open closet, but door won't open.*) What's the matter with this door? (*She puts her jacket on table.*)

SALLY (*Startled*): You mean it won't open?

HILDA (*Suspiciously*): There've been a lot of petty thieves around this neighborhood lately. Maybe one is hiding in this closet right now. Well, no sneak thief is going to get around Hilda Swensen! (*She gives door handle a tremendous yank. Door opens,* HILDA *stumbles back, and* MR. HOLMES *falls forward onto floor.)*

SALLY (*Surprised*): Daddy!

HILDA: Oh, my goodness, gracious me! Whatever were you doing in that closet, Mr. Holmes?

MR. HOLMES (*Sarcastically, getting to his feet*): Hiding! (*He kicks closet door closed.*)

HILDA (*Soothingly*): Now, Mr. Holmes, you just let me fix you a cup of hot tea. Maybe you're feeling a bit feverish.

MR. HOLMES (*Annoyed*): I am not! I'm going downtown to meet Alice for lunch. And you two just keep out of that closet!

SALLY: Whatever you say, Daddy!

HILDA (*Muttering*): He's not himself! (MR. HOLMES *rushes out left.*)

SALLY: I'll come and help you with the cake, Hilda.

HILDA: All right, Sally. But I sure am worried about your dad. He's been working too hard lately. (*They exit right.* PENNY *and* CHRIS *enter left.* CHRIS *is carrying large stuffed eagle,* PENNY *carries driftwood.*)

CHRIS: I wonder why this old stuffed eagle was hidden in the attic—way back under the eaves, too. It's sort of mysterious.

PENNY: Mom will be so surprised. I can't wait to see how it looks on the mantel. (*She puts driftwood on mantel and* CHRIS *sets eagle on it, with great care. They stand back to view mantel.*)

CHRIS: Not bad! Lots better than that dinky little bird at the flower shop.

PENNY (*Pleased*): I'll say! I'm going to put this stuff in the closet before anyone comes. (*She picks up eagle and driftwood, opens closet door, then startled, she steps back hastily, pushing closet door shut with her foot.*) There's something in there, Chris—something with shiny eyes! It looked right at me!

CHRIS (*Disgustedly*): You read too many ghost stories. Penny. Here, let me put those things away. (*He takes driftwood and eagle, opens closet door confidently, then jumps back, quickly closing door.*) I guess we'd better hide it under the sofa. It's sort of crowded in the closet. (CHRIS *hides driftwood and eagle under sofa. Phone rings, and* PENNY *answers it.*)

PENNY (*Into phone*): Hello. . . . Oh, hi, Amy. . . . No, we'll be right over. (*Excitedly*) Listen, Amy, I think we have a ghost in our house. . . . Really! I'll tell you all about it. See you soon. (*Hangs up*) Come on, Chris. Amy's waiting for us. (*They exit left.* HILDA *enters right, tiptoes to closet, and opens door cautiously. She peeks in, then screams and hastily closes door.*)

HILDA: Oh, goodness, gracious me. I don't know what to make of Mr. Holmes. (MRS. HOLMES *enters left, carrying large box.*)

MRS. HOLMES (*Surprised*): Hilda! I thought you'd gone to your sister's.

HILDA: My plans have changed slightly, Mrs. Holmes. (*Pause*) Mr. Holmes left a little while ago. He said he was going to have lunch with you.

MRS. HOLMES (*Shaking her head*): He probably forgot where I told him to meet me. I waited and waited, and finally I had a bite and came home. Fred can be so absent-minded.

HILDA (*Hesitantly*): I don't think he was feeling quite himself today. I—I found him hiding in the closet!

MRS. HOLMES (*Astonished*): Hiding in the closet?

HILDA: That's what he said he was doing.

MRS. HOLMES: If he had anything to hide, it was probably something he picked up at the auction and didn't want us to see. (*She heads for closet.*)

HILDA (*Hastily stepping in front of her*): Oh, no, Mrs. Holmes, you mustn't go in there. Mr. Holmes strictly forbade it.

MRS. HOLMES: Nonsense, Hilda. I don't intend to scold him. I was a little extravagant myself this morning. (*Glancing at box*) We can have a good laugh together over whatever he bought.

HILDA: I'm going back to the kitchen. (SALLY *enters right, as* HILDA *exits.* MRS. HOLMES *has her hand on closet doorknob.*)

SALLY (*Rushing over to* MRS. HOLMES): Oh, Mom, you can't go in there!

MRS. HOLMES (*Exasperated*): You, too? Now my curiosity really *is* aroused. What has your father been up to?

SALLY: Oh, it isn't Daddy, it's something that Roger—oh, well, never mind. (*Pleads*) Just stay out of the closet, O.K., Mom?

MRS. HOLMES (*Smiling*): I guess I can take a hint. Where is Roger, anyway?

SALLY: He went to the store to get some cream for Hilda. She had to lend him the money for it, but he promised to pay her out of his next allowance.

MRS. HOLMES (*Puzzled*): Roger had to pay Hilda for the cream?

SALLY: Well, I'm going to pay for the butter and eggs, so it's only fair for him to pay for the cream. (*Quickly*) I don't have time to explain now, Mom. I'm helping Hilda. See you later. (*She exits.*)

MRS. HOLMES (*Thoughtfully*): Now, I wonder what that was all about. (*Looks toward closet*) And heaven only knows what they have in that closet. Oh, well, I'll think about something pleasant—my new dress. (*She opens box and takes out stylish dress. She holds it up to herself in front of mirror.*) I hope Fred likes it. Of course, it was very extravagant of me, but if he only remembers that I had a dress very much like this on our honeymoon, it may soften the blow. (*Dreamily*) It certainly pleased him then—he said the flowers matched my eyes! I think I'll put it away until tomorrow and surprise him. (*She puts dress back in box, looks around.*) Let's see—where can I put it? (*Suddenly*) I guess I'll just slide it under the sofa for now. (*She starts to push box under sofa, then stops and gets up. Surprised*) Now, how did that old stuffed eagle ever get under there? (*Doorbell rings, and she goes to open door. MESSENGER enters, carrying flower box.*)

MESSENGER: Flowers for Mrs. Holmes.

MRS. HOLMES: Flowers for me? How nice! (*She takes box. MESSENGER exits.*) They must be from Fred. How sweet! (*SALLY enters left, as MRS. HOLMES opens box and takes out red roses.*)

SALLY (*Excitedly*): What gorgeous roses! Who sent them, Mom?

MRS. HOLMES: Your father, of course, dear. Wasn't that sweet of him? (*ROGER enters.*)

ROGER: Wow! Red roses! Who sent them?

MRS. HOLMES: Your father. Here's the card. (*She removes card from envelope, looks at it; puzzled*) Why, this says "With best Mother's Day wishes from *The Daily Bugle*"! The florist must have made a mistake. I'd better call them.

SALLY (*Exchanging meaningful glance with ROGER*): Uh-oh.

MRS. HOLMES: Now, what do you mean by that?

SALLY (*Hastily*): Nothing, Mother—nothing at all, really. Your name is on the card, so they couldn't have made a mistake. Right, Roger?

ROGER (*Eagerly*): Right! It would be sort of like looking a gift horse in the mouth to question it.

MRS. HOLMES (*Doubtfully*): I suppose so. I don't know . . . Maybe it's some newspaper gimmick. There might be something in today's paper about it. I wonder if it's come yet. (*Starts for outside door*)

ROGER *and* SALLY (*Together*): I'll get it, Mom! (*They rush for door.*)

MRS. HOLMES: For heaven's sake, how come you're such eager beavers? I can wait. (ROGER *runs out door.*) Dear me, so much has been going on today, I do believe I'm getting a headache. (*Holds hand to head*)

SALLY: Why don't you go and lie down, Mom? I'll put the roses in water. (*Takes roses from* MRS. HOLMES, *exits right.*)

ROGER (*Popping head in door*): No paper yet. I'll keep my eye out for it.

MRS. HOLMES: Roger has taken a great interest in the paper all of a sudden. . . . I think I will lie down for a few minutes. (*She exits right.* MR. HOLMES *enters left, holding newspaper.*)

MR. HOLMES (*Sighing*): What a day! (SALLY *enters, with roses in vase.*)

SALLY: Hi, Daddy. You look sort of beat.

MR. HOLMES: You can say that again. I'm hungry, too. Your mother never met me for lunch. I don't know where she is.

SALLY: Why, Mom's been here for a long time. Hilda told me *you* didn't meet Mom for lunch. She waited and waited.

MR. HOLMES: She probably forgot where we'd arranged to go. Your mother's getting very absent-minded lately. Where did the flowers come from?

SALLY (*Teasing*): They're Mom's. A secret admirer sent them to her. She was thrilled! (MR. HOLMES *looks puzzled.*) I'll go make you a sandwich, Dad. Be right back! (SALLY *exits right.*)

MR. HOLMES (*Puzzled*): Who could have sent Alice a dozen roses, I'd like to know? (*Strides to telephone, looks up number in directory*) And I'm going to do something about it! (*Dials telephone. Then into phone*) Hello, Anson's Florist? . . . This is Fred Holmes at 59 Park Avenue. I want you to deliver two dozen yellow roses to my wife Alice, at this address. . . . The card is to read, "With the compliments of an admirer—your husband." . . . That's right. Thank you. (*Hangs up*) At least *I* know yellow is her favorite color. (*Picks up newspaper; irritated*) That paper boy is so sloppy! The paper's a mess. (*Starts to look through paper, becoming increasingly irritated*) Where's page two? (*Flips pages*) Page nine is missing, too! (*Groaning*) That does it! (*Shouts*) Alice! Alice! (*Curtain*)

* * * * *

SCENE 2

TIME: *The next morning.*

SETTING: *Same as Scene 1. Vase with yellow roses is on table, center. On table and around it on floor are brightly wrapped gifts. A large placard tacked to table reads,* HAPPY MOTHER'S DAY.

AT RISE: MRS. HOLMES *enters, followed by* MR. HOLMES, SALLY, ROGER, PENNY, *and* CHRIS.

ALL (*Together*): Happy Mother's Day!

MRS. HOLMES (*Slightly overcome*): Oh, my, is all this for me?

PENNY (*Picking up package*): Mom, this is from Chris and me.

MRS. HOLMES (*Starting to unwrap package*): I can't possibly guess what it is. It looks very mysterious. (*She opens package to reveal stuffed eagle attached to driftwood. She is speechless.*)

PENNY: Isn't it great, Mom? Aren't you surprised? We thought it would be perfect for the mantel—we've already tried it there. (MRS. HOLMES *smiles at them, then looks accusingly at* MR. HOLMES, *who tries to conceal a grin.*)

MRS. HOLMES: I'm surprised, all right. I'm positively overcome. I suppose you had your father's help with this?

PENNY (*Proudly*): No, we thought of it all by ourselves, didn't we, Chris?

CHRIS: You bet. We found the eagle in the attic, but we *bought* the driftwood. Wait till you see how great it looks. (*He places eagle on mantel.*)

ROGER (*Eagerly*): Hey, that's not half bad! Goes with my trophy— with my present, I mean.

MRS. HOLMES (*Faintly*): I can hardly wait to see it, dear. (ROGER *drags his present forward.*)

ROGER: You've been wanting something to go over the mantel for a long time, Mom. Just wait till you see this! (MRS. HOLMES *begins to untie package.*) Here, let me help you. (*Opens wrappings and reveals large antlers.* MRS. HOLMES *gasps and sinks back onto sofa.*)

SALLY: No wonder I got poked.

ROGER: Just wait till you see these antlers on the wall, Mom. (*He stands on chair by fireplace.*) Hey, what's this big nail doing here?

SALLY: I put it there to hold the present *I* got Mother!

ROGER (*Hotly*): Oh, no, you don't!

MRS. HOLMES: Oh, dear!

MR. HOLMES: To each his own, my boy. Let Sally have her chance.

ROGER (*Protesting*): But, Dad, *The Daily Bugle* put my picture in the paper yesterday for choosing the most original Mother's Day gift, and they sent Mom those red roses. My gift's *got* to be the best. (*He gets down from chair.*)

MRS. HOLMES: So the newspaper *did* send the roses!

MR. HOLMES: I don't remember seeing your picture in the paper—what was left of it.

ROGER (*Apologetically*): I tore that page out before you saw it, Dad. I was afraid Mom would see it and spoil the surprise. You can have it now, if you want it.

MR. HOLMES: No, thanks. No news is better than stale news.

MRS. HOLMES: Roger, I want to see your picture. Now I can really appreciate my roses. I'm glad I didn't look my gift horse in the mouth.

SALLY (*Impatiently*): If everyone is through with all their irrelevant chatter, I would like to give Mother *my* gift. (*Hands package to* MRS. HOLMES)

MRS. HOLMES: Thank you, Sally. (*Takes gift and opens it, revealing brightly colored oil painting*) Oh, my!

SALLY: Isn't it beautiful, Mother? I knew it would take your breath away. Jeff has painted dozens of pictures, but he feels that this is his masterpiece. He decided to open a studio in his father's garage and have an exhibition and sale. I was his first customer.

ROGER (*Guffawing*): And his last, I'd say!

SALLY: Don't show your ignorance. Jeffrey was voted most likely to succeed in his class.

MR. HOLMES (*Cautiously*): Are you sure you're not holding it upside down? (ROGER *snickers.*)

SALLY (*Indignantly*): Of course not, Daddy. You'll see it better when I hang it on the wall. It's called "Stag at Bay." It's much more effective from a distance.

ROGER: The farther off, the better!

SALLY (*Disdainfully*): At least it's a whole deer, not just the antlers! (*She hangs picture above mantel.*)

CHRIS (*Excitedly*): I see it—I see the stag! There's the head. (*Pointing*)

SALLY (*Disgustedly*): No, Chris, those are some bushes. It all seems perfectly clear to me, doesn't it to you, Mother?

MRS. HOLMES: Oh, yes, dear, yes, perfectly! And it's so—so—ah—colorful!

MR. HOLMES: You must admit it's an eyecatcher, Alice. And that's what you've been asking for. Roger could hang the antlers above the picture and along with my gift to you (*Presents huge package*), you'd have a real focal point, all right. (MRS. HOLMES *unwraps gift, revealing bearskin rug.*)

PENNY (*Screaming*): The ghost—the ghost!

CHRIS: Don't be silly. It's just a bearskin rug!

MRS. HOLMES (*Laughing helplessly*): Oh, Fred! What possessed you?

MR. HOLMES: Sentimental reasons. Don't you remember the bearskin rug in front of the fireplace at Niagara Falls?

MRS. HOLMES: On our honeymoon?

MR. HOLMES (*Nodding*): You said that someday you wanted one just like it.

MRS. HOLMES: I did?

MR. HOLMES (*Huffily*): If you don't like it, Alice, I'll put it out in the garage. I expect it'll come in handy if I'm changing a tire.

MRS. HOLMES (*Reassuringly*): Oh, I didn't say I didn't like it, dear. It was very sweet of you to remember. Let's put it right down in front of the fireplace. (MR. HOLMES *arranges rug, as* MRS. HOLMES *removes box from beneath sofa, takes out dress, and holds it up.* MR. HOLMES *gets to his feet.*) How do you like it, Fred?

MR. HOLMES (*Gazing admiringly at rug, as* MRS. HOLMES *turns back to mirror*): It looks great! (*Dreamily*) Reminds me of our honeymoon, all right.

MRS. HOLMES: Do you think the flowers match my eyes, dear?

MR. HOLMES: Flowers? What are you talking about, Alice? (*Seeing dress for the first time*) Oh, you've got a new dress. (HILDA *enters, carrying tray with coffee cake, dishes, coffeepot, etc.*)

HILDA: That's a mighty pretty new dress, Mrs. Holmes. I'd say the flowers match your eyes.

MR. HOLMES (*Grinning broadly*): Now that you mention it, Hilda, I guess they do. Sort of reminds me of the dress you wore on our honeymoon, dear. (*He puts his arm affectionately around* MRS. HOLMES.)

MRS. HOLMES: You've all given me a wonderful Mother's Day, with lots of loving thought behind it. (*Gazing at the mantel, thoughtfully*) You know, the longer I look at the driftwood, the better I like it. It's—well—it's different! And it's going to be a real conversation piece.

PENNY: Conversation piece? What's that?

CHRIS: It means everybody will be talking about us!

MRS. HOLMES: That's right. I'm sure nobody will have a mantel decoration to equal it! (*Curtain*)

THE END

Mother for Mayor

by Jane McGowan

Striking the right balance between the demands of family and politics . . .

Characters

MARY WEBSTER, *candidate for Mayor of Greenville*
JULIA WEBSTER, *her daughter, 16*
TINA WEBSTER, *her daughter, 12*
JEFF WEBSTER, *her son, 14*
DICK DALY, *a reporter*
TOM SIMMS, *Jeff's friend*
BARRY SIMMS, *Tom's older brother and Julia's boyfriend*
GLORIA CHADWICK, *chairwoman of Independent Women Voters*

SETTING: *Living room of Webster home, comfortably furnished. On table near chair are telephone, pencil, and notepad. Exit right leads to front door; exit left to kitchen and rest of house.*
AT RISE: JULIA *and* TINA WEBSTER *are going through cookbooks and recipe cards as they talk to* DICK DALY.
JULIA: If you'd only wait till my mom comes home, she'd give you exactly what you want.
DALY: Sorry, but I have a deadline to meet. My editor said to round up favorite recipes from all the mayoral candidates, and

313

Ms. Webster's is the only one I'm missing. I've got to make the *Herald*'s morning edition, so could you just pick one out?

TINA: How about her recipe for peanut butter fudge? That's delicious.

JULIA: Tina, we don't want the voters to think Mom feeds her family a diet of peanut butter fudge. We want something nourishing and inexpensive.

DALY: You've got the right idea. We want to get the human interest angle on all the candidates—family life, kids, parental values.

TINA (*Picking out card*): Here's "Shrimp Wiggle." Would that do?

DALY: Sounds pretty revolting to me.

JULIA: I'd feel a lot better about this if Mom were here. She has lots of wonderful recipes.

DALY (*Pulling out card*): What's this? "Mulligan Stew au Gratin."

TINA: Oh, that's good! We always have that when the budget runs short.

DALY (*To* JULIA): What do you think? Is it O.K.?

JULIA (*Hesitantly*): Well, I guess so. It's good, all right, and it's economical.

DALY: Sounds like our dish! Thanks a lot, you two. I've got to run. Sorry to miss your mother, but I'm sure I'll be back for another story—it's not every day that a woman runs for Mayor of Greenville.

JULIA: *Another* story! How many will you be doing?

DALY: That depends on my editor. But your mother is big news right now. That means lots of articles and photos—of her and her kids.

TINA: Big news? She's just "Mom" to us.

DALY (*Scribbling in notebook*): Hey, that's good! "Just Mom to us." Well, thanks again, kids, and good luck! May the best mom win! (*Laughing*) Ha! That's a good one! "May the best mom win!" Tell her she can use that as a slogan, with my compliments. So long. (*He exits.*)

JULIA (*Rolling her eyes*): Thank goodness he's a reporter and not a campaign manager! (*Frowning*) I hope we made a good choice on that recipe. (BARRY SIMMS *enters right.*)

BARRY: Hi, Julia—Tina. The door was open, so I just walked in.

JULIA (*Smiling*): Oh, hello, Barry.

BARRY: Who was that guy that was just here?

JULIA: A reporter from the *Herald.*

BARRY: More headlines for Mamma Webster, I take it. What's the angle this time?

TINA: Mulligan Stew!

BARRY: Huh?

JULIA: They're doing a story on the candidates' favorite recipes.

BARRY: Oh, I get it—human interest stuff! Big politician takes time out to chop carrots for her happy family. (*He mimes taking her photograph.*) Smile and say Mulligan Stew! (*Guffaws*)

JULIA (*Annoyed*): Will you please stop calling my mother a big politician?

BARRY: Aw, loosen up, Julia. She *is* a politician, isn't she?

JULIA (*Heatedly*): Not in the way you mean! Her family's not a photo opportunity. She's a public-spirited citizen who's being drafted into the service of her community.

BARRY: Sorry! My mistake. I was under the impression that your mother's running for mayor of this town.

JULIA: Sure she is—so what?

BARRY: So she's a politician.

JULIA: But people *asked* my mother to run.

BARRY: What's the difference? If she's running and she wants to win, then she'll have to play politics, honey!

JULIA (*Angrily*): Don't you "honey" me, Barry Simms! My mother's not playing at anything. She wants to *work* for the people of Greenville.

BARRY: Look, Julia, I think your mother's great, but she's just like everybody else who goes into politics. She'll have to swap recipes with the old pols. One false move, and she's out.

JULIA (*Coldly*): No, *you're* out—right out the front door. I hope it's still open so you won't have to soil your hands on our political doorknob.

BARRY: Don't be silly. Can't we discuss politics and Mulligan Stew like two grownups?

TINA: You heard what my sister said. Get lost!

BARRY: Julia, I just came over here to see if you want to go to Sue's party on Saturday. Be reasonable.

TINA: She's reasonable, all right. (*Points to door*) Goodbye!

BARRY: Is that how you want it, Julia?

JULIA: That's how it *is*, Barry.

BARRY (*Muttering to himself*): Was it something I said? (*To* JULIA) If you have a change of heart, let me know. You may feel different when you see your mother cross swords with Mrs. Chadwick.

TINA: Who's Mrs. Chadwick?

JULIA: Don't ask questions, Tina. I want him to get out of here fast.

BARRY (*To* TINA): Julia will tell you. In the meantime, so long. (BARRY *exits.*)

JULIA (*Fuming*): He makes me so mad I could spit!

TINA: So who's Mrs. Chadwick?

JULIA: Mrs. Chadwick is chair of the Independent Women Voters.

TINA: Does Mom have to do what she says?

JULIA: Well, sort of . . . I mean (*Irritated*) . . . well, no! No, Tina. All she has to do is be herself. Come on, let's clear this mess away and set the table for supper.

TINA (*Collecting cookbooks*): Do you think Barry is gone forever?

JULIA (*Staunchly*): He'd better be!

TINA: Really? Forever?

JULIA (*Giving in*): Let me put it this way. In my book, forever should last no longer than the day after tomorrow. (TINA *shrugs and exits left. Phone rings and* JULIA *answers it.*) Hello. . . . Oh, hello, Mr. Price! . . . No, my mom isn't at the bank today. She took time off to give a speech. But I'm expecting her soon. . . . No, Jeff isn't home either. What's the matter? Is he in some sort of trouble? . . . All right, I'll have her call you as soon as she gets home. Goodbye. (*Hangs up as* TINA *re-enters*)

TINA: Who was that?

JULIA: Mr. Price, Jeff's teacher. He wants to talk to Mom as soon as she gets home. (*Upset*) I'll bet Jeff's in some sort of trouble at school.

TINA: Not again!

JULIA: You'd think he'd know enough to keep out of trouble when Mom is in the middle of a campaign.

TINA: I'd better go and look for him.

JULIA: Maybe he's at basketball practice. If you find him, tell him to come right home. Much as I hate to do it, I'll call Barry. Jeff might be with his brother.

TINA: O.K. 'Bye. (*She exits.* JULIA *dials phone.*)

JULIA (*On phone*): Hello, Barry? It's Julia. . . . I certainly did *not* call to apologize! I'm trying to find Jeff. Is he there with Tom? . . . (*Concerned*) I wonder where he could be? . . . I'm not sure what's up, but Mr. Price just called, and I have an idea Jeff is in some sort of trouble. . . . Please call me if you see him. . . . (*Angrily*) Of course I'm still mad! Goodbye. (*Hangs up*) I hope I can get this straightened out before Mom gets home. (JULIA *exits left. After a moment,* JEFF WEBSTER *and* TOM SIMMS *enter right.*)

TOM: If you ask me, Jeff, you're nuts.

JEFF: Nobody's asking you. *Your* mother's not running for mayor. The fact is that when somebody in your family is running for office, the least you can do is to keep your nose clean. Wait until word gets out that Mary Webster's son has been suspended from junior high school!

TOM: I don't see how you'll make things any better by running away! The headlines will be even worse.

JEFF: I just want to keep out of Mom's sight till I get another chance to talk to Mr. Price. Let me stay at your house tonight and I'll have another go at him tomorrow.

TOM: All I'm saying is that if you told the truth right away—

JEFF: The truth? Then I'd really be in the soup! And Mom, too!

TOM: But suppose Mr. Price calls her?

JEFF: Mom's pretty hard to catch these days. The worst he can do is get hold of Julia. But I can count on her to stall for me till I straighten things out. Come on, Tom. What do you say?

TOM: I'm sure my mom won't mind if you spend the night at my house, but won't your mother be worried?

JEFF: I'll tell Julia and Tina where I am. (*Calling*) Hey, Julia! Tina! Anybody home? (*To* TOM) Wouldn't you know! Two sisters and neither one around when I need them. Wait here till I get my stuff. If they're not back by then, I'll leave a note. (JEFF *exits*.)

TOM: I'm glad my mom's not running for mayor! (*Phone rings.* TOM *answers it.*) Hello. Yes, this is the Webster residence. . . . Sorry, Mrs. Webster isn't here. (*Pause*) Mrs. Chadwick? Sure, I'll tell her. . . . No, I'm not her son. I'm just a neighbor. Goodbye. (*He hangs up.*)

JEFF (*Entering with overnight bag*): Who was that?

TOM: You'll never believe it. Mrs. Chadwick!

JEFF (*Alarmed*): Oh, no! What did she want?

TOM (*Scribbling on pad*): She said to tell your mother she's coming over.

JEFF: That does it. Let's get out of here.

TOM: What about telling Julia where you are?

JEFF: I'll call her from your house. Come on! Step on it! (*They exit left as* TINA *enters right, carrying a newspaper.*)

TINA (*Calling*): Hey, Julia! Where are you? (*To herself*) Wait till she sees this picture of Mom! (*Reading to herself*) "Candidate Webster Promises Civic Clean-Up. Mary Webster, local civic leader and prominent member of the City Planning Council, proposes plan to make Greenville a safer, better place to raise children. Ms. Webster, Branch Manager at City Bank and mother of three, all students of Greenville Public Schools, announced—" (JULIA *enters.*) Oh, there you are. Look, here's a big article about Mom. Good picture of her, too! (*Shows paper*)

JULIA (*Glancing at paper*): Tina, I'm worried. I can't find Jeff. Did Barry call?

TINA: No, but I just came in.

MS. WEBSTER (*Calling from off right*): Yoo-hoo! Anybody home? (*Enters with an armful of books, notebooks and papers*) Hello, girls! How are my favorite constituents? (*Dumping articles on table and sinking into a chair*) I'm nearly dead. Tina, could you get me a glass of water, dear?

TINA: Sure, Mom. (*She exits left.*)

JULIA: How did the speech go?

MS. WEBSTER: Fine. I was really scared at first, but it was all right after I got started. What's wrong with you? You look worried.

JULIA: Just tired. I have a headache.

Ms. WEBSTER: Oh, no—but isn't this your night with Barry?

JULIA (*Dejectedly*): No, not any more.

Ms. WEBSTER: But it's Tuesday. And how could it be Tuesday without Barry?

TINA (*Entering with water*): I guess we won't be seeing old Barry for a while. Julia blew up at him. (JULIA *glares at* TINA.)

Ms. WEBSTER: But you and Barry never fight. What in the world happened?

JULIA (*Stiffly*): Really, Mom, I don't want to talk about it. Tina had no business mentioning it.

TINA (*Shrugging*): Sorry. Say, Mom, did you see your picture in the paper? That Dick Daly really did a great job! (*Shows paper*)

Ms. WEBSTER: Dick Daly? Since when do you know Dick Daly?

TINA: Oh, he was here this afternoon to pick up a recipe.

Ms. WEBSTER (*Surprised*): A *what–?*

JULIA: He wanted to do a roundup of all the candidates' favorite recipes.

TINA: So we gave him the Mulligan Stew au Gratin!

Ms. WEBSTER (*Alarmed*): Good heavens! You didn't! Not that one!

JULIA (*Groaning*): I knew we should have chosen the Shrimp Wiggle.

Ms. WEBSTER: Mulligan Stew au Gratin is Mrs. Chadwick's secret recipe. She serves it at her Sunday-night suppers, and she gave it to me as a very special favor. If it ever comes out in the paper as *my* specialty, she'll have a fit.

JULIA (*Pointedly*): Why does it matter so much if Mrs. Chadwick has a fit?

Ms. WEBSTER: Why, good heavens, Julia, Mrs. Chadwick heads the Independent Women Voters. I certainly can't afford to have her angry with me right now.

JULIA: So Barry was right.

Ms. WEBSTER: What does Barry have to do with it?

JULIA: Oh, nothing . . . just something he said, that's all. Now it looks as if he might have been right.

Ms. Webster (*Dialing phone*): I've got to call that reporter right away. (*On phone*) Hello, Dick Daly, please. (*Pause*) Hello, Mr. Daly, Mary Webster here. About that recipe you've got. I'm afraid it's not mine to give away. . . . Oh, no! Are you sure you can't stop it? I wouldn't have called if it weren't so important . . . I'll be glad to give you another recipe. . . . Yes, I'll be home until seven. You can come and get it. . . . Thank you. Goodbye. (*Hangs up*) I hope he can keep that recipe out of the morning edition. This is one time when I'll be happy if the *Herald* doesn't have *any* news about candidate Webster.

Julia: Are you as scared as all that of Mrs. Chadwick, Mom?

Ms. Webster: Well, I'm not scared, but naturally I don't want to annoy her. Besides, it would be dishonest to publish that recipe as my own. Don't you understand?

Tina: I understand, Mom. That's not playing politics, Julia. That's just good sense.

Ms. Webster: What's all this about playing politics?

Julia: Nothing. But I think Tina should go into politics. It might teach her not to speak out of turn. (*Doorbell rings*)

Tina: I'll see who it is. (*Exits*)

Ms. Webster: Julia, you're keeping something from me, aren't you?

Julia: There's just so much fuss over this recipe and everything. (Mrs. Chadwick *enters with* Tina.)

Mrs. Chadwick: Hope I'm not intruding, Mary.

Ms. Webster: Hello, Gloria! This is a surprise.

Mrs. Chadwick: The minute I heard the news I thought I'd better dash right over here and have a talk before it was public knowledge. Did you get my message?

Ms. Webster: What message? And what news?

Mrs. Chadwick: Oh, you poor dear! These things are always so hard on a parent. And it's just too bad it had to happen right now . . . especially when your other children have had such splendid records. We'll just try to hush it up as quickly as possible.

Ms. Webster (*Upset*): Gloria, what are you talking about? What do my children have to do with your coming here?

MRS. CHADWICK: I hate to be the one to break the news to you. I had supposed Mr. Price would call you right away.

Ms. WEBSTER: Did Mr. Price call, Julia?

JULIA: Yes, he did. But I haven't had a chance to tell you. He wanted you to call him as soon as you came in.

TINA: It sounded to us as if Jeff is in hot water!

MRS. CHADWICK: He certainly is, Mary. The fact is that Jeff has been suspended from school.

Ms. WEBSTER (*Aghast*): Jeff suspended! But where is he?

MRS. CHADWICK (*Smugly*): I suppose he's afraid to come home.

Ms. WEBSTER: Gloria, I have always raised my children to understand that home is the first place to come when they need help. Girls, do you know where he is?

JULIA: We've looked everywhere, Mom.

Ms. WEBSTER: Where can he be? I'm really worried!

MRS. CHADWICK (*Folding her arms*): So am I, Mary.

Ms. WEBSTER: It's good of you to worry about Jeff, too, and under the circumstances you'll understand that I couldn't possibly keep any speaking engagement this evening . . . not until I can get this problem with Jeff straightened out.

MRS. CHADWICK: Please understand me, Mary. I said I was worried, but not about Jeff. It's you I'm worried about . . . you and the campaign. You must realize that after all the work I've done for you, I certainly won't have it spoiled. You'll have to settle this thing as quickly and quietly as possible. Send that terrible boy to private school if need be.

Ms. WEBSTER (*Astonished*): How can you talk like that when you don't even know what he's done?

MRS. CHADWICK: I know only too well what he's done! I was there—and I was never so amazed in my life. There we were, the whole Executive Council of the P.T.A. with Dr. Farnsworth and three other members of the Board of Education as our guests at a luncheon in the school cafeteria . . . when BANG! We were almost blown out of our chairs. Somebody had thrown one of those giant firecrackers right outside the window!

TINA: Oh, boy! I'll bet Mr. Price exploded!

Ms. WEBSTER: Gloria, why do you think it was Jeff who threw it?

MRS. CHADWICK (*Smugly*): I *know* it was Jeff who threw it, Mary. He admitted it!

MS. WEBSTER (*Skeptically*): Don't tell me he marched in there and gave himself up!

MRS. CHADWICK: Hardly! The firecracker was thrown from the room above. Mr. Price dashed up to the study hall, and Jeff admitted that he had thrown it. So, Mr. Price made him go downstairs and apologize before the whole crowd.

MS. WEBSTER (*In dismay*): I still can't believe it.

MRS. CHADWICK: Mary, I must say your attitude amazes me! Don't you realize that your boy's disgraceful conduct might cost you votes that you can ill afford to lose? This campaign is not going to be easy. Plenty of people are skeptical about a woman mayor. Now Jeff has made you a laughingstock. Just let the papers get hold of this! If my son Eustace had ever done a thing like this, I'd waste no time feeling sorry for him, I can tell you that!

MS. WEBSTER (*More calmly*): Then that's one way in which we differ, Gloria. Jeff is more important to me than any office in the world, and my first concern right now is to find him and help him. (*Doorbell rings.* TINA *exits.*)

JULIA: Good for you, Mom. I knew you could play politics by your own rules! (TINA *enters with* DICK DALY.)

DALY: Sorry to bust in on you like this, Ms. Webster. Oh, good evening, Mrs. Chadwick. (*Pulls out notebook and pen; eagerly*) You two discussing campaign strategies?

MRS. CHADWICK: Good heavens! A reporter! Now look here, sir, Mr. Price assured me there would be no need to smear this whole thing in the papers! It's a matter between the school and the parent.

DALY: Aha! It looks as though I've walked in on a story!

MS. WEBSTER: A very sad story, I'm afraid, Mr. Daly. My son has been suspended from school.

MRS. CHADWICK (*Aghast*): Mary! Don't you realize you're talking to the press?

MS. WEBSTER: Jeff did a very foolish thing this afternoon, but he did not commit a crime. Mr. Daly will have to make up his own mind about the publicity he chooses to give it! Right now I'm concerned only about Jeff. I just can't understand why he doesn't come home.

DALY: Is there anything I can do to help? Has the boy run away?

(BARRY *enters with* TOM *and* JEFF.)

BARRY: At least he didn't run far! No farther than our house!

(Ms. WEBSTER *hurries to* JEFF *and hugs him.*)

Ms. WEBSTER (*Relieved*): Jeff! Thank heavens you're safe.

JEFF (*Weakly*): Hiya, Mom. I'm sorry I got into such a mess.

TINA: Boy, oh, boy! You sure put your foot in it this time, Jeff!

JULIA: Quiet, Tina!

JEFF (*To* Ms. WEBSTER): I thought maybe it would be better if I stayed at Tom's house . . . well, with this election and everything.

MRS. CHADWICK: Young man, you should have thought of this election before you ruined your mother's career!

Ms. WEBSTER: Gloria, I must ask you not to interfere! This is a matter between Jeff and me. As for Jeff's ruining my career . . . that's utterly ridiculous.

JEFF: Listen, Mom. I just wanted to stay clear of home till I could talk Mr. Price into letting me come back to school, and I figured the whole thing would quiet down. I didn't want to drag you into it.

MRS. CHADWICK: That's very noble of you, I'm sure! But I'm afraid Mr. Price will hardly want to be lenient with you.

BARRY: I'm afraid there's more to the story than you know, Mrs. Chadwick.

MRS. CHADWICK: You forget, young man, I was there when he admitted he threw the firecracker out the window!

BARRY: But he didn't say where he got the firecracker, did he?

JEFF (*Warningly*): Barry . . .

BARRY (*Interrupting him*): Do you mind if I ask you a question, Mrs. Chadwick?

JEFF: Please, Barry! Stay out of it!

TOM: Go ahead and ask her, Barry!

BARRY: Mrs. Chadwick, what would you do if you were standing by an open window, and somebody came along and put a lighted firecracker into your hands?

MRS. CHADWICK (*Bristling*): What a ridiculous question!

BARRY: Yes, isn't it? Because the answer is so obvious! You'd drop it or throw it like a hot potato before it could explode in your face.

DALY (*Incredulously*): Do you mean somebody just handed that firecracker to Jeff?

BARRY: That's right. Jeff's only mistake was that he didn't mop up the floor with young Eustace Chadwick.

OTHERS (*Ad lib; surprised*): What? Was Eustace in on this? (*Etc.*)

MRS. CHADWICK: Young man, do you realize what you're implying?

BARRY (*Triumphantly*): That Eustace Chadwick the Third walked into the study hall and handed that lighted firecracker to Jeff—just to see what he'd do with it.

JEFF (*Dismayed*): I had to throw it out the window. But I had no idea there was a luncheon going on downstairs.

MRS. CHADWICK: Well, Eustace couldn't have known that either. It was not deliberate.

BARRY: But he deliberately kept quiet when Mr. Price came in. Jeff had to admit he threw the firecracker. Mr. Price was too mad to ask for any more information, and Good Citizen Chadwick didn't volunteer any.

MRS. CHADWICK (*Indignant*): That's a preposterous story! I don't believe a word of it!

BARRY: It's easy to check, Mrs. Chadwick. Just ask your son . . . or ask any of the kids who were in the room when it happened.

MRS. CHADWICK: Very well, I will! As for you, Mary, I just don't understand your attitude at a time like this!

Ms. WEBSTER: If you mean you can't understand why I'd place my children before my career, then I'll have to run for mayor without your support. And if the rest of the Independent Women Voters feel the way you do, so be it.

DALY: Excuse me for butting in, Ms. Webster, but I don't think you have to worry about that. This town is sure to vote for a woman who can stand up for her principles and for her kids. And I'll be more than happy to show it to our readers.

MRS. CHADWICK: I guess you don't need me any longer. (*Stiffly*) Good night, Mary.

Ms. WEBSTER (*Warmly*): Good night, Gloria. I hope you'll change your mind about me.

MRS. CHADWICK: I intend to have a long talk with Eustace. (*To JEFF; softening*) And if what I've heard this evening is true, I'll be back to make amends. (*Exits*)

BARRY: Julia, I owe you and your mother an apology. She does make her own rules for playing politics. (JULIA *smiles, takes his arm.*)

JULIA: And I'm sorry I got so hot and bothered.

Ms. WEBSTER (*Smiling*): So that's what you two argued about! I think I understand.

DALY: I hate to break things up here, but how about that recipe, Ms. Webster?

TINA: Should I give him the one for peanut butter fudge, Mom? (Ms. WEBSTER *looks alarmed, then laughs and others join in. Quick curtain.*)

THE END

Production Notes

Production Notes

PROLOGUE TO ADVENTURE

Characters: 7 male; 2 female.
Playing Time: 30 minutes.
Costumes: Spanish dress of the late fifteenth century.
Properties: A letter for Perez.
Setting: The sitting room of a small inn outside Granada, Spain. Upstage left center is a door which opens on the yard; upstage right center, a window overlooking the yard. Downstage center is a table, on which is a bowl of apples. To right of table is a bench; to the left, several chairs.
Lighting: No special effects.

A COMPASS FOR CHRISTOPHER

Characters: 6 male; 4 female.
Playing Time: 10 minutes.
Costumes: The girls wear long-sleeved square-necked dresses with long bodices and full skirts. Maria and Susanna wear particularly colorful dresses. Susanna has a small compass in the pocket of her dress. The men and boys wear hose and long-sleeved doublets. Don Pedro wears a cape. Christopher has red hair.
Properties: Net, bolt of blue cloth, small compass.

Setting: The harbor at Genoa, Italy. The only furnishings needed are several kegs. A harbor backdrop might be used. Nets might be hung around the stage, and piles of crates placed in corners.
Lighting: No special effects.

THE NEW BROOM

Characters: 3 male; 7 female.
Playing Time: 20 minutes.
Costumes: Witches wear black robes, black pointed hats, and masks, and all but 4th carry a broom. Other characters wear everyday clothes.
Properties: 4 brooms.
Setting: The living room of an old house should be made as cobwebby and dusty as possible in the beginning. All furniture is covered with dusty pieces of cloth. Cobwebs may be suggested by wispy bits of thread hung here and there. Piles of newspapers and other objects suggest a littered effect. There are entrances right and left, and an entrance from the street at right center of back wall.
Lighting: Dim lighting at beginning suggests the shabbiness and dustiness of the room. After the room has been cleaned by the witches, light should be bright.

THE HOUND OF THE MASKERVILLES

Characters: 7 male; 7 female; as many extras as desired for Masqueraders.

Playing Time: 35 minutes.

Costumes: Witches wear traditional black costumes. Lady Maskerville wears flowing white robes. Footmen are dressed as skeletons, and maids wear appropriate costumes and masks. Ghoulfinger has on a hunting outfit and carries a hunting horn and a leash for Fang, whose costume should be as ferocious and ugly as possible. Heada is dressed in a trailing black dress and garden hat, and wears a half-mask. Gangsters wear everyday clothes and half-masks, and carry a violin case and a briefcase. Mayor has a blanket around his waist and wears a cap with a stuffed toy black cat attached when he first enters. He later puts on a long red robe. Masqueraders wear costumes and masks. If desired, some may have musical instruments, which they play as they enter.

Properties: Black coffin containing pillows and sheet, chest, teacups, notepaper, pen.

Setting: A clearing in front of the witches' cave in Hag Hollow. The entrance to the cave is at right, and over it is a large "Welcome" sign, festooned with orange and black streamers. Nearby are several tree stumps. A large black pot is at right, and a long table set with plates of sandwiches, crackers, paper cups, and Halloween decorations is at left. An exit is left.

Lighting: No special effects.

Sound: Whirring noise, barking and snarling, horn blasts, music.

HAPPY HAUNTING!

Characters: 6 female.

Playing Time: 10 minutes.

Costumes: Halloween costumes, as appropriate, for all.

Properties: Letters for Miss Goblinette; lorgnette for Mrs. Spectre.

Setting: Miss Magicia's office. A desk, with a chair behind it and one beside it, are left center. Four straight chairs are arranged in a semi-circle, right, facing the desk. Pictures and a bookcase filled with books decorate the back wall. There is a door at right.

Lighting: No special effects.

Sound effects: Loud knocking, as indicated in text.

VOTING AGAINST THE ODDS

Characters: 3 male; 3 female.

Playing Time: 20 minutes.

Costumes: Everyday, modern dress.

Properties: Comic books (including one booklet on voting); four large sandwiches; scissors; scraps of felt (letters and pennant may be precut).

Setting: Living room. At one side is a large table holding telephone and pile of comic books. Several chairs are near table. The other furnishings may include easy chairs, lamps, etc. Exits are right and left, one leading to kitchen, the other to front door.

Lighting: No special effects.

Sound: Doorbell, as indicated in text.

HUBBUB ON THE BOOKSHELF

Characters: 6 male; 3 female.

Playing Time: 25 minutes.

Costumes: At rise, Bookworms are identically dressed in white or pale gray sheaths. Old Bookworm is in similar costume, and has long white beard. Later, Young Bookworms change into costumes described in text.

Properties: Scrap of paper, lorgnette, covered basket, guitar, sword, huge spray can with label reading, INSECT REPELLANT, giant-sized comic book.

Setting: An old bookshelf in an attic. Eight large "books" (flats or cardboard cut-outs) form the background. Each "book" has a flap at the bottom for exits and entrances. "Books" are labeled as follows: "Etiquette," "Grimms' Fairy Tales," "Encyclopedia," "Dracula," "Life of a Rock Superstar," "King Arthur and His Knights," "Tales of the Wild West," and "Arithmetic."

Lighting: No special effects.

THE CASE OF THE BEWITCHED BOOKS

Characters: 7 female; 3 male; 12 male or female for Readers, Herald, Dwarfs and Librarian; as many male or female as desired for Stagehands.

Playing Time: 20 minutes.

Costumes: Witch wears black gown, cape and conical hat; Stepsisters, fright wigs, gaudy gowns, junk jewelry and false noses; Wicked Queen, gown, ermine robe, crown and heavy eye make-up; Sleeping Beauty and Cinderella, ball gowns, tiaras, dancing slippers. Snow White wears gown, slippers and small crown. Prince Florian wears a knight's costume; Herald, tunic, tights, boots and hat; Prince Charming, tunic, ermine robe, trousers tucked into boots, and crown. Dwarfs may have white beards, and wear turtleneck sweaters, tunics, breeches tucked into

boots, and elf caps. Chubby's costume is stuffed with a pillow, and Sloppy's buttons are left unbuttoned. Prince Roland has Robin Hood-type costume. Readers and Librarian wear modern, everyday clothing.

Properties: Picket signs for Witch and Wicked Queen reading, FAIRY TALES UNFAIR TO WITCHES and MIRROR, MIRROR ON THE WALL, WE WANT JUSTICE FOR VILLAINS ALL! Sandwich signs for Two Stepsisters reading, SUPPORT YOUR LOCAL STEPSISTERS and STEPSISTERS ARE HUMAN, TOO. Books for Readers, reading, SLEEPING BEAUTY, CINDERELLA, and SNOW WHITE; chair on wheels, chaise on wheels, with sheet, to cover Witch; basket of apples for Wicked Queen.

Setting: Before Rise: This scene is played before curtain. Sign reading, FAIRY TALE FESTIVAL, CHILDREN'S ROOM OF THE PUBLIC LIBRARY is on easel down right. At Rise: Library, with bookcase labeled, FAIRY TALES upstage center, librarian's desk and chair up left, and table with three chairs down right.

Lighting: No special effects.

Sound: Chimes striking twelve; trumpet fanfare.

Music: Musical chords, lullaby, waltz and march music, as indicated in text.

HORN OF PLENTY

Characters: 6 male; 4 female.

Playing Time: 30 minutes.

Costumes: Modern dress. Officers wear uniforms. Sally carries purse.

Properties: Cartons of assorted items, including baseball glove; sporting equipment; small radio; tennis racket; alarm clock; portable typewriter; two coin purses; sousaphone; metal toy bank; old-fashioned tuba; coins; keys; two pies covered with aluminum foil.

Setting: Hill living room. There is table left holding old-fashioned tuba. Desk is up center. Telephone is on small table right, which also has drawer containing change purse. Sofa and chairs complete furnishings. Exit left leads to kitchen and other rooms; exit right leads outside.

Lighting: No special effects.

Sound: Telephone, siren, as indicated.

New-Fangled Thanksgiving

Characters: 4 male; 3 female.

Playing Time: 20 minutes.

Costumes: Mr. Brooks wears suit; Kevin and Billy, jackets and slacks. Vicky and Mrs. Brooks wear dresses; when she first enters, Mrs. Brooks also has on large apron with turkey on it. Grandma and Grandpa wear coats.

Properties: Suitcases.

Setting: Living room of the Brooks' house. Exits are right and left. There is sofa up center, easy chairs right and left. Small tables, lamps, television, books, etc., as required to furnish the room comfortably.

Lighting: No special effects.

The Pilgrim Painting

Characters: 5 male; 4 female.

Playing Time: 20 minutes.

Costumes: Modern clothing for Landis family. Meg wears many-colored dress; David, a red sweater. Mr. Marks wears coat. Pilgrims wear appropriate dark brown or gray Pilgrim costumes.

Properties: Old doll; rubber ball; bowl of fruit, including banana and orange; large cooked turkey in box; check.

Setting: The Landis living/dining room. Table (set for dinner) and four chairs are left, and armchair and end table are right. Door right leads outside; door left to kitchen. At center back are two folding screens behind which is Pilgrim tableau, a long table placed lengthwise with bench behind it facing audience and chairs at either end.

Lighting: Spotlight on tableau, if desired.

The Reform of Benjamin Scrimp

Characters: 5 male; 4 female; 12 male and female for Jitterbug Dancers; 7 male or female for Paper Boy, Delivery Person, Ghosts, Doctor, Band Leader; as many extras as desired for Carolers, Band.

Playing Time: 35 minutes.

Costumes: Penny, Lora, Kim, Mike and Ralph, modern school clothes; later, they wear dresses, suits, may use canes (these outfits may be worn over school clothes). Benjamin Scrimp, black suit and string tie, has checkbook and pen in pocket. Paper Boy, ragged jeans, jacket. Delivery Person, uniform. Ghost of Christmas Present, red and green rock-star costume. Ghost of Christmas Past, red-and-green striped "zoot suit" (thigh-length jacket with wide lapels and padded shoulders, wide peg-top trousers, bow tie), long watch chain. Ghost of Christmas Future, sheet and astronaut's helmet. Doctor, white coat. Debbie Ann and jitterbug girls, pleated skirts, sweaters, bobby socks, saddle shoes; jitterbug boys, slacks, open-necked shirts, sports jackets. Frankie Bing Scrimp, white zoot suit, bow tie. Carolers, red and green robes.

Properties: Easel with sign reading, AUDITORIUM, CHARLES DICKENS JUNIOR HIGH SCHOOL, calculator, stepstool, clipboard, checklist, tape measure, basketball, dolly, large boxes, bandages, cot, stethoscope, decorated Christmas tree, banner reading, CHRISTMAS SOCK HOP, 1955, bandstand, microphone, benches, tray, punch cups, baton, banner reading, CHRISTMAS REUNION, CLASS OF 199-.

Setting: Bare gym with basketball hoop up center. Extra properties are brought on and off stage by stagehands, as needed.

Lighting: Lights dim and flash, as indicated.

Music: Christmas carols, as indicated in text, and any 1950's jitterbug number, live or recorded.

THE CHRISTMAS NUTCRACKER

Characters: 6 male; 4 female; 2 male and or female for Royal Astrologer and Mathematician; offstage voice.

Playing Time: 25 minutes.

Costumes: Old-fashioned German clothing for the Silberhaus family and Dr. Drosselmeyer: rather formal dress, with high collars for boys, long skirts for girls. Doctor has glasses, gray beard and hair at first, then removes beard and has dark hair. Members of the court of King Pudgy Podgy wear traditional fairy tale clothing: King wears royal robes stuffed with pillow, and crown, and his cheeks are red; Princess, a pretty long dress and coronet; Chancellor, long robe and billowy wig; Astrologer, long robe and great pointed hat with suns and moons and stars on it; Mathematician, black robe with numbers and equations on it; Maid, long skirt, blouse, and apron. Mouse King wears mouse costume and tiny gold crown. Nicholas wears page's suit and high boots. There is a nutcracker's mask, which first Princess and then Nicholas wears.

Properties: Music box, toy telescope, large notebook and pencil, cardboard swords, bandage. Nuts, which actors pretend to crack, should be cracked in advance.

Setting: Home of Judge Silberhaus in old German village. There is large lighted Christmas tree right, trimmed with tinsel, toy flutes, candy canes and nuts in small paper baskets. Dolls, toy soldiers, and other wrapped packages are under it, as well as a nutcracker in the shape of a man, with movable jaws (may be made of cardboard). There is a fireplace at left, and near hearth a large armchair. Set in the back wall is a wide alcove with a grandfather clock in it. (If desired, clock may be painted on alcove wall.) There are doors up left and up right in the alcove, and down left and down right.

Lighting: Effect of lightning, if possible, as indicated in text. Lights dim and black out temporarily, as indicated. Green spotlight when Mouse King appears; white spotlight to shine on clock.

Sound: Musical selections from Tchaikovsky's "Nutcracker Suite," sound of music box, thunder.

THE LEFT-OVER REINDEER

Characters: 9 male; 5 female.

Playing Time: 30 minutes.

Costumes: Modern dress for Mr. Marboro and Sylvesters. St. Nick, Jing, and Jang wear Christmas costumes. Others wear clothes appropriate to the early 1900s. Bathrobes, slippers, and outdoor winter clothes should be included in changes for Sandy and Robbie.

Properties: Two cots made up and covered as couches; footstool; volume of 'Twas the Night Before Christmas; paper and pencil.

Setting: Victorian living room, with window and fireplace.

Lighting: Lights dim and black out at points indicated in text. Spotlight on fireplace, as indicated.

THE TWELVE DAYS OF CHRISTMAS

Characters: 36 female; 26 male; 24 female or male; extra singers for Chorus. If the cast must be limited, most of the actors may take several roles.

Playing Time: 20 minutes.

Costumes: Members of the court wear traditional robes and crowns. Jester has on a tight-fitting costume of bright colors, and pointed cap with bells. Pages may wear short, full bloomers and tights, the Maids, short full skirts. Swans wear white leotards and tights, with white feathers in hair. Milkmaids may be dressed in blue and white and wear aprons and small white caps. Drummers and Pipers wear uniforms. Lords and Ladies wear appropriate finery.

Properties: Paper and pen; the following gifts, made of cardboard: partridge in a pear tree, two turtledoves, three hens with bows around their necks, four blackbirds, six geese, five hoops covered with gold paper; pails and stools; eleven pipes; twelve drums; robe and leather purse.

Setting: The throne room. Two thrones on a platform at one side of stage.

Lighting: No special effects.

RANDY, THE RED-HORNED RAINMOOSE

Characters: 18 male or female.

Playing Time: 20 minutes.

Costumes: Randy wears moose costume. His bright red antlers are covered with green felt (or similar material resembling moss) until the end of play—actor playing Randy must be able to remove material quickly and easily. Hustle, Bustle, Fred, and Tissue Elf wear brown tights, green jerkins with wide belts, and elf caps. Weather Elf has three costumes: bright Hawaiian shirt, shorts, sandals, and straw hat, with beach towel draped over his shoulder and bottle of suntan lotion in his pocket; raincoat, rain hat, galoshes, and umbrella; ski jacket, ski cap, snow boots, mittens, and earmuffs. Santa wears traditional costume. Rudolph and the reindeer wear reindeer suits with antlers and brown face makeup. Rudolph has red nose.

Properties: Broom, two clipboards, long sheets of computer paper, wagon with small garbage can in it, several boxes of tissue, can of soda.

Setting: Santa's workshop. There is a workbench covered with tools, boxes, and wrapping paper. Large can reading SLEIGH WAX and tool chest holding screwdriver, flashlight, pliers, large battery, and jar labeled MOMMA ELF'S MAGICAL, MULTI-PURPOSE OVEN CLEANER AND REINDEER FLYING ELIXIR are at rear. Sheet, three white smocks, and three sets of white gloves are hidden under workbench.

Lighting and Sound: No special effects.

I HAVE A DREAM

Characters: 7 male; 2 female; 1 male

or female for M.C.; male and female extras for all other characters.

Playing Time: 20 minutes.

Costumes: Jeff, Susan, Grandfather, Samuel, Other Audience Members and M.C. wear modern, everyday dress. All other characters wear clothes appropriate for the 1950's and early 1960's.

Properties: Shopping bags for Rosa Parks.

Setting: Stage is bare. M.C.'s stand is at one side of stage. At other side are two rows of chairs, angled so that they face the audience. Large sign reading RESERVED FOR WHITES is near chairs in front. Chairs at the back have sign reading COLORED SECTION. Single chair for Bus Driver is in front of the two rows. On the backdrop is a large picture of Martin Luther King. If available, slides of Martin Luther King and activities in which he was engaged may be flashed on backdrop from a projector throughout the play.

Lighting: Spotlights, as indicated.

Music: "We Shall Overcome."

YOUNG HARRIET TUBMAN

Characters: 2 male; 3 female.

Playing Time: 20 minutes.

Costumes: Minty and Martha wear plain, faded dresses; Minty also has piece of cloth wrapped around her shoulders. Both girls' hair is plaited in cornrows or braids. Jim wears pants cut off at knee, and long-sleeved tattered shirt. Ben and Harriet have gray hair. Ben wears heavy work shirt and old trousers; Harriet, a long, homespun dress, shawl, apron, and kerchief around her hair.

Setting: The Ross family's one-room log cabin on plantation near Bucktown, Maryland. Wooden bed with pillow, brightly colored patchwork quilt, and worn blanket, is against wall right. Large, open fireplace, with huge pot hanging over a low-burning fire, is upstage. Rough-hewn table and benches are center; a candle burns low on table. A tiny window is in rear wall beside fireplace. Exit is left.

Lighting: Mostly dim, except for fireplace. Only the small space surrounding the table is fairly well lighted, so the characters can be seen clearly.

Sound: Knocking; laughter; Christmas singing, as indicated in text.

A MAN LIKE LINCOLN

Characters: 5 male; 4 female.

Playing Time: 25 minutes.

Costumes: Modern dress. Mr. Gifford and Mrs. Sullivan wear wristwatches.

Properties: Overcoat for Mrs. Sullivan, letters for Craig, program for Ricky, brief case for Mr. Lazlo.

Setting: Mr. Gifford's library/law office. At center is a large desk with telephone and swivel chair, above which is a painting of Lincoln. Other furnishings include bookcases, filing cabinets, long table with six chairs, pencils, paper, file folder and notebooks, secretary's desk with typewriter or computer, manila folder with contract, and telephone, and a pedestal on which there is a bust of Lincoln.

THE PERFECT TRIBUTE

Characters: 8 male; 1 female or male for Nurse.

Playing Time: 20 minutes.

Costumes: Period dress. Lincoln, black suit, frock coat, high black hat, bow tie, watch chain and watch, beard. Warrington, hip-

length jacket, pantaloons loosely fitted at the ankles, Eton collar, bow tie. Carter, Patients, hospital gowns. Sentry, Union soldier's uniform and Springfield rifle with bayonet, which may be made of cardboard.
Properties: None required.
Setting: Hospital room in a Civil War prison building. There are four cots upstage and a cot downstage which has a table beside it. On the table there are a basin, towel, lamp (with concealed flashlight), Bible, a folded newspaper, an ink bottle, pen, and sheaf of papers. There is a chair next to table.
Sound: No special effects.

LOOKING FOR LINCOLN

Characters: 7 male; 5 female.
Playing Time: 15 minutes.
Costumes: Plain clothes of the period. Graham and Stuart may wear suits. Abe has a straw hat. The women and girls wear long skirts.
Properties: Books, letters (folded sheets of paper), three poles with fish hanging from the ends, man's shirt, jug of maple syrup.
Setting: A Store in New Salem, Illinois. There is a door, up center. Over the door is a sign: GENERAL STORE—SAM HILL, PROP. A counter at left has display of vegetables, seed, furs, cheeses and bolts of material. A counter at right has a sign: POST OFFICE, NEW SALEM, ILLINOIS— A. LINCOLN, POSTMASTER. Guns and tools hang on walls. Down right is a rocking chair. Several wooden kegs may be placed around the store.
Lighting: No special effects.

WHAT RHYMES WITH CUPID?

Characters: 3 male; 4 female.
Playing Time: 25 minutes.

Costumes: Modern dress. Miss Fenmore and Janey wear dresses. Lester wears jacket, then Cupid costume made of white crepe paper, red hearts, and wings; still later he wears heavy woman's overcoat and scarf. Paulette wears scarf. Whelan is dressed in police uniform.
Properties: Greeting cards, valentine tablecloth, plates, cups, paper bags, large red hearts, cardboard "cake" on "table" made of large carton, portfolio, papers, pen, bow and rubber-tipped arrows, pin.
Setting: Higby's Greeting Card store. There are racks of cards left and right, table and several chairs, and counter with telephone on it. Store is decorated with balloons, large bow and arrow, and target with heart in center. Sign reading LET US PLAN YOUR PARTY hangs on wall. Exits lead to street, storeroom, and Miss Fenmore's office.
Lighting: No special effects.
Sound: Telephone ringing, as indicated in text.

THE KINGDOM OF HEARTS

Characters: 5 male; 7 female; 6 male or female for Snow Buntings; as many extras as desired for Children.
Playing Time: 15 minutes.
Costumes: King of Hearts wears a bright red robe trimmed with white to resemble ermine. Queen of Hearts wears bright red dress also trimmed with white. Both wear silver crowns. Knave of Hearts, red slacks and shirts with white neck ruffs. Maids of Hearts, red dresses, white scarves at neck. Herald, red tunic and tights. Jack Frost, silver slacks and shirt, crown of silver icicles. Snow Buntings, white slacks and shirts with silver wings, head-

dresses resembling birds' heads. Children, everyday clothes.

Properties: Parchment scroll; white paintbox and silver paintbrush for Jack Frost.

Setting: Throne Room of the Royal Palace of the King and Queen of Hearts. There are two royal thrones at center stage. Large red heart and silver loving cup are concealed beneath King's throne. There should be a white backdrop on which large red hearts have been pinned. Exits are right and left.

Lighting: No special effects.

Sound: Live or recorded accompaniment for "Frosty the Snowman," "You've Got to Have Heart," as indicated in text.

EXPRESS TO VALLEY FORGE

Characters: 2 male; 4 female.

Playing Time: 25 minutes.

Costumes: All characters are dressed in appropriate costumes of the Revolutionary period.

Properties: Scene 1: Knitting, cups, saucers, plates, cutlery, teakettle. Scene 2: Miniature, letter.

Setting: The kitchen of the Heather Inn. At rear center is a door leading to the yard. On either side of the door are windows. At right is a fireplace. A teakettle hangs in the fireplace and before the fireplace is a bench. At right of fireplace is a large cabinet. Downstage center is a large table with four chairs around it. Near the table is a rocking chair. Door at left leads to rest of house. On rear wall are hooks for hanging clothing.

Lighting: No special effects.

PRELUDE TO VICTORY

Characters: 5 male; 3 female.

Playing Time: 30 minutes.

Costumes: Hessian uniform for Piel, American uniform for Washington. The others wear civilian clothes of colonial America.

Properties: A wooden tray attached to straps, spectacles, needles, pins, spools of thread and a wig for Dick.

Setting: The living room of a house in Trenton, New Jersey. A door, up center, and a window, up right center, open on the street. A coat rack is up left center. Down center, a table, with a chair at each end and another at the back. A door, left center, opens on a bedroom. Down right center is an open fireplace, in front of which is an armchair. A door, up right, opens on the kitchen.

Lighting: No special effects.

Sound: Stamping of feet; knock on door; guns firing.

ATTIC TREASURE

Characters: 4 male; 1 female.

Playing Time: 10 minutes.

Costumes: Everyday dress.

Properties: Key, tissue paper, three-cornered hat, black breeches with buckles, white shirt, blue coat with gold epaulettes.

Setting: An attic. Upstage center is an old trunk. A key hangs on the wall above the trunk. Other typical furnishings, including some curtain rods, are placed around the stage.

Lighting: No special effects.

CINDER-RILEY

Characters: 2 male; 5 female; at least 3 players for Stagehands; as many male and female as desired to be Dancers.

Playing Time: 20 minutes.

Costumes: Leprechaun wears brown tunic, tights, cap and kerchief. He carries a stick and has a red handkerchief in one pocket. Stepmother and Stepsisters wear long gowns, crowns, and comical putty noses. Stepmother wears a cloak. Cinder-Riley wears a long gown, a crown, and silver slippers (the gown should be expendable, since it must be cut). Fairy Godmother wears housedress, two aprons, two mob caps, and two pairs of shoes. Jack wears a crown of potatoes, a tattered shirt, and breeches with green patches. Dancers are in green and white—boys wear gold ties, girls, gold kerchiefs.

Properties: Large portable screen decorated with coat of arms; light card table covered with long tablecloth; papers, quill pen and inkstand (on top of table); broom; reticule containing huge shears for Fairy Godmother.

Setting: The stage is bare, and all necessary furnishings are brought on and removed as indicated in the text. The backdrop may be hung with drawings of large knives, forks, spoons and skillets.

Sound: Piano or recorded music, clock chimes.

BUNNIES AND BONNETS

Characters: 6 male; 8 female; as many players for Bunny Ballet as desired.
Playing Time: 20 minutes.
Costumes: Miss Ambrose, Mrs. Murphy, Mrs. Ross, Mr. Fulton, Miss Blossom, and Mr. Hunter wear modern, everyday clothes. Alice wears Alice in Wonderland costume. All others wear bunny costumes (Bunny Ballet, in appropriate ballet clothing). White Rabbit has pink jacket, wears watch.
Properties: Cardboard carrot covering trumpet; cards; bag holding cookies; bass drum; harmonica; guitar case; briefcase; Easter bas-

ket (wide-brimmed straw hat trimmed with flowers, and used upside down to hold Easter eggs); candy eggs.
Setting: Waiting room of TV studio. Receptionist's desk is left; benches are at rear.
Lighting: No special effects.

A MAN CALLED APPLESEED

Characters: 3 male; 3 female.
Playing Time: 20 minutes.
Costumes: Sarah and Polly Dillon wear long, plain gingham dresses and aprons; Tommy, pants tied with rope belt, flannel shirt; Melody, frilly dress; Johnny, saucepan for hat, loose sacking suit with rope belt and large pockets; Owl's Wing, conventional Indian costume with beads around neck, knife in belt.
Properties: Wood, for Tom; bonnet and basket for Sarah; hoe and sack for Johnny, containing papers, three apples, pouch of seeds.
Setting: A room in a log cabin, with a fireplace at rear and door to outside, left. At rear is door leading inside. There is a table, center, with bowls and utensils on it. Chairs, stools, a bucket and bench are placed about room. A gun hangs on wall. Window is in right wall.
Sound: Wind, thunder, loud crash, as indicated in text.

CONVERSATION PIECE

Characters: 3 male; 4 female; 2 male or female for Messenger and Delivery Person.
Playing Time: 25 minutes.
Costumes: Modern, everyday dress. Hilda wears coat in Scene 1.
Properties: Large package containing antlers, large, flat package containing modern painting; odd-

shaped packages containing drift-wood, bearskin rug, stuffed eagle; feather duster, flower box with red roses and card, newspaper, vase with yellow roses, placard reading HAPPY MOTHER'S DAY, tray holding coffeepot, coffee cakes, cups and saucers, etc., purse, telephone directory.

Setting: Scene 1: The living room of the Holmes family. Mantel, over fireplace rear, has nothing but pair of candlesticks. A sofa, several easy chairs, and telephone on table are center stage. Bookshelves, lamps, paintings, etc., complete the furnishings. Scene 2: Same as Scene 1. Brightly wrapped packages have been arranged on table and on floor nearby. In front of packages is sign reading HAPPY MOTHER'S DAY. Exit left leads outside; exit right, to rest of house. There is closet down left.

Lighting: No special effects.

Sound: Telephone and doorbell.

MOTHER FOR MAYOR

Characters: 4 male; 4 female.

Playing Time: 30 minutes.

Costumes: Modern everyday dress.

Properties: Cookbooks and box of index cards, papers, notebooks, pencils, overnight bag, newspaper, books, glass of water.

Setting: Modern living room, comfortably furnished with chairs, tables, lamps, bookcases, etc. On table near chair is telephone, pencil, and notepad. Exit right leads to front door; exit left to kitchen and rest of house.

Lighting: No special effects.